The Shenandoah Valley
Campaign of 1864

ALSO BY JACK H. LEPA
AND FROM McFARLAND

The Civil War in Tennessee, 1862–1863 (2007)

*Breaking the Confederacy: The Georgia and
Tennessee Campaigns of 1864* (2005)

The Shenandoah Valley Campaign of 1864

Jack H. Lepa

McFarland & Company, Inc., Publishers
Jefferson, North Carolina, and London

The present work is a reprint of the illustrated case bound edition of The Shenandoah Valley Campaign of 1864, *first published in 2003 by McFarland.*

LIBRARY OF CONGRESS CATALOGUING-IN-PUBLICATION DATA

Lepa, Jack H., 1949–
  The Shenandoah Valley Campaign of 1864 / Jack H. Lepa.
    p.   cm.
  Includes bibliographical references and index.

  ISBN 978-0-7864-4583-7
  softcover : 50# alkaline paper

  1. Shenandoah Valley Campaign, 1864 (May–August)
  2. Shenandoah Valley Campaign, 1864 (August–November) I. Title.
  E476.66.L47   2010
  973.7'36—dc22   2003014388

British Library cataloguing data are available

©2003 Jack H. Lepa. All rights reserved

No part of this book may be reproduced or transmitted in any form or by any means, electronic or mechanical, including photocopying or recording, or by any information storage and retrieval system, without permission in writing from the publisher.

Cover art: "Battle of New Market," Benjamin West Clinedinst, oil on canvas 18" × 23", 1914 (VMI Museum, Lexington, VA)

Manufactured in the United States of America

McFarland & Company, Inc., Publishers
  Box 611, Jefferson, North Carolina 28640
    www.mcfarlandpub.com

"We'll always have great men,
but we'll never have better."

Contents

Preface	1
1. A Long Road Ahead	3
2. The Valley	13
3. The Campaign Begins	20
4. The Battle of New Market	33
5. New Commander, Same Plan	46
6. The Battle of Piedmont	53
7. On to Staunton and Lynchburg	60
8. Lynchburg and Retreat	73
9. Early Moves North	84
10. The Battle of Monocacy	95
11. The War Comes to Washington	103
12. Back to the Valley	116
13. Chambersburg and the Turning Point	126
14. A War of Maneuver	135
15. The Battle of Winchester	146
16. The Battle of Fisher's Hill	160
17. The Burning and Tom's Brook	170
18. Camping at Cedar Creek	179
19. Cedar Creek, The Morning	189

20. Cedar Creek, The Afternoon	199
21. To the End	211
Notes	221
Bibliography	235
Index	243

Preface

It has been almost a century and a half since our nation was torn apart by civil war. The terrible tragedy of so much death and destruction happening on our soil is difficult for most of us to comprehend. It is almost as difficult to understand why the war was necessary for the United States to grow and prosper. The Union victory not only eliminated the deplorable institution of slavery but, after many years, finally pulled together the two regions that had so many differences between them that they were one nation in name only.

The goal of this book is to give the reader the opportunity to view the events that occurred in the Shenandoah Valley over the entire year of 1864. Instead of concentrating on one significant battle or event, I believe it is interesting to see the progression of events that turned a garden spot into a burned out shadow of itself—how each event became a link in a chain and how this sometimes brought about an unintended result.

But the real story here is not about strategies that succeeded or failed, or the generals who earned glory or suffered humiliation, but about the regular soldiers who simply did their duty. Much of the information and most of the quotations used in this work came from the men who actually fought the battles: men who were usually tired, hungry, dirty, and scared, but still kept fighting for what they believed in.

I spent many months gathering the information for this book and used many sources. There are many internet sites devoted to the Civil War, but a few that were particularly useful and would be well worth the reader's time to visit include *The Making of America*, which is sponsored by the Andrew W. Mellon Foundation; *The Valley of the Shadow*, a project of the University of Virginia; and the *Virginia Military Institute Archives*.

In addition, three institutions deserve to be mentioned for providing the majority of the references. The Lied Library at the University of Nevada, Las Vegas is where I found a large selection of Civil War books, both recent and 19th Century, and many important multi-volume works. I made several visits to the Honnold/Mudd Library at Claremont Colleges in Claremont, California, which contains an extensive collection of original 19th Century books in excellent condition. These books were a major factor in providing more detailed information about events and the people involved. Last, but certainly not least, I must acknowledge the staff of the Inter-Library Loan Department at the Las Vegas–Clark County Public Library, who were able to locate many hard to find older books, including regimental histories and memoirs. These were an invaluable source of original information about the events covered in the book and provided many of the quotes from the participants in those events.

Jack H. Lepa
Fall 2003

1. A Long Road Ahead

On the first day of 1864, the new year was starting out the same way the old year had ended—the nation was at war with itself. After nearly three years of bloody civil war no one in America could be sure what the next year would bring, except that the end of the terrible struggle was nowhere in sight. What many people originally thought would be a short and glorious little war, with flags flying and bands playing, had turned into a murderous disaster for both sides.

The war had become a test of will, both in the North and in the South. As President Abraham Lincoln told an audience in Gettysburg on November 19, 1863:

> It is for us the living, rather, to be dedicated here to the unfinished work which they who fought here have thus far so nobly advanced. It is rather for us to be here dedicated to the great task remaining before us—that from these honored dead we take increased devotion to that cause for which they gave the last full measure of devotion—that we here highly resolve that these dead shall not have died in vain....[1]

Neither side would or could quit. Neither side wanted to admit that the dreadful cost had been for nothing. And it was bound to get worse before it was over.

The war seemed to have turned in the Union's favor since the previous summer. In July, the best the Confederacy had to offer, General Robert E. Lee's Army of Northern Virginia, was defeated and his invasion of Pennsylvania was turned back in three terrible days at Gettysburg. That same week, after months of maneuvering and siege warfare, Major General Ulysses S. Grant captured Vicksburg, Mississippi, giving the Union virtual control of the entire Mississippi River. This enabled civilian trade and war supplies for the

Union to move freely while preventing the Confederate states west of the river from contributing to the war effort in the east. In November, Grant dealt the Confederates another serious blow when the siege of Chattanooga was lifted by Union victories at Lookout Mountain and Missionary Ridge. But even these great victories might not be enough to convince the people in the North to continue making the sacrifices that would be needed to keep the Union together. They were tired of war and many were ready for peace on any terms, so long as the killing came to an end.

In addition to the war, this year would bring a presidential election. President Lincoln was seeking a second term, and he had made it very clear that he would not end the war until the country was whole again, no matter what it took. In Philadelphia that summer, the president said, "We accepted this war for an object, a worthy object, and the war will end when that object is attained. Under God, I hope it never will until that time."[2] The 1864 election would decide the course of the war and the future of the nation. The Democrats were promising to end the war, although it was not clear how. Some wanted to just end the fighting and grant independence to the Confederacy, others proposed to restore the Union as it was before the war. There would be no such uncertainty if Abraham Lincoln was victorious—the war would continue until the South was defeated and the Union restored.[3]

Across the North, people were wondering if the price to keep the Union together was becoming too high. For some, that point had already been reached. The ranks of the moderates and peace parties were steadily increasing. Many people, including Lincoln himself, felt there was a very real possibility that the president would not be re-elected.[4] The Democrats had nominated George B. McClellan to run against Lincoln. As a former commander of the Army of the Potomac, McClellan had been given the opportunity to end the war with a military victory; now he was running for president by promising to just end it.[5]

In the South, the situation was even worse. The Federal naval blockade was having the desired effect with food and supplies of all kinds in short supply. Slowly, the power of the Union was strangling the Confederacy. It was obvious by now that there would be no foreign allies for the Confederate States of America; the institution of slavery prevented recognition by foreign powers, especially England and France. For almost three years the brilliance of its generals and the courage of its soldiers had kept the Confederacy alive, but now, at least for some, the reality of eventual defeat was setting in.

Throughout the Confederacy, the coming spring campaign would bring new and greater hardships than ever before. The feelings of many in the South were summed up by John S. Wise:

> The winter of 1863–64 was gloomy enough in the Confederacy. Our soldiers no longer returned from the front exuberant with the joys of camp life and of victory. They were worn and ragged, and, if not actually dispirited, were at least sobered and reflective. The thoughtful, the wise, shook their heads sadly at the prospects of the opening spring campaign.[6]

In December of 1863, the military operations of Major General Jubal Early in the lower Shenandoah Valley were turned into a food gathering expedition for the hungry Confederate soldiers when Lee told him to "avail yourself of the present opportunity to collect and bring away everything that can be made useful to the army from those regions that are open to the enemy, using for this purpose both the cavalry and infantry under your command."[7]

Other correspondence by General Lee illustrates his concern about the lack of supplies and what this was doing to the fighting ability of his army. In a letter to his wife, Lee said:

> Provisions for the men, too, are very scarce, and, with very light diet and light clothing. I fear they suffer, but still they are cheerful and uncomplaining. I received a report from one division the other day in which it stated that over four hundred men were barefooted and over a thousand without blankets.[8]

On January 22, Lee wrote to James Seddon, Confederate Secretary of War:

> A regular supply of provisions to the troops in this army is a matter of great importance. Short rations are having a bad effect upon the men, both morally and physically. Desertions to the enemy are becoming more frequent, and the men cannot continue healthy and vigorous if confined to this spare diet for any length of time. Unless there is a change, I fear the army cannot be kept together.[9]

Also on January 22, trying to improve morale, Lee issued General Orders No 7:

> The commanding general considers it due to the army to state that the temporary reduction of rations has been caused by circumstances beyond the control of those charged with its support. Its welfare and comfort are the objects of his constant and earnest solicitude, and no effort has been spared to provide for its wants. It is hoped that the exertions now being made will render the necessity of short duration, but the history of the army has shown that the country can require no sacrifice too great for its patriotic devotion.
>
> Soldiers! You tread with no unequal step the road by which your fathers marched through suffering, privations, and blood to independence. Continue to emulate in the future, as you have in the past, their valor in arms, their patient endurance of hardships, their high resolve to be free, which no trial could shake, no bribe seduce, no danger appal, and be assured that the just God who crowned their efforts with success will, in His own good time, send down His blessing upon yours.[10]

Even more important than a shortage of supplies was the inability of the Confederacy to increase the strength of its armies. Early in 1864 it became clear to Confederate officials that even if they increased the age at which citizens could be conscripted into the army and eliminated many of the exemptions, there still would not be enough new fighting men available to make much of an impact in the field. Virginia, for example, had about 90 percent of all males of military age either in the army or performing war-related work. In short, the Confederacy was running out of able-bodied men.[11]

Still, in spite of all the problems confronting the South, there were few, if

Confederate Second Lieutenant John S. Wise (Virginia Military Institute Archives).

any, voices calling for surrender. Many of the troops might be hungry and barefoot, but there was no doubt that they could be counted on to once again follow their tattered flags into battle against the more numerous enemy. The courage of the men and the quality of their leaders had been proven again and again. The men of the Army of Northern Virginia did not know the meaning of the word quit. After the war, a former Confederate soldier wrote about how difficult it was to admit even the possibility of defeat:

> We were convinced, beyond the possibility of a doubt, of the absolute righteousness of our cause, and in spite of history we persuaded ourselves that a people battling for the right could not fail in the end. And so our hearts went on hoping for success long after our heads had learned to expect failure.[12]

And, despite all the problems facing the South, there was still hope. The center of the South was still firmly under Confederate control. From Virginia to Georgia, this area contained the primary sources of food, manpower and industry. In the Shenandoah Valley, with its fertile farms and well-used route for invading the North, the most Federal forces had been able to accomplish were brief raids and then quick retreats. Daring blockade runners were still able to bring in small amounts of needed goods through ports such as Charleston and Mobile. While outright victory now appeared unattainable, a stubborn defense of what was left of the Confederacy might just keep the bloodletting going long enough for the North to tire and give up.[13]

In the North there were different problems to overcome. The Federal troops had plenty of food and other supplies. So far in the war, the Federal problem was leadership, or rather the lack of it. Now, Major General Ulysses S. Grant appeared to be the solution—at least almost everyone hoped he was. The Congress of the United States had recently revived the rank of lieutenant general and it was no secret that Grant was soon to become the highest ranking military officer in the country, and with that rank, general-in-chief of all the armies.[14]

Throughout the Federal Army the highest rank had been that of major general. In each army or military department, the most senior major general, or the one with the best political connections, was named as the commander, giving him authority over other officers of the same rank. Unfortunately, this system sometimes produced resentment and less than enthusiastic support by men who, at least in their own minds, possessed superior military talents. With a formal act of Congress promoting Grant above all other officers as the only lieutenant general, no one could question or ignore his orders.[15]

Ulysses S. Grant looked like a rural Midwesterner who had been less than successful at his previous endeavors. This is exactly what he was. He was short and unimpressive looking with a red, bristly beard and the face and eyes of a man who had seen more than his share of trouble and failure, but who refused to quit when things got tough. He was careless about his appearance and was uninterested in the pomp and ceremony that accompanied his high rank.[16] On meeting Grant for the first time, one of his aides saw "a general officer, slight in figure and of medium stature, whose face bore an expression of weariness."[17]

He had remarkable self-control and few men ever saw him lose his temper or panic in a crisis. If a plan did not work out as anticipated, he did not get dismayed or make rash mistakes, but simply developed another plan. Grant was able to combine two traits that were indispensable for a military man and had served him well so far: ruthless determination and plain common sense.[18]

The people in the North believed that he was the man who at last was going to win the war. He had refused to admit defeat at Shiloh and was able to salvage at least a draw. At Fort Donaldson and again at Vicksburg, he had captured whole Confederate armies, and at Chattanooga the forces under his command attacked and routed the enemy from what was thought to be an impregnable position. James Longstreet, commander of the First Corps in the Army of Northern Virginia and one of Grant's oldest friends, had warned some of his associates not to underestimate the new Federal commander:

> I believe I know him through and through; and I tell you that we cannot afford to underrate him and the army he now commands. We must make up our minds to get into line of battle and to stay there; for that man will fight us every day and every hour till the end of this war.[19]

Finally, the nation had found the right man to direct the war effort. The days of replacing one inept general with another inept general, with disaster the usual result, were over.

When Grant took command there were 19 independent military departments, with the Army of the Potomac considered a separate command. It was this lack of organization of the vast Federal military effort that caused much of the confusion that was hampering the war effort. Part of the problem as Grant saw it was that "Before this time these various armies had acted separately and independently of each other, giving the enemy an opportunity often of depleting one command, not pressed, to reinforce another more actively engaged. I determined to stop this."[20]

Improving the efficiency of the military administration would help, but devising an overall strategy that would defeat the superb Confederate armies was Grant's main concern. During the past three years the Federal government had been unable to come up with a comprehensive plan to win the war. They had sufficient manpower and materials, the men were brave and willing to go through hell for their cause, but the Federal authorities seemed unable to get their armies to work together. The North had the military strength to win the war. What had been missing was someone who knew how to use it properly.[21]

A few months earlier in a message to Major General Henry W. Halleck, Grant had proposed an attack in the Deep South. "It seems to me this move would secure the entire States of Alabama and Mississippi and a part of Georgia, or force Lee to abandon Virginia and North Carolina. Without his force the enemy have not got army enough to resist the army I can take."[22] He knew that they did not have enough manpower to be strong everywhere at the same time and it was now time to take advantage of that weakness. Grant clearly understood the basic premise of war; victory came by killing or capturing the enemy's soldiers. He also realized, however, that this war was more than just a struggle between the armies in the field. To end the war it would be necessary to destroy the will of the Southern people to continue to support the fighting, and to achieve this, he was willing to use economic and psychological weapons that had not been used before. Not only their armies, but the farms, railroads and factories of the South were now targets. There would be no rest for the Rebel armies, there would be no quiet areas from which to take reinforcements, the Confederacy was to be worn out and crushed under the weight of continuous aggression by the stronger Federal forces. Grant was going to bring total war to the South.[23]

Just as important as formulating a winning strategy was another, potentially crippling, problem for the Federal authorities to overcome. A large number of the troops currently in the army had enlisted for three years when the government called for volunteers in the summer of 1861. In a few months, tens of thousands of these men would come to the end of their term of enlistment and could simply leave the army and go home. The spring campaign would begin in April or May, and just as the fighting got started the Union army could begin to lose most of its best soldiers.[24]

These veteran troops had experienced everything about war that would make any sane human being want to call it quits. They had survived horrible battles like Antietam and Fredericksburg, Chancellorsville and Gettysburg and dozens of smaller, deadly fights. They had made grueling marches in scorching heat, cold rain and mud. They had spent months in dirty, unhealthy camps where thousands died of disease. And, as in all armies, it would be the veteran regiments led by experienced commanders that would be called on to lead the attacks that spring. After almost three years of fighting, the veterans knew full well that many of them would not survive another campaign.[25]

The federal government faced the very real possibility that these veterans, who had certainly done their duty, would now do the smart thing and go home while they could. This meant that the fighting would be left to the new draftees and men who joined the army to collect the generous bounties being offered by the federal and state governments. If this were to happen, the Union could very likely lose the war, as it was doubtful that these new, untried men would be able to defeat the tough, battle hardened veterans of Lee's Army of Northern Virginia.[26]

It is truly amazing that so many of these veterans decided to continue to risk their lives for their country. One of the incentives used to keep the men in the army was a thirty-day leave to go home. This proved so popular that, overall,

> the plan for re-enlisting veterans was instantly vitalized and proved eminently successful. Over 136,000 tried soldiers, who would otherwise ere this have been discharged, were secured for three years longer, organizations which would have been lost to the service were preserved and recruited, and capable and experienced officers were retained in command.[27]

In the Army of the Potomac alone, its commander, Major General George G. Meade, reported that "The total re-enlistment of veterans up to and including the 28th instant in this army was 26,767."[28] After all they had suffered it appears that most of them just wanted to see the job through to the end, and victory.

General Grant's plan for the coming campaign would take advantage of the Federal superiority in men and material. This superiority had always existed, but had never been used the way Grant was going to use it. Simply put, he was going to attack everywhere at the same time with "co-operative action of all the armies in the field, as far as this object can be accomplished."[29] One expedition was to move toward Mobile, Alabama, to close that important port (later canceled by President Lincoln in favor of an expedition into Texas). Major General William T. Sherman was heading through Georgia to capture Atlanta. In the Shenandoah Valley, Major General Franz Sigel was to destroy the railroads that brought supplies to Richmond and Lee's army. Major General Benjamin Butler was to move toward Richmond from the east.[30]

Another significant change from previous campaigns was how Grant was going to use the Army of the Potomac. No longer was the capture of Richmond their goal; now the objective was the Army of Northern Virginia. In a letter to General Meade, Grant gave him one simple, overall instruction for the coming campaign: "Lee's Army will be your objective point. Wherever Lee goes, there you will go also..."[31] Meade had to get close to Lee's army and maintain contact. There were two very good reasons for this change: Lee would not have the freedom of movement to launch one of his lightning attacks anywhere else, and he would be unable to detach significant numbers of troops to reinforce other Confederate armies. Meade might not actually be able to beat Lee's army, but eventually his superior manpower would wear them out. The Army of the Potomac could pay a high price, but in the end, winning the war would be worth it.[32]

The Federal authorities were not alone in making plans for the coming campaign. General Lee was not just sitting idly by waiting for the blow that he knew was coming. With his limited resources, he did everything humanly possible to increase the strength and efficiency of his army. He knew full well that the Union was putting together an enormous force to crush the Confederacy.

Robert Edward Lee was, and still is, one of the most revered men in American history, and for good reason. Lee's father was "Light Horse Harry" Lee, a hero of the Revolutionary War and close friend of George Washington. His wife was Mary Custis, a direct relation of Martha Washington, and their estate outside Washington, D.C., is now part of Arlington National Cemetery. Well before the war Lee had freed his own slaves and was opposed to secession. He had been superintendent of West Point and was so respected as a military leader that President Lincoln had offered him command of the U.S. Army, but when the war came Lee could not fight against his beloved Virginia. He had led the Army of Northern Virginia against the vastly superior Federal armies, beating them over and over with brilliant tactics and the nerves of a riverboat gambler, until Gettysburg. He was worshipped by his men and even his enemy held him in high esteem.

Never one to let the enemy dictate his actions, Lee wrote to Jefferson Davis, President of the Confederate States of America, on February 3:

> If we could take the initiative & fall upon them un-expectedly we might derange their plans & embarrass them the whole summer.... We are not in a condition, & never have been, in my opinion, to invade the enemy's country with a prospect of permanent benefit. But we can alarm & embarrass him to some extent & thus prevent his undertaking anything of magnitude against us....[33]

Despite being outnumbered by his opponent, Lee's confidence in the courage and ability of his army was never shaken. In another letter to Davis, he states that if Butler's movement toward Richmond could be stopped, "I have no uneasiness as to the result of the campaign in Virginia."[34]

In March, Lee again wrote to the Confederate president:

> Since my former letter on the subject, the indications that operations in Virginia will be vigorously prosecuted by the enemy are stronger than they then were. General Grant has returned from the army in the West. He is, at present, with the Army of the Potomac, which is being organised and recruited... Every train brings recruits, and it is stated that every available regiment at the North is added to it.... Their plans are not sufficiently developed to discover them, but I think we can assume that, if General Grant is to direct operations on this frontier, he will concentrate a large force on one or more lines, and prudence dictates that we should make such preparations as are in our power....[35]

Unfortunately for the Confederacy, there were too few preparations that could be made. With the usually weaker army, Lee had been forced to take the greater risks to achieve victory. Time and again he had gambled and won. But by the spring of 1864, the Confederacy's supply of time and luck were running out. Grant's analysis that winter was absolutely correct: they did not have enough army.

In addition to being responsible for the military aspect of the war, Grant also had to operate within the political realities of a civil war where party politics and the influence of powerful individuals had to be considered. Unlike most of his predecessors, his calm disposition and lack of personal political ambition enabled Grant to work within these boundaries. For the first time, the Federal effort had something that never existed before—complete trust between the president and the commanding general.[36]

This mutual trust is shown in an exchange of letters at the end of April when Lincoln wrote to Grant wishing him success:

> Not expecting to see you again before the Spring campaign opens, I wish to express, in this way, my entire satisfaction with what you have done up to this time, so far as I understand it. The particulars of your plans I neither know, or seek to know. You are vigilant and self-reliant; and, pleased with this, I wish not to obtrude any constraints or restraints upon you. While I am very anxious that any great disaster, or the capture of our men in great numbers, shall be avoided, I know these points are less likely to escape your attention than they would mine. If there is anything wanting which is within my power to give, do not fail to let me know it.
> And now with a brave Army, and a just cause, may God sustain you.[37]

To this Grant replied:

> Your very kind letter of yesterday is just received. The confidence you express for the future, and satisfaction with the past, in my military administration is acknowledged with pride. It will be my earnest endeavor that you, and the country, shall not be disappointed. From my first entrance into the volunteer

service of the country, to the present day, I have never had cause of complaint, have never expressed or implied a complaint, against the Administration or the Sec. of War, for throwing any embarrassment in the way of my vigorously prossecuting what appeared to me my duty. Indeed since the promotion which placed me in command of all the Armies, and in view of the great responsibility, and importance of success, I have been astonished at the readiness with which every thing asked for has been yielded without even an explanation being asked. Should my success be less than I desire, and expect, the least I can say is, the fault is not with you.[38]

Unlike some of his predecessors, Grant did not talk about what he was going to accomplish or complain about constant interference from Washington. He accepted the responsibility for his decisions, exonerated the administration in advance, and ordered the armies to open the campaign of 1864.

2. The Valley

One Union soldier from New York described his first sight of the Shenandoah Valley as a panorama that "stretched as far as the eye could reach. Bordered with the blue mountains on either side, carpeted with alternate field and forest, and interspersed here and there with small town and villages, it looked a perfect paradise on earth."[1]

Sheltered between the western side of the Blue Ridge Mountains and the eastern edge of the Alleghenies, the Shenandoah Valley, commonly referred to as "the Valley," starts deep in Virginia at Lexington and angles northeast for about 165 miles, ending near Harpers Ferry. From Lexington the Valley gradually descends as it moves toward Harpers Ferry and the Potomac River. Most of the Valley is twenty to thirty miles wide except for the area between Harrisonburg and Strasburg, where a massive rock known as Massanutten Mountain towers over the landscape for about forty-five miles. To the west of Massanutten lies the main part of the Valley, ten to fifteen miles wide, and on the east is the narrower Luray Valley, containing more wooded and difficult terrain only a few miles wide. The two forks of the Shenandoah River run around each side of Massanutten and join together near Front Royal. The only good road over the mountain winds its way through a gap near New Market. South of the gap there were no roads over the mountain and to the north only a few narrow, rugged roads that were unsuited for large bodies of troops. It was a land made for small armies and fast striking units of cavalry who could hit their targets and then quickly run to the safety of the mountains. With such a wide variety of plains and mountains so easily accessible in the same small area, it was difficult for the military commanders to use conventional strategies. Those with the most intimate knowledge of the area, usually the Confederates, had a distinct advantage over their opponents.[2]

Long before the madness of the Civil War had begun, pioneers from Maryland and Pennsylvania were moving into the Valley. This new land proved to be exceptionally fertile and soon the generations that followed filled the Valley with productive and prosperous farms. Many of these settlers were Quakers and Dunkers, devout and industrious, more than willing to work from dawn to dusk clearing the land and tilling the fields. However, their religious beliefs taught them that violence, for any reason, was wrong. They refused to volunteer for military service and Confederate authorities soon learned that attempting to draft these conscientious objectors was a waste of effort. A plan was developed that allowed them to avoid military service on payment of a $500 tax, which also kept them working the land to produce the much needed food for Confederate armies in Virginia.[3]

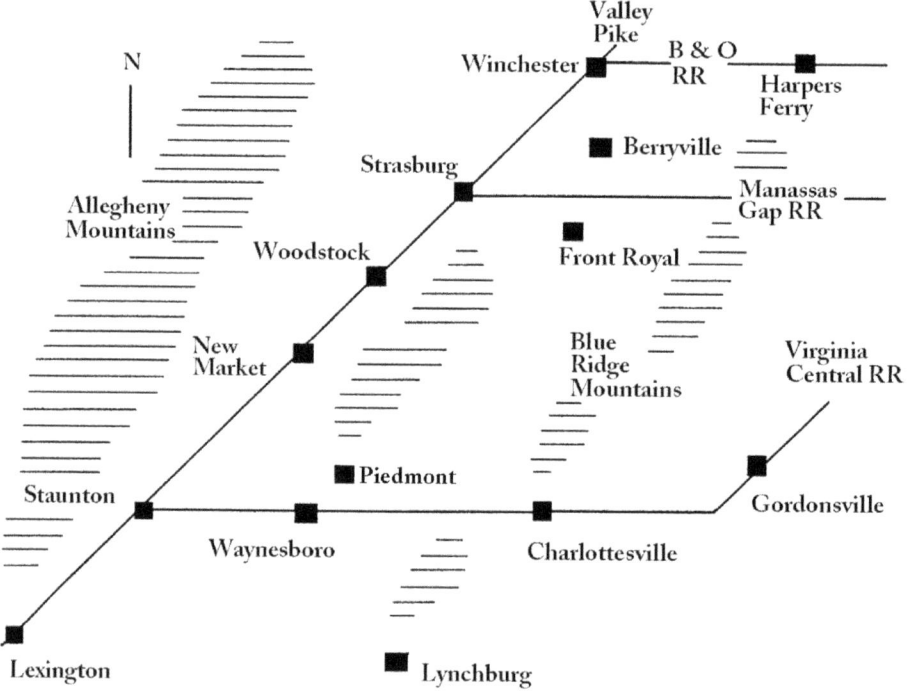

Shenandoah Valley

During the first three years of the war, many areas of the Valley were subjected to occupation by troops of both sides. It wasn't unusual for a territory to be under Confederate control one day and Union control the next. For the local residents who just wanted to visit relatives or go into town for supplies, this meant that they were frequently crossing enemy lines, subject to harassment by Union troops and possible attacks by marauders or deserters from both sides. Another problem facing Valley residents in areas that came under Federal control was that some Union soldiers saw little reason to respect their rights as American citizens. After all, they were in rebellion against the nation whose laws provided those rights. This was enemy territory. Personal valuables, livestock and even their homes were sometimes taken for use by the occupying forces.[4]

To meet the needs of the Confederate armies, the farms of the Valley provided large amounts of food for the soldiers and forage for animals right from the opening of the war. In fact, so much was sent east that during the winter of 1863–64, the local forces stationed in the northern part of the Valley began to suffer from shortages of some of their basic needs. The lack of supplies was so serious that unusual steps had to be taken to try to ensure that the men and animals assigned to defend the Valley would be able to fulfill their duty. The commander of the Confederate forces, Brigadier General John D. Imboden, wrote to the *Staunton Spectator* making a public request for supplies, coupled with a warning of what might happen if they were not forthcoming:

> We cannot haul feed from the upper country, 75 or 100 miles, to feed our horses when on duty to the front. I might possibly obtain a supply by sending my Quartermasters to your barns and cribs with orders to take whatever they might find.... If on the other hand supplies cannot be had at all, and the troops are obliged to fall back on that account, and the Yankees ride over your country, stealing and plundering as they go, and living off the very supplies we could not get, I shall be cursed from one end of the Valley to the other for falling in my duty.... To meet the whole difficulty and surmount it, I think you have but to act in concert, and promptly.[5]

Many times during the conflict farmers planted and cared for their crops only to see them trampled under the feet of thousands of soldiers as the contending armies moved up and down the Valley. When the armies clashed, the toil and sacrifice of past generations could be wiped out in just a few hours, along with whatever dreams the family might have been nurturing for the future. But for many citizens, the possibility of death or injury from fighting on their property and the loss of homes and farms were only part of the tragedy. In the aftermath of a battle the dead and wounded had to be cared for, and the residents of the nearest town were usually pressed into service to assist the frequently overwhelmed military medical staffs. Public buildings, barns and sometimes private homes served as hospitals. Tending to the wounded as nurses, many local women learned firsthand the horrors of war.[6]

The romantic notions of war quickly vanished as the people of the Valley became acquainted with its reality. Southern patriotism and support for the rebellion soon were tempered as the dead and wounded soldiers were returned to their families. It would not be too long before the residents of the Shenandoah Valley became closely acquainted with the death and destruction and misery that is war. Almost every family lost a relative or friend before the fighting ended.

The military value of the Shenandoah Valley during the Civil War can hardly be overestimated. Control of Virginia was the key to victory for both sides and control of the Valley was necessary for a successful campaign in Virginia. The geography of the Valley gave the greatest advantage to the Confederate forces. Moving northeast, down the Valley, a Rebel army could emerge from behind the mountains and quickly move into Pennsylvania and Maryland.[7] Perhaps more importantly, the entire Valley north of Strasburg was above Washington, D.C. A quick moving Confederate force could easily cross the Potomac River and threaten the capital from the rear. The Blue Ridge Mountains concealed the invading force as it advanced and cavalry could easily block the few passes through the mountains, thus enabling the Confederates to move toward their target before the Union forces could be sure of their destination, as Lee had done during his invasion that ended at Gettysburg. The Valley was a natural invasion route for the Confederacy. The Federal forces could also take advantage of the concealment the route provided. However, when they marched up the Valley toward the southwest, they were headed nowhere important, because they were actually moving away from Richmond and Lee's army.[8]

There was another military factor that made control of the Valley so important for both sides. The main theatre of action in eastern Virginia was less than one hundred miles away. A small army moving quickly through the gaps in the Blue Ridge could deliver a devastating flank attack on their enemy. Neither side could have a successful campaign in eastern Virginia unless they controlled the Valley. A prime example of how the Confederates were able to use their control of the Valley was Thomas "Stonewall" Jackson's brilliant campaign in 1862. Jackson made his home at Lexington and used his knowledge of the mountains and control of New Market Gap to move back and forth over Massanutten to defeat or at least halt the advance of three Union armies in succession. Not knowing where Jackson might strike next confused and intimidated the Federal commanders and was a factor in bringing George McClellan's advance toward Richmond to a halt.[9]

As much as the geography of the land affected the strategic thinking of the military commanders of both sides, what the Valley contained was of utmost importance to the Confederate war effort. The Virginia Central Railroad, one of the main links from Eastern Virginia to the west, crossed the Valley and maintained the largest railroad depot in the region at Staunton. The Virginia & Tennessee Railroad wound its way from the west to Richmond through the Blue Ridge and Lynchburg. The Manassas Gap Railroad moved north from the center of the Valley before turning east at Strasburg and moving through the mountains near Front Royal. The James River and Kanawha Canal provided links to Lynchburg and Richmond. In addition, the macadamized Valley Turnpike, one of the best roads in the nation before the war, provided a year-round route to move troops and supplies between Staunton and Martinsburg. Besides the railroad facilities, Staunton was home to large military warehouses and several hospitals where Confederate wounded were sent to recover in what so far had been a safe area, far away from most of the fighting.[10]

Even more important than the man-made assets in the Valley was the land itself, some of the best, most fertile soil on the continent. In 1864 the Shenandoah Valley was already widely known for its vast wheat and corn harvests and high quality livestock. The richness of the land and the high productivity of the Valley farmers could guarantee ample supplies of food and fodder to the Confederate armies in Virginia, but only if the transportation system was able to move the supplies to where they were needed. Almost everyone in the Valley owed his or her livelihood to the amazing productivity of the region one way or another. The many streams and rivers that flowed through the region ran mills that processed the grain and the railroads carried it in all directions. It was not an overstatement that the Shenandoah Valley was "the Breadbasket of the Confederacy," as it was commonly called.[11]

In the areas that hadn't yet been ravaged by the war, the Valley farms produced as much food and grain as ever, but shortages of some items affected the daily lives of virtually all the Valley residents. Years after the war, a local resident and former Confederate doctor wrote:

> Our country had never known such seasons as we had during the four years of war. Whatever was put in the ground grew in profusion. Wheat, corn, oats, rye, and grass yielded large crops, with little cultivation. The orchard bore heavily, small fruits and the nuts on the trees were in the greatest abundance.... Our people relied on these food supplies in the scarcity of flour and cornmeal.[12]

The Confederacy could not afford to neglect the defense of such a valuable region. Right from the start of the war, ways to protect and use the Valley were an important part of the Confederate war plans.

Control of the Shenandoah Valley was almost as important to the Federal war effort as that of the Confederates. Besides the military aspects mentioned above, the northern part of the Valley contained the Baltimore and Ohio Railroad, the most important transportation link between the Ohio and Potomac rivers, and the Chesapeake and Ohio Canal. The main line of the Baltimore and Ohio ran through Martinsburg and Harpers Ferry on its way east. The portion of the track that lay south of the Potomac River was an easy target for Confederate raiders who frequently disrupted service on this heavily used route. Despite the efforts of the Federal authorities to protect the railroad, it wasn't until after Sheridan's victory at Winchester that the ability of Confederates to raid the area at will was finally removed.[13]

During the first three years of the war, every Federal expedition into the Valley was thwarted. These movements were usually confined to the northern part of the Valley so that the area south of Winchester and Southwest Virginia were spared, at least temporarily, from the destruction that was all too common in eastern Virginia. Time after time the Federal soldiers started out with high hopes, only to see them dashed by clever and daring Confederate commanders, "Stonewall" Jackson prime among them. A soldier of the Federal 19th Corps wrote later that

> the very name of the Shenandoah Valley had long since passed into a byword as the Valley of Humiliation, so often had those fair and fertile fields witnessed the rout of the national forces; so often had the armies of the Union marched proudly up the white and dusty turnpike, only to come flying back in disorder and disgrace.[14]

If the Federal war effort in Virginia was to succeed, this situation had to change. To end the war the Army of Northern Virginia had to be eliminated;

there was no way around this simple fact. General Grant knew that if he could not destroy Lee's army in battle he would have to slowly grind it down to impotence. One of the keys to this strategy was removing the Valley from Confederate control, or at least preventing the region from continuing to provide the supplies that fed Lee's army. There were three ways to accomplish this: take control of the Valley to prevent the movement of supplies and the threat of flank attacks that would siphon off troops from the main Federal effort, destroy the means of transporting the supplies east or, simply eliminate the source of the problem by destroying the Valley itself. One way or another, the Shenandoah Valley had to be taken out of the war, and it would not be an easy task.

There was one other factor that was to have a major effect on the plans and conduct of both sides in the Shenandoah Valley. Throughout the war, small parties of Confederate irregulars or guerrillas continually harassed the Federal forces in and near the Valley. These men would make surprise attacks on small Union detachments and outposts, killing or capturing a few men, destroying or capturing supplies, stealing horses and anything else they could find that might be useful, then return to their homes or hide out in the mountains.[15] The effectiveness of these bands was debatable. A few contained efficient and brave fighters, but most were made up of men looking for booty and trying to avoid service in the regular army. In January Brigadier General Thomas Rosser wrote a stinging indictment to General Lee:

> They are a nuisance and an evil to the service. Without discipline, order, or organization, they roam broadcast over the country, a band of thieves, stealing, pillaging, plundering, and doing every manner of mischief and crime. They are a terror to the citizens and an injury to the cause. They never fight; can't be made to fight. Their leaders are generally brave, but few of the men are good soldiers, and have engaged in this business for the sake of gain. The effect upon the service is bad, and I think, if possible, it should be corrected.[16]

The only generally accepted exception to this would be the partisans commanded by John Mosby. The famous cavalry leader J.E.B. Stuart called Mosby's men "the only efficient band of rangers I know of...."[17] General Lee agreed with Rosser's assessment, as his own reports show. In forwarding the report to Richmond, he added, "As far as my knowledge and experience extends, there is much truth in the statement of General Rosser. I recommend that the law authorizing these partisan corps be abolished. The evils resulting from their organization more than counterbalance the good they accomplish."[18]

And in April, Lee wrote to Richmond:

> Experience has convinced me that it is almost impossible, under the best officers even, to have discipline in these bands of partisan rangers, or to prevent them from becoming an injury instead of a benefit to the service, and even where this is accomplished the system gives license to many deserters and marauders, who assume to belong to these authorized companies and commit depredations on friend and foe alike. Another great objection to them is the bad effect upon the discipline of the army from the constant desire of the men to leave their commands and enjoy the great license allowed in these bands.[19]

2. The Valley

There was also some question in the ranks of the Confederate high command concerning the quality of the troops and by extension the ability of the local commanders. In February, General Imboden wrote to request a court of inquiry concerning statements made by Jubal Early:

> It has come to my knowledge repeatedly that Maj. Gen. J. A. Early, commanding this district, habitually uses the most disparaging language in respect to my command, and indirectly in regard to myself, in the presence of my own officers and others of the army and citizens indiscriminately, charging in general terms that it is known to every one in the army and to every one in civil life in the valley, where this brigade has been on duty, that it is wholly inefficient, disorganized, undisciplined, and unreliable.[20]

Early forwarded Imboden's request with some comments of his own:

> I am sorry to say that I have found the command generally in a very bad state of discipline, and from what I have seen and heard of it, I should feel great reluctance to have to rely on it in any emergency.... No injury has been done this command in public estimation by any remarks that I have made, or am reputed to have made, for I have found the opinion very generally prevailing in all parts of the country where I have been and the command has operated that it is inefficient and undisciplined. What is the cause of this state of things I can only conjecture, but I think it due in great part to the fact that a large number of the men have been recruited from deserters from other parts of the army.[21]

This lack of confidence in the men and their officers could not have come at a worse time. It was essential for the Confederate war effort that they maintain control of the Shenandoah Valley. They would soon be facing the most serious Federal threat of the war.

3. The Campaign Begins

One of the most important and challenging regions for Federal authorities was the Department of West Virginia. It was composed of West Virginia, the Shenandoah Valley and part of Loudoun County in Virginia, and Maryland west of the Monocacy River. Thus far in the war, Federal efforts to control this large, mountainous area had brought only defeat and embarrassment. In the upcoming spring campaign, General Grant needed someone to command this vital department who, if he could not actually beat the Confederates in open battle and take control of the Valley, would, at the very least, avoid another demoralizing defeat. The main objective was to halt the movement of supplies and troops eastward to Lee's army.[1]

Early in 1864 the department commander was Brigadier General Benjamin F. Kelly. One of Kelly's most important responsibilities was to protect the portion of the Baltimore & Ohio Railroad that ran through his department, a job at which he had been less than successful. The mountainous terrain provided ample opportunity for Confederate raiders to attack the line, which they did frequently, destroying track and disrupting service, then disappearing before the bewildered Federals could find them. Kelly's lack of energetic leadership only helped to compound the problem. For some time now the local authorities had been calling for a new, more aggressive department commander.[2]

Appointing someone to take over this department offered President Lincoln the opportunity to resolve two nagging problems with a single stroke, one political and one military. At that time the Union Army had quite a few inactive major generals. Some were just incompetent, some did not have the right friends in the right places, and some had the misfortune of meeting Robert E. Lee on a field of battle. The one thing that most of them had in common was their constant pressure on the administration for an active command. One of

3. The Campaign Begins

these men was Major General Franz Sigel, one of the most popular and influential Germans in America. German immigrants made up a significant part of the population in several large cities and many thousands of them had enlisted in the Union Army. It did not seem unreasonable to them that at least a few of their fellow Germans should be given positions of leadership, and Sigel was at the top of the list.[3]

Franz Sigel was a prime example of one of the most serious problems facing the Federal war effort—a political general. Many Union officers achieved high rank not because of battlefield accomplishments, but because of political influence in Washington or their popularity with the voters at home which enabled them to convince large numbers of men to join the Union army. Sigel had led troops in several battles since the war began and had exhibited little military ability. Nevertheless, Lincoln approved his appointment as commander of the Department of West Virginia. It would probably be safe to assume that the votes of German immigrants in the upcoming election was a factor in this decision.[4]

Major General Sigel reached his department's headquarters at Cumberland, Maryland, and assumed command on March 11. One of Kelly's staff officers that Sigel retained was Colonel David H. Strother, who described his new commanding officer: "His hair and beard are tawny, his jaws and cheek bones square and angular, his eyes light blue, forehead narrow, and too small for his face. Small in stature and ungraceful."[5] Some officers were optimistic that the change in command would produce positive results. It was also believed by some that after Sigel's experience in command of large numbers of troops in the east, he was well qualified to lead the relatively small army now under his command.[6]

Sigel's new command contained over 22,000 troops, but the numbers did not reflect their quality.[7] His cavalry commander, Brigadier General William W. Averell, wrote in mid–March warning Sigel about the low quality and lack of experience of his officers and men, saying that "The results are want of discipline, neglect of duty, and waste of precious time and valuable material thus far, and I have

Union Major General Franz Sigel (Virginia Military Institute Archives).

apprehensions of more serious results in future...."[8] Inactivity had made the men soft and they were dispersed all over the department protecting a multitude of military and railroad facilities. Sigel could not afford to bring his troops together to practice maneuvers because that would leave the Baltimore & Ohio line even more exposed to guerrilla attacks.

After familiarizing himself with the department and its troops, Sigel displayed a definite lack of optimism in a report to headquarters on March 29:

> Brave as the soldiers may be individually, and with the exception of a few well-drilled and well-disciplined regiments, they have become loose and degenerated by inactivity and garrison life. They may be made soldiers, but at this moment they are very far from understanding their duties.... I will do the best I can under the circumstances prevailing to make the troops efficient, to defend and strengthen my position, and to protect the people.[9]

During the next few weeks Sigel worked hard at organizing and improving the condition of the troops in his department. Unfortunately, during this time he also displayed one of his weaknesses by giving several important posts to unqualified officers, in most cases because they were friends. Sigel also took a strict Prussian approach to discipline and training that did not endear him to the American born troops and led to an even heavier reliance on his fellow Germans.[10] Many officers on his staff could barely speak English. The vast majority of the men in the 28th Ohio Infantry and the 1st New York (Lincoln) Cavalry were Germans who spoke little or no English. This language barrier could have serious consequences when the outcome of a battle, to say nothing of life or death for the men involved, depends on clearly understanding and carrying out orders.[11]

As bad as the situation was in Sigel's department, his opponents were not in much better condition. The Confederate Department of Western Virginia contained the Confederate controlled parts of West Virginia and Kentucky, southwestern Virginia and eastern Tennessee. The Confederate commanders in the region had to contend with the same problems as their foes: politics, inexperienced troops, and a scarcity of leadership. The department commander was Brigadier General Samuel Jones, a less than inspiring officer who was never able to completely please his superiors in Richmond.[12]

General Lee, knowing full well how important this department was to his own army's well-being and the war effort in general, wrote to Confederate President Jefferson Davis twice in January to express his views. On the 13th:

> I think a reorganization of these troops necessary and a change of commanders desirable. The department requires a man of judgment and energy, whose discretion can be depended upon without always awaiting orders. The importance of this command will be augmented in view of the occupation by the enemy of East Tennessee, threatening Southwest Virginia, and demanding able, intelligent, and vigorous management on our part.[13]

Then on the 27th Lee wrote:

> A change, I think, is necessary, both for the sake of the officers in that department and the interests of the country.... If a proper man can be found I think

it would be better to include the Shenandoah Valley in his command, in order that he might concentrate the troops where most necessary. A better discipline should be instituted among the troops themselves.... Unless this is done the resources of that country will be lost to us, both its mineral wealth and provisions. The first step to improvement is an energetic active commander, and no time should be lost in his selection.[14]

The Confederate government acted in February and replaced Jones with Major General John C. Breckinridge. They could hardly have made a better choice. Confederate Secretary of War James A. Seddon wrote to Jones that his replacement was "an officer of distinction in the Western army, who has political as well as military influences to aid his administration."[15]

Virtually everyone in the South, as well as in the North, was familiar with Breckinridge. He was born near Lexington, Kentucky, in 1821 into a distinguished family. He practiced law and later went into politics. In 1856 he was elected vice-president of the United States under James Buchanan. Breckinridge did not approve of slavery and was not in favor of secession. After Lincoln's election, Breckinridge became a United States senator from Kentucky and consistently criticized the president's policies until he was forced to flee to the Confederacy to avoid arrest. He fought well in several major battles and was promoted to major general in late 1863.[16]

General Breckinridge reached the department headquarters at Dublin, in Southwest Virginia, on March 4 and immediately realized that he had a daunting task ahead of him. The department was of vital economic and military importance to the Confederate war effort. Besides the invaluable Shenandoah Valley the most productive lead mines in the Confederacy were in Wythe County in Southwest Virginia. To the east was Saltville, where most of the salt for the Confederate states east of the Mississippi was mined and processed. When Breckinridge took over the department, there were only about 5,000 men under his command and they were scattered all over the region.[17] Like their opponents, few of the Confederate troops had ever participated in a tough campaign and most had grown soft and bored from too many nights of sitting around their campfires.

Immediately after assuming command, Breckinridge left on a 400-mile tour of his department. He personally spoke with many of the troops and his enthusiasm and confidence worked wonders in improving morale. In addition to learning first-hand about the condition of his troops, Breckinridge became familiar with the varied terrain in his department, knowledge which would be very useful when he began to prepare plans to cover the multiple approaches that the enemy might take to attack the important sites he now must defend.[18]

Soon after he returned to Dublin, reports of Federal movements began to come in. Breckinridge quickly began moving troops and building fortifications at the most vital locations along a line of about 140 miles. At the end of April, he reported his dispositions as follows:

> Echols' brigade is on the south side of Greenbrier River, about 7 miles from Lewisburg; Colonel McCausland's brigade at the Narrows of New River and

Confederate Major General John C. Breckinridge (Virginia Military Institute Archives).

Princeton, in Mercer County. Col. W. L. Jackson is covering the country south of the Warm Springs with about 1,000 cavalry (dismounted), and with mounted scouts thrown forward to Huntersville and toward Beverly. I have a little cavalry in Tazewell County, to cover one of the approaches to Wytheville and the lead mines, and a large regiment and fourteen pieces of tolerable artillery at Saltville. A portion of General Buckner's troops are also near the later point.[19]

Although his forces were spread thin, these dispositions would give Breckinridge advance notice of any Federal advance along a broad front, then he could concentrate his forces to meet the threat.

In the Shenandoah Valley, General Imboden was also working hard to prepare a defense if Federal troops moved into the Valley. He had only 2,000 men to defend the entire Valley and at best could only hope to slow the enemy advance until help arrived. The 18th Virginia Cavalry was his largest unit and even though they were constantly on the move, there were just too many places to defend. Imboden admitted, "If Averell comes with 5,000 to 6,000 men and threatens two or three places at once, say Staunton, Lexington, and the Virginia and Tennessee Railroad, we shall be sorely put to meet him...."[20]

At the end of March General Grant sent instructions to Sigel for the coming campaign. There would be two columns advancing from West Virginia at the same time the Army of the Potomac began moving south to engage Lee's army. Major General E. O. C. Ord would lead 8,000 infantry and 1,500 cavalry from Beverly toward the Virginia & Tennessee Railroad, destroying as much of the line as possible, then advance to the Confederate supply depots at Lynchburg. The commander of the second column was Brigadier General George Crook, a highly respected officer who had performed well in several battles. Crook was to lead his column toward the railroad from Charlestown, move to destroy the mines at Saltville and then join Ord in the attack on Lynchburg.[21]

An important part of Grant's overall strategy was the destruction of the Confederate railroads that carried supplies and troops from the west to Lee's army. The Confederate transportation system was still working, but just barely. Lee warned President Davis on April 12:

> My anxiety on the subject of provisions for the army is so great that I cannot refrain from expressing it to Your Excellency. I cannot see how we can operate with our present supplies. Any derangement in their arrival or disaster to the railroad would render it impossible for me to keep the army together, and might force a retreat into North Carolina. There is nothing to be had in this section for man or animals.[22]

The Federal advances from West Virginia were designed to accomplish just such a "derangement."

Problems developed with the Federal plans almost immediately. Although Sigel was the department commander, Grant was well aware of his lack of ability in the field, which is why he chose Ord and Crook to actually lead the advancing columns. Ord was a favorite of Grant's from the western armies and he and Sigel simply did not get along with each other. Ord was probably less than tactful at being chosen to lead the main column instead of the department commander and Sigel must have resented him, the result being constant bickering and lack of cooperation. When Ord made a request for Sigel to meet his column with supplies, Sigel curtly replied, "I don't think I shall do it." This was the final straw for Ord, who asked to be relieved of his command.[23]

With Ord gone, the Union plan was modified so that Crook, with 10,000 men, would advance from the Kanawha to take possession of Lewisburg and to destroy as much of the Virginia and Tennessee Railroad as possible along with the New Creek bridge. General Averell would lead a cavalry force of about 2,000 troopers from Crook's expedition to attack Saltville. Sigel would command a column of about 7,000 men in an advance up the Valley to Cedar Creek, near Strasburg. From here he could either engage the Confederate forces in the Valley or join with Crook. This plan was mostly Sigel's idea and received the blessing of one of Grant's aides who had been sent west to finalize the campaign strategy. "I think General Sigel's plan is the only one by which his force can be used to an advantage at present, and not uncover the Baltimore and Ohio Railroad...." The start of the campaign was set for May 2.[24]

While the bickering with Ord was going on, Sigel also managed to antagonize Grant by using his political connections rather than military channels to get two cavalry regiments returned to his department. Grant's reply, sent through Halleck, made it very clear how he felt about this type of conduct by his subordinates:

> I know no reason why these two regiments should not be ordered to the Department of West Virginia, but it is time General Sigel should learn to carry on his official correspondence through the proper channels and not through members of Congress. Please call his attention to the fact that improper official correspondence will not be tolerated in future.[25]

By the end of April, many of Sigel's officers, even those who had originally welcomed him, were wondering if his appointment might not have been a mistake. Colonel Strother wrote, "Sigel has the air to me of a military pedagogue, given to technical shams and trifles of military art, but narrow minded and totally wanting in practical capacity."[26] Some of the higher-ranking officers had also lost the confidence of their men. "The two Acting Brigadiers—if they are to be judged by the condition of their own regiment ... are poor soldiers."[27]

General Grant had written to his friend Sherman:

> From the expedition from the Department of West Virginia I do not calculate on very great results, but it is the only way I can take troops from there. With the long line of railroad Sigel has to protect he can spare no troops, except to move directly to his front. In this way he must get through to inflict great damage on the enemy, or the enemy must detach from one of his armies a large force to prevent it. In other words, if Sigel can't skin himself he can hold a leg whilst some one else skins.[28]

All Grant really wanted Sigel to accomplish was to keep the Confederate forces in western Virginia busy so that they could not move east and assist Lee's army; any more than that would be considered a bonus.

At least part of Grant's plan had already been accomplished. Breckinridge and Imboden were kept busy organizing their defenses to meet the coming attack and were unable to transfer any troops east; in fact, they were desperately trying to increase their own forces. They knew they were on their own when Lee wrote to Imboden, "I hope you and General Breckinridge will be prepared to unite and beat him back wherever he may come, and drive him across the Potomac. I shall be so occupied, in all probability, that I shall be unable to aid you."[29] Defending the Valley and protecting Lee's left flank would stretch their resources to the limit, but they had no choice. Losing the Valley could mean disaster for the cause. However, the Confederate prospects took a turn for the better when Brigadier General Gabriel C. Wharton arrived on April 30 with his brigade of 1,000 veterans. In addition, the cavalry brigade of Brigadier General John Hunt Morgan was ordered to assist Breckinridge.[30]

There was more help on the way, although from an unexpected source. Major General Francis H. Smith, superintendent of the Virginia Military Institute, wrote to Breckinridge offering him the services of the cadets at the school. There were about 250 to 300 boys under age eighteen ready for duty along with two cannon. Breckinridge did not seriously consider putting these boys into a real battle, but under the circumstances he could not afford to refuse any offer of assistance. If needed, they could be used to replace veteran soldiers in non-combat jobs.[31]

Early on the morning of April 29, Franz Sigel's troops marched out of Martinsburg and headed south. It was a warm spring day and the men were confident and glad to finally begin what they hoped would be the final campaign. The first day's march of twelve miles took them to Bunker Hill, where they spent the next day in camp. On May 1 they moved toward Winchester, a small town of considerable military importance for both sides. A Federal army occupying the town was in a position to guard the Baltimore and Ohio Railroad and protect Washington at the same time. From Winchester, the Federals could also threaten the important Virginia Central Railroad and Staunton, about one hundred miles up the Valley. Confederate control of Winchester gave them easy access to the Baltimore & Ohio Railroad and an opening to raid into Pennsylvania and Maryland, or toward Washington.[32]

3. The Campaign Begins

As the Federal troops moved south, they encountered the devastation from previous campaigns. One of the soldiers who made this march wrote:

> Everywhere could be seen the destructiveness and paralyzing effects of the war. Fences were torn down, farms stripped of live stock, high grass was growing up to the edge of the towns, and it seemed as if the country was deserted by its inhabitants. Everything and the condition of things generally were object lessons teaching of the baleful effects of war.[33]

Ruined farms and abandoned homes were not the worst sights the men saw as they moved south. Along both sides of the Valley Pike lay the bones of dead animals and the graves of Union soldiers who had come before them:

> All along the pike from Martinsburg to Winchester on the march between the two towns, could be seen the graves of soldiers of the one or the other side who had fallen as victims of the cruel, bloody, wicked war. There was perhaps not a mile of the whole route over which we passed along which there could not be seen a soldier's grave; and at Winchester there were thousands buried.[34]

They marched past the site of the Second Battle of Winchester that had been fought the previous June and was a disaster for the Union forces. After the battle, the Confederates had hastily buried most of the Union dead in shallow graves. On many of these graves wind and rain had washed away the light covering of dirt and the bones of their dead comrades were exposed and whitening in the sun, a disturbing sight for men marching down the same road to an unknown fate.[35]

The Federal troops marching down the Valley Pike would have been even more apprehensive had they known how little their commanding general knew about what was ahead of them. As late as May 1, Sigel had no idea of the number of Confederate troops he might soon be fighting. In a message to Grant, he admitted, "I have no positive information yet whether a large force of the enemy is in the Shenandoah Valley. From all reports received I believe that there is not."[36]

On the same day that Sigel left Martinsburg, Crook and Averell began their own advances, which meant that Breckinridge had to choose which of the Federal columns to defend against. Imboden had concentrated about 2,500 veteran troops and local reserves near Woodstock, but this force could not be expected to stop Sigel.[37] General Lee had no real choice but to tell Breckinridge, "For the present you will take the general direction of affairs and use General Imboden's force as you think best. He has been ordered to report to you."[38]

The movement of the Federal columns caused great concern, not just in the Valley but also to Lee. "I do not know whether Staunton is the threatened point, but all the force sent west seem to have returned east, and are now coming up by Front Royal or the Valley. These are the forces I wish you to meet, or by some movement to draw back before they get on my left."[39]

Imboden's task was to stay in front of Sigel, slowing him if possible, but avoiding a pitched battle until Breckinridge arrived. In the meantime, the Confederate partisan groups had to do whatever they could to disrupt the Federal advance. One of these groups was led by Lieutenant Colonel Mosby, who had recently crossed the Blue Ridge to harass Sigel. Almost as soon as Sigel reached Winchester, Mosby's men went to work by capturing eight of his wagons near Bunker Hill.[40] The guerrillas caused nothing but trouble for the Federal army. They disrupted the flow of supplies and hampered communications by bushwhacking messengers. The Valley Pike became so dangerous that on May 2 Sigel sent an order to his supply officers:

> When any trains are about to leave Martinsburg for this place, you will immediately notify me of the fact, that I may order a sufficient escort, unless you have a sufficient force to send with them, in which case your escort will accompany the trains to Bunker Hill, where a relief will be stationed or sent to come on with them. In the mean time you will not suffer any trains to leave Martinsburg for Winchester until you have a sufficient force to accompany them....[41]

General Sigel kept his army in Winchester for over a week, spending much of the time drilling and holding reviews. The highlight was a mock battle held on May 5. There was little or no organization, as many of Sigel's staff were unable to communicate well in English, and whole regiments were marched off in the wrong direction. The exercise was a disaster. This fiasco caused a great deal of damage to Sigel's image and noticeably lowered the army's confidence in their commander's ability to lead them in a real battle.[42]

While Sigel was sitting in Winchester, the Confederates were working hard to slow down his already unhurried advance. One of the partisan leaders, Captain John H. McNeill, took his company on a remarkable raid. He reported:

> I left this place with sixty men on the night of the 3d instant. Reached Bloomington, on the Baltimore and Ohio Railroad, on the morning of the 5th at daydawn. Captured a freight train; put some of my men on board. Went one and a half miles below to Piedmont, my cavalry following on behind. We captured that place with a small garrison, which surrendered without resistance. We burned some seven large buildings filled with the finest machinery, engines, and railroad cars; burned nine railroad engines, some seventy-five or eighty burthen cars, two trains of cars heavily laden with commissary stores, and sent six engines with full head of steam toward New Creek. Captured the mail and mail train and 104 prisoners on the train, and burned the railroad bridge across the North Branch of the Potomac leading to Cumberland.[43]

The results from this spectacular raid were everything the Confederates could have hoped for. The railroad lost several hundred thousand dollars worth of valuable equipment. The damage was repairable but service was disrupted. More importantly, the raid induced Sigel to weaken his main force.[44]

On May 6 Colonel Jacob Higgins and 500 men from the 2nd Pennsylvania and the 15th New York Cavalry regiments left Winchester to try and intercept McNeill on his return trip. Imboden learned of the expedition from the signal station on Massanutten Mountain and on May 8 he led the 18th and 23rd Virginia Cavalry to intercept the Federal force. Higgins missed McNeill's raiders, but on their way back to Winchester the Federals were ambushed and routed by Imboden on the 9th at Lost River Gap.[45]

With Breckinridge now responsible for defending the Valley as well as his own department, he was able to consolidate the Confederate efforts to oppose the multiple Federal attacks and dramatically improve their chance for success. Imboden overlooked no opportunity to increase his manpower:

> I had ordered General Wm. H. Harman at Staunton to notify the "reserves" of Rockingham and Augusta Counties, consisting of men over forty-five and boys between sixteen and eighteen years of age.... A similar notification was sent to General Francis H. Smith, Commandant of the Virginia Military Institute at Lexington, where there were about three hundred cadets under eighteen years of age at school.[46]

The young cadets at the institute had impatiently been waiting for their turn to join the war effort. Graduates of VMI had compiled an excellent record during the conflict, by the end of the war seventeen would become general officers, and the cadets were determined to uphold this tradition of service and courage.[47] They were ready when Breckinridge wired on May 10, "Sigel is moving up the Valley—was at Strasburg last night. I cannot tell you whether this is his destination. I would be glad to have your assistance at once with the cadets and the section of artillery."[48] By 7 A.M. the next day Commandant of Cadets Colonel Scott Ship and 264 cadets with two pieces of artillery marched out of Lexington to join the Confederate army defending their valley.[49]

Sigel finally moved his army out of Winchester on the morning of the 9th, slowly moving past Strasburg and arriving at Woodstock on the 11th. Even after the delay at Winchester, scouts reported that only a few hundred enemy cavalry were between Sigel and Staunton. Sigel was being offered a splendid opportunity if only he could see it. If Crook's expedition had been successful, Sigel could easily occupy Staunton, then continue on to join with Crook to form a force that would be nearly triple the size of the enemy. But, as so often happens in war, things did not go as planned.[50]

On May 9, Crook attacked a smaller Confederate force under Brigadier General Albert Jenkins at the base of Cloyd's Mountain near Dublin. After desperate fighting with heavy casualties for both sides, Jenkins was killed and the survivors now commanded by Brigadier General John McCausland withdrew to Dublin and New River Bridge, where he received reinforcements. Crook attacked again the next day and captured and burned the bridge, but McCausland escaped again. Short of food and ammunition, Crook turned back when he found McCausland again blocking his route to Salem. General Averell's expedition to Saltville met a disappointing end when his cavalry force of about 2,000 men ran into about 4,000 troops under John Morgan and W. E. Jones and was forced to turn back to Wytheville.[51]

When Sigel arrived at Woodstock, his troops drove the Confederates out of town before they were able to destroy all the sensitive documents in the telegrapher's office. In an incredible stroke of good luck, among the surviving messages were Breckinridge's dispatches from the past week. Sigel now knew where the Confederates were, how many troops they had, and where they were headed. He had been given an opportunity that most commanders only dream about. The main purpose of his expedition had been to draw Breckinridge away from Crook. Having accomplished this, he could have moved south to New Market Gap, cross the mountain before Breckinridge could get there from Staunton, and cause any number of problems in Lee's rear and flank, the very thing that the Confederates were most afraid of. Instead, Sigel wasted an excellent opportunity and decided to play it safe and stay in Woodstock.[52]

Sigel's cautious nature is revealed in a message from Woodstock on the 13th, reporting:

> My forces are insufficient for offensive operations in this country, where the enemy is continuously on my flank and rear. My intention, therefore, is not to advance farther than this place with my main force, but have sent out strong parties in every direction. Skirmishing is going on every day. If Breckinridge should advance against us I will resist him at some convenient position.[53]

Breckinridge did not know that his correspondence with Imboden had been captured and still believed that Sigel was unaware of his approach. He had concentrated his troops at Staunton and when joined with Imboden's men at New Market, the Confederate army would number about 5,300 men and eighteen guns. They were still outnumbered, but at least they now had a fighting chance to stop the Federal advance and hold New Market Gap. The most obvious and safest strategy that would allow Breckinridge to compensate for his inferior numbers was to find a good defensive position and let Sigel attack, assuming that the federal commander would attack. Instead, Breckinridge wanted to confront the invaders. He was confident that Sigel was unaware of the Confederate concentration and decided to advance toward the enemy and fight him wherever and whenever the circumstances would be favorable. Early on the morning of the 13th, the small Confederate army moved out toward New Market.[54]

On the 11th, Sigel had sent Colonel William Boyd with two hundred cavalry troopers on an expedition to hunt for guerrillas on the eastern flank of the army and into the Page Valley. Boyd's column reached New Market Gap on the 13th and could see the town and several hundred men camped to the north. It was near sunset and despite the poor light and the warnings of several of his officers that the troops could be the enemy, Boyd ordered his men down into the Valley.[55]

The troops north of New Market were in fact Imboden's force waiting for Breckinridge on Rude's Hill. The Confederates were momentarily surprised to see Federal cavalry coming through the Gap, but Imboden quickly sent the 23rd Virginia Cavalry through New Market to hold the bridge at Smith's Creek at the base of the Gap. Leading the 18th Virginia Cavalry south, Imboden got behind Boyd's men and caught them in a vise. Within a few minutes the

Federal cavalry was scattered. Imboden wrote to Breckinridge, "We pitched into him, cut him off from the roads, and drove him into the Massanutten Mountain. Numbers have been captured, together with about half of all their horses. They are wandering in the mountain to-night cut off." Sigel had lost another cavalry detachment with nothing to show for it.[56]

While Sigel waited in Woodstock, the weather grew worse. It had been raining constantly and was unseasonably hot and humid. Except for the Valley Pike, the roads were rivers of mud and the streams nearly all flooded and difficult to ford.[57] Scouts had reported that only Imboden's small force was at New Market. The obvious importance of taking Mount Jackson and the crossroads at New Market was too much for even the cautious Sigel to resist, so he violated one of the cardinal rules of military tactics—he split his army in the face of the enemy. On the 14th Colonel August Moor, commander of the First Infantry Brigade, was sent with three regiments of infantry and 1,000 cavalry, over 2,300 men altogether, twenty miles ahead of the rest of the army toward New Market.[58]

Imboden and Breckinridge met at Lacey Springs on the afternoon of the 14th. Well aware of Sigel's slow approach, Imboden believed that there was little immediate risk that the Federal commander would try to force his way into New Market. Their dinner was interrupted by a courier reporting that fighting had broken out and the Confederate forces were being pushed back. Imboden hurried back to join his troops with instructions to hold New Market until dark and then fall back to Shirley's Hill. Breckinridge was trying to lure the Federals south of the town to a stronger position, where he would then stand and fight on ground of his own choosing.[59]

Near New Market that morning, Major Timothy Quinn and about six hundred New York cavalry troopers were engaged with Imboden's men. By noon the Federal skirmishers had crossed Meem's Bottom and were over Rude's Hill. Quinn continued to press the Confederates until they were slowly forced back into New Market by late afternoon. Colonel Moor's force, consisting of the 1st West Virginia, 34th Massachusetts, and 123rd Ohio Infantry regiments, along with about three hundred cavalry troopers under Colonel John E. Wynkoop, arrived on the scene at about the same time.[60] It was early evening before Colonel Moor had all his infantry up and moved forward in line of battle, pushing the Confederates out of New Market. Imboden knew he could not hold the town even if he wanted to, and following his orders, he fell back to the south and established a defensive line on Shirley's Hill down to Smith's Creek.[61]

During the evening there was some light skirmishing and Imboden sent his troops forward twice. Colonel Moor reported that "At about 8 P.M. a line of rebels approached across an open field on my right front with the evident purpose to turn the position I had occupied before sunset.... About two hours later my whole front was attacked and for a few minutes the firing became general."[62] Both attacks were easily repulsed and the Federal army was in control of New Market.

In May of 1864, the town of New Market was a sleepy little village of about one thousand inhabitants. The north fork of the Shenandoah River flowed behind a range of low hills northwest of the town. The rain had made the river unfordable and high bluffs on its eastern bank formed a natural barrier. From the crest of the bluffs, the ground sloped gently east toward the Valley Pike, the town's main street. About a mile southeast of the pike flows Smith's Creek at the foot of Massanutten Mountain. A narrow, muddy road crossing the mountain through a depression about four miles to the east was the reason the town was so important. New Market Gap was the only access to the other side of the mountain and could easily be blocked by a small force. With the gap under Federal control, it would take Breckinridge at least two days to march around the mountain. By that time Sigel's army could cross the Blue Ridge and advance on Lee's left flank with a two-day head start, a potential disaster for the Confederates.[63]

The residents of New Market were unaccustomed to the sounds and sights of war. Some people left town as quickly as they could while others stayed and tried to find places to hide themselves and their personal treasures. Stories of Yankee brutality spread rapidly, frightening the townspeople and causing farmers to drive their livestock into the countryside to keep them from being confiscated by the invaders. When Imboden's men retired through the town, the remaining citizens secured their homes as best they could and grimly awaited the arrival of the coming enemy. Apprehensive parents took their children down into their cellars and tried to stay awake in case they had to flee during the night.[64]

Everyone in and around New Market had a pretty uncomfortable night. The Federal troops were already cold and tired from marching all day and now they had to make camp in the muddy fields. Even worse, the rain was still falling, so there could be no fires to cook dinner. The Confederates were no better off and they did not even have the chance to rest during the night. Breckinridge's army had left Lacey Springs and was rapidly moving through the rain toward New Market.[65]

4. The Battle of New Market

In the early morning hours of May 15, the main bodies of both armies made their way toward New Market. The Confederates marched most of the night and arrived before daylight, wet and weary. Breckinridge's original plan was to form a defensive line on a series of hills running along the west side of the pike. Anchoring his line on Williamson's Hill, he hoped the Federals would attack this fortified position. The Confederates had their defensive position completed a little after dawn. Wharton's Brigade was on the left with Echols' Brigade to their right. A reserve force was formed up behind the first line with Colonel George M. Edgar's 26th Virginia Battalion and the VMI cadets.[1]

Breckinridge had told Colonel Ship he "did not wish to put the Cadets in if he could avoid it, but that should occasion require it, he would use them very freely."[2] It was a good plan that would favor the outnumbered Confederates. The only problem was that Colonel Moor refused to be pulled farther away from the rest of the Federal army and did not attack.

Sigel and the rest of the Federal army left Woodstock about 5 A.M. that same morning. It had been raining off and on for days: the roads were soaked and the fields like marshes. As they moved south, the cavalry was in the lead with the infantry struggling to keep up as they waded through the muddy ground alongside the road. Inevitably, the column gradually lengthened as units fell behind and the army lost all semblance of cohesion.[3]

Colonel Moor's defensive line ran along the Old River Road to the Lutheran church. On the far left was the West Virginia Horse artillery. Moving east was the 18th Connecticut, the 123rd Ohio and the 1st West Virginia. Snow's Maryland Battery was stationed in the church cemetery while the 34th

Massachusetts was east of the Pike. Moor's refusal to attack the Confederates showed good judgment, but he knew that his position could not withstand a heavy assault, and reinforcements were still far to the north. About 8:30 A.M. Major General Julius Stahel arrived with the rest of the cavalry and assumed command. Wanting to shorten the distance between Moor's troops and the rest of the Federal army, he decided to abandon New Market and withdraw to the north. An example of the confusion of the Federal commanders was that the 34th Massachusetts moved back, then was ordered forward, and finally moved back again to a position near Bushong's Hill.[4]

General Breckinridge decided that he had waited long enough. It was well after 10 A.M. and it was obvious that the Federals were not going to attack. Unaware of the size of the approaching Federal army, Breckinridge decided to take the initiative. He quickly took in the lay of the land and decided to scrap his original plan to fight a defensive battle. He enthusiastically told Imboden, "We can attack and whip them here, and I'll do it."[5]

About the same time that Breckinridge made his decision to move forward, General Sigel arrived at Mount Jackson and then rode forward to check on the troop dispositions. He later wrote, "Believing that a retreat would have a bad effect on our troops, and well aware of the strategical value of New Market.... I resolved to hold the enemy in check until the arrival of our main forces from Mount Jackson and then accept battle." After a brief discussion with his staff, Sigel decided to move the army forward toward New Market.[6]

The decision to advance with most of the army spread out over several miles was the first of several blunders by the Federal commanders this day. Colonel Moor now had four infantry regiments, most of the cavalry and about half of the artillery with him at New Market. Two other regiments, the 54th Pennsylvania and the 12th West Virginia, less several companies assigned to guard a wagon train, had not yet reached the field but were moving up rapidly. However, two more regiments of infantry, the 28th and 116th Ohio, and Captain Henry DuPont's Battery of the 5th U.S. Artillery were with Brigadier General Jeremiah Sullivan and the baggage trains, still several miles from New Market.[7]

While Sigel was deciding what to do, Breckinridge had his troops move forward to Shirley's Hill and aligned in a staggered line that made them look more numerous than they were. Wharton's Brigade was in two lines; on the west was Lieutenant Colonel John P. Wolfe's 51st Virginia, then Lieutenant Colonel J. Lyle Clark's 30th Virginia Battalion, Colonel George Smith's 62nd Virginia Mounted Infantry, and Colonel Robert White's dismounted 23rd Virginia Cavalry extending the line to the Pike. Behind this first line, the 26th Virginia Battalion and the VMI cadets formed another line. Echol's Brigade, composed of the 22nd Virginia Regiment and the 23rd Virginia Battalion, were stationed behind and to the right of Wharton's first line and extended across the Pike to link the main formation with Imboden's cavalry covering the area to Smith's Creek.[8]

From his vantage point on Shirley's Hill, Breckinridge could clearly see that the field in front of him was almost perfect for what he had in mind.

There was little risk of being attacked on either flank; the river protected the left and Smith's Creek the right. A small force could cover the marshes between the town and the creek, allowing Breckinridge to use most of his troops for the assault. On the right there were several positions for the artillery that would allow them to support the infantry as they advanced. Shortly after 11 A.M., Breckinridge ordered them to move out and behind a thin screen of skirmishers Wharton's battle line came over the crest of Shirley's Hill and started down toward the Federals.[9]

Confederate Brigadier General Gabriel Wharton (Virginia Military Institute Archives).

Through the rain, the Union troops could see the Confederate skirmishers moving toward their line. The veterans among them knew that these advance troops would be followed by a heavier formation, but when they saw the lines of enemy troops that advanced down the hill, the realization of what they were now facing came as quite a surprise. Until now Sigel's men believed that the only enemy troops in the area were Imboden's cavalry and perhaps a small infantry force. They had not been expecting to engage so many of the enemy. With the rest of their army spread out for several miles behind them, Colonel Moor's small force was suddenly facing disaster.[10]

The Confederates quickly moved to the valley between Shirley's Hill and Manor Hill. Most of the men of the first line got there unscathed, but by the time the reserve and VMI cadets in the rear of the formation arrived, the Federal gunners had found the range and they suffered their first casualties. Briefly resting and adjusting their formation, they soon pushed forward up the slope of Manor Hill. Even though the Confederates were slowed by deep mud, the Federal resistance was light along most of the line except where the 51st Virginia ran into the 18th Connecticut, which held out briefly, but the 123rd Ohio gave way almost immediately. The 18th Connecticut and the 123rd Ohio fell back about 400 yards and set up another line to resist the advancing enemy while the 1st West Virginia and Snow's artillery were ordered back to Bushong's Hill. It was now about 12:30 P.M. and the Confederate army had regained control of New Market and was poised to continue the attack.[11]

Soon after arriving at the front, Sigel realized that the Confederates would

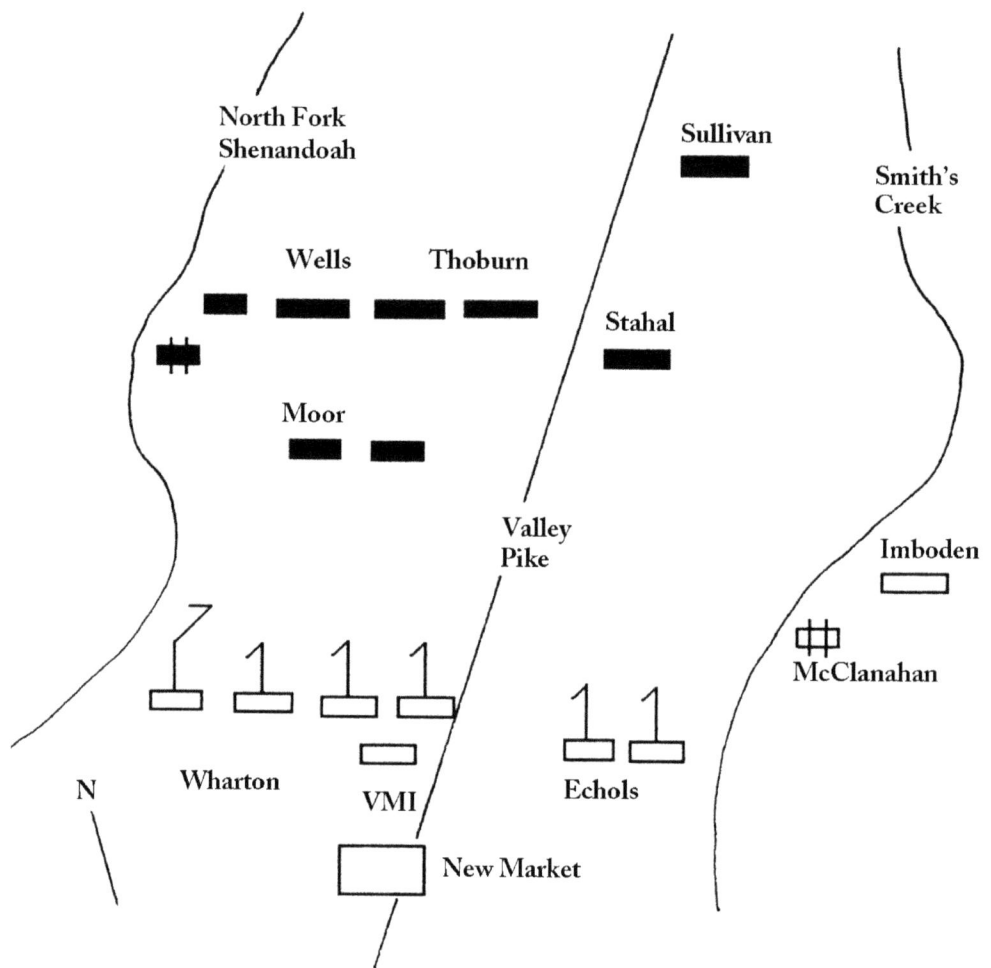

Battle of New Market

probably overrun Moor's line before the rest of the army could arrive. He ordered his troops to concentrate on the higher ground of Bushong's Hill. This was actually a very good position, with the flanks protected by the North Fork of the Shenandoah River and Smith's Creek. The ground in front was muddy and offered a clear field of fire with few trees or buildings.[12] Most importantly, by shortening the distance that the troops had to travel, it would allow the Federal army to concentrate sooner. Sigel had sent word for Sullivan to head for Bushong's Hill, but nothing seemed to be going right that day. DuPont later wrote:

> A second order arrived directing Sullivan to move at once with his infantry, but to my extreme surprise and disappointment, he interpreted this order literally and, as my battery was not specifically mentioned, directed it to remain where it was, but said he would send for it as soon as he reached the front, which he failed to do.[13]

4. The Battle of New Market

While the Confederates were regaining control of the town, the Federal cavalry, back under Stahel's command, had moved to the far left of their line to protect against a flanking movement. Even after the losses suffered by Higgins and Boyd, there were still about 2,000 troopers available. While they were waiting for orders in a large field, Imboden had moved a battery of artillery across Smith's Creek to support the infantry advance. The commander of this battery, Captain John H. McClanahan, set up his guns on a low hill about one thousand yards from the Federal cavalry. Imboden later wrote:

> The position was a magnificent one for our purpose.... A large part of his cavalry, and that nearest to us, was massed in column, close order, squadron front, giving our gunners a target of whole acres of men and horses. The guns were rapidly worked, whilst my cavalry kept on slowly down the creek as if aiming to get in the enemy's rear. The effect was magical.[14]

McClanahan opened a devastating barrage on the exposed cavalry, forcing Stahel to pull his troopers back out of range, and away from the main portion of the field.[15]

Sigel positioned his troops in two battle lines. The first line contained the 18th Connecticut on the right with the 123rd Ohio and von Kleiser's six twelve-pounders along the Pike. Colonel Moor commanded the first line, about three-fourths of a mile from his original line. This front line was to soften the Confederate attack and delay their advance until more of the army could arrive. Several hundred yards behind Moor's troops, Sigel had established his main formation on Bushong's Hill with Carlin's West Virginia Battery closest to the Shenandoah bluffs, then Snow's Maryland Battery. The infantry line contained the 34th Massachusetts closest to the artillery with the 1st West Virginia and the recently arrived 54th Pennsylvania extending the line to the Pike. The remaining troops of the 12th West Virginia were put in reserve on the right, behind the 34th Massachusetts and the artillery.[16]

At two o'clock the battle resumed in earnest. Breckinridge had positioned his artillery on the right, where several low hills allowed the guns to fire without endangering his men. He directed most of the battle from this vantage point. The Confederate battle line moved forward as the continuing rain turned the ground into a field of mud. In Moor's first line, the men of the 123rd Ohio and the 18th Connecticut could see that the Confederate formation coming toward them was much larger than their own. They fired at the enemy for a brief time and then quickly fell back toward Bushong's Hill. An officer in the 18th Connecticut wrote, "It being apparent that the line of the enemy greatly outnumbered our own, and that farther stay in that position was worse than useless."[17] Some of these troops reformed at the main line as they were supposed to, but many just keep going, "our skirmishers and infantry in front came back on the double-quick, some of them running through and over" the main Federal line, causing confusion among their comrades who were waiting to face the advancing enemy.[18]

As the Confederates approached the main Union line, Colonel George D.

Wells of the 34th Massachusetts described the tense scene as his men waited for the enemy to reach them:

> The rebels advanced in three lines of battle, each, I think, as heavy as ours, with masses on the right and left.... Their yelling grew steadily nearer.... The officers in the line were giving their orders in low tones, and every man stood, his gun at the ready, his finger on the trigger, waiting to see the face of his foe.[19]

Near the buildings on the Bushong land the ground rose slightly, which gave the 26th Virginia and most of the 51st Virginia some protection from the fire of the Federal troops. But when they reached the top of the rise they ran into a heavy, concentrated fire from muskets and artillery. Loaded with canister and grapeshot, the Federal artillery had a devastating effect on the right side of the Confederate line. At this point on the field, the course of the Shenandoah River curved east and forced the 26th Virginia to slow down and then fall behind the 51st Virginia. This part of the line slowed and then stopped as the men wavered under the intense fire, causing some of the troops to their right to also stop advancing. Gradually the right side of the 51st Virginia began to fall back. The 30th Virginia Battalion had gone out in front of the line as skirmishers and were blasted by the Federal artillery and forced back on the right of the 51st Virginia. This opened a gap between them and the 62nd Virginia as the other parts of the Confederate line advanced.[20] Colonel Wells wrote, "Our front fire was heavy, and the artillery had an enfilading fire, under which their first line went down. They staggered, went back, and their whole advance halted."[21]

The 62nd Virginia easily moved forward until they also ran into the Federal artillery fire. Passing by the Bushong house on the east, they marched into a slight depression with the VMI cadets right behind them. Instead of providing some protection against the Federal fire, this little ravine quickly became a slaughterhouse. Of over 200 casualties suffered by the 62nd Virginia during the entire battle, most of them occurred in this one spot. Colonel Smith realized that his regiment would be destroyed if they remained here. He pulled them back to take cover at a fence and wait for help before attempting to continue the attack.[22]

The Confederate attack was not progressing much better on the east side of the Pike. Colonel George S. Patton's 22nd Virginia and Lieutenant Colonel Clarence Derrick's 23rd Virginia Battalion had also run into heavy resistance. The ground on this side of the battlefield was more difficult to cross with several ridges and ravines. As the 23rd moved over the crest of a ridge, they ran into the Federal cavalry. They poured a heavy fire into the Confederate line, forcing them to stop and hug the ground to hold their position. Patton's troops soon halted and since there was no reserve force, the attack on this side also became stalled.[23]

The Confederate attack had ground to a halt and most of the first line was pinned down by heavy fire. A potential disaster was building as a gap between the 51st and 62nd opened almost in the middle of the line. The men in the front line could not move to close this opening. The only possible chance to close it before the Federals could take advantage of it and launch a counterattack was to send in the closest troops in the second line, the cadets of VMI. Breckinridge never really planned to send the cadets into combat, and certainly not against enemy fire that had stopped his veteran regiments, but he really had little choice. Reluctantly, he gave the order for them to advance.[24]

Union Colonel George Wells (Library of Congress).

The gap in the line that the cadets had to close was almost directly in their front. Moving past the Bushong house, they were exposed to the full force of the Federal fire and casualties quickly mounted as they moved through the orchard. Colonel Ship reported, "The fire was withering. It seemed impossible that any living creature could escape; and here we sustained our heaviest loss, a great many being wounded and numbers knocked down, stunned and temporarily disabled."[25] Despite the losses, the cadets forged their way through the orchard to a fence on the other side, closing the gap in the line. Years later a former cadet who was there wrote about that day: "I honestly believe that if the Battalion had not have been there and had not have acted the gallant part they did, there would have been another tale to tell."[26]

This was the decisive moment of the battle. Although the Confederate line was whole again, their casualties were mounting and Wharton's men were just barely hanging on. On the right, Breckinridge could see that the Federal cavalry was massing for a charge up the Pike and there were clear signs that Sigel was trying to organize his infantry to launch a counterattack against their struggling enemy.[27]

Over on the left of the Union line, General Stahel could see that the Confederate assault had stalled and that they were having a difficult time holding their present positions. Yet for some reason he had been slow to take advantage of the enemy's difficulties. It wasn't until about 2:45 P.M. that he decided to launch a cavalry attack against the struggling Confederate line. Massed in squadrons, nearly 2,000 Federal troopers rode toward the Confederate right in a wave of blue. As they approached, Patton's and Derrick's men held their fire until the troopers were close and then let loose a devastating combination of musket and artillery fire. By the time Stahel's men were within 300 yards of the Confederate line, they were being ripped apart by fire from both flanks and the front.[28]

The charge was broken before the Federals got near the Confederate line. Stahel tried to order a withdrawal, but few of his men could hear him over the noise of the battle. The scene became even more ghastly when the rain came pelting down harder and thunder and lightning added to the confusion. Singly, and then in groups, the cavalrymen began to turn and flee for their lives. The rout of the Union cavalry gave the Confederates a much-needed boost at a critical time. As Stahel rode west to report to Sigel, he could see his command retreating down the Pike in mass confusion.[29]

Despite the fact that Moor's troops had been pushed back, overall the battle had been going pretty well for Sigel before the cavalry debacle. Despite the mistakes made by the Federal commander, his main line was holding and inflicting heavy casualties on the enemy. If Sigel had been able to launch an attack against the gap between the 51st Virginia and the 62nd Virginia, he might have been able to rout Breckinridge's beleaguered army. Perhaps in the confusion and smoke from all the musket and cannon fire Sigel didn't see the opening in the enemy line, or perhaps he was simply too slow to grasp the opportunity that was presented. When he finally did decide to act, a coordinated infantry and cavalry attack might have destroyed the Confederates, but now there was no cavalry force available.[30]

It was now about 3:00 P.M. and Sigel finally decided it was time to attack. However, there was confusion among the Federal commanders. "Sigel seemed in a state of excitement and rode here and there with Stahel and Moor, all jabbering in German. In his excitement he seemed to forget his English entirely, and the purely American portion of his staff were totally useless to him," wrote Colonel Strother.[31] The order for the infantry to advance was given. However, the delay had given the Confederates time to regain their composure. The cadets were holding firm behind the fence in the orchard and the veterans around them were re-formed behind rails and building small walls of stones and wood. They were ready.[32]

The Federal attack was confused and uncoordinated, as if each regiment was acting on its own instead of advancing together using the full weight of a massed attack. The 1st West Virginia moved out first, with no support on either side. They advanced only a short distance before running into heavy fire from the 62nd Virginia and the cadets. With their flanks exposed, and seeing no other troops advancing with them, they were soon headed back to their own lines.[33]

Colonel Jacob M. Campbell led the 54th Pennsylvania forward about the same time the West Virginians started falling back. As they moved over a rise that had provided some protection, they ran into the same heavy fire. Trying to hold their position and advance, Campbell saw Confederate troops under Patton and Derrick moving around his left toward the rear. With the 1st West

Virginia being pursued by the enemy as they fell back on the right, Campbell could see that his troops would soon be surrounded:

> The enemy, however, pressed forward his right, which extended some distance beyond our left, and was rapidly flanking me in that direction despite the most determined resistance, when my attention was called to the fact that the regiment on my right (owing to the overwhelming numbers brought against it) had given way, and the enemy was advancing at almost right angle with my line and extending beyond the rear and right of my regiment. A few minutes only would be required to completely surround my regiment, and in the absence of any appearance of advancing support I was reluctantly compelled to order my command to retire.[34]

The final Federal regiment to advance was the 34th Massachusetts. They could see very little of the field because of the smoke, but they cheered as Colonel Wells led them forward. After the 1st West Virginia pulled back, the 34th went on alone into a storm of bullets. In only a few minutes they advanced halfway to the Bushong house with killed and wounded dropping everywhere. Colonel Wells later wrote:

> As we neared the crest of the hill we met the entire rebel force advancing and firing. The regiment on my left, which first met the fire, turned and went back, leaving the Thirty-fourth rushing alone into the enemy's line. I shouted to them to halt but could not make a single man hear or heed me, and it was not until they had climbed an intervening fence, and were rushing ahead on the other side, that I was able to run along the lines, and, seizing the color bearer by the shoulder, hold him fast as the only way of stopping the regiment.[35]

The Federal attack was a complete failure. Breckinridge now had his artillery increase its fire on the Federal guns to force them back to the base of Rude's Hill. The failed Union attacks by both the cavalry and infantry and now the decrease in artillery fire gave the advantage to the Confederates. Breckinridge did not hesitate to seize the opportunity. As the rain and thunder and lightning grew more severe, the Confederates surged forward in an unstoppable wave.[36]

Colonel Smith's 62nd Virginia, with the VMI cadets, and Colonel Patton with his 22nd Virginia advanced together against the Union line and the 23rd Infantry moved on the flank. Colonel Campbell and his Pennsylvania troops were totally exposed when the 1st West Virginia retreated after a token resistance. The 54th Pennsylvania put up a gallant but short fight against these overwhelming odds, the regiment losing nearly a third of its men by now.[37]

Over on the left the 51st Virginia and the 26th Virginia concentrated on Colonel Wells and his 34th Massachusetts. The Confederate fire was like a storm of bullets, shredding branches and leaves in a grove behind their position. In minutes the cadets were firing into the Federals' left, part of the 51st Virginia was flanking the right and Colonel Wells could do nothing but withdraw or lose his entire command.[38]

> I ordered a retreat, but they either could not hear or would not heed the order. I was finally obliged to take hold of the color bearer, face him about, and tell him to follow me, in order to get the regiment off the field. They fell back slowly, firing in retreat, and encouraging each other not to run. But the rebels were coming on at the double-quick and concentrating their whole fire upon us. I told the men to run and get out of the fire as quickly as possible....[39]

General Sigel had remained on the right throughout the fighting. He may have been a poor general, but he was no coward. Seeing the collapse of his line, Sigel ordered the artillery to pull out and save as many guns as possible. Then the beaten general rode toward the Pike to try and salvage something of his demoralized army, now in full retreat. The Valley Pike was crowded with wagons, cannon, and fleeing men.[40]

The victorious Confederates pursued their beaten enemy for about three miles until they approached Rude's Hill, where Sigel's artillery began shelling them and Breckinridge ordered his men to halt. His men were as exhausted as the Federals and also nearly out of ammunition. They had a brief rest while the supply wagons brought more ammunition. It was now about 5 P.M. and Breckinridge was planning one more attack to completely destroy what remained of the Federal army.[41]

While the beaten Union army was streaming backwards, General Sullivan and his two regiments finally arrived and set up a line on Rude's Hill. Still hoping to salvage something from the disaster, Sigel tried to rally as much of his fleeing army as he could and set up a defensive line anchored by the 28th and 116th Ohio regiments. But it was too late. Both Ohio regiments had virtually run nearly four miles to arrive at Rude's Hill and were exhausted, the 28th had only about half its men present, the rest strung out behind them too tired to move.[42] Colonel Moor later reported that their commander "had ordered bayonets to be fixed to clear his way on the pike up to the battle-field through disgraceful fleeing masses of cavalry and straggling infantry." These new arrivals were in no condition to put up a fight.[43]

On Rude's Hill, Sigel consulted with Sullivan and his staff. It was obvious that considering the heavy losses already suffered and the exhausted condition of those still in the ranks, the Federals could not withstand another Confederate attack. Another defeat could bring on total disaster since the only escape route was the single bridge over the badly swollen North Fork of the Shenandoah. Sigel wrote that:

> When this new and last line was forming I met General Sullivan, and after some consultation we came to the conclusion not to await another attack, for the reason that our losses were severe; that the regiments that had sustained the brunt of the fight were nearly out of ammunition and would have no time to receive it from the train, which was in the rear, beyond the bridge; that our position was not a good one, being commanded by the enemy's guns, posted on the hill in front of our left; and that in case of defeat we could not cross the swollen river, except by the bridge.[44]

He ordered the army to continue the retreat.

After being left behind when Sullivan moved forward, Captain DuPont decided to make his way to the front without orders. His initiative proved important to the retreating Federals, as it was his battery that provided much of the fire to keep the Confederates, who were now moving forward again, at bay.[45]

DuPont's battery was "in the open and entirely without support, but a thick curtain of smoke which hung over the field prevented the Confederates from discovering this fact, and it seemed necessary to risk the loss of some of my guns in order to cover and protect the retreat...."[46]

DuPont's guns slowed the Confederate pursuit enough so that by 7 P.M. the dispirited Union army was able to make good its escape over the Shenandoah bridge. Captain DuPont's guns and a cavalry escort were the last Federal units to cross the river to safety, burning the bridge to prevent the Confederates from following.[47]

Sigel kept his weary men moving until they were about a mile north of the river. After setting up the artillery for defense, the men were finally able to get a couple of hours' rest before resuming the retreat. This was their first real break from marching or fighting since early morning and most were too tired to do much but sit and talk about the battle and their missing comrades. Most of the men stoically accepted their defeat. They believed they had put up a good fight but were simply beaten by better troops under a better commander.[48] Colonel Strother also felt that the men were not to blame for the defeat. "The campaign was conducted miserably by Sigel.... I came to the conclusion that Sigel is merely a book soldier acquainted with the techniques of the art of war but having no capacity to fight with troops in the field."[49]

On the other side of the river the victors began to celebrate. But the battle had taken a heavy toll on both the Confederates and their beaten foe, and it was a busy night for both the military and civilian doctors in and around New Market. Most of the large buildings in town were pressed into service as hospitals. Many of the townspeople volunteered to help the wounded as they lay in the fields with the rain still coming down. An Article in the *Rockingham Register* stated:

> The conduct of the people of New Market, during the fight and after the conflict terminated was above all praise. A better people—more generous, self-sacrificing and devoted to the Confederate cause, does not live. The ladies stood in the doors of their dwellings with refreshments for the wounded and hungry soldiers as they came from the battle-field, and some of them assisted in dressing and binding up the wounds of the poor fellows who had come to defend their home from invasion and desecration.[50]

For both the Confederate soldiers and the townspeople, the death and suffering of the wounded tempered the joy of victory.

That evening both commanders sent messages to their headquarters. As could be expected, they were as different as were the men. Breckinridge sent a simple, businesslike message to Lee reporting that "two miles above New Market, my command met the enemy, under General Sigel, advancing up the Valley, and defeated him with heavy loss. The action had just closed at Shenandoah River. Enemy fled across North Fork of the Shenandoah, burning the bridge behind him."[51]

In his report Sigel took severe liberties with the facts:

> A severe battle was fought to-day at New Market between our forces and those of Echols and Imboden, under Breckinridge. Our troops were overpowered by superior numbers. I, therefore, withdrew them gradually from the battle-field, and recrossed the Shenandoah at about 7 P.M. Under the circumstances prevailing I find it necessary to retire to Cedar Creek. The battle was fought on our side by 5,500 in all against 8,000 to 9,000 of the enemy. We lost about 600 in killed and wounded, and 50 prisoners.[52]

The grim task of totaling up casualties began the morning after the battle. Breckinridge had lost fewer than fifty killed and over 500 wounded or missing out of just under 5,000 men who took part. The Federal losses were larger, with nearly 100 killed, over 500 wounded and just under 200 missing out of a little over 5,000. With the casualties from the two ill-fated cavalry expeditions added to the total, Sigel lost over 1,000 men for the campaign. The Confederates also collected a great deal of equipment and supplies, including five cannon that they would put to good use against their former owners.[53]

On the 17th Sigel sent an ambulance loaded with medical supplies to aid in the care of his wounded in Confederate hands. Breckinridge had previously asked for help in burying the Federal dead but Sigel refused this request. The Confederate dead were laid to rest in St. Matthew's cemetery but the local residents didn't want any of the hated enemy buried there. The tired Confederates had to bury them along the Pike or where they fell. In a few days the continuing rain would wash away the few inches of soil covering the dead and parts of bodies would be exposed all along the road.[54]

General Lee, whose army was fighting for its life with Grant, sent a brief message of congratulations. "I offer you the thanks of this army for your victory over General Sigel. Press him down the Valley, and, if practicable, follow him to Maryland."[55] The destruction of the bridge over the Shenandoah prevented an immediate pursuit and Lee instructed Breckinridge to bring his troops east to reinforce the troops facing Grant's relentless attacks. "If you can follow Sigel into Maryland, you will do more good than by joining us. If you cannot, and your command is not otherwise needed in the Valley or in your department, I desire you to prepare to join me."[56]

Before learning of Sigel's defeat General Grant had wired to Halleck asking, "Cannot General Sigel go up Shenandoah Valley to Staunton?" Halleck replied, "I have sent the substance of your dispatch to General Sigel. Instead of advancing on Staunton he is already in full retreat on Strasburg. If you expect anything from him you will be mistaken. He will do nothing but run. He never did anything else."[57]

This was close to the truth, as it took only one day for the retreating Federal army to reach Strasburg, compared to the five days it took to march the thirty-two miles from Strasburg to New Market.[58] The partial success of Averell's raid on the rail lines in Southwest Virginia gave Colonel Strother the opportunity to write with more than a trace of bitterness, "We are doing a good

4. The Battle of New Market

business in this department. Averell is tearing up the Virginia and Tennessee Railroad while Sigel is tearing down the Valley turnpike."[59]

While the number of men who fought at New Market was small compared to the armies in Eastern Virginia, the battle was still very important for several reasons. The Confederate victory gave them control of the Valley for a few more weeks, providing time to harvest the crops that were feeding Lee's army at Petersburg. Most importantly, the Confederates kept control of the mountain passes and were able to protect Lee's flank. Imboden later wrote:

> If Sigel had beaten Breckinridge on the 15th of May General Lee could not have spared the men to check his progress.... without exposing Richmond to immediate, and almost inevitable capture. In view of these probable consequences, there was no secondary battle of the war of more importance than that of New Market.[60]

Breckinridge did a superior job as both department commander and battlefield leader. He exhibited excellent organizational skills and motivated his troops by example. On the battlefield, he held nothing back at the critical moment and had the courage to accept the risks necessary to achieve victory. Franz Sigel, on the other hand, exhibited excessive caution and committed the major sin of splitting his command in the face of the enemy, inviting defeat. Colonel Strother's assessment of Sigel's leadership was severe:

> I had hoped when he first came into the department that he was at least honest and enthusiastic for an idea, but I think now he was an adventurer and speculator, venal and intriguing. We can afford to lose such a battle as New Market to get rid of such a mistake as Major General Sigel.[61]

5. New Commander, Same Plan

After the fiasco at New Market, Grant, Halleck and Secretary of War Edwin M. Stanton all agreed that Sigel should be replaced. Grant was disgusted by the affair and when Halleck suggested Major General David Hunter, Grant replied, "By all means I would say appoint General Hunter, or anyone else, to the command of West Virginia."[1] The administration wasn't sure what to do with Franz Sigel. Obviously, they could not give him another field command, but they also feared the political impact of his removal. Hunter solved the problem by assigning him to command the reserve troops protecting the Baltimore and Ohio Railroad, well away from the main theatre of action.[2]

Born in Princeton, New Jersey, in 1802, David Hunter came from patriotic stock. His father was a chaplain in the Revolutionary Army and his mother, Mary Stockton, was the sister of Richard Stockton, a signer of the Declaration of Independence. General Hunter took the war against the South much more personally than most of the men in the Union. Hunter had served in Kansas before the war and witnessed atrocities that convinced him that the institution of slavery, and its supporters, were evil and had to be destroyed. Friends in the administration helped him rise in rank but several times Hunter allowed his personal feelings to get him in trouble. As the commander of the Department of the South, part of South Carolina, Georgia and Florida, Hunter issued an order freeing all slaves, which was quickly rescinded by the president.[3]

Captain DuPont wrote:

> Upon assuming command of the Department of West Virginia, General Hunter was only two months short of sixty-two years of age. A man of

middle height, with broad shoulders and very swarthy complexion, the expression of his somewhat prominent features was stern and severe; but he was free from affectation and his manner was tranquil except when disturbed by fits of sudden anger which were by no means infrequent. Unfortunately, his mentality was largely dominated by prejudices and antipathies so intense and so violent as to render him at time quite incapable of taking a fair and unbiased view of many military and political situations. Aspiring, energetic and self-reliant, his bold and rather aggressive temperament, as well as his intolerant ideas, often gave rise to unpleasant relations with others, whom he did not hesitate to criticize and denounce in the plainest terms....[4]

Union Major General David Hunter (Library of Congress).

Hunter was to follow the same basic plan that Sigel had tried; move south to Staunton, capturing the city and destroying as much railroad equipment and military supplies as possible. Crook and Averell were to meet Hunter at Staunton and the combined army was then to move toward Charlottesville or Lynchburg, depending on the strength of the Confederate opposition.[5] As a wire to Halleck shows, Grant was hoping for a major blow at the Confederate supply lines, but apparently he really did not expect much more from this expedition than he had from Sigel's failed attempt:

> The enemy are evidently relying for supplies greatly on such as are brought over the branch road running through Staunton. On the whole, therefore, I think it would be better for General Hunter to move in that direction; reach Staunton and Gordonsville, or Charlottesville, if he does not meet too much opposition. If he can hold at bay a force equal to his own he will be doing good service.[6]

The Army of the Shenandoah that Hunter took over had been beaten but still had plenty of fight in it. The men were as brave as any others and hungry for victory, but they needed capable and energetic leadership, traits that were not too common in this army. General Hunter was not satisfied with many of his subordinate commanders and felt that the cavalry was "utterly demoralized from frequent defeats by inferior forces and retreats without fighting, and it most urgently needs a commander of grit, zeal, activity, and courage.... It would be impossible to exaggerate the inefficiency of General Stahel."[7] Trying to get Stahel and Sullivan replaced, Hunter requested that:

> two efficient and energetic brigadiers might be sent immediately to this department to report to me in the field.... General Stahel, in command of the cavalry, has had but little experience as a cavalry officer in this country, nor am I aware that he has had any experience with cavalry elsewhere. General Sullivan, in command of the infantry, may be a very excellent officer, but is also of limited experience, and I, therefore, urgently need two additional brigadiers of experience, energy, and reliability."[8]

On May 23 General Halleck sent two messages responding to Hunter's request for replacements and offered important information on Confederate troop movements. "Energetic and efficient brigadiers are scarce. Name any you want who are available and you shall have them. General Grant telegraphed last evening that Breckinridge had joined Lee."[9] The second was more specific:

> There are no vacancies of brigadier-general of volunteers. You have three generals of cavalry in your department, Stahel, Duffié, and Averell, certainly enough for your cavalry force. If any are worthless recommend them to be mustered out and I will indorse it. No one can be appointed till some one else is mustered out."[10]

While Hunter was getting his army ready for its next campaign into the Shenandoah Valley, guerrillas were busier than ever in the rear areas. Part of the reason for Sigel's failure was that the long supply lines needed when advancing into the Valley were easily broken. Realizing how difficult it was to catch the partisans, Hunter decided to focus attention on the support they received from the local civilian population. An attack on a wagon train passing through the town of Newtown brought a swift response and a warning.[11] On May 24th Major Timothy Quinn of the 1st New York Cavalry was ordered to

> proceed at once with your command to Newtown, ascertain the house from which our train was fired upon last night, and burn the same with all the outbuildings pertaining thereto. Notify the inhabitants of the town and along the pike if our trains or escorts are fired upon in that way again, that the commanding general will cause to be burned every rebel house within five miles of the place at which the firing occurs.[12]

The Army of the Shenandoah, reorganized and with a new commander, moved south from Cedar Creek on the morning of May 26. The next day they camped near Woodstock, producing pandemonium among the residents who hardly expected to see a Federal army so soon after the defeat at New Market. Colonel Strother wrote, "The whole town was squalling with women, children, chickens, and geese."[13] Hunter waited for two days in Woodstock for a supply train to catch up and bring badly needed shoes. While there the troops busied themselves by gathering food and threatening to burn the town to the ground.[14]

Almost immediately after the New Market victory, General Lee had ordered Breckinridge and his troops to join him in the life or death struggle with Grant. This left General Imboden to face the approaching enemy alone. When he learned of Hunter's advance, Imboden wrote to Lee, "His cavalry outnumbers ours two to one; his infantry four to one; his artillery four to one. He is moving on my flank, and will compel me to fall back. There is no point this side of Mount Crawford where I can successfully resist him, and there it is very doubtful...."[15]

The response to Imboden's pleas for help was certainly not what he was hoping for, but must not have been much of a surprise considering the desperate fighting going on to the east between Grant and Lee:

> General Lee informed me that he could not then send me any assistance from the army near Richmond, but would direct General William E. Jones, who was in Southwestern Virginia, to come to my aid with every available man he could raise; and that I might retard Hunter's advance as much as possible, he ordered me to call out the "reserves" of Rockingham and Augusta counties.[16]

These troops were poorly armed militia consisting of men over fifty and boys between sixteen and eighteen. Concerned that the Federal cavalry might outflank and destroy his small force, Imboden was unable to do anything other than retreat in front of the Federal army while trying to slow them with harassing tactics until General Jones arrived with reinforcements.[17]

General Jones was a native Virginian, 40 years old with black hair. Although short in stature with a high-pitched voice, he was fearless in battle. His proven courage under fire and readiness to suffer the same hardships his men faced while on the march earned Jones the respect of his troops. He was also a chronic complainer, had little patience and was not afraid to criticize superiors.[18]

Imboden later wrote:

> He was an old army officer, brave as a lion, and had seen much service, and was known as a hard fighter. He was a man, however, of high temper, morose and fretful to such a degree that he was known by the soubriquet of "Grumble Jones." He held the fighting qualities of the enemy in great contempt, and never would admit the possibility of defeat where the odds against him were not much over two to one.[19]

On the 28th Hunter sent a message to Sullivan exhibiting a change in his early opinion of the infantry command:

> I am much pleased with the infantry, who must form the main reliance of every army. They are fine, stalwart, soldierly young fellows for the most part. You will have a beautiful division with proper care, and if we can only inspire them with confidence by teaching them their own strength, and every man is determined to do his whole duty, we are sure, under God's blessing, of complete victory. Impress on all your officers and men the importance of strict and unhesitating obedience to orders. In this is the true strength of every army...."[20]

The Federal army left Woodstock on May 29. As they moved through the Mount Jackson area there was an increase in Confederate harassment, but Hunter easily crossed the North Fork of the Shenandoah River and arrived at New Market the next day. There the troops came upon a sickening sight. The exhausted Confederates had not actually buried most of the Federal dead from the battle on the 15th, but rather hastily covered them with just a few inches of dirt where they had fallen. This thin layer of soil had been subsequently washed away in the continuing rain. Parts of bodies were exposed and the stench of decay was intense. Burial details were organized and the fallen men were given proper graves with markers.[21]

Early on the morning of June 2, the Federal army left New Market heading south on the Valley Pike. As the troops moved out, they got a rousing sendoff with bands playing and the cheers of their comrades who had been wounded on the 15th and were still being cared for. This encouraging start didn't last long. Imboden's men began harassing the column soon after leaving the town and the first serious skirmishing occurred at Lacy Springs a few miles north of Harrisonburg.[22]

As the Union troops moved south, it became obvious that as the length of the supply lines increased, so did the opportunity for guerrilla attacks. This made it difficult, if not impossible, to supply the army by wagon trains. Hunter was following the same basic orders that Grant had given to Sigel before his ill-fated campaign began. In these instructions, Grant wrote that the Federal troops should live off the land whenever possible. "In this latter case, however, indiscriminate marauding should be avoided. Nothing should be taken not absolutely necessary for the troops, except when captured from an armed enemy."[23]

These good intentions would prove to be difficult to enforce when faced with the necessity of feeding thousands of hungry men. As there had been few military operations in the upper Valley, Hunter expected that supplies would be available. He was apparently unaware that forage and grain were so scarce in Shenandoah and Rockingham counties that even the Confederate forces had trouble obtaining an adequate supply. Many of the Federal troops were on short rations already and incidents of pillaging grew more common as they moved south.[24] Colonel Strother wrote that in Harrisonburg:

> The requisition on the town for meat and flour has created great consternation and disgust. It seems hard but it is necessary as the army must feed. The soldiers in addition are plundering dreadfully from all accounts. This is not necessary and should not be permitted, especially as there are some wounded Union soldiers here who have been well treated by the citizens.[25]

On the 3rd the Federal army moved out early in the morning and advanced in the direction of Mount Crawford, where the Confederates were waiting for them in a strong defensive position. Imboden's force numbered about 3,000, and although vastly outnumbered, the defenders were in a strong position.[26] An assault would probably prove too costly for any result that it might achieve and, more importantly, might force a delay in reaching their main objective at

5. New Commander, Same Plan

Staunton. Colonel Strother wrote that he advised Hunter to "move by way of Port Republic, cross the river there, and take Waynesboro with his cavalry, thereby cutting off stores and railroad stock at Staunton. He would also cut off the enemy that way, which would demoralize him greatly."[27]

That night troops from General Jones began arriving and Imboden was disappointed in their numbers, about 2,000, and their quality:

> To my dismay I found they were not generally organized in bodies larger than battalions, and in companies and fragments of companies ... and in large part indifferently armed. Indeed, many of the men were convalescents taken from the hospitals, and furloughed dismounted cavalrymen who had gone home for a remount, and were taken possession of by General Jones wherever he could find them...."[28]

During the day of the 4th, General John C. Vaughn arrived with a small brigade of less than 800 men. These men brought the Confederate army total to over 4,000 with eleven pieces of artillery.[29] Imboden later described the dire circumstances now facing the small Confederate army:

> Hunter, with eleven thousand superbly-appointed troops of all arms, was only eight miles distant in our front, and Crook and Averill, with seven thousand more, only two days' march in our rear; the two bodies rapidly approaching each other, and we between them ... and with no hope of further assistance. Obviously our policy was to fight Hunter at the earliest moment, and possibly defeat him, and then turn upon Crook and Averill and do the best we could.[30]

If both Federal columns were to combine, there was no Confederate force anywhere near that could stop Hunter from taking Staunton and possibly Lynchburg.

When General Jones arrived at the Confederate headquarters at Mount Crawford, he assumed command as the senior officer. He approved of Imboden's deployment of the improvised little army and they went about the business of organizing their forces as much as possible. Imboden and Vaughn's brigades were left intact and the rest of the infantry had been formed into two brigades with each containing about 1,000 men. The men who formed these patched together units had no time to become familiar with each other or their leaders, and there was no time to correct the deficiencies in organization and discipline.[31]

Imboden had the defenses at Mount Crawford ready and he "fully expected an attack early on the morning of the 4th."[32] When no attack came, Imboden sent out cavalry patrols, who soon found that Hunter had left the Valley Pike and was moving southeast toward Port Republic. Both Jones and Imboden did not believe the initial reports of the Federal change in direction, thinking it might be a trick to maneuver the Confederates out of a good defensive position, but soon it was confirmed that Hunter had outflanked them.[33] Colonel Strother wrote, "The enemy evidently did not expect us to move by this route and so far have had no information of our line of march."[34]

Imboden took his cavalry to try and delay Hunter's advance so that the rest of the army would have time to reach and fortify a position between Port Republic and Staunton:

> As we were in my native county, Augusta, I knew every road, and almost every farm over which Hunter would pass. I did not, therefore, hesitate to urge on General Jones to let me select the point of conflict with Hunter. He consented to this, and I chose the crest of what is known as "Mowry's hill," an eminence overlooking the beautiful little vale of Long Meadow run, about eight miles northeast of Staunton.[35]

Mowry's Hill ran perpendicular to the road that Hunter would have to take to reach Staunton. From this position the Confederates could block the path of the Federal army and partially offset their superior numbers. Jones and Vaughn agreed with Imboden's proposal and the Confederate plan seemed to be set.[36]

Between Hunter's army and the location Imboden had picked out to make their stand lay the small village of Piedmont, about thirteen miles east of Staunton and situated among rolling hills and forests. It had just one row of houses along the East Road going from Port Republic to Staunton. The Middle River ran along the west of the village with several smaller streams flowing through the area into the river. There were several large, prosperous farms in the area, most of whose owners objected to the war and slavery on religious grounds and considered themselves neutral, but the war was coming to their peaceful little village anyway.[37]

6. The Battle of Piedmont

Just after dawn on June 5, the Federal cavalry left Port Republic and moved down the road to Staunton. About 7 A.M. the 18th Virginia Cavalry, commanded by Colonel George Imboden, brother of the general, engaged the 1st New York Cavalry and the 21st New York Cavalry as the Federals were moving toward Piedmont. The fighting went back and forth with the Confederates doing their best to delay the Union troopers. After a short but violent fight, Imboden's troopers had to fall back before they were overwhelmed by superior numbers. Among the captured Confederate cavalrymen was another of the Imboden brothers, Frank.[1]

General Imboden wrote that "we came in collision with his cavalry so unexpectedly that I became more seriously engaged than I intended or my instructions warranted, and had great difficulty in extricating my command from what, for a little while, was a most perilous position."[2]

Imboden and Vaughn both believed that Jones had agreed with them to make a stand at Mowry's Hill, but when Jones arrived at Piedmont he changed his mind and decided to fight there. General Imboden continued, "Our next stand was made near Piedmont, where, to my amazement and against my solemn and angry protest, General Jones had decided to fight, instead of at Mowry's Hill, three miles further back."[3] Jones was not the type to have his orders questioned and when Imboden and Vaughn protested the change in plans, he ordered them to move their cavalry to the right side of the army, take up position on Round Top Hill and await further orders, which the two disgusted veterans did.[4]

Despite the objections of his subordinates, General Jones had picked a very good defensive position. The main Confederate line was positioned between a bend in the Middle River and the East Road. Colonel Beuhring

Jones, commanding the First Brigade, was on the right with the right flank of the 60th Virginia Regiment on the East Road. The Second Brigade, commanded by Colonel William Browne, filled the line across the front and to the left with its left resting on a steep bluff at the river. This "L" shaped formation protected both flanks and made good use of the terrain. The 3rd Battalion Valley Reserves were stationed behind a wooded area to the rear of the main line. General Vaughn's troopers were stationed behind the Cross Road and on the right of East Road with Imboden further south toward Round Top Hill to protect the flank and rear. The infantry built up palisades of fence rails and timber, called "railpens," across their front and the East Road. The only flaw in the position was that Vaughn's troopers were drawn up to the right and a little behind the reserves, leaving a gap of about five hundred yards between the infantry and Vaughn's cavalry.[5]

Colonel Strother described the position as

> strong and well chosen. It was on a conclave of wooded hills commanding an open valley between and open, gentle slopes in front. On our right in advance of the village of Piedmont was a line of log and rail defenses very advantageously located in the edge of a forest and just behind the rise of a smooth, open hill so that troops moving over this hill could be mowed down by musketry from the works at short range and to prevent artillery being used against them. The left flank of this palisade rested on a steep and impracticable bluff sixty feet high and washed at its base by the Shenandoah. Just behind this work was the village itself, a single street of wooden houses, and nearly a mile in the rear was another line of rail defenses also located in the border of a wood crossing the valley and terminating with the twenty-pounder battery on the ridge to their extreme right.[6]

As Hunter's army came up to the Confederate position, Colonel Moor's Brigade, with the 18th Connecticut, 28th Ohio, 116th Ohio and part of the 5th New York Heavy Artillery, arrived first and formed between the cavalry on the far right along the river and the road from Port Republic. Colonel Joseph Thoburn's Brigade with the 54th Pennsylvania, 34th Massachusetts and 12th West Virginia arrived soon after and deployed to the left on higher ground near the East Road. Captain DuPont also positioned his twenty-two guns on the left where they could fire on both sides of the Confederate defenses from a ridge near Thoburn's troops. Around 10:00 A.M., Moor had his troops in line and began to advance against the enemy skirmishers, forcing them to fall back over the hill and into the main Confederate line in the woods just north of the village. Fighting dismounted the 21st New York Cavalry. The 14th Pennsylvania Cavalry helped the infantry to force the enemy back, but could not overcome the Confederate defenses. General Hunter arrived about 11 o'clock and after a quick inspection of the field ordered the men to advance.[7]

It was warm and the sun was shining when the Federal line moved out. Moor's troops, led by the 18th Connecticut, pushed forward into a hail of bullets from the Confederate railpens and were stopped cold. General Jones then reinforced his left and launched a counterattack. Surging down the hill, the Confederates of the 45th Virginia Infantry Regiment and the 45th Virginia

6. *The Battle of Piedmont*   55

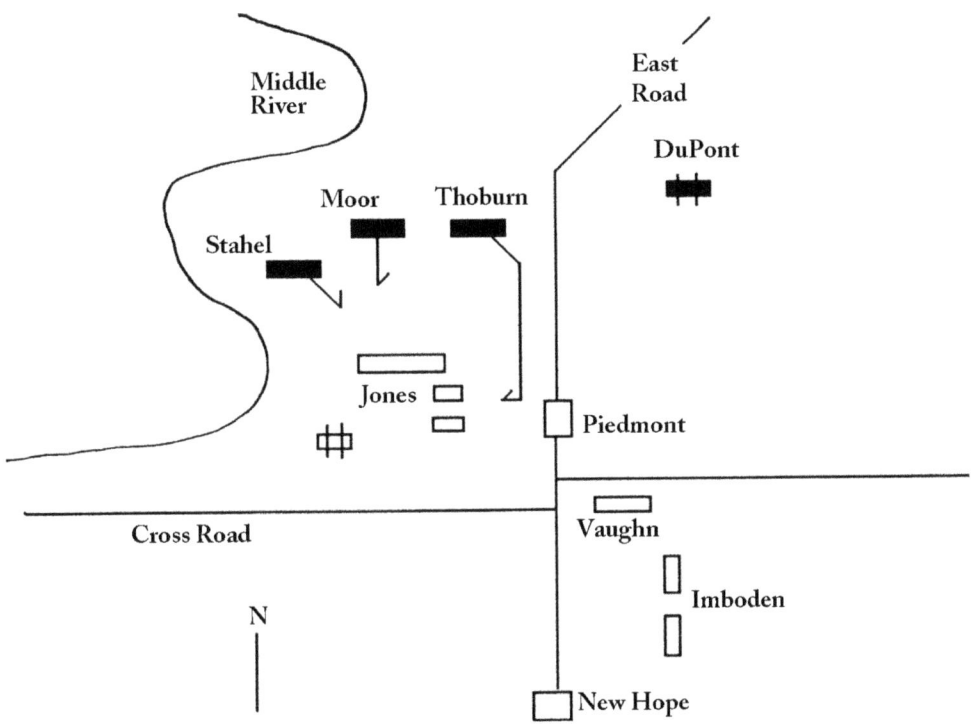

Battle of Piedmont

Battalion broke the Federal attack and forced them back. The right of Moor's brigade faced a critical test as the Confederates began to overlap their line, but the 116th Ohio came up on the far right just in time to blunt the counterattack. With Captain DuPont pouring artillery fire into the Confederates and the 116th standing firm, they were forced to stop and then slowly had to fall back to the protection of the railpens on the heights.[8]

Colonel Moor reorganized his troops and sent them forward again only to be repulsed again. The Confederates quickly launched their own counterattack, but they too were halted and thrown back. By now it was obvious that the Federal infantry could make no headway against the fortified enemy positions. Two cannon from Von Kleiser's battery were brought up to support the 18th Connecticut and the 5th New York. They were able to get close enough to the Confederate railpens to have a devastating effect by "knocking the rail pens in splinters amid great slaughter."[9] But even though damaged, the railpens still provided protection from infantry fire for the stubborn defenders.

About 2 P.M. the Confederates scrambled out from behind their shelters and launched yet another attack on Moor's Brigade. This third attack was the most serious and there was desperate fighting, especially around Von Klieser's guns, before the Confederates were forced to return to their lines. By now

Hunter was so worried that the Confederates might launch a mass attack that would overwhelm the right side of his line that he ordered the wagon trains turned around so they would have a better chance to escape if necessary.[10]

So far the battle had gone well for the Confederates. Hunter's troops had attacked the nearly impregnable railpens three times only to be driven back each time, and the last Confederate counterattack had come close to breaking the Union line. Jones must have been feeling optimistic that he could at the very least hold this position and halt the Federal advance toward Staunton, and there was a possibly of a great victory if he could beat Hunter's army outright.

While the fighting on the Union right was going back and forth, Hunter had ordered Colonel Thoburn to move farther to the left to try and exploit the gap between the Confederate infantry and cavalry. Thoburn led his men through a heavily wooded area until they arrived undetected on the Confederate right flank. DuPont's artillery opened a heavy barrage on the railpens along East Road and about 3 P.M. Thoburn's men advanced up the slope to surprise the 60th Virginia as the Union troops rushed their position. The 34th Massachusetts was on the left and rapidly overlapped the Confederate entrenchments attacking the flank and rear of the stunned defenders. Jones immediately sent the reserves forward to try to stem the Union attack. Desperate hand-to-hand fighting took place.[11]

Colonel Jacob Campbell of the 54th Pennsylvania described the attack:

> We advanced up to the brow of the hill, where my regiment lay down on the ground, discharging a volley into the enemy, and immediately charged into the woods on the right flank and rear of the enemy's intrenched position. Here for a short time a most desperate struggle took place, bayonets and clubbed guns were used on both sides, and many hand-to-hand encounters took place. So sudden and apparently so unexpected to the enemy was our movement on their flank that they were soon compelled to give way in great confusion, despite all the efforts of their officers to rally them. About 100 yards from the front of the woods was a fence running from the left of the line, and parallel with it, extending along the front of the regiment on my left. Along this fence to protect their flank the enemy had a strong force posted. This appeared to be the key to their position, and they held it most obstinately for some time, partially checking the advance of the regiment in front of them. It was here that Brigadier-General Jones commanded in person, and was killed while encouraging and rallying his troops.[12]

While Thoburn's men were advancing on the left, Hunter ordered Moor to launch his brigade against the front. Within minutes they were plunging through the Confederate defenses.[13]

Colonel Weddle of the First (West) Virginia Infantry

> saw the opportunity and called on the First, "Boys, there's Colonel Thoburn doubling up the enemy on the right, let's meet him in the defences. Charge!" The men responded with a cheer, and steadily the regiment advanced, increasing the pace to the double-quick, and, as the distance decreased, into a run, arriving at the fortifications, jumping and clambering over them, and gaining the inside of the works, giving the defenders little or no time to rally,

commenced a hand-to-hand contest, pushing them back and putting them to flight in a short time.[14]

With their commanding general dead, Union infantry attacking from front and flank, and Colonel Wynkoop leading a cavalry attack on the right, what was left of the Confederate line soon broke and began to flee in panic.[15] In his report, Colonel Campbell stated, "Those who were not captured were driven through the woods and down a steep bank into the river.... So numerous were the captures made of the enemy, that I was compelled to stop taking them to the rear, and simply disarm them and turn them out over the barricade to be taken charge of by the cavalry...."[16]

As the fleeing Confederates tried to escape to the south and west, Federal cavalry under Colonel Wynkoop followed to exploit the victory. Vaughn and Imboden finally left their position on Round Top Hill to form a rear guard to cover the withdrawal of the surviving infantry. A small body of infantry along with McClanahan's battery made a stand near New Hope and with the help of their cavalry, the Confederates were able to halt the Union pursuit and allow the remainder of the army to escape.[17]

That evening Vaughn informed General Lee of the defeat and sent a message to Secretary of War Seddon from Fisherville giving him the bad news. "My command is much scattered. The enemy is pursuing. I fear I will be forced to leave the Valley. Staunton cannot be held."[18] Later that evening Imboden joined Vaughn and they decided that since there was no chance of getting any meaningful reinforcements in time to stop Hunter from taking Staunton, the only realistic avenue open to them was to continue to withdraw to Waynesboro.[19]

The casualties at Piedmont were high considering the relatively small numbers of men engaged, a sign of the ferocity of the fighting. General Hunter reported about 500 killed and wounded, and the defeated Confederates' loss was "over 1,000 prisoners in our hands, including 60 officers. The killed and wounded are estimated at 600 men." Assuming that Hunter's casualties were estimated too low and there was some inflation in the Confederate loss, it was still a lopsided victory for the Federal army in the Shenandoah Valley.[20]

Finally, after three years of war, a Federal army had won a clear-cut victory in the upper Shenandoah Valley. Although Jones had a reserve mainly made up of local militia, his main force consisted of experienced infantry veterans who had seen plenty of action. Hunter's army clearly outnumbered the Confederates, but the 16th Ohio and 123rd Ohio did not see action and were held in reserve, so the difference in numbers was between 1,000 and 2,000 men. Even with fewer men, the good defensive position Jones had laid out and the solid protection offered by the railpens could have easily resulted in a Confederate victory. Their defeat was a result of two glaring lapses: the gap between the infantry and cavalry on the right, and the failure of the cavalry to take action when the Union troops attacked through that gap.[21]

The fatal gap between the cavalry and the far right infantry position could have resulted because Jones was not familiar with the topography of the area, or he might not have been exact in his orders to Vaughn and Imboden. It is also possible that Vaughn could have misunderstood his orders and posted his men too far south and Imboden simply extended his line as he was ordered. These are problems that can easily occur on any battlefield.

The failure of the cavalry to participate in the action on the right is much more difficult to understand. As the Federal troops swept around the right flank of the Confederate infantry, they presented their own flank to Vaughn and Imboden, who did nothing. The Confederate cavalry outnumbered Thoburn's infantry and a charge could have destroyed them and probably won the battle. Imboden believed that the orders he received from Jones gave him no latitude for independent action and were a strict prohibition of his engaging the enemy without further orders. It is likely that Vaughn also interpreted the order the same way, in other words, don't move unless ordered to do so. There was a serious breakdown in communications between the three commanders and both Vaughn and Imboden denied having received any orders from Jones to attack the Federal left. Even if they both felt that they had to hold their positions, it is difficult to understand why they did not act when they could clearly see their comrades being overwhelmed. It is unlikely that, if presented with the flank of attacking enemy infantry, that J.E.B. Stuart or George Custer would have just sat there, orders or no orders.[22]

General Jones didn't give any reasons for his deciding to meet Hunter at Piedmont rather than at Mowry's Hill. Imboden later speculated:

> I never learned the reason for his change of plans, but infer that it was occasioned by a telegram he had received the night before from General Lee, and which the enemy found on his body, to the effect that no additional troops could be sent to the Valley for several days, and he must therefore fight Hunter as quickly as possible, and beat him back before Crook's and Averill's advent on the scene; and as Hunter had the day before flanked our position at Mount Crawford, making considerable detour by way of Port Republic, I think Jones concluded that his opponent sought to evade a conflict till the last possible moment, thus increasing the probabilities of a junction with Crook and Averill; and that if such was his purpose he would either not attack us at Mowry's hill, or would seek to flank it by another detour either to the right or left. Reasoning thus, and entirely confident that if he could engage Hunter anywhere that day he could beat him, he disregarded topographical considerations of advantage, and sought his enemy at the nearest point.[23]

One of Hunter's major complaints when taking command of the army was the quality of his subordinate commanders. He tried to replace generals Sullivan and Stahel, but on this day they performed as well as anyone could have asked. Sullivan's infantry assaulted the formidable Confederate railpens time after time, and fought off their ferocious counterattacks. During the battle Sullivan had three horses killed under him.[24] Stahel received a painful wound in the arm but later left the hospital to lead his men in the final attack, earning the Congressional Medal of Honor. Captain Henry DuPont's handling of his artillery also played a large part in the victory. He showed great skill in massing his fire when needed and then concentrating on certain points with remarkable accuracy when called for.[25]

6. The Battle of Piedmont

In a congratulatory telegram, Secretary Stanton wrote:

> These brilliant achievements wipe out the antecedent disasters to our arms in former campaigns in the Shenandoah Valley, and induce strong hope that, led on by the courage and guided by the experienced skill of its commander, the army of the Shenandoah will rival our other gallant armies in the successful blows against the rebels.[26]

Hunter's victory was much more than revenge for the loss at New Market. Like New Market, the relatively small number of men involved did not indicate the importance of the battle. For the first time in the war there was no organized Confederate resistance to Federal forces in the Shenandoah Valley. Not only was the Valley and Western Virginia open to Federal occupation, but there was nothing to prevent Federal forces from moving into central Virginia, which would pose a serious threat to General Lee's left flank. And, of more immediate importance, the road to Staunton, with its vital railroad facilities and supply depots, lay open to Hunter's army.[27]

7. On to Staunton and Lynchburg

The road to Staunton was wide open for Hunter's victorious army as they moved south early Monday morning. There was no organized Confederate force to resist them and had Hunter moved quickly, he might have been able to catch up with Vaughn and Imboden at Waynesboro. But the long-sought prize of Staunton was too much to pass up, and Crook and Averell were already on their way to Staunton to join their forces with Hunter's.[1]

At Staunton, the newly appointed commandant, Colonel Edwin G. Lee, received word of the Confederate defeat at Piedmont and immediately began transporting military supplies south by rail and wagon trains. Lee was able to save "900 sacks of salt, a large lot of leather, &c. All the ammunition was saved, all the bacon, and most of the quartermaster's stores." Even though the townspeople were allowed to take some of the remaining supplies, a great deal was left behind when Lee finally left just ahead of Hunter's men.[2]

On June 6 the first Federal army to reach Staunton marched into town with bands playing and flags waving. A few citizens seemed glad to see them, but most only watched with disbelief or hatred as the blue-clad invaders filed past.[3] The next day, Colonel Strother met with the mayor and some of the prominent citizens of the town and informed them:

> We were warring according to the rules of civilized nations, that all warlike stores, manufactures, and buildings which appertained to the Confederacy would be destroyed but that private property and noncombatants would be respected. The schools and charitable institutions would be carefully protected. I warned them that disorders might take place such as were to be expected among an ill-disciplined soldiery, but that no pains would be

spared to keep peace and order in the town and I hoped these efforts would be successful.[4]

There were only a few incidents on the first day, but on Tuesday morning the pillaging and destruction began. The Union troops were already short of supplies and their hunger and just plain vandalism led to many unfortunate acts of violence against the civilian population. Grocery and dry goods stores were broken into and their contents stolen by mobs of soldiers and residents.[5] When Strother rode into town that morning, he

> found everything in shocking confusion. They were burning the railroad property and public stores and work shops. A mixed mob of Federal soldiers, Negroes, Secessionists, mulatto women, children, Jews, and camp followers and the riff raff of the town were engaged in plundering the stores and depots. Quantities of army goods were found, blankets, clothes, a thousand saddles, shoes, tobacco, etc., without end. These stores were distributed among our people *ad libitum* and plundered as freely by Negroes, Confederate bummers, and citizens.[6]

Gradually the troops were brought under control, but not before extensive damage was done to the town. The military property could be considered legitimate targets but the destruction and theft of civilian property in Staunton was just a taste of what was soon to come.

Colonel Strother later totaled the destruction in Staunton, at least that which could be considered war materials:

> To sum up what was accomplished at Staunton, we took five hundred wounded and invalid prisoners and paroled them. We destroyed one thousand stands of small arms and three guns, one thousand cavalry saddles, horse equipment and shoes and leather, several woolen factories and quantities of grey cloth and other stores, and some ammunition. The depot buildings and fifty miles of the Virginia Central railroad were destroyed.[7]

On June 8 General Crook's infantry and General Averell's cavalry forces arrived at Staunton, swelling the ranks of Hunter's army. The commanders agreed that it was time to proceed with the main objective of capturing Lynchburg, but there was disagreement on how to do it. General Crook wanted to take his division on a forced march to Lynchburg and quickly seize the city before it could be reinforced. He believed that Lee would do everything possible to keep such a valuable supply base from falling into enemy hands. Hunter wanted to wait for badly needed supplies, then attack with the full force of the combined armies.[8] Confident that no Confederate force in the area could stand against his army, Hunter decided that the entire force would "move south immediately to perform our work."[9]

General Crook was exactly correct in his assessment of how Lee would react to a Federal move toward Lynchburg. The only Confederate force that could oppose Hunter's army at present was a small cavalry brigade under General John McCausland, and these men were tired and demoralized. General Lee was faced with a dilemma—he could not afford to lose Lynchburg and he could not spare the men to defend it without endangering his own army. In a letter to Jefferson Davis on June 6, he wrote: "The only assistance I can give from this army as I wrote you last night would be to send back Wharton's & Echols' brigades numbering now about 2100 muskets." In the same letter, Lee stated the reality of the situation. "It is apparent that if Grant cannot be successfully resisted here we cannot hold the Valley. If he is defeated it can be recovered. But unless a sufficient force can be had in that country to restrain the movements of the enemy, he will do us great evil...."[10]

The Federal army left Staunton on June 9, on their way to Lexington, the home of the cadets of the Virginia Military Institute who played such a large role at New Market. Hunter started out with "twenty thousand men and thirty-six cannon. Our cavalry numbered about five thousand. We moved on four parallel roads with orders to concentrate at Lexington on the second day and to move toward any point where the sound of cannon indicated a serious engagement."[11]

As they moved south, there was constant skirmishing with Confederate cavalry under McCausland, who "was ordered to keep in front of Hunter, and delay and harass him as much as possible, a task which he performed with signal ability, skill, and bravery."[12] The small Confederate force was nearly helpless against the much larger numbers they were facing. In Achilles J. Tynes' letter he said: "We were in what may be called a very tight place. If we turned our backs 'twas a ruinous rout; if we moved back fighting, slowly, the flanking columns, one, two thousand, & their other fifteen hundred strong [cavalry] would pass & engulf us. Here was a dilemma."[13]

On the morning of the 11th, McCausland tried to defend the approaches to Lexington, but with the small number of men available, it was a wasted effort and the delay was negligible. About the only thing he accomplished was to get the town bombarded by Hunter's artillery. One resident wrote, "I seemed to have spent a lifetime in one day. I never before had an idea of the terror caused by the shelling of a town, never seemed to realize what it meant."[14] Colonel Strother noted that "The enemy had burned the bridge and were attempting a defense with artillery and sharpshooters."[15] The destroyed bridge had fallen into the river, allowing the Federal infantry to cross over on the wreckage while under fire from the opposite bank and buildings of the Virginia Military Institute. While the infantry was struggling to cross the river, "Averell with a brigade crossed by a ford above and flanked them to the right. Perceiving the movement in time, the enemy retired hastily," leaving Lexington open to Hunter's army.[16]

The Federal occupation of Lexington was marked by the destruction of many public and private buildings and pillaging by the soldiers. Although primarily an educational institution, VMI was considered a military target because, as Colonel Strother wrote, "The professors and cadets had taken the field against government troops, as an organized corps. The buildings had been used as a Rebel arsenal and recently as a fortress.... The order was given to fire the building and all the houses and outbuildings."[17]

7. On to Staunton and Lynchburg

As Hunter wrote in his report:

> On the 12th I also burned the Virginia Military Institute and all the buildings connected with it. I found here a violent and inflammatory proclamation from John Letcher, lately Governor of Virginia, inciting the population of the country to rise and wage a guerrilla warfare on my troops, and ascertaining that after having advised his fellow-citizens to this course the ex–Governor had himself ignominiously taken to flight, I ordered his property to be burned under my order, published May 24, against persons practicing or abetting such unlawful and uncivilized warfare.[18]

The former governor had left the area, but his wife and family were still occupying the residence. They were given only a few minutes to gather up what belongings they could before the buildings were set on fire. Many of the Federal officers were dismayed at the destruction of non-military property and the homes of private citizens, as well as the stealing and vandalism by the troops.[19]

Captain DuPont wrote:

> In my judgment, as well as in that of every other Union officer who expressed himself on the subject, the destruction of the cadet barracks was fully justified by the laws of war, but the burning of the buildings containing the library, the philosophical apparatus, the large and extensive mineralogical collection and other objects used solely for educational purposes, was entirely unnecessary, besides being contrary to the conventions of civilized warfare which respect as far as possible the property of institutions of learning.[20]

VMI buildings after Hunter's raid (Virginia Military Institute Archives).

The conduct of the troops got so bad that General Crook was forced to issue two separate orders to bring them under control:

> The general commanding regrets to learn of so many acts committed by our troops that are disgraceful to the command, such as breaking open trunks of private citizens, &c., the utter disregard of General Orders, No. 11, by troops of this command. Brigade commanders must hold their officers responsible that this order is enforced. Supplies must not be taken by individuals, as their supplies are being collected by the division quartermaster for issue.[21]
>
> Hereafter foraging parties will be sent out under the direction of the division commissary and quartermaster. Eighteen good men with three sergeants from each brigade and one sergeant from each battery will be detailed each day for this purpose, and will be provided with passes from the officer in charge. All other persons foraging will be arrested and marched under guard during the day and reported to the division provost-marshal upon arrival in camp.[22]

In addition to the shortages of food, the battle of Piedmont and the constant harassment by Confederate cavalry had depleted the army's supply of ammunition. On the 12th, Hunter sent orders to Sigel that nothing "except ammunition, be sent forward to this army in any train coming.... In the next train coming you will only send, besides the ammunition for the army, a scant supply of subsistence for the escort, as they can supply themselves with meat from the country as they go along."[23]

The destruction of homes and other private buildings during Hunter's move toward Lynchburg evoked an undying hatred in the Valley residents. Writing to a friend, a VMI cadet who fought at New Market tells how the destruction by the Federal troops affected his family and his own attitude toward the enemy:

> Mother lost absolutely everything she had, and is now a refugee here, sick too, they not only stole all provision, and stock she had, but went about the house breaking up what they could find and then had the assurance to ask my sister if she could not furnish them with a snack of ham. Roller, if I am ever spared to get into yankee land, I will respect nothing but a woman's person, I'll break, pillage and plunder. My Mother, from living in luxury at home, is now forced to the necessity of borrowing a wagon to get home in, and I don't know what she is going to live on after she gets there.[24]

While Hunter's army was moving south and creating long-standing hatreds, General Grant had been busy creating new ways to destroy Lee's supply lines. He decided to send Major General Philip H. Sheridan, Cavalry Commander of the Army of the Potomac, with two divisions of his troopers on a raid to destroy the Virginia Central Railroad connections between Richmond and the Valley. After destroying the railroad, Sheridan was to head to Charlottesville, where Grant believed Hunter to be going, and then join forces destroying more of the railroad and the James River and Kanawha Canal on their way back to the Army of the Potomac. In the orders for Hunter that Grant sent with Sheridan, he left on doubt as to what he wanted accomplished. "The complete destruction of this road and of the canal on James River is of great importance to us.... Lose no opportunity to destroy the canal."[25]

General Lee learned of Sheridan's expedition almost immediately and sent two cavalry divisions commanded by Major General Wade Hampton and Major General Fitzhugh Lee to intercept the raiders and protect the vital transportation links to the Valley. The two forces met on the 11th near Trevilian Station and after a daylong series of fierce charges and counter-charges, darkness halted the fighting. Sheridan learned from prisoners that Hunter was not headed toward Charlottesville and that the infantry force under Breckinridge was already on its way there. The next day there was no serious fighting but several fierce skirmishes. With his ammunition running low and not knowing where to find Hunter anyway, Sheridan decided to return to the Army of the Potomac.[26]

Although Sheridan's raid did not accomplish the main part of its mission, Grant still derived a major benefit. With virtually all his cavalry gone, Lee was unable to properly watch his opponent. In a move that took the Confederates by surprise, the Army of the Potomac left its trenches at Cold Harbor during the night of the 12th and was moving unopposed on Lee's right flank toward the James River, which had been Grant's objective since the start of the campaign. At the same time, the Federal move gave Lee's army a break from the constant pressure that Grant had been applying since the campaign began.[27]

General Lee was now faced with one of his most important and difficult decisions of the war, and he came up with one of his most audacious plans. Despite horrendous casualties, Grant continued to attack the Army of Northern Virginia and now had swung around Lee's right and was heading for Petersburg, a rail center and gateway to Richmond that the Confederates could not afford to lose. Sherman was moving slowly but steadily toward Atlanta. If Hunter captured Lynchburg, there would be devastating effects on the flow of supplies to Lee's army and the capital. Grant's war of attrition was daily cutting into Confederate manpower and replacements were almost nonexistent. Lee had to find a way to save Lynchburg and at the same time relieve the pressure on the capital and the Army of Northern Virginia. He believed that he could hold his heavily entrenched lines with fewer men and that he could spare one of his corps in a desperate gamble to stave off defeat.

On June 12 Lee sent for Lieutenant General Jubal Anderson Early, commander of the Second Corps, and gave him one of the most extraordinary assignments of the war. The Second Corps was currently being held in reserve but Lee could not have picked a better unit to fulfill this vital mission. This was the old Army of the Valley that Stonewall Jackson had led to glory. The men were familiar with the region and had no fear of hard marching and hard fighting. The corps contained about 8,000 of the finest veteran soldiers in Lee's army and two battalions of artillery with 24 guns. The only question mark was its commander.[28]

Jubal Early was born near Lynchburg in 1816 and graduated from West Point in 1837. He became a lawyer and served in the Mexican War. He was a delegate to the Virginia Convention in 1861 and strongly opposed secession, but quickly volunteered for service when the war started. He was an aggressive fighter from the beginning of the war and participated in most of the major campaigns in the east. Early earned a reputation for strict discipline and extraordinary courage and coolness under fire, wherever he commanded his men were tough and hit hard.[29]

A staff officer who served both Jackson and Early wrote, "Of all the generals who made for themselves a reputation in the Army of Northern Virginia, there were none of General Lee's subordinates, after the death of General Jackson, who possessed the essential qualities of a military commander to a greater extent than Early."[30]

John Wise wrote that Early was:

> eccentric in appearance, in voice, in manner of speech. Although he was not an old man, his shoulders were so stooped and rounded that he brought his countenance to a vertical position with difficulty. He wore a long, thin, straggling beard. His eyes were very small, dark, deep-set, and glittering, and his nose aquiline. His step was slow, shuffling, and almost irresolute. I never saw a man who looked less like a soldier. His voice was a piping treble, and he talked with a long-drawn whine or drawl.[31]

Along with his courage and aggressiveness, Early had other, less admirable traits: "He received with impatience and never acted upon, either advice or suggestion from his subordinates. Arbitrary, cynical, with strong prejudices, he was personally disagreeable; he made few admirers or friends either by his manners or his habits...."[32]

Another man noted:

> His opinions were expressed unreservedly, and he was most emphatic and denunciatory, and startlingly profane. His likes and dislikes he announced without hesitation, and, as he was filled with strong and bitter opinions, his conversation was always racy and pungent. His views were not always correct, or just, or broad; but his wit was quick, his satire biting, his expressions were vigorous, and he was interestingly lurid and picturesque.[33]

He sometimes acted too quickly based on his own hunches. Once he made a decision he was usually inflexible and bold to the point of being rash. Despite his many faults, he was considered a man of integrity and honor by those who knew him, whether they liked him or not. His nickname was "Old Jube," but it was not considered a term of respect or affection.[34]

General Early's two-part assignment was both daring and necessary. The Second Corps was to reinforce Lynchburg to prevent its capture and then, if possible, destroy Hunter's invading army, a pretty straightforward task. The second part of Lee's plan, however, was among the most audacious of his career. After disposing of the threat to Lynchburg, the Second Corps would combine with Breckinridge's troops and Early was to lead a daring invasion northward through the Shenandoah Valley. The objective was to threaten, or if they were really lucky, capture Washington, D.C. Lee believed, and justly so as his two previous invasions had proven, that any threat to the capital would produce panic in the north and might pressure Federal authorities into making a mistake. Grant might be forced to send troops north to save the capital and weaken his grip on Lee's Army at Petersburg, opening the way for a breakout by the besieged Confederates, or believing that Lee was substantially weaker because of the detached corps, Grant might be induced to try another assault on the still-strong Confederate lines, resulting in high casualty lists and more despair in the North. Either result would prolong the war and increase the number of people in the North who wanted an end to the fighting, and also increase the chance that Lincoln would not be re-elected. And if Early were able to actually capture Washington, even for a day or two, the results could be fantastic. Besides the huge amounts of food and weapons that might be carried away, the occupation of the Federal capital would prove to the world that the Confederacy was still very much alive and give an enormous boost to the morale of its beleaguerd people.[35]

David Hunter led his Army of West Virginia out of Lexington on the morning of June 14. The weather was hot and dry and it was a long, tough march to Buchanan, which the lead units reached at dusk. By the time they stopped for the night, the men were pretty well played out from the march itself and the constant harassment from McCausland's troopers. The defenders did anything they could to slow down the Federal advance. They cut down trees to block the roads and set up ambushes to force the column to halt, then melted back into the woods to do it again farther down the road.[36]

The Union soldiers were not the only ones facing exhaustion. It was just as hard for the Confederates, as Captain Achilles Tynes wrote to his wife on June 13th, "so rapidly have events chased each other & so wearying has been the last ten or fifteen days. In all my experience of war I have never been so chased, pursued, dogged."[37]

Early the next morning the Federal army was on the move again and crossed the Blue Ridge Mountains between the Peaks of Otter. Again there was frequent contact with McCausland's men but Hunter kept moving steadily forward, destroying railroad tracks, mills and many other buildings along the line of march. The town of Liberty was occupied that afternoon, the army marching in with flags flying and bands playing. As soon as they had control of the town the destruction began. Private homes were plundered and even an empty building used as a hospital was destroyed. This was enemy territory and David Hunter had no problem with destroying any and all property of his country's enemies.[38]

So far, Hunter's campaign had gone about as well as could be hoped for. He had won a small but important victory at Piedmont, the capture of Staunton was a long-sought after prize, they had destroyed large amounts of Confederate supplies, railroad equipment and miles of track, and his army was tired but intact and far larger than any opposition in the vicinity. They had just come through the Blue Ridge, the last natural obstacle, and were within about twenty-five miles of the grand prize: Lynchburg.

There was a direct road from Liberty to Lynchburg and although the terrain was rough and hilly, the only thing to stop the Union army was the worn

Confederate Lieutenant General Jubal A. Early (Massachusetts Commandery Military Order of the Loyal Legion and U.S. Army Military History Institute).

out forces of McCausland and Imboden, and at best they could only slow the Federal advance. Now was the time to press forward. Instead, Hunter decided to spend the day in and around Liberty destroying railroad tracks and concentrating his units. By the evening of Thursday, the 16th, the Union army had advanced only a few more miles to Big Otter Creek. The slowness of the advance was beginning to worry Colonel Strother. "I feel a vague uneasiness as to the result of our move," he wrote, "Lee will certainly relieve Lynchburg if he can. If he cannot, the Confederacy is gone up. If he does succeed in detaching a force, our situation is most hazardous."[39]

That night Hunter grew more and more cautious. Rumors of Confederate strength ahead only caused more confusion. This is clearly illustrated in Hunter's own words:

> Neither from this scouting party nor from other sources could we obtain any clear or reliable information in regard to the enemy. Through rebel channels we had exaggerated rumors of disasters to our armies both under Sherman and Grant. Some reported that Sheridan had been defeated near Louisa Court-House, while others said that he was already in Lynchburg. Negro refugees just from the town represented that it was occupied only by a few thousand armed invalids and militia, and that its inhabitants in the greatest panic were fleeing with their movable property by every available route. At the same time, from other sources equally worthy of respect, we were assured that all the rebel forces of West Virginia were concentrated there under Breckinridge, and that Ewell's corps of veteran troops, 20,000 strong, had already re-enforced them.[40]

While Hunter had been slowly approaching Lynchburg from the west, the Confederates were feverishly working to reinforce the city and make his worst fears come true. The first of these reinforcements was General Breckinridge's arrival on the night of the 15th.[41] When the remainder of his small force arrived, the people of Lynchburg welcomed them as heroes. Sergeant John H. Worsham wrote:

> Much to the surprise of the men we found the town in great excitement, because the enemy, under the command of Gen. Hunter, had advanced to

within two miles of the place. There was a small force in his front and the citizens expected immediately to see the enemy march into the town. Our presence brought an immediate change. We were cheered to the echo, and the ladies waved their hands and gave us lunches and cool water as we marched through the city.[42]

At about 2:00 A.M. on the 13th, the Second Corps began its march west. They tramped through Mechanicsville, Louisa Court House, and Gordonsville. The weather was hot and dry, the roads dusty, but the men moved quickly. When Early first departed he had no information of Hunter's whereabouts or his destination, although it was assumed that Lynchburg was the target. He had wired Breckinridge from Louisa Court House, asking, "What is the state of things in the Valley?"[43]

Early arrived at Charlottesville on the 16th. Starting at 11:40 A.M. he sent a series of messages to Breckinridge confirming his intention to move toward Lynchburg as quickly as possible:

> Send off at once all engines and cars of Orange and Alexandria Railroad to this place, including everything at its disposal. I will send troops as soon as I get cars.... My first object is to destroy Hunter, and the next it is not prudent to trust to telegraph. Hold on and you will be amply supported.[44]

Patience was not one of Jubal Early's virtues and after commandeering all the rolling stock he could find, he sent another message to Breckinridge at 12:30 P.M.:

> Let me know what the railroad agents can and will do. Everything depends upon promptness, energy, and dispatch. See that agents use all these, and if they fail take the most summary measures and impress everything that is necessary in the way of men or means to insure the object. I have authority to direct your movements, and I will take the responsibility of what you may find it necessary to do. I will hold all railroad agents and employees responsible with their lives for hearty co-operation with us.[45]

In another message at 2:20 P.M., Early said, "I shall come as soon as trains from Lynchburg arrive. I cannot start sooner for fear of interruption on the roads if trains start in both ways, besides my troops marched twenty miles to-day.... If you can hold out till morning and the railroad does not fail all will be well."[46]

Also on the 16th, the incapacitated Breckinridge sent a message informing Vaughn that he was to take command until Early arrived. With this message was a private note meant to boost the confidence of Vaughn and through him, the worn-out Confederate troops. "There is no occasion for any disorder. The enemy is advancing slowly. We will have General Early and large reenforcements to-morrow morning, and if the enemy comes in earnest he will be destroyed."[47]

Early later wrote:

> The railroad and telegraph between Charlottesville and Lynchburg had been, fortunately, but slightly injured by the enemy's cavalry, and had been repaired. The distance between the two places was sixty miles, and there

were no trains at Charlottesville, except one which belonged to the Central road, and was about starting for Waynesboro. I ordered this to be detained, and immediately directed, by telegram, all the trains of the two roads to be sent to me with all dispatch, for the purpose of transporting my troops to Lynchburg. The trains were not in readiness to take the troops on board until sunrise on the morning of the 17th, and then only enough were furnished to transport about half of my infantry. Ramseur's division, one brigade of Gordon's division, and part of another were put on the trains as soon as they were ready, and started for Lynchburg. Rodes' division, and the residue of Gordon's, were ordered to move along the railroad, to meet the trains on their return. The artillery and wagontrains had been started on the ordinary roads, at daylight.[48]

Although the railroad had been repaired, the line was still old and decrepit and the trip to Lynchburg was agonizingly slow. When Early reached Lynchburg he found the locals excited and worried. Since the defeat at Piedmont, the residents had been expecting a Federal attack and were well aware that the city's defenses were inadequate. Early found Breckinridge bedridden from a previous injury and unable to supervise the defense. "As General Breckinridge was unable to go out, at his request, General D. H. Hill, who happened to be in town, had made arrangements for the defence of the city, with such troops as were at hand."[49]

Early found the fortifications of the city to be totally inadequate:

> I rode out with General Hill to examine the line selected by him, and make a reconnaissance of the country in front. Slight works had been hastily thrown up on College Hill, covering the turnpike and Forest roads from Liberty, which were manned by Breckinridge's infantry and the dismounted cavalry of the command which had been with Jones at Piedmont. The reserves, invalids from the hospitals, and the cadets from the Military Institute at Lexington, occupied other parts of the line. An inspection satisfied me that, while this arrangement was the best which could be made under the circumstances in which General Hill found himself, yet it would leave the town exposed to the fire of the enemy's artillery, should he advance to the attack, and I therefore determined to meet the enemy with my troops in front.[50]

As Early's Confederates were moving into Lynchburg on the afternoon of the 17th, Averell's cavalry was slowly pushing McCausland back toward the city until he established a defensive position near New London. Fortunately, they were joined by Imboden and his command and the Federal advance was stalled. Imboden then sent McCausland north where Brigadier General Alfred A. Duffié was pushing forward on the Forest Road in the oppressive heat.[51]

Duffié reported that after

> proceeding a short distance on this road, I met the enemy at 1:30 P.M., strongly posted in the woods. I immediately engaged him, with my men dismounted in the woods. The road was narrow, and the woods so dense as to forbid the use of cavalry. The engagement of my division lasted about two hours, during which we drove the enemy a short distance. Mean time the infantry immediately on my right became engaged, and the firing was heavy along the whole line. The enemy fell back slowly.[52]

Duffié's troopers pushed McCausland back until they reached Blackwater Creek. Here the Confederates had established a strong position on high ground and Duffié decided not to continue the attack, ending the fighting for the night.[53]

Earlier that afternoon Early found Imboden near the Quaker meetinghouse engaged with Averell's troopers. Imboden's men were holding their own until the arrival of Crook's infantry threatened to flank and overwhelm the small Confederate force. Early quickly ordered Maj. Gen. Stephen D. Ramseur to reinforce the position and two of his brigades arrived in time to contain the Federals. Soon Ramseur's other brigade and part of Maj. Gen. John B. Gordon's division arrived and the Confederates launched a counter-attack. The Federal advance was halted and both sides settled down for the night. This attack by the men of the Stonewall Brigade was the first indication that Hunter was not facing a small force of cavalry and convalescents, that he could overwhelm without too much difficulty, but the tough veterans of the Second Corps of the Army of Northern Virginia, quite another matter. That night the exhausted Federal army rested wherever they were when the fighting ended: Averell's cavalry on the right, Crook and Sullivan with their infantry divisions in the center, and Duffié's cavalry on the left.[54]

That night Early cleverly used an old trick to create the illusion that he was constantly receiving reinforcements. While his men were strengthening and extending their fortifications, Early had an engine and a few cars run in and out of the city to create the impression that more troops were arriving during the night.[55]

The Federal troops heard the trains and Hunter reported:

> During the night the trains on the different railroads were heard running without intermission, while repeated cheers and the beating of drums indicated the arrival of large bodies of troops in the town, yet up to the morning of the 18th I had no positive information as to whether General Lee had detached any considerable force to the relief of Lynchburg.[56]

During the night both commanders wrestled with the decision of what they should or could do in the morning. Only Early knew how weak his force really was, Major General Robert E. Rodes' division and part of Gordon's as well as the artillery had not yet arrived. Most of the men of the Second Corps were exhausted from the forced march to Lynchburg. McCausland and Imboden's troopers were played out from the constant fighting, heat, and lack of rest while they had been trying to slow the Federal advance. If Early attacked in the morning he might catch the enemy by surprise, but he didn't have enough men to take advantage of an initial success. If the attack failed, his command might be destroyed and Lynchburg would fall into enemy hands. As much as he must have disliked the idea, Early decided to strengthen his defenses and wait for Hunter to attack.[57]

For David Hunter the night brought only indecision. He had no idea how many enemy troops he might be facing, but he could certainly hear the trains bringing Confederate reinforcements. The fierce attack that halted Crook's men that afternoon told Hunter that he was facing tough, experienced troops.

His own men were tired and hungry, ammunition was already running low, and just the thought that he might now be facing a superior force wore down Hunter's resolve. Sometime during the night he may have started thinking more about not losing than winning. It is seemingly small difference, but in war, one that frequently separates the victor from the vanquished.

8. Lynchburg and Retreat

The fate of Lynchburg would be determined on June 18. Besides being a test of military power between the two opposing forces, there would be a test of will and character between the two commanders. The combination of McCausland's delaying tactics and the time wasted by Hunter in plundering towns and burning houses had allowed the Confederates the time to reinforce Lynchburg, but Hunter had no idea of the enemy strength. The lines of the opposing armies stretched about three miles from Forest Road to across the Salem Pike. The ground was full of short, steep hills with thick woods in many places and streams with high banks running through the entire area, excellent ground for defense. Caution and indecision gripped Hunter and he could not bring himself to order an all-out attack. For most of the morning the Federals did nothing more than test the Southern lines, looking for a weak spot.[1]

Hunter reported:

> Their works consisted of strong redoubts on each of the main roads entering the town about three miles apart, flanked on either side by rifle-pits protected by abatis. On these lines the enemy could be seen working diligently as if to extend and strengthen them. I massed my two divisions of infantry in front of the works on the Bedford road ready to move to the right or left as required, the artillery in commanding positions, and Averell's cavalry division in reserve. Duffié was ordered to attack resolutely on the Forestville road, our extreme left, while Averell sent two squadrons of cavalry to demonstrate against the Campbell Court-House road on our extreme right. This detachment was subsequently strengthened by a brigade. Meanwhile I reconnoitered the lines, hoping to find a weak interval through which I might push with my infantry, passing between the main redoubts, which appeared too strong for a direct assault.[2]

Early got little rest that night, rising at 2 A.M. to inspect the work being done to improve his lines. Even though the trains had been running all night, all his troops had still not arrived and it was obvious that it would be late in the day before his corps would be at full strength. Early fully expected a Federal attack soon after dawn. Controlling his naturally aggressive nature, he wrote:

> On my arrival at Lynchburg, orders had been given for the immediate return of the trains for the rest of my infantry, and I expected it to arrive by the morning of the 18th, but it did not get to Lynchburg until late in the afternoon of that day. Hunter's force was considerably larger than mine would have been, had it all been up, and as it was of the utmost consequence to the army at Richmond that he should not get into Lynchburg, I did not feel justified in attacking him until I could do so with a fair prospect of success.[3]

On the Federal left, Duffié had been out of contact with headquarters, isolated by the rough terrain between the Forest Road and the Salem Pike. He did not receive Hunter's orders to attack up the Forest Road, which didn't really matter because that was exactly what he was doing. A small infantry force under General Wharton had reinforced McCausland, but the Confederates on this end of the line were still outnumbered. About 9 A.M. Duffié's men began their advance and forced the enemy back over a railroad bridge about four miles from Lynchburg. After receiving a message from Averell to continue the attack, the dismounted troopers advanced slowly in three columns, one on the road and one on each side in the woods. Gradually the defenders were forced back across Backwater Bridge, about two miles from the city, but here the Federal advance again stalled at the steep banks of the creek.[4] Later in the day Duffié sent a courier to tell Hunter that he had been "engaging the enemy on the extreme left. I attacked him at 12:30 P.M., and drove him into his fortifications. Have been fighting ever since. Two charges have been made, and the enemy's strength fully developed in our front. His force is much superior to mine. All my force is engaged."[5]

In the center of the Union line along the Salem Pike, the day began with light skirmishing and occasional artillery fire, but as the morning progressed fire from both sides was getting more intense. Colonel Strother later wrote:

> I called on Sullivan who was with Colonel Thoburn lying on the ground on some boards. Sullivan said he had heard the railroad trains coming and going all night, also cheering and military music which indicated the arrival of troops in the town. Since morning the lines were very much strengthened and were pressing him hard. He was sustaining himself with difficulty. He said he was ready to attack if ordered but he felt assured it would end in disaster. Thoburn spoke in the same strain and in somewhat more decided language.... I reported to General Hunter Sullivan's views as I heard them. He seemed dissatisfied and at the same time hesitated to order the advance.[6]

The expected Federal attack had not materialized and by 11 A.M. Early was beginning to lose his patience. Like Hunter, he decided to test his enemy's lines, hoping that the movements against the flanks had weakened the center.

8. Lynchburg and Retreat

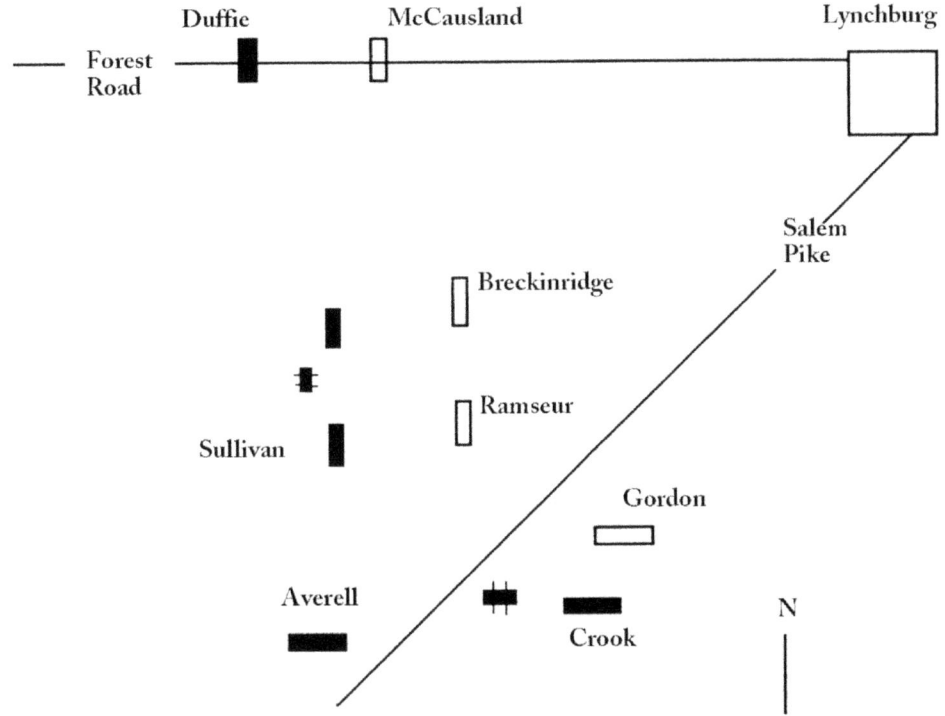

Battle of Lynchburg

Suddenly Confederate artillery opened up a heavy barrage on the Union center near the Salem Pike. About one o'clock Ramseur and Gordon launched their attack, taking the Federal troops in the front lines by surprise.[7] Captain DuPont remembered, "Leaping over their defences, the enemy's infantry, with terrific yells, assaulted the Union left and center.... So serious and prolonged, however, was the Confederate attack, that Hunter became apprehensive and ordered Crook to return at once."[8]

In the center of the Federal line, Sullivan's infantry had a difficult time containing the fierce assault and were being gradually forced back. Fortunately, Crook, who had been moving to the right to find a way around the Confederate flank, was on his way back and had already dispatched reinforcements on his own initiative before receiving Hunter's order.[9]

On the left of the Federal line, the rough terrain filled with woods and underbrush contributed to intense back-and-forth fighting. Colonel Wells led his brigade in a counterattack that stopped the Confederate advance, pushing them back into their fortifications. As they pursued the retreating enemy, the 116th Ohio and the 5th West Virginia followed them too far and ended up in the Confederate works. Without support from other Federal units, they were unable to penetrate any farther and were forced back to their original line.[10]

In the center of the Federal line Colonel Thoburn could hear the heavy fighting on the left and moved the 18th Connecticut in that direction, where they helped to repel two Confederate attacks. When Ramseur's men moved out, they were met with heavy fire from the 12th West Virginia and forced back before they got close to the Federal line.[11]

On the Federal right, Gordon's men charged toward DuPont's guns but were met with heavy artillery fire that brought their advance to a standstill. From the right, the 54th Pennsylvania, moving through rough terrain, "found the enemy strongly posted in a deep ditch, concealed by thick weeds and underbrush, lining both banks. Upon this discovery, we immediately charged the enemy and drove him in confusion from his position." The Pennsylvanians suffered heavy casualties but the danger to Hunter's army was over, for now.[12]

Union soldier William G. Watson wrote in his memoirs:

> At day break the enemy commenced the woods we were in. The roar of their artillery & the bursting of shells as they tore thru the woods breaking off limbs which fell among us in showers was deafening & some what appalling.... By this time twas believed one third of Genl. Lee's veterans were in our front sent from Richmond during the past 24 hours. And they were now ready to assume the offensive. So they began not by firing a few spattering shots like the big rain drops which precede a thunder shower, but in one grand outburst so unexpected & deafening that for a moment we were paralyzed.[13]

On the far right of the Union army, Averell's cavalry continued to skirmish with Imboden's men around Campbell Court House, but they could make only slow headway against the stubborn defenders. Averell believed that "It was evident that too many lives must be expended to carry the enemy's position." By early afternoon it was obvious that no real progress could be made in that direction and the fighting ended without accomplishing much other than an increase in casualties.[14]

To the north, Duffié had been slowly advancing against stubborn resistance and had moved to within about two miles of the city, but his troops were exhausted and unable to penetrate the Confederate line any farther. About 5 P.M. the Confederates began a heavy fire from artillery and muskets that drove his men back across Backwater Creek and put the Union troops on the defensive for the first time that day.[15]

Duffié later wrote:

> From my position on the field I could see numerous re-enforcements marching down the hill from the city, and could hear the whistle of the cars as they came in and the playing of bands of music. This led me to the belief that large bodies of re-enforcements were arriving and being thrown into my front.[16]

Duffié had not received any communication from Hunter all day and knew nothing of what was happening on his right except for hearing heavy firing several times during the day. Lack of information about the rest of the army and fear of being attacked by a superior enemy force convinced Duffié to suspend further offensive moves and just try to hold on where he was.[17]

8. Lynchburg and Retreat

By late afternoon, the fighting in the center had died down and Hunter was able to consider the situation facing his army:

> From prisoners captured we obtained positive information that a portion of Ewell's corps was engaged in the action, and that the whole corps, 20,000 strong, under the command of Lieutenant-General Early, was either already in Lynchburg or near at hand. The detachment sent by General Averell to operate on our right had returned, reporting that they had encountered a large body of rebel cavalry in that quarter, while Duffié, although holding his position, sent word that he was pressed by a superior force. It had now become sufficiently evident that the enemy had concentrated a force of at least double the numerical strength of mine, and what added to the gravity of the situation was the fact that my troops had scarcely enough of ammunition left to sustain another well contested battle. I immediately ordered all the baggage and supply trains to retire by the Bedford turnpike, and made preparations to withdraw the army as soon as it should become sufficiently dark to conceal the movement from the enemy.[18]

General Hunter had never really intended to occupy Lynchburg. He planned to destroy the town and then withdraw back over the mountains. A frontal assault on the Confederate fortifications would almost certainly be a costly failure and attempts to find a way around had been repulsed. And now Hunter was more worried than ever about a possible Confederate attack that might destroy his army. Even though Early's attack had failed, it had achieved his ultimate goal. It was obvious that the Union army would not be able to capture Lynchburg, so there was really only one thing left to do. Captain DuPont summed up the situation: "With but little ammunition and less food, we now found ourselves in a hostile country several hundred miles from our base, from which we were entirely cut off. As it was perfectly clear to me that our safety lay in an exceedingly prompt and rapid retreat."[19]

After dark the Federal troops began to withdraw from their main lines. There were no fires that night and the men were warned to be as quiet as possible as they pulled out and headed west. To cover the movements, a picket line was set up to keep in contact with the Confederates until midnight, when they also fell back to rejoin the main body. Many of the men could not understand why they were retreating. They had not been beaten in battle; in fact, they had repulsed the ferocious Confederate attacks and their lines were intact. The Army of West Virginia had dominated the enemy since the campaign began, but now it was suddenly sneaking off in the dark.[20] William Watson wondered:

> Why are we retreating. The reason will be told us bye and bye we thought, not now. Silently we withdrew careful to not leave anyone though it required severe shaking to waken tired out sleepers. Through strips of woods and fields we stumbled along till we reached a pike and halted to await the passing of Infantry Regts. We were now told that Genl. Lee had sent a large force from Richmond who were now trying to surround us. Besides we hadn't enough ammunition to last through another days fighting. Worse yet, our commissary train with our rations had been unable to reach us.[21]

Jubal Early was always ready to fight, but he had to wait for the rest of his troops to arrive before taking any major offensive action. The remainder of the Second Corps infantry arrived late in the afternoon and had hurried forward to the main lines, but the artillery was still en route. Even though Early knew he was outnumbered, he also knew that the Federal army was scattered and they appeared exhausted and content to just sit behind their works, waiting to see what would happen next. All of Early's instincts told him now was the time to attack, perhaps one more hard blow delivered in the right spot could bring a great victory, but he held back. Now, for the first time, he faced the responsibilities of an independent command. It was crucial for the Confederacy that the enemy be kept out of Lynchburg. If Early launched an attack before his men were ready, he could lose the battle and the city. Even if he won the battle, a tough fight with heavy casualties could delay or even prevent him from carrying out the second part of the plan. Most of his troops were exhausted and needed a break from marching and fighting. Making the difficult but necessary decision, Early issued orders to rest for the night and prepare for an offensive in the morning.[22]

As the Federal army slipped away from Lynchburg during the night, in addition to the pickets who gave the appearance of holding the lines, they also left behind Duffié's command along the Forest Road. About 7:00 P.M. a messenger arrived to inform Duffié that the army was withdrawing to the west and that he was to hold his position to protect the flank until notified that it was safe for his cavalry to withdraw. His command was nearly out of ammunition and any serious attack would have resulted in disaster. Duffié was understandably nervous as he waited for the order to withdraw, but it never came:[23]

> Having held my position until 10 p. m., I took upon myself the responsibility of falling back. This was effected in perfect order, my forces being withdrawn in the same order in which I advanced in the morning. Falling back for three miles, I re-established my line of battle, in order to ascertain if the enemy were following. At the same time I sent Captain Ricker, of my staff, to the headquarters of General Hunter. He returned two hours later, informing me that he could not find General Hunter's headquarters, and that the whole army had left the field.[24]

Convinced that his command was unsupported and in serious danger, Duffié continued to fall back. After marching all night, the tired troopers met up with the rear guard of the army a few miles from Liberty.[25]

An army the size of Hunter's could not just leave without being noticed, and Early wrote later:

> Sometime after midnight, it was discovered that he was moving, though it was not known whether he was retreating, or moving so as to attack Lynchburg on the south where it was vulnerable, or to attempt to join Grant on the south side of James River. Pursuit could not, therefore, be made at once, as a mistake, if either of the last two objects had been contemplated, would have been fatal.[26]

8. Lynchburg and Retreat

By daylight the direction of the Federal troops had been confirmed and the Second Corps was off in hot pursuit.

On the 19th Early wired General Lee:

> Last evening the enemy assaulted my lines in front of Lynchburg and was repulsed by the part of my command which was up. On the arrival of the rest of the command I made arrangements to attack this morning at light, but it was discovered that the enemy were retreating, and I am now pursuing. The enemy is retreating in confusion, and if the cavalry does its duty we will destroy him.[27]

Union soldier Watson wrote about the first night after leaving Lynchburg:

> Sleepy tired and hungry, to that add Depression of spirits which always follow defeat. Our pride was on furlough. We would have willingly traded rank and honor with a mule driver for a full meal and a wagon ride. But we plodded along, keeping bunched together, wishing for daybreak and a halt.... Slowly we trudged on in compact form, our feet made sore by crossing streams – a few of us were beginning to limp, wishing for daylight even though skirmishing would be resumed, we could then see around us. The Rebs were cautious, fearing a trap. We halted a short time for breakfast though we had but a few mouthfuls of crumbs to eat with a handful of sugar.[28]

The Confederate pursuit was hampered by confusion and mistakes. Early wanted his cavalry to converge on Liberty and block Hunter's escape route:

> Imboden, who was on the road from Lynchburg to Campbell Court House ... was to have moved on the left towards Liberty, but orders did not reach him in time. The enemy's rear was overtaken at Liberty, twenty-five miles from Lynchburg, just before night, and driven through that place, after a brisk skirmish, by Ramseur's division. The day's march on the old turnpike, which had been very rough, had been terrible. McCausland had taken the wrong road and did not reach Liberty until after the enemy had been driven through the town.[29]

The opportunity to cut off the retreating Federal army was lost, now it would be a chase from behind with little hope of overtaking the enemy and forcing more than a rear guard action.

Duffié's cavalry had secured Buford's Gap and after a hard march the infantry arrived there on the morning of the 20th. Early wrote:

> The pursuit was resumed early on the morning of the 20th, and on our arrival in sight of Buford's, the enemy's rear guard was seen going into the mountain on the road towards Salem.... The enemy was pursued into the mountains at Buford's Gap, but he had taken possession of the crest of the Blue Ridge, and put batteries in position commanding a gorge, through which the road passes, where it was impossible for a regiment to move in line.... We tried to throw forces up the sides of the mountains to get at the enemy, but they were so rugged that night came on before anything could be accomplished, and we had to desist, though not until a very late hour in the night.[30]

The men in both armies suffered from hunger and exhaustion. An Ohio artilleryman, J.O. Humphreys, wrote in his diary on June 20th: "At one and a half o'clock A.M. we were aroused for the march and at 3 o'clock we pulled out, and marched on along the railroad toward Salem. Skirmished all day in rear. Marched seventeen miles."[31]

On the 21st he wrote, "All last night we marched and how tired and sleepy! We were attacked on the flank, but the rebs did not succeed in their design to capture our two Batteries.... Crossed one high mountain today and are supposed to be safe. Thirty miles, and camp and rest came welcome, thrice welcome."[32]

The Confederates were just as worn out as their opponents. There had been no time to rest since the forced march from Cold Harbor. They had gone directly into the line at Lynchburg and now were racing after the retreating enemy. Early had left Lynchburg in such a hurry that his supply trains were unable to keep up and many of the men had not been issued rations for two or three days. Gradually hunger and fatigue took its toll and the men of the Second Corps simply could not move fast enough to catch up with Hunter's army. The Confederate cavalry was the only force that could effectively engage the enemy to slow them enough for the infantry to catch up, but McCausland had been unable to get ahead of the Federal advance guard of cavalry.[33]

Hunter's army marched with Duffié's cavalry in the lead, followed by the artillery and its ammunition train with the main body of infantry next and Averell's cavalry as rear guard.[34]

C.J. Rawling, in *History of the First Regiment Virginia Infantry,* wrote:

> The road at this time being traversed was a very bad one. What road was not bad throughout that region? In consequence of this the column was a very long one, the men being much scattered, and taking considerable time to collect them made a defence very difficult, the enemy at the same time watching his opportunity to capture men and material when ever chance offered.[35]

On the afternoon of the 21st, a detachment of McCausland's cavalry slipped behind Duffié's troopers and ambushed the artillery trains. Both Duffié from the front and Averell from the rear sent troopers to protect the wagons, but they arrived too late. The Confederate troopers were able to capture two batteries and then destroyed the carriages and stole the horses. With no way to move the guns, the Federals had to abandon eight of the precious artillery pieces. This was the worst loss from action during the retreat.[36]

After a brief pursuit of the raiders, Hunter's exhausted men began the climb up the imposing Catawba Mountain. It was three miles to the top of the mountain over a steep and rough road. The march would have been tough enough for a well-rested army, and soon the roadside became littered with equipment, broken-down wagons, and exhausted animals. Many men were just too worn out to make the climb and collapsed by the side of the road, some were able to continue with help from their comrades and others just sat down, waiting for whatever fate had in store.[37]

On June 22, Colonel Strother realized that "Our position will be a gloomy one if the reports we hear are confirmed. Worn out with fatigue, without supplies in a country producing little at best and already wasted by war, the troops are beginning to show symptoms of demoralization...."[38]

It was of the utmost importance that Hunter select the correct route of retreat for his exhausted troops. If the Confederates caught up and forced a general engagement, the Union army could very well be destroyed. At Sweet Springs on the 23rd, Hunter held a conference with his commanders:

> From this point it was suggested that we should move northward by the Warm Springs and the Valley of the South Branch of Potomac, a route lying west of and running parallel to the Valley of the Shenandoah. By this route the army would have reached the Baltimore and Ohio Railroad at New Creek and Cumberland. It was objected that by this road the troops would find it impossible to collect necessary supplies and run risks of being cut off by the enemy coming in by way of Staunton and Harrisonburg. In favor of the route via Lewisburg to Charleston, Kanawha, it was urged that the road was clear and practicable, and that while the country would furnish little or nothing in the way of supplies, yet we had ample stores at Meadow Bluff and Gauley River. As the question of supplies was one that involved the existence of the army the Kanawha route was decided upon, and messengers immediately sent forward to have supplies sent out from these points to meet the troops.[39]

The Union army was finally safe, at least from a major battle.

A frustrated Early later wrote:

> As the enemy had got into the mountains, where nothing useful could be accomplished by pursuit, I did not deem it proper to continue it farther. A great part of my command had had nothing to eat for the last two days ... and I knew that the country through which Hunter's route led for forty or fifty miles, was, for the most part, a desolate mountain region; and that his troops were taking everything in the way of provisions and forage which they could lay their hands on.... I had seen our soldiers endure a great deal, but there was a limit to the endurance even of Confederate soldiers. A stern chase with infantry is a very difficult one, and Hunter's men were marching for their lives, his disabled being carried in his provision train which was now empty. My cavalry was not strong enough to accomplish anything of importance, and a further pursuit could only have resulted in disaster to my command from want of provisions and forage.[40]

Early also was aware that his men needed some rest before starting out on the long march to complete the second part of Lee's plan.

The next several days were a blur of fatigue and hunger for the Federal troops. Watson, one of the men who made the march, remembered:

> Stragglers strung out whom we tried to urge along. Our mounted men coaxed, encouraged and threatened them even driving them. So exhausted were they that nearly all fear of Rebel prison or death barely aroused them. Men were staggering along half asleep, occasionally falling down on their faces with an effort to get on their feet again. Were hardly awake when we had to face about and repel a Rebel dash. They were very alert trying to pick up stragglers. Our troubles were increased by attacks on our right and rear at the same time....

> Stragglers every where. A few had thrown their muskets away too tired to carry them. Discipline was forgotten. We halted often and made coffee. At night when we camped coffee and sugar was set down in barrels for us to take all we wanted. How soundly we slept, undisturbed, till sunrise. Our condition was no worse. We marched slowly. We heard our destination was Charleston on the big Kanawha, from where we started. We made up our minds to get there sometime and in any way.[41]

The Federal retreat through West Virginia continued for several more miserable days until, on the 28th, Hunter reported to headquarters:

> I have the honor to report that our expedition has been extremely successful, inflicting great injury upon the enemy, and victorious in every engagement. Running short of ammunition, and finding it impossible to collect supplies while in presence of an enemy believed to be superior to our force in numbers and constantly receiving re-enforcements from Richmond and other points, I deemed it best to withdraw, and have succeeded in doing so without serious loss to this point, where we have met abundant supplies of food and forage.... The command is in excellent heart and health, and ready, after a few days' rest, for service in any direction.[42]

Hunter obviously put a more positive light on the campaign than circumstances would seem to allow. He was later roundly criticized for withdrawing west instead of going down the Valley, where his mere presence would have helped to deter Early's raid. Of course, at the time no one could have guessed at the audacious move that Lee had planned. Even Grant seemed to be unconcerned about Hunter's route when he wrote to Meade on the 21st: "The only word I would send General Hunter would be verbal, and simply to let him know where we are, and tell him to save his army in the way he thinks best...."[43]

Although it ended in a desperate retreat, Hunter's campaign had been the most successful Federal foray into the Valley so far in the war. Coming after the loss at New Market and the terrible casualties of Grant's campaign, the victory at Piedmont provided a much-needed boost to Union morale. Hunter also destroyed much valuable railroad equipment and large amounts of military supplies, and forced Lee to considerably weaken his army to save Lynchburg.

On the other hand, Hunter's campaign against civilian property served only to create an unending hatred of him in the Valley and turn many neutrals into enemies. A woman whose house had been burned wrote Hunter a scathing letter that said, in part:

> I ask who, that does not wish infamy and disgrace attached to him forever, would serve under you! Your name will stand on history's page as the Hunter of weak women and innocent children; the Hunter to destroy defenseless villages and refined and beautiful homes – to torture afresh the agonized hearts of the widows....[44]

One Confederate officer wrote about what they found behind the fleeing Federal army:

8. Lynchburg and Retreat

> It was a scene of desolation. Ransacked houses, crying women, clothes from the bed chambers and wardrobes of ladies, carried along on bayonets and draggled in the road, the garments of little children, and here and there a burning house marked the track of Hunter's retreat. I had never seen anything like this before and for the first time in the war I felt that vengeance ought not be left entirely to the Lord.[45]

On June 26 General Lee sent the following letter to Confederate President Jefferson Davis, briefly touching on Hunter's retreat, plans for Early's army and the possible consequences of supply problems at Petersburg:

> General Hunter has escaped Early, and will make good his retreat, as far as I can understand, to Lewisburg. Although his expedition had been partially interrupted, I fear he has not been much punished except by the demoralization of his troops and the loss of some artillery. From his present position he can easily be reorganized and re-equipped, and, unless we have sufficient force to resist him, will repeat his expedition. This would necessitate the return of Early to Staunton. I think it better that he should move down the Valley if he can obtain provisions, which would draw Hunter after him, and may enable him to strike Pope[?] before he can effect a junction with Hunter. If circumstances favor, I should also recommend his crossing the Potomac. I think I can maintain our lines here against General Grant.... I am less uneasy about holding our position than about our ability to procure supplies for the army. I fear the latter difficulty will oblige me to attack General Grant in his intrenchments, which I should not hesitate to do but for the loss it will inevitably entail. A want of success would, in my opinion, be almost fatal, and this causes me to hesitate, in the hope that some relief may be procured without running such great hazard.[46]

The relief Lee was hoping for was now firmly set on Jubal Early's stooped shoulders.

Although Early had not been able to destroy Hunter's army, the results could hardly be better for the Confederates. The most dangerous Federal incursion in the Valley had been beaten back and the absence of the enemy would allow the all-important crops to grow and be harvested to supply the armies. Early was now closer to the Valley Pike and the Potomac than Hunter, and the Confederate commander was just the man to take advantage of the situation. Disappointed that they had missed a battlefield victory. Early was still hopeful that they could soon strike a heavy blow where the enemy least expected it.

9. Early Moves North

On Wednesday, June 22, Early called off the pursuit of Hunter's army:

> My command had marched sixty miles, in three days pursuit, over very rough roads, and that part of it from the Army of Northern Virginia had had no rest since leaving Gaines' Mill. I determined, therefore, to rest on the 22nd, so as to enable the wagons and artillery to get up, and prepare the men for the long march before them ... and the cavalry was sent through Fincastle to watch the enemy and annoy him as he passed through the mountains....[1]

When Early reviewed the situation, he must have liked what he saw. Hunter was effectively out of the war for several weeks and there was a clear road down the Valley toward the Potomac and Washington. The route Early would take was long and much of the food in the area had been taken by Hunter's troops. There was forage for the animals, but supplies for the troops would have to come from Richmond and Lynchburg. In anticipation of their needs, Early requested that supplies be forwarded to several locations along the route.[2]

Back on June 18th, Lee had written that "Grant is in front of Petersburg. Will be opposed there. Strike as quick as you can, and, if circumstances authorize, carry out the original plan, or move upon Petersburg without delay."[3] The final decision was Early's, but there was no doubt that Lee wanted the Army of the Valley to move north. Detaching Early's corps was a desperate gamble by Lee, but saving Lynchburg and the possibility that a raid toward the Federal capital might relieve the pressure on Petersburg was worth almost any risk. Early's army was small, probably about 12,000 to 13,000 infantry and cavalry,[4] but as a staff member wrote, "The audacity of Early's enterprise was its safety; no one who might have taken steps to oppose or cut him off would believe his force was so small.... Jackson being dead, it is safe to say no other General in either army would have attempted it against such odds."[5]

In his report to the Confederate War Department, General Lee explained why he decided to send Early north:

> Finding that it would be necessary to detach some troops to repel the force under General Hunter, which was threatening Lynchburg, I resolved to send one that would be adequate to accomplish that purpose effectually, and, if possible, strike a decisive blow. At the same time General Early was instructed, if his success justified it, and the enemy retreated down the Valley, to pursue him, and, if opportunity offered, to follow him into Maryland. It was believed that the Valley could then be effectually freed from the presence of the enemy, and it was hoped that by threatening Washington and Baltimore General Grant would be compelled either to weaken himself so much for their protection as to afford us an opportunity to attack him, or that he might be induced to attack us.... In addition to these considerations there were other collateral results, such as obtaining military stores and supplies, that were deemed of sufficient importance to warrant the attempt.[6]

On June 23rd Early's army began the long march down the Valley Pike. Although these men were battle-hardened veterans, many were shocked by the destruction committed by Hunter's troops. There was always some damage that occurred as armies marched through the countryside or during battles, but seldom were civilian property and homes targeted as Hunter had.[7]

Early wrote:

> The scenes on Hunter's route from Lynchburg had been truly heart-rending. Houses had been burned, and helpless women and children left without shelter. The country had been stripped of provisions and many families left without a morsel to eat.... We now had renewed evidences of the outrages committed by Hunter's orders in burning and plundering private houses. We saw the ruins of a number of houses to which the torch had been applied by his orders.[8]

They reached Staunton on the 26th, where they rested, received supplies, and:

> Another telegram was received here from Gen. Lee, stating that the circumstances under which my original orders were given had changed, and again submitting it to my judgment, in the altered state of things, whether the movement down the Valley and across the Potomac should be made. The accession to my command from Breckinridge's forces had not been as great as General Lee supposed it would be, on account of the disorganization consequent on Jones' defeat at Piedmont, and the subsequent rapid movement to Lynchburg from Rockfish Gap, but I determined to carry out the original design at all hazards, and telegraphed to General Lee my purpose to continue the movement.[9]

Not all the Confederate soldiers were enthusiastic about the prospects of a long, hard march to raid the north. Most were still worn out from the march to Lynchburg and the pursuit of Hunter. The men needed more than one day to rest. While in Staunton, Thomas Winton Fisher wrote home:

> The whole march from the time we got off the cars at Waynesboro till we arrived here yesterday evening is about 225 miles and from what I can hear, we will start in the morning on a long march again, one which I don't like, viz: to make a raid on the Yankees. I fear it will not pay. We are in a fair way of defeating Grant at Richmond and mark my prediction if we attempt to go into Maryland and Pennsylvania the fat is turned into the fire. In the first place, our men and stock are not fit for a raid from the effects of long hard marching and in the second place, it never has paid either party to raid and if we attempt it I should not be surprised if half of us are captured. We have a pretty large force though and will be hard to stop.[10]

On June 28 the Army of the Valley left Staunton and started the march north with seven days of rations and high hopes. Many of the men were clad in old clothing that resembled rags more than uniforms and almost half had no shoes. But they moved swiftly with the gait of old soldiers who knew how to make long marches on empty stomachs.[11]

The next day, Lee wrote to Jefferson Davis explaining that the general goal of Early's movements was to "draw the attention of the enemy to his own territory. It may force Grant to attack me, or weaken his forces. It will also, I think, oblige Hunter to cross the Potomac or expose himself to attack. From either of these events I anticipate good results." Lee also mentioned that there was still plenty of time to either change the direction of Early's march or end the movement before he reached the Potomac River. In addition, "He could not be withdrawn from the Valley without inviting a return of Hunter's expedition. To retain him there inactive would not be advantageous...."[12]

The weather was hot and dry as Early's men pressed forward as quickly as their tired legs could carry them. He later wrote:

> On the 2nd of July we reached Winchester, and I here received a dispatch from General Lee, directing me to remain in the lower Valley until everything was in readiness to cross the Potomac, and to destroy the Baltimore and Ohio Railroad and the Chesapeake and Ohio Canal as far as possible. This was in accordance with my previous determination, and its policy was obvious. My provisions were nearly exhausted and if I had moved through Loudon, it would have been necessary for me to halt and thresh wheat and have it ground, as neither bread nor flour could be otherwise obtained; which would have caused much greater delay than was required on the other route, where we could take provisions from the enemy. Moreover, unless the Baltimore and Ohio railroad was torn up, the enemy would have been able to move troops from the West over that road to Washington.[13]

While Early was in Winchester, he received the first reliable information on Federal forces in the area. Franz Sigel was at Martinsburg with about 5,000 men of the Reserve Division. His job was to protect the Baltimore & Ohio Railroad and provide occupation troops for the lower Valley. Julius Stahel, who had been re-assigned after being wounded at Piedmont, commanded the division's cavalry. In order for Early to continue toward Washington, he had to capture the massive Federal supply depot at Martinsburg and remove Sigel's troops from his path. He split the small Confederate army into three separate wings to surround Martinsburg and destroy Sigel's command. McCausland led his cavalry west to destroy the Baltimore & Ohio railroad bridge at Back Creek and the North Mountain supply depot, then move to Martinsburg. Bradley Johnson's troops were to move around Martinsburg to the east and then join with McCausland to cut off Sigel's avenue of retreat. Finally, Breckinridge advanced toward the town on the Martinsburg Pike.[14]

On the morning of July 3rd, J. W. Garrett, president of the Baltimore & Ohio Railroad, sent a message to Secretary of War Stanton relaying information he had received earlier:

> General Sigel telegraphs at 12:50 this A.M. that there are indications of the advance of the enemy down the Valley, and that his cavalry met ours at Winchester. He has ordered one hundred and fifty cars to be sent at once to remove this A.M. all Government stores from Martinsburg, and that all our rolling-stock in that region should be sent west. I apprehend the information recently sent you of heavy forces in the Valley is about to prove correct.[15]

Later that same day, the railroad man was to be proven more correct than he knew.

As Early approached Martinsburg early on the morning of the 3rd, he believed that he would trap Sigel between the advancing infantry and the cavalry sent out earlier. But Early gave too much credit to Sigel, who did not wait for the Confederates to reach the town but had already ordered an evacuation. The Confederate cavalry was unable to close the trap and Sigel's troops and much of the supplies were able to get safely away. Sigel reported that "Colonel Mulligan fought the enemy all day, but was compelled to retire, necessitating our evacuation of Martinsburg. Our losses are not known, but great damage will be done to the railroad."[16]

Early later recalled:

> On the approach of Breckinridge, Sigel, after very slight skirmishing, evacuated Martinsburg, leaving behind considerable stores, which fell into our hands. McCausland burned the bridge over Back Creek, captured the guard at North Mountain depot, and succeeded in reaching Haynesville; but Johnson encountered a force at Leetown, under Mulligan, which, after hard fighting, he drove across the railroad, when, Sigel having united with Mulligan, Johnson's command was forced back just before night, on Rodes' and Ramseur's divisions, which had arrived at Leetown, after a march of twenty-four miles. It was too late, and these divisions were too much exhausted, to go after the enemy; and, during the night, Sigel retreated across the Potomac....[17]

So far Early's campaign had yielded somewhat disappointing results. Even though Hunter had been forced out of the Valley, he suffered few casualties and his army was still intact. Now Sigel had escaped destruction and was heading for Harpers Ferry to join forces with Brigadier General Max Weber, who defended the town and occupied a formidable position at Maryland Heights across the Potomac from the town. Early had two chances to destroy Federal armies and missed them both. But there was nothing more the weary Confederate infantry could do after days of marching in the scorching heat.

After entering Martinsburg in the late afternoon, they went into camp for the night.[18]

The Fourth of July was a day of rest for most of Early's infantry. The always-hungry Confederates feasted on the supplies they found in Martinsburg? John Worsham wrote:

> The next morning was the Fourth of July, 1864! Gen. Early did not move us at the usual early hour, but issued to the men the good things captured the evening before. They were divided among the men as fairly as possible, F Company getting a few oranges, lemons, cakes and candy, and a keg of lager beer. We certainly enjoyed the treat, and celebrated the day as well as we could for our hosts, and regretted they did not stay to preside for us. We drank [to] their health with the wish that they would do the like again. This was the biggest Fourth of July picnic celebration we enjoyed during the war.[19]

The celebration didn't last for long, as there was still serious work to be done and Early was not a commander to put things off. He recalled, "On the 4th, Shepherdstown was occupied by a part of Ransom's cavalry. Rodes' and Ramseur's divisions moved to Harpers Ferry, and the enemy was driven from Bolivar Heights, and the village of Bolivar, to an inner line of works under the cover of the guns from Maryland Heights."[20]

Approaching from the southwest, Harpers Ferry was guarded by several hills, the highest being Bolivar Heights. But the real key to the area was Maryland Heights, which rose straight out of the opposite side of the Potomac. This peak bristled with Federal artillery and commanded the terrain for miles, making capturing and holding Harpers Ferry out of the question. Early decided to shell the Federal positions, bring up his infantry, and see how the Union commander, Max Weber, reacted. He didn't have to wait long, because "During the night of the 4th, the enemy evacuated Harper's Ferry, burning the railroad and pontoon bridges across the Potomac."[21]

Here was the first real obstacle that Early had encountered on his march north:

> My desire had been to manoeuvre the enemy out of Maryland Heights, so as to enable me to move directly from Harper's Ferry for Washington; but he had taken refuge in his strongly fortified works, and, as they could not be approached without great difficulty, and an attempt to carry them by assault would have resulted in greater loss than the advantage to be gained would justify, I determined to move through the gaps of South Mountain to the north of the Heights.[22]

Once again he showed his growth as a commander by curbing his combative nature and putting the goal of the mission first. Early had an almost open road ahead, he could not afford any unnecessary delays, Washington was waiting.

Back on July 3rd Halleck had warned Grant that at the present there was not much that could be done to oppose Early if he chose to continue advancing:

> General Sigel reports that Early, Breckinridge, and Jackson, with Mosby's guerrillas, are said to be moving from Staunton down the Shenandoah Valley. I ordered General Hunter up to the line of the Railroad, but he

has replied to none of my telegrams, and has made no report of his operations or present condition.... The three principal officers on the line of the road are Sigel, Stahl, and Max Weber. You can, therefore, judge what probability there is of a good defense if the enemy should attack the line in force.[23]

The Confederate capture of Martinsburg was proof that Early was not going to return to Petersburg but was heading north with a force that was large enough to cause serious problems. If Early kept going and crossed the Potomac, he would be in a good position to threaten both Washington and Baltimore, and the Union high command was well aware that the defenses of both cities were in poor condition and feebly manned. For months before launching the summer offensive, Grant had been taking troops from wherever he could find them to build up the Army of the Potomac. He did not hesitate to transfer into the infantry, garrison troops that were just sitting out the war including artillerymen from the forts around Washington. Since the campaign began, he was constantly trying to find men to replace those lost in the terrible fighting, and he hated to part with a single man. General Lee was well aware of this and in fact was counting on the defenses of Washington being undermanned. He said, "At this time, as far as I can learn, all the troops in the control of the United States are being sent to Grant, and little or no opposition could be made by those at Washington."[24]

On the 5th, Halleck wired Grant to inform him that

There has been no telegraphic communication with Harper's Ferry since yesterday, a little after noon; but we learn through the railroad company that Sigel had reached Maryland Heights and withdrawn all troops from south of the river, destroying the bridges. We can learn nothing whatever of Hunter.... We have nothing reliable in regard to enemy's force. Some accounts, probably very exaggerated, state it to be between 20,000 and 30,000. If one-half that number we cannot meet it in the field till Hunter's troops arrive. As you are aware, we have almost nothing in Baltimore or Washington, except militia, and considerable alarm has been created by sending troops from these places to re-enforce Harper's Ferry....[25]

By this time Grant had heard enough. He sent a message to Meade, telling him, "The enemy have got to the Baltimore and Ohio road and have destroyed the railroad bridges from Patterson's Creek to Harper's Ferry. Send in one good division of your troops and all the dismounted cavalry, to be forwarded at once."[26]

Also on the 5th, Grant received a message from Meade that information obtained from Confederate deserters, which was remarkably accurate, confirmed the worst. "They state it to be currently reported at Richmond and in Petersburg that Early, in command of two divisions of Ewell's corps, with Breckinridge's command and other forces, was making an invasion of Maryland with a view of capturing Washington, supposed to be defenseless."[27]

Now the Union high command realized that they were facing a serious situation. A Confederate army north of Washington called for an immediate and decisive response. Following Grant's order, Meade had immediately ordered

Brigadier General James B. Ricketts with his veteran Third Division from the 6th Corps, nearly 5,000 infantry, along with almost 4,000 dismounted cavalrymen, to head north as soon as possible. This relief force was on its way by the 6th.[28]

While Grant knew that protecting Washington was of the utmost importance, he also could see that the invasion was a golden opportunity to put troops south of Early and prevent him from returning to join Lee at Petersburg. As much as he wanted to keep a stranglehold on the Confederate forces at Petersburg, the chance to destroy an entire corps of Lee's veteran troops was too important to pass up. He wired Halleck on the 5th, "We want now to crush out and destroy any force the enemy have sent north. Force enough can be spared from here to do it."[29]

Unfortunately, both General Halleck and Secretary Stanton seemed to be unable to take any initiative on their own. Halleck sent a mixed force of militia, artillerymen and dismounted cavalry to reinforce Maryland Heights. All Halleck could think of to do when Washington was being threatened was to send troops someplace else while waiting for the slow-moving troops of General Hunter to arrive. Secretary Stanton, who normally was his most active in times of danger, appeared calm and discounted the rumors of invasion, possibly because the War Department didn't know enough about what was going on to realize how dangerous the situation really was.[30]

In their tattered uniforms, the men of the Second Corps sent clouds of dust into the air as they marched. On the afternoon of July 5th, they began splashing across the Potomac and moving through the lush fields of Maryland. Near Shepherdstown, Breckinridge's men crossed the river at Boteler's Ford. Some of them would remember that they had crossed the river here before, on the way to the bloodbath at Antietam. Once again a Confederate army was invading the north, but this time there were no bands playing or flags waving in the breeze. Twice before they had crossed this river, on the way to Antietam and Gettysburg, only to be thrown back with heavy losses and shattered hopes. But this time was different—the war had changed them and the earlier enthusiasm had given way to desperation.[31]

Foragers quickly went to work in the countryside with Confederate money and impressment certificates. Early did not like to commandeer supplies from civilians and was concerned about the lapses in discipline that had already occurred. In the past, the Confederate army had maintained excellent discipline and pillaging had been held to a minimum in enemy country. But now, some of the men were not above taking revenge for Hunter's destruction in the Valley. Early had learned of the sacking of warehouses in Martinsburg and on the 5th he issued a tactful rebuke to Breckinridge for not maintaining discipline:

> I have very deplorable accounts of the plundering and confusion at Martinsburg, and hope it may turn out to be untrue. You will direct all officers of every grade to remain and camp with their commands.... It is absolutely necessary that the most rigid discipline be enforced, else disgrace and disaster will overtake us.[32]

9. Early Moves North

That same day, Early issued a general order to the army:

> In entering the enemy's country the lieutenant-general commanding would remind the officers and men of this army that they are engaged in no marauding expedition, and are not making war upon the defenseless and unresisting, and he confidently appeals to them to emulate their behavior upon former similar occasions.... The strictest discipline must be preserved, and all straggling, marauding, and appropriation of property by unauthorized parties must be prevented.
>
> Such supplies as are needed for the army will be taken by or under the direction of the chiefs of the various departments, and payment made therefor or certificates given as the owner may prefer; and any officer or man found committing depredations of any sort will be at once arrested and summarily punished.[33]

While Early kept busy trying to accumulate enough supplies for his troops, he also was active in trying to confuse the Federal authorities as to the size and destination of his command. John Imboden was sent to the South Branch Valley to destroy railroad track in an effort to prevent Hunter from returning too soon and blocking the way home. Although Imboden became sick and the damage to the track was minor, Early had no reason to worry, Hunter was moving too slowly to be a factor in the near future. General Gordon occupied the attention of the Union troops at Maryland Heights while work parties did as much destruction as possible to the Chesapeake and Ohio Canal, damaging the locks and destroying boats. Early also had cavalry troopers move out in several directions simultaneously, creating the illusion of a large force threatening all Maryland and even parts of Pennsylvania. Reports of Rebel raids from both military and civilian sources created even more confusion at the War Department, deepening the concern about the raiders' objectives but producing few proposals to stop them.[34]

The situation was even worse than Stanton or Halleck imagined. Hunter was still too far away to help and in any event, it wasn't clear where Early was or where he was going, Baltimore or Washington. Since most of the able-bodied troops had been taken by Grant and Sherman, the government was reduced to asking neighboring states to call up short-term militia forces to defend the capital. And finally there was a growing flood of refugees fleeing the Confederate raiding parties and spreading all sorts of rumors:

> The people of Western Maryland and Southern Pennsylvania, who had already received two unpleasant visits from the Rebels, fled in haste towards Baltimore and Harrisburg. The panic was widespread. Extravagant stories were told of the force of the enemy: Lee's whole army was advancing; he had outgeneraled Grant; he had sixty thousand men across the Potomac; Washington and Baltimore were to be captured.[35]

On the sixth, Early received a letter from General Lee. Early was to assist in an attempt to free Confederate prisoners being held south of Washington at Point Lookout.[36] There were thousands of veteran troops incarcerated at the prison camp and the release of these men could provide desperately needed reinforcements for Lee's army, and if they joined with Early there was no telling what he might accomplish. The possibilities were too promising not to make an attempt. At the end of June, Lee wrote to Jefferson Davis and suggested:

> Great benefit might be drawn from the release of our prisoners at Point Lookout if it can be accomplished.... The dismounted cavalry with the released prisoners of that arm could mount themselves on the march, and the infantry would form a respectable force. Such a body of men under an able leader, although they might not be able without assistance to capture Washington, could march around it and cross the upper Potomac where fordable.... The subject is one worth of consideration....[37]

Early on the morning of the 7th, the Eighth Illinois Cavalry under Lieutenant Colonel David Clendenin, out on a scouting mission, engaged Bradley Johnson's cavalry outside the village of Middletown. After heavy fighting, the Federals were pushed back to Frederick City, Maryland. The fighting continued until dark when the Confederates discontinued the attack. They had learned all they needed to know and further fighting was unnecessary. The main roads to Washington and Baltimore were being defended by only small units of Federal troops and, even more importantly, they were not from the Army of the Potomac; none of Grant's veterans had arrived.[38]

About three miles southeast of Frederick City, at Monocacy Junction, Major General Lew Wallace was waiting to learn the outcome of the fighting at Middletown. It was Wallace who sent the cavalry forward trying to find out anything he could about the invaders, although the simple fact that there was fighting in the area meant trouble. Wallace was the commander of the U. S. Army's Middle Department with headquarters in Baltimore. Far away from the battle lines, the department was used primarily to train new recruits and garrison the city: most of the men had never been in battle. The early rumors of Confederate activity had reached Wallace, but since they were out of his jurisdiction, he did not get too excited. However, all that quickly changed when Harpers Ferry fell and word was received that Confederate cavalry was already north of the Potomac.[39]

If the Confederates had crossed into Maryland, Wallace believed, they were either unusually reckless or they came in large enough numbers to do serious damage, perhaps even make a dash for the capital. Wallace later wrote, "It was questionable whether the enemy had Washington for his objective, or Baltimore. Enough that I believed it Washington. Then when I ran over all the consequences of the capture of that city, they grouped themselves into a kind of horrible schedule."[40]

If the Confederates were able to enter Washington there would be targets galore. At risk were huge warehouses full of supplies and ordnance for the Army of the Potomac, as well as the wealth of the treasury and the buildings from which the government of the United States was run, to say nothing of how even the temporary occupation of the nation's capital would affect the support for the war. At the very least, the Union war effort might be brought to a temporary halt if the Confederates could cause enough destruction.

9. Early Moves North

For the time being, the only body of Federal troops between Early and Washington was the 2,500 men commanded by Wallace. Not knowing where the Confederates were ultimately heading, Wallace decided to make a stand at Monocacy Junction, where both the Georgetown Pike to Washington and the National Road to Baltimore, along with a bridge for the Baltimore & Ohio, crossed the Monocacy River. Wallace's small force would have to cover about two miles of riverfront to protect the bridges and several fords that crossed the river.[41] E.M. Haynes said, "Perhaps the near proximity of the rebels to Baltimore and Washington, and their defenceless condition, warranted the attempt to throw a small force across the intended track of a much superior force, and delay its advance as long as possible."[42] But Wallace would need help if he hoped to do anything other than get his command destroyed for no good reason.

The help that Wallace needed was on its way in the form of General Ricketts' veterans. About the only information Ricketts had been given on leaving Petersburg was that there was some sort of enemy threat near Washington. He arrived at Baltimore on the 7th with virtually no information about where the enemy was, where they might be heading, or what he was supposed to do about it. The same chaos and indecision that gripped Washington was also present in Baltimore. Since Wallace was calling for help from Monocacy Junction and seemed to have some knowledge of the enemy's whereabouts, that is where Halleck ordered Ricketts to go. "As fast as your division arrives it will move by Baltimore and Ohio Railroad to Point of Rocks, or mouth of Monocacy...."[43]

Ricketts and two of his brigades joined Wallace's small command on the 8th, increasing the Federal force to a little over 5,000 men.[44]

Also on the 8th, General Halleck telegraphed Grant:

> [The] latest dispatches state that a heavy column of the enemy has crossed the Monocacy and is moving on Urbana. Sigel and Couch say that scouts, prisoners and country people confirm previous reports of enemy's force—that is, some 20,000 or 30,000. Until more forces arrive we have nothing to meet that number in the field, and the militia is not reliable even to hold the fortifications of Washington and Baltimore. It is the impression that one-third of Lee's entire force is with Early and Breckinridge, and that Ransom has some 3,000 or 4,000 cavalry. None of the cavalry sent up by you has arrived nor do we get anything from Hunter. Troops sent from the James River should come here, not to Baltimore, where they cannot be supplied or equipped. If you propose to cut off this raid and not merely to secure our depots we must have more forces here. Indeed, if the enemy's strength is as great as represented, it is doubtful if the militia can hold all of our defenses. I do not think that we can expect much from Hunter. He is too far off and moves too slowly. I think, therefore, that very considerable re-enforcements should be sent directly to this place.[45]

The increasingly pessimistic information reaching Grant finally forced him to take further action. The Nineteenth Corps was already on its way north from New Orleans and the First Division would be arriving at Fort Monroe any day now. Grant was well aware of how few trained soldiers manned the defenses of Washington; most of them had been transferred to the Army of the

Potomac. A series of messages to Halleck on the 9th illustrate his growing concern for the safety of the capital:

> If you think it necessary, order the Nineteenth Corps as it arrives at Fortress Monroe to Washington. About the 18th or 20th is the time I should like to have a large force here; but if the rebel force now north can be captured or destroyed I would willingly postpone aggressive operations to destroy them, and could send in addition to the Nineteenth Corps, the balance of the Sixth Corps.[46]

At 5:30 p.m:

> I have ordered the remainder of the Sixth Corps to Washington. On account of scarcity of transportation I do not send wagons or artillery, but they will follow if you say it is wanted. I think most of the 3,000 cavalry sent are fit for duty. They certainly must have reached Baltimore with the other troops. If the Nineteenth Corps reached Fortress Monroe in time you can take it also if you deem it advisable.[47]

Then at 6:00 P.M.:

> Forces enough to defeat all that Early has with him should get in his rear south of him, and follow him up sharply, leaving him to go north, defending depots, towns, &c., with small garrisons and the militia. If the President thinks it advisable that I should go to Washington in person I can start in an hour after receiving notice, leaving everything here on the defensive.[48]

While Grant was sending messages to Washington on July 9, Wallace and Ricketts were doing their best to defend Monocacy Junction as if the safety of their nation's capital was at stake, which it most certainly was.

10. The Battle of Monocacy

It was Saturday, July 9, and the sun rose on a clear and hot summer day. Early in the morning Confederate cavalry and Ramseur's infantry pushed the Federal skirmishers back through Frederick to the Monocacy River. Most of Early's troops moved around the town while the Federal rear guard was engaged. Beginning about 9 A.M., there was only skirmishing and light artillery fire as Early was trying to get his men into position for the attack. While Early's artillery fired on the Federal positions, the leaders of Frederick were informed that unless they contributed $200,000 to the Confederate cause, their town would be destroyed. The payment was made.[1]

Lew Wallace had pulled his troops back to the heights on the east side of the river. Wallace quickly saw that it was a very good defensive position since "the river covers its entire front. In a low stage of water the fords are few, and particularly difficult for artillery, and the commanding heights are all on the eastern bank, while the ground on the opposite side is level and almost without obstructions." He also noted that if the army were forced from this position, the road to Baltimore was easily accessible and they could retire and prepare to defend that city.[2]

Based on the direction Early was moving, Wallace decided that

> it seemed to disclose a purpose to obtain the pike to Washington, important to the enemy for several causes, but especially so if his designs embraced that city, then in no condition, as I understood it, to resist an army like that attributed to Early by General Sigel. I claim no credit for understanding my duty in such a situation; it was self-apparent. There was no force that could be thrown in time between the capital and the rebels but mine, which was prob-

ably too small to defeat them, but certainly strong enough to gain time and compel them to expose their strength.[3]

Wallace placed his least experienced troops, commanded by Brigadier General Erastus B. Tyler, on the right side of the Federal defensive line. On the northern end of the line was a stone bridge for the Baltimore Pike defended by the 144th and 149th Ohio National Guard. Troops from the Third Regiment Potomac Home Brigade, Maryland Volunteers and First Maryland Potomac Home Brigade were stationed to defend a ford about midway between the stone bridge and the Baltimore & Ohio Railroad bridge. The Eleventh Maryland was on the southern end of Tyler's line near the railroad bridge and connecting with Ricketts' troops. The stone bridge on the Baltimore Pike was especially important, because as Lew Wallace said, "Upon the holding of that bridge depended the security of my right flank, and the line of retreat to Baltimore."[4]

The veteran troops from the 6th Corps were placed farther south in two lines to cover the railroad bridge and the bridge for the Georgetown Pike leading toward Washington. A detachment of cavalry under Colonel Clendenin was on the far left to guard the flank. Wallace placed a skirmish line on the west bank of the river, screening the approaches to the bridges with his artillery and covering them from the heights on the east side of the river. They were defending a front of nearly two miles with fewer than 6,000 men and only six cannon. It was obvious to both Ricketts and Wallace that the most exposed part of the line, where Early was most likely to attack if he could find a ford across the river, was on the left. That was why the veterans of the Sixth Corps were assigned to protect that flank.[5]

When Early arrived to survey the situation and plan his next move, he was not happy with what he saw:

> The enemy, in considerable force under General Lew Wallace, was found strongly posted on the eastern bank of the Monocacy, near the Junction, with an earthwork and two block houses commanding both the railroad bridge and the bridge on the Georgetown pike. Ramseur's division was deployed in front of the enemy, after driving his skirmishers across the river, and several batteries were put in position, when a sharp artillery fire opened from both sides. Rodes' division had come up from Jefferson and was placed on Ramseur's left, covering the roads from Baltimore and the crossings of the Monocacy above the Junction. Breckinridge's command, with the trains, was in the rear between Frederick and the Junction, while the residue of the cavalry was watching a force of the enemy's cavalry which had followed from Maryland Heights.[6]

Early had to be careful. He hadn't brought his little army all this way only to smash it against such a formidable position by a foolish frontal assault. "The enemy's position was too strong, and the difficulties of crossing the Monocacy under fire too great, to attack in front without greater loss than I was willing to incur."[7] He could see that the Federal position was already set and could not be extended much further. It was obvious that an attack on the enemy's left flank was the only realistic option for success. Also, Early needed to get

10. The Battle of Monocacy

control of the road to Washington, which was on the Federal left. The decision was made for him, cross the river and attack the enemy's flank and rear. "I therefore made an examination in person to find a point at which the river could be crossed, so as to take the enemy in flank. While I was engaged in making this examination to my right, I discovered McCausland in the act of crossing the river with his brigade."[8]

McCausland's troopers quickly dismounted and attacked the exposed Federal left flank. However, instead of the untrained militia that they believed occupied the position, the Confederate cavalry had run into Ricketts' experienced veterans. Colonel William Emerson, of the 151st New York, reported, "A heavy skirmish line of the enemy's cavalry and infantry appearing on the left and front..." forced the Federal line to extend more to the left.[9] McCausland pressed his attack with vigor but was unable to dislodge the Sixth Corps troops. Early could see that "McCausland's movement, which was very brilliantly executed, solved the problem for me, and, as soon as I discovered it, orders were sent to Breckinridge to move up rapidly with Gordon's division to McCausland's assistance, and to follow up his attack."[10]

Union Brigadier General James B. Ricketts (Library of Congress).

As General Gordon wrote later:

> My hope and effort were to conceal the movement from Wallace's watchful eye until my troops were over, and then apprise him of my presence on his side of the river by a sudden rush upon his left flank; but General McCausland's brigade of Confederate cavalry had already gallantly attacked a portion of his troops, and he discovered the manoeuvre of my division before it could drag itself through the water and up the Monocacy's muddy and slippery banks. He at once changed front and drew up his lines in strong position to meet the assault.
>
> This movement presented new difficulties. Instead of realizing my hope of finding the Union forces still facing Early's other divisions beyond the river, giving my isolated command the immense advantage of the proposed flank attack, I found myself separated from all other Confederate infantry, with the bristling front of Wallace's army before me.[11]

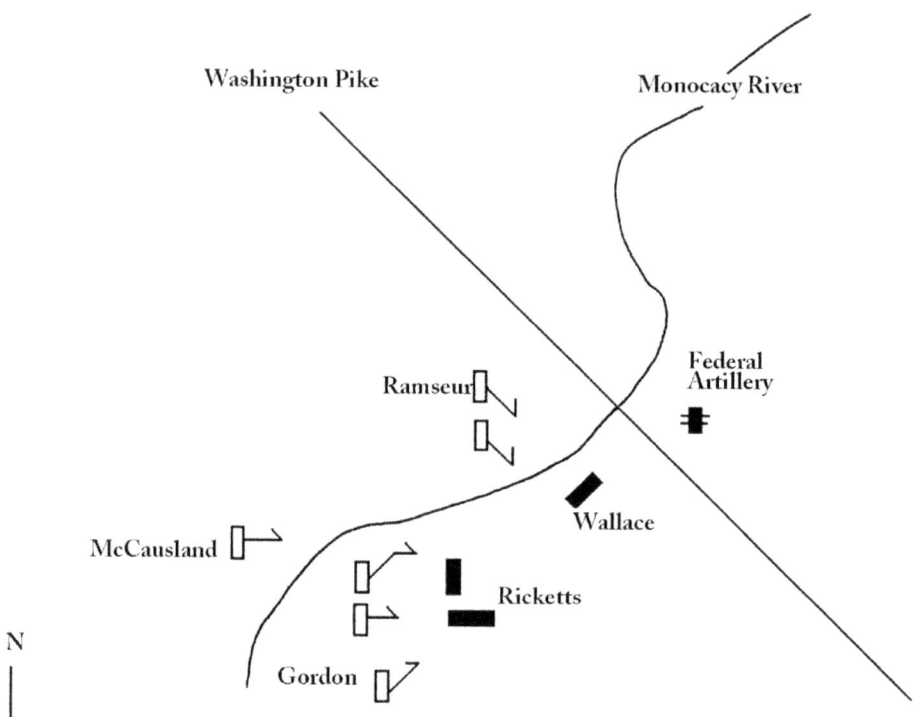

Battle of Monocacy

Seeing the enemy crossing the river in large numbers, Ricketts had changed the position of his line and now was formed with the right of the division near the river bank and the left bending back to cover the Washington Pike, stretching his ranks dangerously thin. Earlier, as the Confederates moved south to flank his line, Wallace had ordered the wooden bridge for the Georgetown Pike and the blockhouses burned and the defenders were sent to assist Ricketts, but there would be no more help.[12] While surveying the terrain where he would attack, Gordon saw that "the enemy was posted along the line of a fence on the crest of a ridge running obliquely to the left from the river. In his front lay an open field, which was commanded by his artillery and small-arms to the extent of their range...."[13]

When the Confederates advanced about 2 P.M., the two leading brigades, commanded by Brigadier Generals Clement A. Evans and Zebulon York, were met with a deadly fire and suffered heavy casualties:

> The troops emerged from the woods 700 yards in front of the enemy's left under heavy fire from infantry and artillery, and had advanced but a short distance when, on account of the wounding of one brigade commander (Evans), to whom explicit instructions had been given as to the movement

of his (the leading) brigade, and the killing of several regimental commanders, and the difficulty of advancing in line through a field covered with wheat-shocks and intersected by fences, the perfect alignment of this brigade was necessarily to some extent broken.[14]

General Gordon later described the difficulties facing his men on that day:

> As we reached the first line of strong and high fencing, and my men began to climb over it, they were met by a tempest of bullets, and many of the brave fellows fell at the first volley. But over they climbed or tumbled, and rushed forward, some of them halting to break down gaps in the fence, so that the mounted officers might ride through. Then came the grain-stacks. Around them and between them they pressed on, with no possibility of maintaining orderly alignment or of returning any effective fire. Deadly missiles from Wallace's ranks were cutting down the line and company officers with their words of cheer to the men but half spoken.[15]
>
> At this point the Louisiana brigades, under the command of Brigadier-General York, became engaged, and the two brigades (Evans and York's) moved forward with much spirit, driving back the enemy's first line in confusion upon his second. After a brief halt at the fence from which this first line had been driven I ordered a charge on the second line, which was equally successful.[16]

Part of the Federal second line ran along a branch of the river where the fighting was especially heavy. Gordon noted that "So profuse was the flow of blood from the killed and wounded of both these forces that it reddened the stream for more than 100 yards below."[17]

The Sixth Corps veterans had been bloodied and battered but still stubbornly held their position protecting the road to Washington. Ricketts had been forced to adjust his line more to the left as the Confederates were coming from that direction and the reserve troops of the Tenth Vermont Volunteers were brought up on the left, "orders being received to hold the position at all hazards." But Gordon was not to be denied and soon he was advancing again.[18]

With his casualties mounting, Gordon ordered Brigadier General William R. Terry's brigade

> who as yet had not been engaged, to attack vigorously that portion of the enemy's line nearest the river, and from which my troops were receiving a severe flank fire. This brigade advanced with great spirit and in excellent order, driving the enemy from his position on a portion of the line. He still held most stubbornly his strong position in front of the other two brigades and upon my right.[19]

It was now mid-afternoon and so far the Federal troops had been able to hold their own against the larger Confederate army. Ricketts' men on the left had borne the brunt of the heavy fighting and although the attackers had pushed them back in places, the Federal line had not broken. On the other end of the Federal position, Ramseur's troops had been skirmishing all day with the troops defending the iron railroad bridge and a nearby blockhouse, but had been unable to make any headway against the determined Federal resistance.[20]

Confederate Major General John B. Gordon (Library of Congress).

General Gordon now ordered an attack all along the Federal left flank. General Terry's brigade changed position and attacked the Federal right. "This movement, promptly executed with a simultaneous attack from the front, resulted in the dislodging of their line, and the complete rout of the enemy's forces. This battle, though short, was severe...."[21]

One of the Confederate soldiers wrote that as Gordon led his men forward, he tried to calm them down and keep the formation together until the cry went up from the men, "Charge them! charge them!" It was useless for Gen. Gordon to try to stop it now,—nothing but a shot through each man could have done it,—and with a yell, we were at the fence. A volley from our guns,—and that magnificent body of men who were taking their places in line were flying! The other men of our brigade came up as fast as they could run and delivered their fire at the fleeing enemy.[22]

Years later General Gordon wrote a tribute to the courage and determination of his men who made the final charge:

> It was one of those fights where success depends largely upon the prowess of the individual soldier. The men were deprived of that support and strength imparted by a compact line, where the elbow touch of comrade with comrade gives confidence to each and sends the electric thrill of enthusiasm through all. But nothing could deter them. Neither the obstructions nor the leaden blast in their front could check them.[23]

Ricketts' troops had been hit with a ferocious attack by Terry's men on their right and York's men on the left that finally broke the Federal line. Lieutenant Colonel O. H. Binkley, of the 110th Ohio Volunteer Infantry, later reported, "Having received orders to fall back when we could hold the position no longer, and seeing the enemy coming down upon us in overwhelming numbers with imminent danger of having my command annihilated, I gave the order to fall back."[24] Ricketts' men fell back across the Washington Pike toward the road to Baltimore, which had been designated as the route of escape.

With the left part of the Federal line gone, Wallace could not hold the rest of his line and had to order the remainder of his troops to fall back. "The stone bridge held by Colonel Brown now became all important; its loss was the loss of my line of retreat, and I had reason to believe that the enemy, successful on my left, would redouble his efforts against the right." Ramseur did exactly that, crossing the river on the iron railroad bridge and joining Gordon's men in pursuing the beaten enemy as they fled north toward the Baltimore road, capturing several hundred prisoners.[25]

Colonel Allison L. Brown of the 149th Ohio Infantry reported that he "received an order from Major-General Wallace to hold the bridge over the Monocacy at that point to the last extremity, and when I was pressed so hard that nothing more could be done, to command my men to disperse and to take care of themselves."[26]

By 5 P.M. the battle was over. What was left of Wallace's command was streaming down the National Road toward Baltimore. Early quickly decided not to pursue the fleeing enemy past the immediate battlefield. His men were exhausted and there were many casualties to tend to. The main goal of removing the last organized body of the enemy between the Confederate army and Washington had been accomplished and the road ahead looked clear. Rounding up more Federal prisoners would only slow down the march to the capital.[27]

Considering the relatively small numbers engaged, the Battle of Monocacy produced a high number of casualties. In his official report, Wallace states, "My casualty list will be quite severe, but cannot possibly equal that of the enemy, as they charged several times in close lines, and with a recklessness that can be justified only upon the ground that they supposed my command consisted of raw militia."[28] For the Confederates, Gordon reported 698 casualties from his division alone. Although Early stated that the loss for his entire army was virtually the same number, it would be reasonable to put the total at about 800 to 900. Wallace lost about 1,300 men with about 550 taken prisoner or missing.[29]

Early made his headquarters across the river near the railroad bridge and immediately began to plan the next phase of the advance. Discovering that units of the Sixth Corps had been present for the battle was a double-edged sword for Early. He must have been pleased that the Union high command was worried enough for Grant to send some of his best troops from Petersburg to protect the capital, and Early had heard reports that more were on the way. Forcing Grant to reduce his strength at Petersburg was one of the main goals that Lee had in mind when forming the plan to create a diversion. On the other hand, if enough Federal troops had been sent north it would be difficult, if not impossible, for Early to accomplish the rest of his task—the capture of Washington. The fortifications around the capital were known to be as strong as any ever built in this country. The only way the small Confederate army had a chance of breaching them was if there were too few defenders to properly protect the city.

Time was the critical factor. If Early could get to Washington before it was heavily reinforced, there was a good chance of capturing the city. If, however, Early delayed, or the reinforcements were closer than believed, the Confederate army could be destroyed in a futile attack against veteran troops manning impenetrable fortifications, or be caught from behind by Hunter, who was slowly but steadily moving east. All these factors had to be considered. But for now, it was too late in the day to do anything but care for the wounded and rest the army so they could resume the march early the next morning.[30]

For Lew Wallace, James Ricketts, and their troops, the battle had been a costly defeat, but the price paid was worth it. Now there was definite information about the numbers and intentions of the invaders. Wallace reported that Early's force was about 18,000 strong.[31] Even if this number was too high, there were enough Confederates to actually threaten the capital if the fortifications were not properly manned. Wallace's little army had done its job and the delay of Early's troops at the Monocacy turned out to be very important indeed. As Grant wrote later:

> If Early had been but one day earlier he might have entered the capital before the arrival of the reinforcements I had sent. Whether the delay caused by the battle amounted to a day or not, General Wallace contributed on this occasion, by the defeat of the troops under him a greater benefit to the cause than often falls to the lot of a commander of an equal force to render by means of a victory.[32]

11. The War Comes to Washington

Jubal Early had his men on the road to Washington by daylight on the day after the battle. It was Sunday and the conditions were terrible. "On the morning of the 10th I moved toward Washington, taking the route by Rockville, and then turning to the left to get on the Seventh-street pike. The day was very hot and the roads exceedingly dusty...."[1]

The sun baked the men in stifling heat as choking dust billowed up from the bone dry roads, forcing many to fall behind or just collapse by the roadside, hoping to catch up to their comrades later. Despite their fatigue, they still covered over twenty miles, about half the distance to Washington, by the time the army halted at sunset:[2]

> We moved at daylight on the 11th; McCausland moving on the Georgetown pike, while the infantry, preceded by Imboden's cavalry, under Colonel Smith, turned to the left at Rockville, so as to reach the 7th street pike which runs by Silver Spring into Washington. Jackson's cavalry moved on the left flank. The previous day had been very warm, and the roads were exceedingly dusty, as there had been no rain for several weeks. The heat during the night had been very oppressive, and but little rest had been obtained. This day was an exceedingly hot one, and there was no air stirring. While marching, the men were enveloped in a suffocating cloud of dust, and many of them fell by the way from exhaustion. Our progress was therefore very much impeded, but I pushed on as rapidly as possible, hoping to get into the fortifications around Washington before they could be manned.[3]

Long before noon, however, veterans who had endured some of the hardest marches of the Second Corps were falling out of ranks. "Probably the day was hotter than the preceding, and we had been marching faster too. Consequently there was more straggling. Our Division was stretched out almost like skirmishers, and all the men did not get up until night." Early tried to push his men on, but even his zeal could not keep the column closed or the men in their place.[4]

As the weary Confederates approached Washington, they moved through Silver Spring, home of some of Washington's social and political leaders. The condition of these homes when they left the area depended mostly on who the owners were. Confederate officers, who took care not to unduly damage the property, occupied the home of well-respected Francis P. Blair. Nearby was the home of his son Montgomery, the current postmaster general; his house was burned to the ground.[5]

At the home of socialite Elizabeth Blair Lee, one of the Confederate officers who occupied her home left a note that he and his comrades "...regrets exceedingly that damage & pilfering was committed in this house.... We wage no ignoble warfare for plunder or revenge, but for all that men hold dearest, & scorn to retaliate in kind the unmentioned outrages committed on our homes by federals...."[6] It might be reasonable to wonder if the lady's last name had something to do with the apology.

Early's cavalry easily dispersed a few Federal cavalry detachments that were out scouting, and they proceeded along the Seventh Street Pike. Early wrote that he "rode ahead of the infantry, and arrived in sight of Fort Stevens on this road a very short time after noon, when I discovered the works were but feebly manned."[7] One of his soldiers wrote in his diary that the men were all wondering what was next, "and all are eager to enter the city. We can plainly see the dome of the Capitol and other prominent buildings, Arlington Heights (General Lee's old home), and four lofty redoubts, well manned with huge, frowning cannon."[8]

Just the fact that this small and now exhausted Confederate army had been able to reach Washington was an amazing achievement. But now that they were in sight of their target, could they make the long, hard march pay off?

Washington, D.C., was more than the capital of a nation. It was the headquarters of the war effort. Grant was the head of all the armies and in theory wherever he was, that was where the military headquarters was located. But he avoided the capital like the plague and stayed in the field at Petersburg; the military bureaucracy that made things work was in Washington. Disrupting the government and the machinery to make war, even for a brief time, could bring disaster to the Union cause.

People had different impressions of the capital that summer. The wife of Union General George A. Custer wrote:

> As I looked at Washington in one light it seemed only a huge hospital encircled with a sad cordon of suffering, for the hospitals had been moved from the heart of the city to the higher and purer air of the slopes. They could hardly be built fast enough to accommodate the long trains of ambulances that brought the wounded from the skirmish lines across the Potomac in Virginia. Another point of view made one feel that the city was only a store-

11. The War Comes to Washington

house, for long trains of supplies were traveling through the streets on the way to the wharves to be shipped to the front.[9]

By the summer of 1864 the people of Washington had become complacent about the war. Like the Confederate capital at Richmond, the Union capital was a target right from the start of hostilities. The Confederates had made several attempts to capture Washington and dictate peace terms to the Union. But now those days of worry were gone. The war was being fought south of Richmond and the enemy was hard pressed to hold on to what was left of the Confederacy. The danger of an invasion of the north had passed. All this changed with the defeat at Monocacy. Suddenly the city was awash in refugees from Maryland fleeing from the invaders with whatever they could load on their wagons or carry on their backs, bringing with them terrifying stories of destruction by a huge Confederate army that could not be stopped.[10]

With good reason, the people of Washington had felt secure behind the massive fortifications that surrounded their city. There were at least fifty forts ringing the city with an excellent system of trenches connecting them, and all the ground in front of the works was commanded by heavy artillery. No enemy could approach the city from any direction without running into this system of modern, seemingly impenetrable fortifications. There was only one problem. There was nowhere near enough soldiers to properly man them.[11]

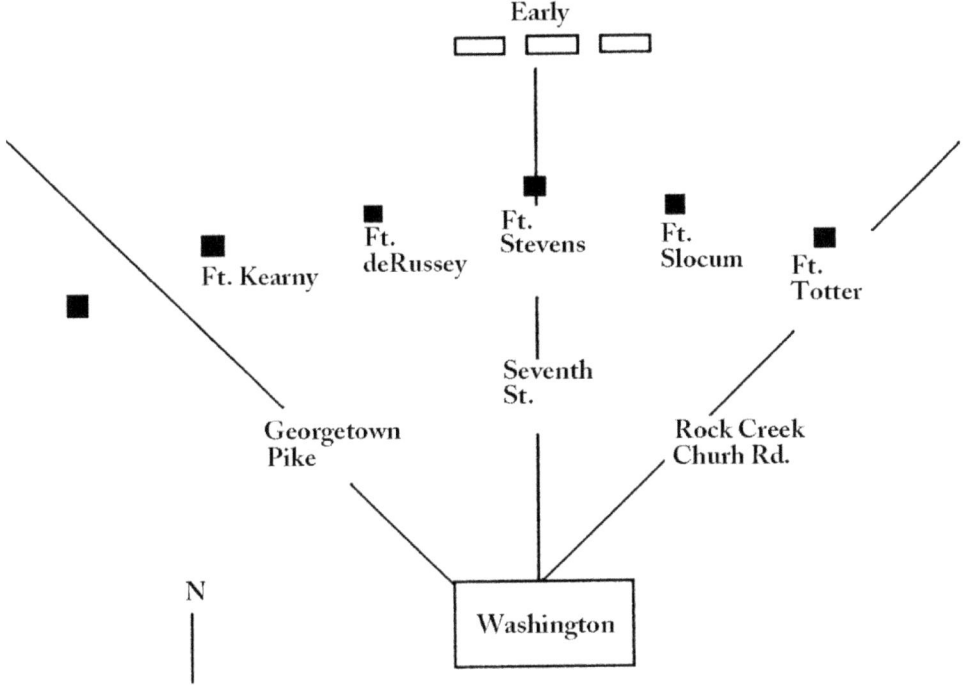

Fortifications of Washington

Major General Christopher C. Augur, a veteran of service in Virginia and Louisiana, commanded the Department of Washington and its Twenty-second Corps. On paper he reported a total of thirty-one thousand men in the department, but fewer than ten thousand of these were available to man the fortifications, the rest being spread out in small detachments outside the city, on guard duty in and around the capital, or not physically fit to fight. Grant had taken most of the able-bodied men to help replace his huge losses. What was left were trainees, inexperienced National Guard troops, some 100-day militiamen from neighboring states, and the Veteran Reserve Corps made up of men who were unfit for normal duty due to wounds or illness. There were not enough men to properly man the forts and none to occupy the trenches between them. Few of these men had ever heard a shot fired in anger and most knew nothing about the heavy artillery that they were supposed to man in case of an attack.[12]

General Halleck had requested an examination be made of the defenses on the bridges crossing the Potomac. On the 6th, he received a distressing report from Lieutenant Colonel B. S. Alexander, aide to General J. G. Barnard, Chief Engineer of the city's fortifications. Alexander reported that on the Chain Bridge above Georgetown, the batteries on the Washington side of the river

> are in charge of Private Spink, One hundred and forty-seventh Ohio National Guard, acting ordnance sergeant. He knows nothing about ordnance or artillery. In fact, no one at the bridge knows how to load the guns. The business of Sergeant Spink is to clean the guns, air the ammunition, and sweep the platforms.

The lieutenant in charge of the sixty-three men defending the bridge said that the bridge was mined, but no one could find the explosives.[13]

On the Aqueduct Bridge, in Georgetown, there were "three block-houses near the south end of this bridge, but the latter are not occupied." The bridge was defended by fifty-eight men under a Veteran Reserve captain who told Alexander, "If a sudden attack was apprehended would close the gates and man the stockade. Did not know whether the bars for securing the gates were on hand or not; did not know whether the bars, if on hand, would fit the staples. Had never tried them."[14]

The Long Bridge was guarded by sixty-four men also under a Veteran Reserve captain, and although they were better organized than the other bridges, the only fort on the Virginia side, Fort Jackson, was dilapidated and there was no artillery on the Washington side. A determined Confederate attack could easily capture any or all of the bridges leading to the capital.[15]

President Lincoln sent Grant a message on July 10 reflecting his concern for the safety of the capital and his opinion of some of the troops that were available to guard it:

> General Halleck says we have absolutely no force here fit to go to the field. He thinks that with the 100-days' men and invalids we have here we can defend Washington, and scarcely Baltimore. Besides these there are about

8,000, not very reliable, under Howe, at Harper's Ferry, with Hunter approaching that point very slowly, with what number I suppose you know better than I. Wallace, with some odds and ends and part of what came up with Ricketts, was so badly beaten yesterday at Monocacy that what is left can attempt no more than to defend Baltimore. What we shall get in from Pennsylvania and New York will scarcely be worth counting, I fear. Now, what I think is that you should provide to retain your hold where you are, certainly, and bring the rest with you personally, and make a vigorous effort to destroy the enemy's force in this vicinity. I think there is really a fair chance to do this if the movement is prompt. This is what I think, upon your suggestion, and is not an order.[16]

In his reply, Grant tried to reassure the president that all would be well:

I have sent from here a whole corps, commanded by an excellent officer, besides over 3,000 other troops. One division of the Nineteenth Corps, 6,000 strong, is now on its way to Washington, one steamer loaded with these troops having passed Fort Monroe to-day. They will probably reach Washington to-morrow night. This force under Wright will be able to compete with the whole force with Ewell (Early). Before more troops can be sent from here Hunter will be able to join Wright, in rear of the enemy, with at least 10,000 men, besides a force sufficient to hold Maryland Heights. I think, on reflection, it would have a bad effect for me to leave here, and with General Ord at Baltimore, and Hunter and Wright with the forces following the enemy up, could do no good. I have great faith that the enemy will never be able to get back with much of his force.[17]

Also on July 10, General Halleck sent his own message to Grant detailing his views on the shortcomings of the quality and quantity of troops for the capital's defense:

Whether you had better come here or remain there is a question upon which I cannot advise. What you say about getting into Early's rear is perfectly correct, but unfortunately we have no forces here for the field. All such forces were sent to you long ago. What we have here are raw militia, invalids, convalescents from the hospitals, a few dismounted batteries, and the dismounted and disorganized cavalry sent up from James River. With these we expect to defend our immense depots of stores and the line of intrenchments around the city; but what can we do with such forces in the field against a column of 20,000 veterans? One-half of the men cannot march at all. The only men fit for the field was Ricketts' division, which has been defeated and badly cut up under Wallace. If the remains can hold Baltimore till we can re-enforce it I shall be satisfied.[18]

In the city confusion reigned supreme, almost no one knew what was happening. The people did not know if they should stay or flee. Some private citizens organized into groups to defend their city, but they had no weapons. Government employees formed volunteer companies, but they were just as confused as everyone else. Even wounded soldiers were called from their hospital beds and sent to the forts. Fortunately, most of the city's residents were unaware that the leaders of their government were just as disorganized.[19] In a letter to his wife on July 11, Colonel Charles Russell Lowell summed up the situation: "There is no end of confusion out here, and very little known of the enemy."[20]

Working hard to man the forts, the authorities took men from wherever they could find them, experience or physical condition were not considered:

> At 9 P.M. Brig. Gen. M. C. Meigs, Quartermaster-General U. S. Army, reported at Fort Stevens with about 1,500 quartermaster employees, armed and equipped. They were at once ordered into position near Fort Slocum, placed on right and left in rifle-pits. At 10 P.M. Colonel Price reported with about 2,800 convalescents and men from hospitals, organized into a provisional brigade composed of men from nearly every regiment of the Army of the Potomac.[21]

Major General Alexander McCook was in command of a portion of the fortifications that included Fort Stevens. He did the best he could with what he had and at least now there were men in the forts and trenches to oppose the enemy. Unfortunately, no matter how brave and willing to fight they might be, the office workers, militiamen, and invalids that were manning the works were still too few. If Early launched a serious attack, his tough veterans probably could have walked into Washington before the end of the day.[22]

As the invading Confederates trudged along the Seventh Street road, the first part of the city's defenses they came to was Fort Stevens. Early could see that the Union works were thinly manned and that all he needed to do was bring up his men and launch an attack and the capital could be his. But his men were strung out along the road and just too exhausted to move into any kind of formation to attack the forts:[23]

> When we reached the right of the enemy's fortifications the men were almost completely exhausted and not in a condition to make an attack. Skirmishers were thrown out and moved up to the vicinity of the fortifications. These we found to be very strong and constructed very scientifically. They consist of a circle of enclosed forts, connected by breast-works, with ditches, palisades, and abatis in front, and every approach swept by a cross-fire of artillery, including some heavy guns.[24]

Early wrote that:

> Rodes, whose division was in front, was immediately ordered to bring it into line as rapidly as possible, throw out skirmishers, and move into the works if he could: ...before Rodes' division could be brought up, we saw a cloud of dust in the rear of the works towards Washington, and soon a column of the enemy filed into them on the right and left, and skirmishers were thrown out in front, while an artillery fire was opened on us from a number of batteries. This defeated our hopes of getting possesion [sic] of the works by surprise, and it became necessary to reconnoitre.[25]

What Early saw were some of the dismounted troopers from the Second Division of the Army of the Potomac's Cavalry Corps. Although only about

600 strong, these men were obviously veterans and just the fact that they were in the fortifications made Early pause and reconsider before making an all-out attack.[26]

While Early's men were coming up, the forts had opened fire with long-range artillery. A Union soldier noted: "This artillery practice, marked by the bursting shells, was the poorest I ever saw. It was evident that the department clerks or the 100-day men were serving the guns. The Confederates did not pay the slightest attention to this fire."[27]

While Early was waiting for his troops to form up:

> Rodes' skirmishers were thrown to the front, driving those of the enemy to the cover of the works, and we proceeded to examine the fortifications in order to ascertain if it was practicable to carry them by assault. They were found to be exceedingly strong, and consisted of what appeared to be enclosed forts of heavy artillery, with a tier of lower works in front of each pierced for an immense number of guns, the whole being connected by curtains with ditches in front, and strengthened by palisades and abattis. The timber had been felled within cannon range all around and left on the ground, making a formidable obstacle, and every possible approach was raked by artillery. On the right was Rock Creek running through a deep ravine which had been rendered impassible by the felling of the timber on each side, and beyond were the works on the Georgetown pike which had been reported to be the strongest of all. On the left, as far as the eye could reach, the works appeared to be of the same impregnable character. The position was naturally strong for defence, and the examination showed, what might have been expected, that every appliance of science and unlimited means had been used to render the fortifications around Washington as strong as possible.[28]

Early wasn't the only one impressed by the strength of the Federal works. One of the men who could soon be risking his life in an assault wrote, "As far as the eye could reach to the right and left there were fortifications, and the most formidable looking I ever saw.... The enemy had a full sweep of the ground for at least a mile in their front, and if their works were well manned, our force would not be able to take them...."[29]

Early spent most of the afternoon inspecting the Federal works and weighing the risk to his army against the potential rewards:

> The rapid marching, which had broken down a number of the men who were barefooted or weakened by previous exposure, and had been left in the Valley and directed to be collected at Winchester, and the losses in killed and wounded at Harper's Ferry, Maryland Heights and Monocacy, had reduced my infantry to about 8,000 muskets. Of those remaining, a very large number were greatly exhausted by the last two days marching, some having fallen by sunstroke, and I was satisfied, when we arrived in front of the fortifications, that not more than one-third of my force could have been carried into action. I had about forty pieces of field artillery, of which the largest were 12 pounder Napoleons, besides a few pieces of horse artillery with the cavalry. McCausland reported the works on the Georgetown pike too strongly manned for him to assault. We could not move to the right or the left without its being discovered from a signal station on the top of the "Soldiers Home," which overlooked the country, and the enemy would have been enabled to move in

his works to meet us. Under the circumstances, to have rushed my men blindly against the fortifications, without understanding the state of things, would have been worse than folly.[30]

Jubal Early had a tough decision to make. Clearly the fortifications were too strong for him to take if they were properly manned, and even if they did break through, then what? The small Confederate army was not large enough to take and occupy Washington, the best that could be hoped for was to destroy as much Union property and war supplies as possible, then try to escape back to Virginia. Early also realized that Federal troops in his rear and those on the way had the potential to trap him north of the Potomac and destroy his entire force, a loss that the Confederacy could not afford.[31]

But, on the other hand, what a prize was within his grasp. Early was well aware of how tired his men were, but he was also confident that they could not be stopped by untried troops and invalids, no matter how strong the fortifications. Even if they only occupied Washington for a short time, the damage to the Union cause would be severe, to say nothing of the mountains of supplies his men could carry away. In the end Early decided that he hadn't brought his men all this way, risking so much, just to look at the enemy's capital.

Back in city the confusion and fear were intensifying. Refugees were everywhere, with their tales of death and destruction, few people in the administration had any accurate information as to what was going on and the military authorities were rushing anyone in a uniform out to the forts. About all anyone knew for sure was that no one knew anything for sure.[32]

Amid all the fear and chaos in the city, the sound of cheering suddenly coming from the Sixth Street docks seemed out of place. Since Grant's offensive had begun, most of the ships docking at Washington were bringing back the hordes of wounded from Virginia. But now strong, tanned men in faded blue uniforms were flooding out of the transports and forming their ranks in the streets: the Sixth Corps had arrived. As word spread, people came out to see and cheer their saviors. Several times in the past three years the men of the Sixth Corps had moved through Washington on their way to Virginia, but never were they as welcomed as now.[33] These tough veterans quickly got into formation and moved out towards the forts. They had the casual look of professionals on their way to work as they marched, but they rapidly moved through the city streets. One soldier wrote of

> hearing the people who crowded upon the sidewalks exclaiming, "It is the old Sixth corps!" "Those are the men who took Marye's Heights!" "The danger is over now!" We had never before realized the hold which the corps had upon the affection of the people. Washington, an hour before was in a panic; now as the people saw the veterans wearing the badge of the Greek cross marching through their streets, the excitement subsided and confidence prevailed.[34]

Major General Horatio Wright, commander of the Sixth Corps, rode ahead of his men to Fort Stevens. At first General McCook wanted to keep the Sixth

11. The War Comes to Washington

Corps men in reserve just behind the forts, but Wright knew that behind the Confederate skirmishers a much heavier line of troops might be approaching that could overwhelm the inexperienced defenders.[35]

Wright reported to General Augur that the Confederates had not yet made an attack on Fort Stevens, but they were close enough to see what the defenders were doing and that it would be a good idea to try and push them back. "I believe it to be only a very light skirmish line, and with your permission will send a brigade out against it and try to clean it out. General McCook's men are not as good as mine for this purpose."[36]

It took some time for Wright to receive permission to move up and it was late afternoon by the time he was ready. McCook reported:

> The enemy, on retiring their line on the evening of the 11th, seized and retained possession of a house on the right of the Silver Spring road, situated on an elevated piece of ground, surrounded by an orchard and large shade trees(Rives), which afforded excellent cover for sharpshooters, and commanded our advance line. They also posted sharpshooters in Mrs. Lay's house to the left of the road. From these two points our skirmish line was very much annoyed by the enemy, they killing and wounding about 30 of our skirmishers during the day. I determined these two points must be carried.[37]

Brigadier General Frank Wheaton commanded the troops who went out of the works to recover the ground in front and "at about 6 P.M., the two positions held by the enemy were vigorously shelled from Fort Stevens. Then at a signal Wheaton's troops dashed forward, and, after a spirited contest, gained the ground."[38] That ended the fighting and both sides settled down to long-range skirmishing and occasional artillery fire for the rest of the night.

The people of Washington had been hearing and reading about the fighting for the last three years and now the enemy was at their doorstep. Curiosity got the better of many and a short ride out Seventh Street brought them to the front. When they arrived at the forts they found that confusion reigned out here as well as back in town. Federal officials, including President Lincoln, who were able to get up to Fort Stevens witnessed the evening skirmishing. They saw and heard the musket fire, the roar of the artillery,

Union Major General Horatio G. Wright (Library of Congress.)

and the men falling wounded and dead. All in all they were treated to a nice little fight.[39]

Not everyone was pleased with the events of the day. Assistant Secretary of War Charles Dana telegraphed Grant's Chief of staff, Brigadier General John A. Rawlins:

> Indeed until Wright reached the scene yesterday evening McCook had had no skirmishers out at all but had allowed the rebel sharpshooters to get up near [the] line and pick the men off at the embrasures of the fort. Along this part of the lines there was no general commander, no real knowledge of what was in the front, nothing but wild imagination and stupidity. From what I can hear the same system reigns throughout the whole length of the lines. I do not exaggerate in the least when I say that such a lamentable want of intelligence energy and purpose was never before seen in any command. I cannot learn that Augur had personally visited any part of the line, and I [am] sure that he knows as little respecting them as I did before I went out. Indeed the Secretary has very sharply reprimanded him for his want of attention to his duties. Halleck seems to be about as well informed as Augur and I judge that he contributes quite as much as the latter to the prevailing confusion & inefficiency....[40]

Early had seen the Sixth Corps troops coming into the fortifications that afternoon. He had earlier "determined at first to make an assault, but before it could be made it became apparent that the enemy had been strongly re-enforced...."[41] After the Confederates lost their advance positions in front of the forts, Early decided to take no more action and talk it over with his division commanders:

> After dark on the 11th, I held a consultation with Major Generals Breckinridge, Rodes, Gordon and Ramseur, in which I stated to them the danger of remaining where we were, and the necessity of doing something immediately, as the probability was that the passes of the South Mountain and the fords of the upper Potomac would soon be closed against us. After interchanging views with them, being very reluctant to abandon the project of capturing Washington, I determined to make an assault on the enemy's works at daylight next morning, unless some information should be received before that time showing its impracticability, and so informed those officers. During the night a dispatch was received from Gen. Bradley Johnson from near Baltimore, informing me that he had received information, from a reliable source, that two corps had arrived from Gen. Grant's army, and that his whole army was probably in motion. This caused me to delay the attack until I could examine the works again....[42]

As soon as it was light on the morning of the 12th, Early was peering at the Federal fortifications. In the soft light of dawn he "rode to the front and found the parapets lined with troops."[43] After inspecting the forts once more, Early decided that even a successful assault "would be attended with such great sacrifice as would insure the destruction of my whole force before the victory could have been made available, and, if unsuccessful, would necessarily have resulted in the loss of the whole force."[44]

He didn't really have much of a choice after seeing how many defenders were in the forts. "I had, therefore, reluctantly to give up all hopes of capturing Washington, after I had arrived in sight of the dome of the Capitol, and given the Federal authorities a terrible fright."[45]

During the day Early sent out a heavy skirmish line and formed his troops in a wooded area in case the Federals came out of their fortifications to attack him. The firing was sometimes heavy and two houses which Confederate sharpshooters were using for cover were blown apart by artillery fire. While this was going on Fort Stevens received an unexpected visitor—President Lincoln, who had once again come out to see a little of the war. General Wright, not thinking of the possible consequences, asked the president if he would like to view the fighting. Mr. Lincoln quickly got up on the parapet to watch, towering over everyone in the vicinity with his stovepipe hat, the perfect target for Confederate sharpshooters. Realizing that the president of the United States was just as exposed as the lowest private, Wright tried to talk the president down[46]: George Stevens of the Sixth Corps noted:

> While the battle was in progress, President Lincoln stood upon the parapet of the fort watching, with eager interest, the scene before him. Bullets came whistling around, and one severely wounded a surgeon who stood within three feet of the President. Mrs. Lincoln entreated him to leave the fort, but he refused; he, however, accepted the advice of General Wright to descend from the parapet and watch the battle from a less exposed position.[47]

The sporadic firing continued for most of the day until about 6 P.M. when the Third Brigade, commanded by Colonel Daniel Bidwell, moved out of the fortifications to clear the field in front and a section of woods. A member of the Vermont Brigade remembered: "The pseudo-soldiers who filled the trenches around the Fort were astounded at the temerity displayed by these war-worn veterans in going out before the breast-works, and benevolently volunteered most earnest words of caution...."[48] Bidwell's men advanced until they approached the woods and the hidden Confederates opened fire:

> In magnificent order and with light steps they ran forward, up the ascent, through the orchard, through the little grove on the right, over the rail fence, up to the road, making straight for the first objective point, the frame house in front. The rebels at first stood their ground, then gave way before the impetuous charge.[49]

Another soldier wrote, "Our brave men charged handsomely, for they meant business and knew how it was done ... the dignitaries in the Fort returned to their homes, having witnessed as pretty and well conducted a little fight as was seen during the whole war."[50]

Early hated to leave any field to the enemy, but he finally recalled his skirmishers and after dark began the long retreat back to Virginia. In his official report, Early explained:

> As it was evident preparations were making to cut off my retreat, and while troops were gathering around me I would find it difficult to get supplies, I

determined to retire across the Potomac to this county before it became too late. I was led to this determination by the conviction that the loss of my force would have had such depressing effect upon the country, and would so encourage the enemy as to amount to a very serious, if not fatal, disaster to our cause. My infantry force did not exceed 10,000, as Breckinridge's infantry (nominally much larger) really did not exceed 2,500 muskets. A considerable part of the cavalry has proved wholly inefficient. Sigel was at Maryland Heights. Hunter was making his way to get in my rear, and Couch was organizing a militia force in Pennsylvania. If, therefore, I had met a disaster I could not have got off, and if I had succeeded in the assault, yet my force would have been so crippled that I could not have continued their active operations so necessary in an expedition like mine.[51]

Major Henry Kyd Douglas recorded:

> Some while after dark that night I was sent for by General Early. Generals Breckinridge and Gordon were with him. He seemed in a droll humor, perhaps one of relief, for he said to me in his falsetto drawl: "Major, we haven't taken Washington, but we've scared Abe Lincoln like h—!"
> "Yes, General," I replied, "but this afternoon when that Yankee line moved out against us, I think some other people were scared blue as——'s brimstone!"
> "How about that, General?" said Breckinridge with a laugh.
> "That's true," piped General Early, "but it won't appear in history!"[52]

Jubal Early's raid brought the South high hopes and then bitter disappointment, all in the space of a week. Once again a Confederate army had crossed the Potomac, seized a victory at Monocacy, had the enemy's capital within reach, with staggering possibilities for the Confederacy, then retreated without a battle. A. L. Long, Early's chief of artillery, later wrote:

> This campaign is remarkable for having accomplished more in proportion to the force employed, and for having given less public satisfaction, than any other campaign of the war. The want of appreciation of it is entirely due to the erroneous opinion that the city of Washington should have been taken; but this may be passed over as one of the absurdities of public criticism on the conduct of the war.[53]

Early did fail to achieve the main goals of the raid, or at least what were believed to be the goals. He did not capture Washington and Grant did not abandon the lines at Petersburg. But were these goals attainable to begin with? Major Douglas later wrote:

> It has been said that if Early had moved more rapidly and assaulted at once (presuming, I suppose, that his men were all centaurs) he might have gone into Washington. I do not believe it. If he had I am sure he never would have gotten out again. In fact I am satisfied neither he nor any officer with him ever expected to take Washington.[54]

It is also highly unlikely that anything could have forced Grant to pull enough troops from Petersburg to give Lee an opportunity to break the siege.

Despite these apparent failures, Early did accomplish much that he deserves credit for. He saved Lynchburg from destruction; he cleared the Shenandoah Valley of Federal troops so that the invaluable grain harvest would be available to feed Lee's army; his was the only Confederate army to come within sight of the Federal capital; he destroyed or captured vast amounts of badly needed supplies, "An immense amount of damage has been done the enemy. Our cavalry has brought off a very large number of horses. Over 1,000 have been brought off and $220,000 in money was levied and collected in Hagerstown and Frederick...."[55] In addition, the movements of his little army confused and paralyzed the Union high command and he demonstrated to the war-weary people of the north that despite the enormous casualties the Union armies had suffered, the Confederacy was not yet ready to give up.[56]

12. Back to the Valley

Thanks to the timely arrival of the reinforcements from the Sixth and Nineteenth corps, the capital had been saved and the invading Confederates were headed back to Virginia. Now was the time to make them pay for their audacity. Grant wanted Early's army crushed before they could make good their escape and return to the Valley or return to Lee at Petersburg. Unfortunately, as happened so often in the past, the issuing of orders did not mean that they would be carried out as expected. What Grant could not see from his headquarters in the field was the almost total lack of organization by the commanders in and around the capital. Grant soon learned that "Wright's pursuit of Early was feeble because of the constant and contrary orders he had been receiving from Washington."[1]

On July 12, Grant received the following in a message from Assistant Secretary of War Dana, who had come up from City Point to act as observer for Grant:

> No attack on this city or Baltimore. General McCook has been firing artillery all night from Forts Reno and Massachusetts, which remain within his command, General Wright having relieved him at Fort Stevens. He telegraphs this morning that he is about to drive the rebel skirmishers away from his front, after which the artillery will cease. Nothing can possibly be done here toward pursuing or cutting off the enemy for want of a commander. General Augur commands the defenses of Washington, with McCook and a lot of brigadier-generals under him, but he is not allowed to go outside. Wright commands his own corps. General Gillmore has been assigned to the temporary command of those troops of the Nineteenth Corps in the city of Washington. General Ord to command the Eighth Corps and all other troops in the Middle Department, leaving Wallace to command the city alone. But there is no head to the whole, and it seems indispensable that you should at once

appoint one. Hunter will be the ranking officer if he ever gets up, but he will not do. Indeed, the Secretary of War directs me to tell you in his judgment Hunter ought instantly to be relieved, having proven himself far more incompetent than even Sigel. He also directs me to say that advice or suggestions from you will not be sufficient. General Halleck will not give orders except as he receives them; the President will give none, and until you direct positively and explicitly what is to be done, everything will go on in the deplorable and fatal way in which it has gone on for the past week.[2]

That same day Grant tried to solve at least part of the problem by ordering Halleck to put General Wright in command of all the troops pursuing Early:

> Give orders assigning Maj. Gen. H. G. Wright to supreme command of all troops moving out against the enemy, regardless of the rank of other commanders. He should get outside the trenches with all the force he possibly can and should push Early to the last moment, supplying himself from the country. This will not place General Wright over General Augur, who commands the defenses, but will place him in command of such of his troops and commanders as may be sent outside. The Sixth Corps has all reached Washington and Baltimore, and two divisions of the Nineteenth Corps must reach there during to-morrow, besides the dismounted corps sent from here. This, with Hunter's force, must be sufficient to guard all our fortifications and leave an abundant force to go outside.[3]

By the morning of the 13th it became clear that Early had not simply pulled back to attack elsewhere, but was taking his men home. General Wright and two divisions of the VI Corps set out in pursuit hoping to catch the Confederates before they could make good their escape. During the first day of pursuit, Wright's response to urgings from Secretary Stanton made it clear that his force "will be pushed forward to the limits of the endurance of the men.... I can assure yourself and the President that there will be no delay on my part to head off the enemy, and that the men I have will do all that the number of men can do. They have been well tried and never found wanting."[4]

Having "marched forty miles in twenty four hours"[5] as one exhausted soldier recorded, Wright stopped at Poolesville, Md. on the afternoon of the 14th to report to Halleck:

> I have sent the cavalry forward to see whether anything can be done against the rear guard, but presume it will be too late. The enemy had and kept about twenty-four hours the start of us, which gave him full time to secure his crossing of the river.
>
> I have not been able to get any intelligence from General Hunter's command, and have, therefore, for further operations only the two divisions of my corps, numbering perhaps 10,000, and some 500 possibly of the Nineteenth Corps, which, unless I overrate the enemy's strength, is wholly insufficient to justify the following up of the enemy on the other side of the Potomac. I presume this will not be the policy of the War Department, and I shall, therefore, wait instructions before proceeding farther, which I hope to receive by the time the Nineteenth Corps arrives.[6]

As it turned out, Wright actually had little chance to stop Early from escaping. The pursuit went through four different military departments, and Wright did not have the authority to compel cooperation from any of them. The War Department was the only place where this authority resided and it resisted any policy that did not make the protection of Washington the first priority. After the war, Grant wrote:

> It seemed to be the policy of General Halleck and Secretary Stanton to keep any force sent there, in pursuit of the invading army, moving right and left so as to keep between the enemy and our capital; and, generally speaking, they pursued this policy until all knowledge of the whereabouts of the enemy was lost.[7]

Jubal Early had no such problems as he quickly made his way south:

> Passing through Rockville and Poolsville, we crossed the Potomac at White's Ford, above Leesburg, in Loudoun County, on the morning of the 14th, bringing off the prisoners captured at Monocacy and everything else in safety. There was some skirmishing in the rear between our cavalry and that of the enemy which was following, and on the afternoon of the 14th, there was some artillery firing by the enemy across the river, at our cavalry which was watching the fords. Besides the money levied in Hagerstown and Frederick, which was subsequently very useful in obtaining supplies, we brought off quite a large number of beef cattle, and the cavalry obtained a number of horses, some also procured for the artillery.[8]

Early had made good his escape.

On July 15 Grant sent Colonel Comstock to Washington with instructions for Halleck.

> It would seem from dispatches just received from Mr. Dana, Assistant Secretary of War, that the enemy are leaving Maryland. If so, Hunter should follow him as rapidly as the jaded condition of his men will admit. The Sixth and Nineteenth Corps should be got here without any delay, so that they may be used before the return of the troops sent into the Valley by the enemy. Hunter moving up the Valley will either hold a large force of the enemy or he will be enabled to reach Gordonsville and Charlottesville. The utter destruction of the road at and between these two places will be of immense value to us. I do not intend this as an order to bring Wright back while he is in pursuit of the enemy with any prospect of punishing him, but to secure his return at the earliest possible moment after he ceases to be absolutely necessary where he is. Colonel Comstock, who takes this, can explain to you fully the situation here.... If the enemy has left Maryland, as I suppose he has, he should have upon his heels veterans, militiamen, men on horseback, and everything that can be got to follow to eat out Virginia clear and clean as far as they go, so that crows flying over it for the balance of this season will have to carry their provender with them.[9]

Grant's emissary got nowhere with Halleck. The chief-of-staff was one of the figures in the War Department who disapproved of Grant's strategy to fight Lee wherever he was and not stay between the enemy and Washington.

Halleck, and others in the War Department, feared that Early would return to the capital if the two corps that Grant wanted were sent back to Petersburg, so he simply ignored Grant's request. Without a direct order Halleck would do nothing.[10] He did find time to write a complaining letter to General Sherman:

> *Entre Nous*, I fear Grant has made a fatal mistake in putting himself south of James River. He cannot now reach Richmond without taking Petersburg, which is strongly fortified, crossing the Appomattox and recrossing the James. Moreover, by placing his army south of Richmond he opens the capital and the whole north to Rebel raids. Lee can at any time detach 30,000 or 40,000 men without our knowing it till we are actually threatened. I hope we may yet have full success, but I find that many of Grant's general officers think the campaign already a failure. Perseverance, however may compensate for all errors and overcome all obstacles.[11]

Lee certainly did not have 30,000 to 40,000 men to send to Early. Grant knew this, but all too frequently the military situation in the field seemed unable to seep through the fog at the War Department.

For the men in Wright's little army, the orders that came out of Washington for the rest of July only resulted in a mixture of exhaustion and confusion. A soldier from the Fifteenth Maine wrote that

> our forces engaged in a "neck-and-neck" race with the rebel raiders, pursuing Early through Leesburg and Snicker's Gap and the Shenandoah River, fording streams, fighting guerillas, climbing mountains, marching and countermarching, and enduring fatigues and hardships rarely surpassed in so brief a campaign. The boys marched night and day, over rocky roads, through mountain gorges, fording streams and rivers, with feet wet and sore, until, further to endure, many a weary soldier was compelled to fall out by the way, either to be cared for by the ambulance corps or picked up by the guerillas constantly hovering about our rear and flanks.[12]

Samuel Dunton, of the 19th Corps, described their continuous marching in a letter home:

> On our first march, we crossed the Potomac at Whites Ford, passed through Leesburg and through the Blue Ridge Mountains at Sinker's [Snicker's] Gap, crossed the Shenandoah and went four or five miles beyond, returned by the same route to Leesburg. From there we went to the right and crossed the Potomac at Chain Bridge. We went into camp for two days, then started for Harpers Ferry, by the way of Tenallytown, Rockville, Frederick City, then took the Gettysburg and went about five miles, went into camp, staid one day, then marched back to Frederick and about four miles beyond on the Washington Road, went into camp....[13]

The story was the same in the Thirteenth Maine. They arrived at Washington ten days prior and since then "the regiment had marched over one hundred and fifty miles, had forded the Potomac once and the Shenandoah twice, and had twice crossed the Blue Ridge. The marching was very hard owing to the heat and dust ... and when marching in the road the dust would almost stop one's breath."[14]

Not only did the heat and dust affect the men physically but the useless marching back and forth for no apparent reason began to wear on their morale and confidence in the military command. David Hunter Strother said, "I have never felt so entirely discouraged and disgusted with the condition of public affairs as at present. Folly, faction, and feebleness seem to be more in the ascendant than ever."[15]

Another man commented on the lack of organization:

> I may be a little blue and down spirited this morning, but I tell you the thing looks pretty dark to me. We have never faired so poorly, since we have been in the service, as we have since we arrived in Washington. But I think we will fair better as soon as they get things properly assigned. They ought to be prepared in a place like Washington to accommodate thirty or forty thousand troops at any time. I have never seen so much confusion amongst troops and the management of them, as I have since we left Louisiana.[16]

All was not hardship, however, there were some lighter moments. A soldier from the 149th Ohio Volunteer Infantry remembered:

> We marched to Edwards Ferry, on the Potomac, which we forded about five o'clock in the evening, disrobing, we tied our clothes around our guns, and at "right shoulder shift arms" entered the water. It was an amusing sight to look up and across the river, at the boys struggling through the water, it was about waist deep and some current. The rocks on the river bottom were slippery, and every little while a boy would go down, gun, clothes and all under water, to struggle on again amid the cheers and laughter of his comrades.[17]

In a letter to his sister on July 19, Brigadier General Emory Upton describes his view of the Shenandoah Valley:

> We are encamped on the west side of the Blue Ridge, and hold the east bank of the Shenandoah, while the enemy holds the west bank. I wish you could enjoy this scenery. From our camp on the Blue Ridge the Great Valley of Virginia, with its surrounding streams, its groves, its fertile fields, and elegant mansions, is spread out like a beautiful landscape. Seldom does the tourist meet with a view so enchanting. A glance of the eye comprehends the Blue Ridge, the Alleghanies [sic], Maryland Heights, and innumerable smaller mountains dotted here and there throughout the Valley, lending additional charms to the scenery.[18]

On July 17 Halleck sent a message to the wayward General Hunter informing him that Grant wanted him to pursue Early all the way to Charlottesville if possible. Halleck also made clear that Grant wanted the Valley protected, repeating his orders that "if compelled to fall back you will retreat in front of the enemy toward the main crossings of the Potomac, so as to cover Washington, and not be squeezed out to one side, so as to make it necessary to fall back into West Virginia to save your army." If Hunter could not cut the railroads at Charlottesville, he was to head south in the Valley and destroy as much stock and provisions as possible. Halleck also repeated Grant's order that Hunter's troops should "eat out Virginia clear and clean as far as they go, so that crows flying over it for the balance of the season will have to carry their provender with them." Grant was making it perfectly clear that he wanted to actually destroy the means of supporting the enemy's army in the field.[19]

Grant was even more specific in this telegram to Halleck on July 18:

> Before the Sixth and Nineteenth Corps can get to Washington the enemy will have developed his intentions by stopping, if he thinks of returning to Maryland. In that case Hunter should stop at Winchester, keeping his cavalry as far out as he can, watching the movements of the enemy. If he has not the force to attack with he should not attack, but move forward only as the enemy moves back, and always be prepared to get north of the Potomac without loss when advanced upon by a superior force.... If the enemy have not gone up the Valley, of course Hunter should not go that way. The idea is, he should be between the enemy and Washington, going as far out as he can, never allowing himself to be drawn into an unequal fight south of the Potomac and outside of our defenses.[20]

On July 19 Halleck sent Grant a rather long and less than enthusiastic assessment of the current situation, once again displaying Halleck's disapproval of Grant's strategy:

> General: The recent raid into Maryland seems to have established several things, which it would be well for us to keep in mind:
> First. It has proved that while your army is south of the James River and Lee's between you and Washington, he can make a pretty large detachment unknown to us for a week or ten days and send it against Washington, or into West Virginia, or Pennsylvania, or Maryland.
> Second. General Hunter's army, which comprises all troops north of Richmond that can go into the field, is entirely too weak to hold West Virginia and the Baltimore and Ohio Railroad, and at the same time to resist any considerable rebel raid north of the Potomac.
> Third. We cannot rely upon aid from the militia of the Northern States. They will not come out at all, or will come too late, or in so small a force as to be useless.
> Fourth. The garrisons of Washington and Baltimore are made up of troops entirely unfit for the field and wholly inadequate for the defense of these places. Had it not been for the opportune arrival of the veterans of the Sixth Corps both cities would have been in great danger. So long as you were operating between Washington and the enemy your army covered Maryland and Pennsylvania, and I sent you all the troops from here and the North which could take the field or guard your depots and prisoners of war. But the circumstances have now most materially changed, and I am decidedly of opinion that a larger available force should be left in this vicinity....[21]

While Wright was chasing Early around northern Virginia, Hunter's army had finally arrived in the area after its circuitous route from the Valley. General Crook had taken command of the troops in field while Hunter stayed in the department's headquarters at Monocacy Junction. Crook's force contained three infantry divisions and two cavalry divisions and with the artillery, the total force was not quite 10,000. They were to join with Wright's troops in pursuing Early and protecting the capital.[22]

On the afternoon of the 18th, Colonel Thoburn received orders from Crook to remove a force of Confederate cavalry that was holding the hills above Snicker's Ferry. Thoburn commanded the two brigades of the First Division and the Third Brigade of the Second Division. As the Federals started across the river, heavy fire from the opposite bank held them up until Colonel Wells' brigade was able to cross some distance down river, capturing several of the enemy. The rest of Thoburn's force moved over the river and the prisoners informed him of a much larger Confederate force nearby. This information was relayed to General Crook, who ordered Thoburn to stay where he was and wait for reinforcements from the Sixth Corps.[23]

Colonel Thoburn set up a defense and waited:

> I posted my command in two lines near the riverbank, the Second Brigade, then commanded by myself, on the right, the First Brigade, commanded by Colonel Wells, on the left, and the Third Brigade, commanded by Colonel Frost, in the center.... After lying in this position about one hour, the enemy advanced a heavy skirmish line upon my front and flanks, at the same time a heavy force was moved forward upon my right flank, moving in two lines of battle at nearly right angles to our lines....[24]

General Breckinridge brought Gordon and Echol's troops forward in the center while Rodes attacked on the left. Thoburn had to swing the Second Brigade around to meet the attack on his right and after some fierce fighting, the first line was forced back. On the right, the second line was mainly composed of about 1,000 dismounted cavalry under the command of Lieutenant-Colonel Young of the Fourth Pennsylvania Cavalry. These men had been pulled together from various detachments and the veteran Confederate infantry soon broke this line, sending the cavalrymen and many of the infantry from the first line back across the river.[25]

The reinforcements from the Sixth Corps never joined in the fighting, although they had arrived at the river crossing before the battle ended. General Ricketts, who was in command, could see what was going on and he "did not think it prudent under the circumstances to cross his men...."[26]

On the left of the Federal line, Colonel Wells faced only a line of skirmishers and was able to hold his place and cover the flank of the retreating men until he was ordered to fall back across the river before dusk. The fight at Snicker's Ferry was short but costly. Colonel Thoburn reported, "Our loss was 65 killed, 301 wounded, 56, missing; total 422. The enemy's loss, at their own estimate was over 600 killed and wounded."[27]

While the infantry fight at Snicker's Ferry was taking place, Duffié's cavalry was ordered to head for Ashby's Gap and try to get around Early's army. Duffié reported, "On the 19th of July I reached Ashby's Gap, at about 10 A.M., my advance encountering and driving out a small force of the enemy. Pushing on to the ford, I crossed a part of my command, when they were met by a heavy fire from the enemy, who were posted in a wood and behind a stone fence."[28]

12. Back to the Valley

The Twentieth Pennsylvania Cavalry under Major Anderson made it across the ford but was unable to advance. The Second Brigade commanded by Lieutenant-Colonel Middleton attempted to cross the river but was met with heavy fire also and was forced to turn back. Soon Anderson's men were pushed back and had to retreat back across the river before being overrun. The problem for Duffié was that "A force of riflemen from the enemy, posted behind a stone fence, completely commanded the ford and the river-bank with their long-range rifles."[29]

Later in the day Duffié tried to force his troopers over the river:

> About 5 P.M. I again attempted the crossing of the river. The Twenty-first New York Cavalry, of Colonel Tibbit's (First) brigade, was ordered to charge across the ford and attack the enemy's position, and, if possible, to dislodge them. This movement was superintended by one of my staff in person. The regiment, under Lieutenant-Colonel Fitz Simmons, charged gallantly across the ford and up to the very mouths of the enemy's cannon. They were met by a very destructive fire from the rebel riflemen and artillery, and compelled again to recross the river.[30]

On the 20th, General Averell, with a mixed detachment of infantry and cavalry, defeated a Confederate force a few miles north of Winchester:

> My artillery was placed in position, the infantry regiments in column were thrown forward into line, cavalry skirmishers covering my entire front were withdrawn rapidly to the flanks, the concentrated fire of the twelve guns was opened upon the enemy's center, and the infantry advanced and became hotly engaged, while the cavalry entered into a fierce struggle on each flank.... The enemy, unprepared for such a vigorous onset, after a short but determined resistance, were thrown into confusion, driven from the woods and along the road and across the fields toward Winchester, leaving 4 guns, 73 killed, and 130 wounded on the field. Seventeen officers and 250 men were captured. Our loss was 53 killed, 155 wounded, and 6 missing.[31]

The result of these fights was that nothing whatever was accomplished except to increase casualties. Lack of coordination hampered the Federal effort yet again. Early moved his army near Strasburg and made camp, giving his men a well-deserved rest. On the 22nd General Crook brought his troops over from Berryville to combine with Averell and Duffié, and took overall command. The entire Federal force then left Winchester and made camp a couple miles away near Kernstown.[32]

On the 23rd of July Early's tired men were getting a rare day of rest when

> a report was received from the cavalry in front, that a large portion of the force sent after us from Washington was returning, and that Crook and Averill [sic] had united and were at Kernstown, near Winchester.
>
> On reception of the foregoing information, I determined to attack the enemy at once; and early on the morning of the 24th, my whole force was put in motion for Winchester.... Ramseur's division was sent to the left, at Bartonsville, to get around the enemy's right flank, while the other divisions moved along the Valley Pike, and formed on each side of it. Ransom's cav-

alry was ordered to move in two columns; one, on the right, along the road from Front Royal to Winchester; and the other on the left, and west of Winchester, so as to unite in rear of the later place, and cut off the enemy's retreat.[33]

At about 7:30 on the morning of July 24, General Duffié "received word from Colonel Tibbits that the enemy were advancing, apparently in force, and that his skirmishers were warmly engaged just beyond Kernstown."[34] Duffié informed Crook of the attack and was ordered forward to reinforce the thin Federal picket lines. In the infantry camps, the firing could be heard in the distance while Crook's men were having breakfast and getting ready for an inspection. They quickly formed ranks and headed out to join the fight.[35]

When Duffié reached the battlefield, he deployed one brigade on each side of the pike to try and hold back the Confederate skirmishers until the infantry could be brought up to the front. There was some brisk fighting for about an hour until the infantry began to arrive to replace the hard pressed troopers.[36] The Federal line consisted of Colonel Hayes' brigade on the far left with Colonel Mulligan's two brigades in the center and two brigades under Colonel Thoburn on the right. The cavalry was spread out with Averell on the far left across the pike. Duffié's division was split with Colonel Higgins' brigade west of the pike protecting the left flank of the infantry and Colonel Tibbit's brigade to the right of Thoburn's infantry.[37]

A Confederate soldier described the scene:

> The enemy's line when we drew up in front of them extended from southwest to northeast.... It was evident to the minds of the Confederates, as soon as the skirmishing began, that aggressive leadership was lacking in the ranks of the enemy, and that victory would be easy.
>
> But that was not what Early wanted. It was his purpose to capture the whole force sent against him and show the authorities at Washington his contempt for their effort to take him and his army. His plan was to make a heavy demonstration along the whole line except on the enemy's extreme left, where General Breckinridge was to face on them in a rapid charge, so as to get into their rear, when the whole line would move forward and rout the enemy, thus cut off from any way of escape toward the Potomac and safety.[38]

As his skirmishers advanced, at about noon Early followed up with a series of attacks. Soon after the fighting began, Early discovered that the Federal left was exposed near Kernstown and ordered Breckinridge to move a division commanded by General Wharton to attack that flank. The Confederates were able to use some ravines as cover and struck the Federal left flank "in open ground, doubling it up and throwing his whole line into great confusion."[39]

On the Federal left, Colonel Hayes tried to meet Breckinridge's attack:

> An effort was made to change front to meet this attack, but the fire was so heavy and destructive that the left was doubled back in confusion on the right of the brigade. A new line was soon formed, however, in rear of a stone fence, perpendicular to the original direction, the right resting near the point reached by the right of the brigade at the time the enemy attacked us on the left. A

fire was opened on the enemy and his course checked long enough to enable a great part of the wounded to be got to the rear. It was now discovered that the enemy, with his greatly superior force, enveloped the troops on our right, and that they had been driven back. The First Brigade moved back up the hill, when I was ordered by Major-General Crook in person to hold the enemy in check long enough to enable one of our batteries, which was very much exposed, to withdraw, and then to fall back slowly, bearing to the right of Winchester going north, and protect the line of retreat on the Martinsburg road.[40]

Over on the other end of the Union line, Colonel Wells reported that he could see enemy skirmishers on his far right and was afraid that if a larger force were behind them he would be cut off from the Williamsport Pike. Considering the number of Confederate troops already engaged and the poor condition of his own men, Wells "was certain that we could not repulse his attack, and that if we awaited for it we should be driven back in confusion.... Under these circumstances I thought it proper to fall back at once when I could do so in order and without loss."[41]

Colonel Thoburn received orders from Crook to fall back to a new position on a hill south of Winchester and establish a line to hold the enemy back as long as possible. With both Hayes and Thoburn falling back, the brunt of the Confederate attack fell on Mulligan's brigade in the center. During the fierce fighting Mulligan was killed and his men were soon heading for the rear.[42]

Duffié's troopers covered the retreating infantry along the pike until near Winchester, when the lines started to falter against the rapidly advancing Confederate infantry. When the Union infantry broke and ran to the rear, Duffié ordered his cavalry to charge the advancing Confederate line to provide a temporary pause in their rush and allow the infantry to escape and save its ambulance train. Meanwhile, on the extreme left flank of the army, Averell's cavalry division collapsed and was forced back by fierce Confederate attacks. The Federal troops fled past Winchester and continued through the night until they reached Bunker Hill, although Early's men ended their pursuit at Stephenson's Depot.[43]

A Louisiana soldier wrote that Crook's men "were perfectly demoralized though we captured but few as they were Hunter's men & they think we will kill the last one of them as they treated our citizens so outrageous down about Lynchburg."[44]

The official number of casualties for Crook's army was 100 killed, 606 wounded, and 479 missing, for a total of 1,185.[45] Early reported only that "Our loss in this action was very light."[46] Once again a Federal army had been chased out of the Shenandoah Valley.

13. Chambersburg and the Turning Point

After the debacle at Kernstown, the Federal army continued its retreat north to the Potomac and safety. Early halted his army at Martinsburg to rest and destroy recently repaired railroad track. While there, he decided that the destruction and burning of civilian property by Hunter and other Federal commanders had gone on long enough without some response:[1]

> I now came to the conclusion that we had stood this mode of warfare long enough, and that it was time to open the eyes of the people of the North to its enormity, by an example in the way of retaliation.
> The town of Chambersburg, in Pennsylvania, was selected as the one on which retaliation should be made, and McCausland was ordered to proceed, with his brigade and that of Johnson and a battery of artillery, to that place, and demand of the municipal authorities the sum of $100,000 in gold, or $500,000 in United States currency, as a compensation for the destruction of the houses named and their contents; and, in default of payment, to lay the town in ashes, in retaliation for the burning of those houses and others in Virginia, as well as for the towns which had been burned in Southern States.... I desired to give the people of Chambersburg an opportunity of saving their town, by making compensation for part of the injury done, and hoped that the payment of such a sum would have the desired effect, and open the eyes of the people of other towns at the North, to the necessity of urging upon their government the adoption of a different policy.[2]

General McCausland led about 4,000 men across the Potomac and entered Chambersburg early on the 30th. He met with several of the leading citizens and presented them with Early's demands. The townspeople negotiated for hours, claiming that the amount of money demanded was beyond their means, but to no avail. Late that afternoon the talking ended.³

McCausland had given the townspeople six hours to decide if they would pay or not, at the end of that time they refused to comply with the Confederate demands and so "the destruction was begun by firing the most central blocks first, and after the inhabitants had been removed from them. Thus the town was destroyed, and the citizens driven to the hills and fields adjacent thereto. No lives were lost among the citizens...."⁴

Early later wrote:

> The demand was not complied with, the people stating that they were not afraid of having their town burned, and that a Federal force was approaching. The policy pursued by our army on former occasions had been so lenient that they did not suppose the threat was in earnest this time, and they hoped for speedy relief. McCausland, however, proceeded to carry out his orders, and the greater part of the town was laid in ashes.⁵

The citizens of the North were outraged at the ruthless destruction of Chambersburg and McCausland was widely condemned.

A few years later Early made it clear that he was the only person responsible for the decision to burn the town, "the officers engaged in it were simply executing my orders, and had no discretion left them. Notwithstanding the lapse of time which has occurred, and the result of the war, I am perfectly satisfied with my conduct on this occasion, and see no reason to regret it."⁶

For many in the South the burning of Chambersburg was just retribution for all the destruction done by Federal troops. Josiah Gorgas wrote: "The burning of Chambersburgh by Early gives intense satisfaction. General McCausland seems to have been in command of the troops who did the deed,—a very good one."⁷

Considering the wholesale destruction that was soon to occur in the Valley and the swath of desolation Sherman left behind him in Georgia, the people of the North were probably fortunate that Early's act of revenge was an isolated incident.

McCausland's troopers left what remained of Chambersburg and headed west, reaching Hancock the next evening. They rested for several hours but had to keep moving because they had learned that General Averell and a large body of Federal cavalry were following. The Confederates then attacked Cumberland, but the defenses under General Kelly proved to be too strong and they had to retire. On August 1, McCausland captured a significant amount of supplies at Old Town, Maryland, on the Potomac. After crossing the river the Confederates moved into West Virginia. They attacked the railroad at New Creek on the 4th, but were unable to do any significant damage and headed for Moorefield to rest men and horses in what seemed a relatively safe location.⁸

During the night of the 6th, Confederate scouts warned McCausland that Averell was nearby and that they could expect to be attacked the next day. Despite this information, it appears that Bradley Johnson's men were not prepared for what happened next.⁹

Averell's troopers came upon the Confederates early on the morning of the 7th:

> Without a moment's halt or delay my advanced brigade, under Major Gibson, Fourteenth Pennsylvania Cavalry, deployed, and with an eager shout dashed forward upon the enemy's lines with such impetuosity that, waiting only to fire a few shots, they broke, fled in the wildest confusion, leaving two pieces of artillery, a large number of horses, and throwing away whatever impeded their flight. Giving them no time to reform, Gibson pursued them hotly to the river, precipitating them over its steep banks across and into the ranks of McCausland, who, with another brigade, was posted upon the south bank. There, as I anticipated, the enemy endeavored to make a stand. Colonel Powell, of the Second Virginia Cavalry, commanding Second Brigade, was immediately ordered forward, and, crossing the river in the face of a severe fire, soon routed the enemy a second time, rolling the tide of fugitives back toward Moorefield.[10]

After trying to make another stand about a mile from the river, McCausland was again routed and forced to flee. Averell reported the capture of 4 pieces of artillery, 420 prisoners and over 400 horses with an unknown number of dead and wounded. The Federal loss was only 9 killed and 32 wounded.[11] Even more important than the loss of men and equipment was the effect of the defeat on the men's morale. Early admitted, "The balance of the command made its way to Mount Jackson in great disorder, and much weakened. This affair had a very damaging effect upon my cavalry for the rest of the campaign."[12]

The burning of Chambersburg may have satisfied Early's desire for revenge, but in addition to the disaster to McCausland's force, the raid brought about results that he could not have anticipated. McCausland's raid had again produced panic in the capital and Pennsylvania and Maryland. But the Federal reaction was to change the way the war was being fought in the Valley, which became a significant factor in the months ahead. To start with, Grant ordered the Sixth and Nineteenth corps back to the Valley, soon to be followed by large cavalry reinforcements to form the largest and best equipped army ever seen in the region. Even more important than the numbers of Federal soldiers sent to destroy Early was the appointment of a new commander unlike any who had preceded him.[13]

General Grant realized that the confusion caused by so many different commanders being involved with the pursuit of Early in July could not be allowed to occur again. On July 18 he had written to Halleck on the subject of combining several departments under one commander:

> To prevent a recurrence of what has just taken place in Maryland I deem it absolutely necessary that the Departments of the Susquehanna, West Virginia, and Washington be merged into one department and one head, who shall absolutely control the whole. What are now departments will be districts or corps. The one commander will then control all troops that co-operate in any movement of the enemy toward Maryland or Pennsylvania. I should name Maj. Gen. W. B. Franklin for such commander.[14]

13. Chambersburg and the Turning Point

President Lincoln objected to Franklin being given the position and nothing was done about the situation. Grant tried again a week later, writing to the president on July 25:

> I still think it highly essential that these four departments should be in one command. I do not insist that the departments should be broken up, nor do I insist upon General Franklin commanding. All I ask is that one general officer, in whom I and yourself have confidence, should command the whole. General Franklin was named because he was available and I know him to be capable and believe him to be trustworthy. It would suit me equally as well to call the four departments referred to, a "Military Division," and to have placed in command of it General Meade. In this case I would suggest General Hancock for command of the Army of the Potomac, and General Gibbon for the command of the Second Corps. With General Meade in command of such a division, I would have every confidence that all the troops within the military division would be used to the very best advantage from a personal examination of the ground, and (he) would adopt means of getting the earliest information of any advance of the enemy and would prepare to meet it.[15]

The need for change was even more apparent to the men who did the marching and fighting. Private Wilber Fisk wrote home on August 1st:

> Nobody knows where we shall go to next and some of the boys are of the opinion that it does not matter, so that we keep marching. We marched from Washington, in the first place, to the Shenandoah Valley, then returned to Washington again. After stopping there just long enough to brush the dust off our clothes, and out of our eyes, and get the pay due us for the last four months' service, we started for the Shenandoah Valley again.
> It is terrible hot marching now. The men cannot endure it. Many fell out in our march yesterday, and several died from sunstroke. Straggling may be a serious evil to an army, but under such circumstances as those of yesterday it is as much without remedy as casualties on a battle-field.[16]

Nothing much happened with Grant's proposal to change the command situation until the Chambersburg raid, Sheridan later wrote:

> The President and Secretary Stanton seemed unwilling to adopt his suggestions, and one measure which he deemed very important—the consolidation into a single command of the four geographical districts into which, to relieve political pressure no doubt, the territory had been divided—met with serious opposition. Despite Grant's representations, he could not prevail on the Administration to approve this measure, but finally the manoeuvres of Early and the raid to Chambersburg compelled a partial compliance, though Grant had somewhat circumvented the difficulty already by deciding to appoint a commander for the forces in the field that were to operate against Early.[17]

Grant knew of one officer who had never let him down, who was competent to lead a large body of men, and who was aggressive enough to tackle Early and his tough veterans. On July 31 Grant called Major General Philip H. Sheridan, Cavalry Commander of the Army of the Potomac, to headquarters at City Point and offered him a new command. Instead of making a suggestion or requesting approval from the War Department, Grant simply informed Halleck of his decision:[18]

> I am sending General Sheridan for temporary duty whilst the enemy is being expelled from the border. Unless General Hunter is in the field in person, I want Sheridan put in command of all the troops in the field, with instructions to put himself south of the enemy and follow him to the death. Wherever the enemy goes let our troops go also. Once started up the Valley they ought to be followed until we get possession of the Virginia Central Railroad. If General Hunter is in the field give Sheridan direct command of the Sixth Corps and cavalry division.[19]

Grant later wrote, "The President in some way or other got to see this dispatch of mine directing certain instructions to be given to the commanders in the field, operating against Early, and sent me the following very characteristic dispatch."

> I have seen your dispatch in which you say "I want Sheridan put in command of all the troops in the field, with instructions to put himself south of the enemy, and follow him to the death. Wherever the enemy goes, let out troops go also." This, I think, is exactly right, as to how our forces should move. But please look over the despatches you may have received from here, even since you made that order, and discover, if you can, that there is any idea in the head of any one here, of "putting our army *south* of the enemy," or of "following him to the *death*" in any direction. I repeat to you it will neither be done nor attempted unless you watch it every day, and hour, and force it.[20]

In this message the president exposed one of the major problems that had plagued the Federal war effort since the very beginning of the conflict. Too often in the past, opportunities had been missed because of excessive caution at the War Department. Actions were not taken because the potential risks were given more weight than the potential rewards. This attitude came from the top, Secretary Stanton and General Halleck, and filtered down through the department. In the end no one, including the president, could make the War Department take action if it didn't want to.[21]

One example of the hesitation of anyone in Washington to take on any responsibility was Halleck's message to Grant on August 4. In talking about Hunter and Sheridan, he volunteered that he would have been happy to offer his advice and opinions about the two men if Grant had only asked, "but I must beg to be excused from deciding questions which lawfully and properly belong to your office. I can give no instructions to either till you decide upon their commands. I await your orders, and shall strictly carry them out, whatever they may be."[22]

Grant understood the implications of the president's message and took immediate action:

> I replied to this that "I would start in two hours for Washington," and soon got off, going directly to the Monocacy without stopping at Washington on

my way. I found General Hunter's army encamped there, scattered over the fields along the banks of the Monocacy, with many hundreds of cars and locomotives, belonging to the Baltimore and Ohio Railroad, which he had taken the precaution to bring back and collect at that point. I asked the general where the enemy was. He replied that he did not know. He said the fact was, that he was so embarrassed with orders from Washington moving him first to the right and then to the left that he had lost all trace of the enemy.[23]

Knowing that Early would have to react to any Federal movement toward the Valley, Grant decided to act:

I then told the general that I would find out where the enemy was, and at once ordered steam got up and trains made up, giving directions to push for Halltown, some four miles above Harper's Ferry, in the Shenandoah Valley. The cavalry and the wagon trains were to march, but all the troops that could be transported by the cars were to go in that way. I knew the valley was of such importance to the enemy that, no matter how much he was scattered at that time, he would in a very short time be found in front of our troops moving south.[24]

Grant didn't want to embarrass Hunter by relieving him of command and it seemed a good compromise to have Sheridan command the troops in the field while Hunter stayed at headquarters in overall command but mainly restricted to administrative work. But Hunter had had enough:

The general replied to this, that he thought he better be relieved entirely. He said that General Halleck seemed so much to distrust his fitness for the position he was in that he thought somebody else ought to be there. He did not want, in any way, to embarrass the cause; thus showing a patriotism that was none too common in the army. There were not many major-generals who would voluntarily have asked to have the command of a department taken from them on the supposition that for some particular reason, or for any reason, the service would be better performed. I told him, "very well then," and telegraphed at once for Sheridan to come to the Monocacy, and suggested that I would wait and meet him there.[25]

Sheridan took a special train from Washington and met with Grant in the station at Monocacy on the 6th. The troops were already on their way south so only Grant, Hunter and a few staff officers were waiting for Sheridan. Grant gave him the same instructions that had been written out for Hunter:[26]

From Harper's Ferry, if it is found that the enemy has moved north of the Potomac in large force, push north, following and attacking him wherever found; following him, if driven south of the Potomac, as long as it is safe to do so. If it is ascertained that the enemy has but a small force north of the Potomac, then push south with the main force, detaching, under a competent commander, a sufficient force to look after the raiders and drive them to their homes.... In pushing up the Shenandoah Valley, as it is expected you will have to go, first or last, it is desirable that nothing should be left to invite the enemy to return. Take all provisions, forage, and stock wanted for the use of your command; such as cannot be consumed, destroy. It is not desirable that the buildings should be destroyed; they should rather be protected; but the people should be informed that so long as an army can subsist among them recurrences of these raids must be expected, and we are determined to stop them at all hazards. Bear in mind the object is to drive the enemy south, and to do this you want to keep him always in sight. Be guided in your course by the course he takes.[27]

Before arriving at Monocacy Junction to assume his new command, Sheridan had stopped in Washington to meet with President Lincoln and Secretary Stanton. The reception he received was less than encouraging. The president informed Sheridan that Stanton was not in favor of his appointment because he was too young and did not have enough experience for independent command. The president went on to say that he agreed with Stanton, but, then he said: "since General Grant had 'ploughed round' the difficulties of the situation by picking me out to command the 'boys in the field,' he felt satisfied with what had been done, and 'hoped for the best.'"[28]

Despite any criticism or hesitation from the president or War Department, Grant was sure he had picked the right man to clear the enemy out of the Shenandoah Valley. On August 7 he wrote to Sheridan:

Do not hesitate to give commands to officers in whom you repose confidence, without regard to claims of others on account of rank.... What we want is prompt and active movements after the enemy in accordance with instructions you already have. I feel every confidence that you will do the very best, and will leave you as far as possible to act on your own judgment, and not embarrass you with orders and instructions.[29]

It took a special man to earn such trust from Ulysses Grant, and Phil Sheridan was just such a man. He was born on March 6, 1831, but the location could have been Albany, New York, or Somerset, Ohio, or somewhere in between, there is simply no record of his birth. He grew up in Somerset and received an appointment to the U.S. Military Academy, graduating in 1853. He then served almost eight years in the Pacific Northwest, helping to subdue the native Indians and learning how to lead men by example.[30]

When the Civil War broke out, Sheridan received an appointment as captain in the Thirteenth United States Infantry. He spent most of the first year of the war as a bookkeeper and then quartermaster in the Department of the Missouri commanded by Henry Halleck. During this time he uncovered some less than ethical practices by his superiors, which threatened to put his career on the shelf. Fortunately, in March of 1862, the governor of Michigan offered Sheridan a commission as colonel of the Second Michigan Cavalry, the fighting command he longed for.[31]

It was as a commander of men in combat that Sheridan found his calling. His performance in several skirmishes and small battles earned a promotion to brigadier general in the fall of 1862. While in command of an infantry division in the Army of the Ohio, he exhibited a superior ability to lead large bodies of men in combat at the battles of Perryville and Stones River and was soon promoted to major general in March 1863. At Chickamauga that fall, his division

13. Chambersburg and the Turning Point

was nearly destroyed by the violent attack of Longstreet's corps, but no blame was attached to Sheridan. In November he led his division up Missionary Ridge in a spectacular charge that broke the back of the supposedly impregnable Confederate position. Grant was so impressed by the performance of the young general that when he became general-in-chief in the spring of 1864, Sheridan was brought east as the commander of cavalry for the Army of the Potomac.[32]

Physically, Philip Sheridan looked nothing like a dashing cavalry commander. He stood only about five feet, six inches tall with dark hair and an odd shaped head that seemed to stick out in the back. His eyes were dark and became almost black when he was angry. His arms were too long and legs too short; he was altogether an odd looking man. But it wasn't his looks that took Sheridan to the heights he achieved.[33]

Union Major General Philip H. Sheridan (U.S. Army Military History Institute).

It was on the battlefield that Sheridan's greatness became apparent. Sylvanus Cadwallader, a news correspondent, wrote:

> Probably no living soldier was ever more terrible in battle than Sheridan. With the first smell of powder he became a blazing meteor, a pillar of fire to guide his own hosts. The rather small short, heavily built man rose to surpassing stature in his stirrups, to the sublimity of heroism in action; and infused a like spirit in his troops. I think it no exaggeration to say that America never produced his equal, for inspiring an army with courage and leading them into battle. Absolutely fearless himself, with unwavering faith in his cause and his plans, he always raised the courage and faith of others, to the level of his own; passed from rank to rank in action, flaming, fiery, omnipresent, and well-nigh omnipotent.
>
> But Sheridan's claim to great generalship does not rest on his admitted courage. He gave abundant proof of extraordinary military ability on every field to which he was assigned, and in every official position he ever held. It was well-known to Gen. Grant's intimates, that he considered Sheridan incomparably the greatest general our civil war produced. Other generals might be equally good under ordinary circumstances, under the eyes of an able superior commander, and up to the point of a given or limited number of men. Sheridan he believed could be more safely trusted with an independent army than any of them; and he often said in private confidential conversation, that no army would ever be raised on this continent so large that Sheridan could not competently command it.[34]

W.F.G. Shanks wrote of Sheridan:

> He may be said to be an Inspiration rather than a General, accomplishing his work as much, not to say more, by the inspiring force of his courage and example as by the rules of war.... He was born a belligerent. His natural element is amidst the smoke, his natural position in the front line of battle. He fights vigorously and roughly, and when the tide of battle flows and ebbs most doubtingly he holds on most grimly.[35]

This is the man that was about to be unleashed on Early and the Shenandoah Valley.

General Grant was well aware of how much depended on Sheridan being able to accomplish his task:

> The Shenandoah Valley was very important to the Confederates, because it was the principal store-house they now had for feeding their armies about Richmond. It was well known that they would make a desperate struggle to maintain it. It had been the source of a great deal of trouble to us heretofore to guard that outlet to the north, partly because of the incompetency of some of the commanders, but chiefly because of interference from Washington.... I determined to put a stop to this.[36]

The last campaign in the Shenandoah Valley was about to begin. Grant had decided it was time to play for keeps and was sending a veteran army commanded by his most aggressive general to make sure that the Valley was taken out of the war for good. Lee had gambled and lost, Early had not captured Washington, Grant had not weakened his force at Petersburg enough to make any difference, and now Early and the Valley would have to suffer the consequences. The stakes were high for both sides, as it was apparent that if the stalemate in Eastern Virginia were to be broken, it would have to happen in the Shenandoah Valley.[37]

14. A War of Maneuver

In the first report Sheridan sent to Grant on taking command of the Army of the Shenandoah, he stated, "I find affairs somewhat confused, but will soon straighten them out."[1] Sheridan's new command consisted of the Sixth Corps under General Wright, one division of the Nineteenth Corps under Brig. Gen. William Emory, Crook's Army of West Virginia, now designated as the Eighth Corps, and a division of cavalry commanded by Brigadier General Alfred T. A. Torbert. In a few weeks two more cavalry divisions under Brigadier Generals Averell and Wesley Merritt and the Second Division of the Nineteenth Corps were added. The total manpower would be over 45,000, but due to the number of men needed to escort trains and to stay behind to perform guard duty, Sheridan never had that many men available for combat.[2]

The quality and experience of Sheridan's men varied widely. It was going to take some time to pull them together into an efficient fighting force. The Sixth Corps was as good as any corps in the army. They had plenty of experience and were led by brave and competent officers. They were also exhausted from the pointless chasing after Early and morale was at a new low. Crook's troops were not in much better condition, and most of their battle experience had been on the losing side. The Nineteenth Corps had originally been brought up from Louisiana for duty at Petersburg but had been sent instead to confront Early at Washington. They had not seen as much heavy fighting as the Sixth, but at least they were used to winning their battles, Of course, they had not yet met the Army of Northern Virginia.[3]

Sheridan knew he had the advantage of Early in manpower but was also aware that he had to exercise caution:

> The difference of strength between the two armies at this date was considerably in my favor, but the conditions attending my situation in a hostile

region necessitated so much detached service to protect trains, and to secure Maryland and Pennsylvania from raids, that my excess in numbers was almost canceled by these incidental demands that could not be avoided, and although I knew that I was strong, yet, in consequence of the injunctions of General Grant, I deemed it necessary to be very cautious; and the fact that the Presidential election was impending made me doubly so, the authorities at Washington having impressed upon me that the defeat of my army might be followed by the overthrow of the party in power, which event, it was believed, would at least retard the progress of the war, if, indeed, it did not lead to the complete abandonment of all coercive measures ... I determined to take all the time necessary to equip myself with the fullest information, and then seize an opportunity under such conditions that I could not well fail of success.[4]

As soon as Sheridan took command, the men of the Army of the Shenandoah began to notice an improvement in almost all things. Food and other supplies were more readily available, marches were more organized and it just seemed as if things were being managed better. As C.M. Keyes explained, "Everything now assumed an air of business and preparation; clothing and shoes, which were much needed by the men, were issued in abundance, and our boys again felt that spirit of confidence which is a sure prelude to success."[5] Another thing the men liked was that their new commander made do with very few comforts for himself, unlike the pomp and ceremony that was common in the Army of the Potomac.

Sixth Corps Soldier George T. Stevens said:

> One thing pleased us at the start. Our new general was visible to the soldiers of his command; wherever we went he was with the column, inhaling the dust, leaving the road for the teams, never a day or two days behind the rest of the army, but always riding by the side of the men. His watchful care of the details of the march, his interest in the progress of the trains, and the ready faculty with which he brought order out of confusion when the roads became blocked, reminded us of our lamented Sedgwick.[6]

Sheridan did not force any action before he was ready. After taking command, he spent several days with Lieutenant John R. Meigs, an expert on the geography of the Valley, studying maps and becoming familiar with the lay of the land. Sheridan admitted, "It always came rather easy to me to learn the geography of a new section, and its important topographical features as well; therefore I found that, with the aid of Meigs, who was most intelligent in his profession, the region in which I was to operate would soon be well fixed in my mind."[7]

On August 10 the Army of the Shenandoah left Harpers Ferry and started south toward Berryville. Early, who had been keeping an eye on the Federal army from Bunker Hill, moved his forces toward Winchester to protect that vital position. The next day the Federals moved toward the Opequon and closer to Winchester while Early shifted his forces to keep between Sheridan and the Valley Pike. There was cavalry skirmishing both days as each side tried to control key roads. On the 12th, Sheridan reached Cedar Creek and there was a brisk infantry skirmish as he tried to move forward, but Early then took up position at Fisher's Hill and both armies settled down to see what the other might do.[8]

While this maneuvering was going on, reinforcements that Early had requested were moving closer. "I had received information a few days before, from General Lee, that General Anderson had moved with Kershaw's division of infantry and Fitz Lee's division of cavalry to Culpepper C. H.; and I sent a dispatch to Anderson, informing him of the state of things, and requesting him to move to Front Royal...."[9]

Sheridan had received unconfirmed reports concerning just such a movement and he knew full well the serious problems it could cause. There was the possibility that an enemy force advancing through Front Royal could attack the rear of the army and cut him off from Harpers Ferry. Even worse, they could move around Massanutten Mountain and attack the Federal flank in a combined assault with Early on Fisher's Hill.[10]

On the 14th Sheridan received the following message from Grant, confirming that enemy forces were heading his way and reminding him to be careful: "It is now positive that Kershaw's division has gone, but no other infantry has. This re-enforcement to Early will put him nearer on an equality with you in numbers than I want to see, and will make it necessary for you to observe some caution about attacking. I would not, however, change my instructions, further than to enjoin caution."[11]

Believing that the Confederate reinforcements would give Early an advantage in manpower, Sheridan searched for a position where he could establish a defensive line. The only satisfactory place he could find was in front of Harpers Ferry at Halltown. He discovered that "there was no other really defensive line in the Shenandoah Valley, for at almost any other point the open country and its peculiar topography invites rather than forbids flanking operations."[12]

Sheridan thought about it for a day and then ordered the army to begin heading back north on the night of the 15th. On the way back to Halltown, orders went out to initiate the planned destruction of anything that might be of use to the Confederate armies. The cavalry was to bring up the rear, and on the 16th Sheridan told Torbert:

> You will make the necessary arrangements and give the necessary orders for the destruction of the wheat and hay south of a line from Millwood to Winchester and Petticoat Gap. You will seize all horses, mules, and cattle that may be useful to our army. Loyal citizens can bring in their claims against the Government for this necessary destruction. No houses will be burned, and officers in charge of this delicate, but necessary, duty must inform the people that the object is to make this Valley untenable for the raiding parties of the rebel army.[13]

Sheridan, like Grant, believed in waging total war:

> It was time to bring the war home to a people engaged in raising crops from a prolific soil to feed the country's enemies, and devoting to the Confederacy its best youth. I endorsed the programme in all its parts, for the stores of meat and grain that the valley provided, and the men it furnished for Lee's depleted regiments, were the strongest auxiliaries he possessed in the whole insurgent section. In war a territory like this is a factor of great importance, and whichever adversary controls it permanently reaps all the advantages of

> its prosperity. Hence, as I have said, I endorsed Grant's programme, for I do not hold war to mean simply that lines of men shall engage each other in battle, and material interests be ignored. This is but a duel, in which one combatant seeks the other's life; war means much more, and is far worse than this. Those who rest at home in peace and plenty see but little of the horrors attending such a duel, and even grow indifferent to them as the struggle goes on, contenting themselves with encouraging all who are able-bodied to enlist in the cause, to fill up the shattered ranks as death thins them. It is another matter, however, when deprivation and suffering are brought to their own doors. Then the case appears much graver, for the loss of property weighs heavy with the most of mankind; heavier often, than the sacrifices made on the field of battle. Death is popularly considered the maximum of punishment in war, but it is not; reduction to poverty brings prayers for peace more surely and more quickly than does the destruction of human life, as the selfishness of man has demonstrated in more than one great conflict.[14]

The war in the Valley would be different from now on. One soldier from Ohio saw that "A new state of war-fare was now inaugurated. The Rebels of the beautiful valley were to be taught a lesson which they would never forget...."[15]

As the army moved north, the cavalry spread out across the landscape and did their best to destroy or carry away everything that could conceivably aid the Confederate war effort: barns, crops, mills, and animals. The soldiers were supposed to leave the farmers enough food and forage for their personal use, but any extra that could be sent to the Confederate armies was put to the torch.[16]

A cavalryman from Pennsylvania recalled August 17:

> The day had been an unpleasant one; the weather was hot and the roads very dusty, and the grief of the inhabitants, as they saw their harvests disappearing in flame and smoke, and their stock being driven off, was a sad sight. It was a phase of warfare we had not seen before, and though we admitted its necessity, we could not but sympathize with the sufferers.[17]

Of course, for the farmers the pieces of charred wood that had once been a barn or grist mill and the empty field where their livestock formerly grazed represented not only the loss of a lifetime's work, but probable hunger for their families in the coming winter. As Early's soldiers followed behind the Federal army, they were greeted with scenes of destruction that few had thought possible. Revenge was in the hearts of many. The burning in August brought a revival of the roving bands of guerillas that had plagued other Federal campaigns. The partisans had never really gone away and had been harassing Sheridan's men from the start of the campaign, but now their ranks were swelled by local residents out for some pay-back. Many of these guerrillas were little more than thieves looking to grab whatever they could under the guise of fighting the hated Yankees. They were innocent, peaceful farmers most of the time until called together for a raid. Then they would secretly gather and fall upon an unsuspecting Federal picket line, wagon train, or any lightly defended target they could find.

All too frequently Federal stragglers were found with their throats cut or shot in the back. Unfortunately for the residents of the Valley, most of whom really were peaceful farmers, this guerrilla activity only encouraged increasingly harsh reprisals by the Federal authorities.[18]

One of the few groups of partisans that were considered by many Union commanders as being at least semi-military was John Mosby's band. His men were members of the 43rd Battalion, Virginia Cavalry, and had been usually, but not always, considered regular soldiers and treated as such when captured. Most of the other bands, however, were considered nothing more than outlaws and frequently were summarily hanged or shot when captured. The general feeling in the Federal ranks was that if a man wanted to fight, he should put on a uniform and join the army. If he hid behind a facade of a peaceful citizen, then went out and murdered Federal soldiers doing their duty, there would be no mercy for them or their supporters.[19]

Mosby was the most successful partisan leader of the war and one of the few who survived the war almost universally recognized as a brave fighter and first class leader of men. His men struck so often that eventually the Federal authorities referred to all partisans as "Mosby's men." He later wrote that:

> During this campaign of 1864, my battalion of six companies was the only force operating in the rear of Sheridan's army in the Shenandoah Valley. Our rendezvous was along the eastern base of the Blue Ridge, in what is known as the Piedmont region of Virginia. Fire and sword could not drive the people of that neighborhood from their allegiance to what they thought was right, and in the gloom of disaster and defeat they never wavered in their support for the Confederate cause.... We lived on the country where we operated and drew nothing from Richmond except the gray jackets my men wore. We were mounted, armed, and equipped entirely off the enemy, but, as we captured a great deal more than we could use, the surplus was sent to supply Lee's army.[20]
>
> As we operated in Sheridan's rear, the railroad that brought his supplies was his weak point and consequently our favorite object of attack. For security it had to be closely guarded by detachments of troops, which materially reduced his offensive strength. We kept watch for unguarded points, and the opportunity they offered was never lost.[21]

The changing face of the war and the frustration caused by the guerrillas is illustrated in two messages Grant sent to Sheridan on August 16. In one, he said, "The families of most of Mosby's men are known, and can be collected. I think they should be taken and kept at Fort McHenry, or some other secure place, as hostages for the good conduct of Mosby and his men. Where any of Mosby's men are caught hang them without trial."[22] He also wrote: "If you can possibly spare a division of cavalry, send them through Loudoun County, to destroy and carry off the crops, animals, negroes, and all men under fifty years of age capable of bearing arms. In this way you will get many of Mosby's men. All male citizens under fifty can fairly be held as prisoners of war, and not as citizen prisoners. If not already soldiers, they will be made so the moment a rebel army gets hold of them."[23]

Sheridan's retreat back to Halltown looked as if he had been scared out of the Valley and caused considerable alarm to people throughout the North, and especially in Pennsylvania and Maryland:

> Mutterings of dissatisfaction reached me from many sources, and loud calls were made for my removal, but I felt confident that my course would be justified when the true situation was understood, for I knew that I was complying with my instructions. Therefore I paid small heed to the adverse criticisms pouring down from the North almost every day, being fully convinced that the best course was to bide my time, and wait till I could get the enemy into a position from which he could not escape without such serious misfortune as to have some bearing on the general result of the war.[24]

With the Union army dug in at Halltown, they could protect the roads leading north and the arsenal at Harpers Ferry. It was a good defensive position with rivers protecting the flanks and strong fortifications across the front. Although there had been no really heavy fighting between the main armies, there were plenty of signs that Early was facing a tougher enemy than had confronted him before. As an example of this new toughness in the Federal ranks, there was a small but deadly fight at Cedarville on the 16th. Forces from Anderson's corps attacked the First Cavalry Division, commanded by General Merritt, which was guarding the flank as the Union infantry withdrew to Halltown.[25]

> A force of cavalry under Fitz Lee, supported by a brigade of Kershaw's division, made a descent on Devin's brigade. General Fitz Lee drove in the cavalry pickets and attacked Devin with great violence. This force was scarcely repulsed when a brigade of infantry was discovered moving on the opposite bank of the Shenandoah River toward the left of the cavalry position. One regiment of Custer's brigade, dismounted, was moved up to the crest of a hill near the river-bank to meet this force, while the rest of the brigade, mounted, was stationed to the right of the hill. At the same time the Reserve Brigade under General Gibbs was summoned to the field. The enemy advanced boldly, wading the river, and when within short carbine range was met by a murderous volley from the dismounted men, while the remainder of the command charged mounted. The Confederates were thrown into confusion and retreated....[26]

While Sheridan and Early watched and waited for the other to make a move with his main force, there were several clashes away from the main lines. One Union officer believed that these small battles played an important part in the fight for control of the Valley:

> These affairs between the Union cavalry and the enemy's infantry were of more importance than might appear at first glance. They gave the cavalry increased confidence, and made the enemy correspondingly doubtful even of the ability of its infantry, in anything like equal numbers, to contend against our cavalry in the open fields of the Valley.[27]

Sheridan had to curb his natural aggressiveness during this period and be very careful to avoid a defeat since there were political as well as military ramifications to consider. The war was not going well for the Union that summer and the high hopes of spring had been dashed by the lack of Union victories accompanied by the horrendous casualties in Virginia. One more serious defeat and President Lincoln could lose the coming election, which might mean that all the sacrifices made so far would have been for nothing.

As an example of how careful Sheridan was being, he reported to Grant on the 22nd:

> Yesterday morning the enemy crossed Opequon Creek at different points in the vicinity of Smithfield or Middleway and advanced on my position at Welch's Spring, about two miles west of Charlestown. Skirmishing took place during the day in front of both General Crook's command and the Sixth Army Corps. The skirmishing was at one time rather sharp in front of the latter command, as the line was pressed forward and drove the enemy from a crest in our front which they occupied early in the day.... As my position at best in front of Charlestown was a bad one, and much being dependent on this army, I withdrew my command without loss or opposition last night and took up a new line in front of Halltown.[28]

For many in the administration and the War Department, the static situation in the Valley was probably just the way they liked it—low risk. But for General Grant this was not at all what he envisioned when he appointed Sheridan to command. There had recently been some serious fighting at Petersburg that caused heavy casualties on both sides. Grant hoped that this might force Lee to recall some of the troops he had sent to Early. On August 26, he wrote to Sheridan reiterating his plans for the Valley:

> I now think it likely that all troops will be ordered back from the Valley except what they believe to be the minimum number to detain you.... Watch closely, and if you find this theory correct push with all vigor. Give the enemy no rest, and if it is possible to follow to the Virginia Central road, follow that far. Do all the damage to railroads and crops you can. Carry off stock of all descriptions, and negroes, so as to prevent further planting. If the war is to last another year, we want the Shenandoah Valley to remain a barren waste.[29]

On the same day, Early received a communication from General Lee:

> I am much pleased at your having forced the enemy back to Harper's Ferry. This will give protection to the Valley and arrest the travel on the Baltimore and Ohio Railroad. It will, however, have little or no effect upon Grant's operations, or prevent re-enforcements being sent to him. If Sheridan's force is as large as you suppose, I do not know that you could operate to advantage north of the Potomac. Either Anderson's troops or a portion of yours might, however, be detached to destroy the railroad west of Charlestown, and Fitz Lee might send a portion of his cavalry to cross the Potomac east of the Blue Ridge, as you propose. I cannot detach at present more cavalry from this army; the enemy is too strong in that arm. I am aware that Anderson is the ranking officer, but I apprehend no difficulty on that score.... I am in great need of his troops, and if they can be spared from the Valley, or cannot operate to advantage there, I will order them back to Richmond. Let me know.[30]

From the end of August to mid-September, there was little heavy fighting as the antagonists maneuvered around to find any opening to inflict real damage on one another. A soldier from Vermont remembered:

> It was a zigzag, tiresome game they played there with the wily enemy, for Gen. Early did not propose to quit that region till he had severely worried his antagonist, even though he failed to carry a secession flag into the capital of the United States. At that stage of affairs, therefore, the only mode of dealing with him was to follow him closely, and keep the hostile army at bay as far as possible.[31]

As one Confederate described it, "We had been all the summer marching back & forth, up & down the valley, now to Harper's Ferry, & back to Charlestown, over to Berryville then back to Winchester. Sometimes to draw the enemy up the Valley & then chase them back."[32]

Early later wrote about the weeks when he and Sheridan were testing each other:

> I knew my danger, but I could occupy no other position that would have enabled me to accomplish the desired object. If I had moved up the Valley at all, I could not have stopped short of New Market, for between that place and the country in which I was, there was no forage for my horses; and this would have enabled the enemy to resume the use of the railroad and canal, and return all the troops from Grant's army to him.... The events of the last month had satisfied me that the commander opposed to me was without enterprise, and possessed an excessive caution which amounted to timidity. If it was his policy to produce the impression that his force was too weak to fight me, he did not succeed, but if it was to convince me that he was not an able or energetic commander, his strategy was a complete success, and subsequent events have not changed my opinion.[33]

During the time the two commanders were feeling each other out, Early apparently decided that Sheridan had no appetite for a real fight. Although there had been several opportunities, Sheridan had avoided bringing on a general engagement. Early, in a word, became overconfident. He believed that Sheridan lacked initiative and was not bold enough to risk his army in the open field. Early soon developed the same sort of contempt for Sheridan and his army that he had previously felt for Hunter and Wallace. He was guilty of underestimating his opponent before seeing him in action, one of the worst mistakes a military commander can make.[34]

One of the few real fights between infantry occurred on September 3 when Anderson, who was trying to return to Petersburg, ran into Crook's lines near Berryville and

> a bitter little fight ensued, in which the Confederates got so much the worst of it that they withdrew toward Winchester. When General Early received word of this encounter he hurried to Anderson's assistance with three divisions, but soon perceiving what was hitherto unknown to him, that my whole army was on a new line, he decided, after some slight skirmishing, that

Anderson must remain at Winchester until a favorable opportunity offered for him to rejoin Lee by another route.³⁵

The fight near Berryville was the last engagement of any size for about two weeks. Sheridan decided to wait for Kershaw's division to return to Petersburg before taking any major offensive action. Early found that the passes through the mountains and the Potomac crossings were all defended by Federal cavalry and there was no realistic chance that he could successfully attack Sheridan's army in its fortifications. Both sides decided to wait and see what happened.³⁶

While there was a lull in the action, Colonel Charles Russell Lowell found time to write letters. He wrote to his wife on September 5th:

> By the way, I like Sheridan immensely. Whether he succeeds or fails, he is the first General I have seen who puts as much heart and time and thought into his work as if he were doing it for his own exclusive profit. He works like a mill-owner or an iron-master, not like a soldier,—never sleeps, never worries, is never cross, but isn't afraid to come down on a man who deserves it.³⁷

And on September 10 Lowell wrote to a friend explaining how Sheridan had earned the respect and confidence of the army. "He works at this business as if he were working for himself, watches everything himself (except his trains occasionally) and keeps his officers pretty well up to their work. If the campaign does not succeed, it will not be for want of interest and energy on his part."³⁸

In an attempt to curb some of the foraging and theft by his soldiers, which was a one of the major reasons that some of the local residents joined in partisan activity, Sheridan issued the following orders on September 8:

1. No private property whatever will be seized, except horses, mules, forage, and fresh beef, or, in case of actual necessity, flour and bacon.

2. For all private property seized under this order, brigade or detachment quartermasters will give vouchers to the owners, stating explicitly the amount and character of property taken, the order for so taking it, and that on proof of loyalty to the United States Government the claim will be paid.

3. The quartermasters will take up on their returns and account for all property seized under this order.³⁹

It is unlikely that the men who were doing most of the pillaging paid much attention to this order, and soon it wouldn't matter.

The pressure that Grant had been putting on Lee's extended lines at Petersburg finally paid off, when, "On the 14th, General Anderson again started, with Kershaw's division and Cutshaw's battalion of artillery, to cross the Blue Ridge by way of Front Royal, and was not molested."⁴⁰ Sheridan had no intention of molesting Anderson's move, as this is exactly what he had been hoping for.

A message from General Lee had prompted this significant move:

> I have been very anxious to recall General Anderson with Kershaw's division to me. But a victory at this time over Sheridan would be greatly advantageous to us, and I feared that your corps would be insufficient for the purpose.... It is my intention to send to you Rosser's brigade of cavalry as soon as I can discover the intentions of General Grant. I then think you will be able to spare Kershaw. In the meantime I wish you to defeat Sheridan if your strength is sufficient. He seems disposed to protect himself under his intrenchments. If you could draw him up the Valley and fall upon him suddenly, or throw a body of troops behind him, you might succeed in defeating him. If you think it best for you to remain on the defensive and can spare Kershaw, send him to me as secretly as you can, for I will then take the offensive myself.[41]

Sometime earlier Sheridan had learned of a young woman named Rebecca Wright who was a schoolteacher in Winchester and a loyal Union sympathizer. He wrote to her asking for any information she could obtain. He could hardly have known how important she would be:

> It was the evening of the 16th of September that I received from Miss Wright the positive information that Kershaw was in march toward Front Royal on his way by Chester Gap to Richmond. Concluding that this was my opportunity, I at once resolved to throw my whole force into Newtown the next day, but a despatch from General Grant directing me to meet him at Charlestown, whither he was coming to consult with me, caused me to defer action until after I should see him.[42]

Grant had decided that it was time for Sheridan to take some action. He started for the Valley on the 15th to encourage Sheridan to attack Early or try to maneuver him out of the Valley. Grant decided to go in person rather than just send a message, because, "I knew it was impossible for me to get orders through Washington to Sheridan to make a move, because they would be stopped there and such orders as Halleck's caution (and that of the Secretary of War) would suggest would be given instead, and would, no doubt, be contradictory to mine."[43]

Sheridan described the brief but eventful meeting with Grant:

> I went over the situation very thoroughly, and pointed out with so much confidence the chances of a complete victory should I throw my army across the Valley pike near Newtown that he fell in with the plan at once, authorized me to resume the offensive, and to attack Early as soon as I deemed it most propitious to do so....[44]

What Sheridan didn't know at the time was that Grant was fully prepared to order him to begin the campaign. Grant wrote, "Before starting I had drawn up a plan of campaign for Sheridan, which I had brought with me; but, seeing that he was so clear and so positive in his views and so confident of success, I said nothing about this and did not take it out of my pocket."[45]

The meeting took place on Friday and Sheridan said he could make the attack on the following Monday. On the way to the meeting Grant had met Robert Garrett, the president of the Baltimore and Ohio Railroad, who was concerned about when it might be safe for the tracks to be repaired. As a sign of how much confidence Grant had in his subordinate, when he again met Garrett on the return trip he advised him, without informing him of Sheridan's plans, that the repairs could begin the following Wednesday, after Sheridan had won the coming battle.[46]

Although Early was well aware of the strength of Sheridan's army, he very obligingly scattered his own troops:

> On the 17th of September I moved two divisions (Rodes' and Gordon's) from Stephenson's Depot, where they, together with Breckinridge's division, were encamped (Ramseur being at Winchester to cover the road from Berryville), to Bunker Hill, and on the 18th I moved Gordon's division, with a part of Lomax's cavalry, to Martinsburg, to thwart efforts that were reported to be making to repair the Baltimore and Ohio Railroad. This expedition was successful, and the bridge over Back Creek was burned by a brigade of cavalry sent there. On the evening of the 18th Rodes was moved back to Stephenson's Depot and Gordon to Bunker Hill, with orders to start at daylight to return to his camp at Stephenson's Depot, which place he reached at a very early hour next morning.[47]

When Sheridan learned of Early's surprising movements, he "decided to change my plan and attack at once the two divisions remaining about Winchester and Stephenson's depot...."[48]

Henry Douglas, on Early's staff, was also surprised at his commander's decision to split his army in the face of the enemy:

> My own anxiety is expressed, briefly, in these extracts from my diary:
> Sept 17. Genl Early, in these bold movements seems to rely too much upon the caution and timidity of Sheridan.
> Sept 18. A quiet, beautiful day. The Yankees to our satisfaction did not molest us. I shall be glad if tomorrow passes away as quietly.[49]

15. The Battle of Winchester

At two o'clock on the morning of September 19, Brigadier General James Wilson's Third Cavalry Division opened the battle as they advanced across the Opequon and engaged the Confederate outposts. A trooper in the 5th New York remembered that

> a splendid force of infantry, cavalry and artillery, was advancing toward Winchester. The 2nd New York had the advance, followed by the Fifth. Before daylight the Rebel cavalry pickets were charged at the Opequon, and driven hastily before us. Believing that this was nothing more than a repitition of the many reconnoissances and raids, we had recently made, the Jonnies were scarcely prepared for the onset that was made upon them....[1]

The fords where the Federals crossed the Opequon were about six miles east of Winchester. One Union soldier described the rough terrain:

> Opequon Creek flows at the foot of a broad and thickly wooded gorge, with high and steep banks. The ravine through which the Berryville road rises to the level of the rolling plain, in the middle of whose western edge stands Winchester, is nearly three miles long. Here and there the high ground is covered with large oaks, pines, and undergrowth, and is intersected by many brooks, called runs. Of these the largest is Red Bud Run, which forms a smaller parallel ravine flanking the defile on the north, while a still larger stream, called Abraham's Creek, after pursuing a nearly parallel course on the south side of the defile, crosses the road not far from the ford, and just below it falls into the Opequon.[2]

15. The Battle of Winchester

With Early's army not yet concentrated, Sheridan knew he had a golden opportunity to overwhelm and destroy the Confederates a piece at a time, if only he could move quickly enough. His orders were for the Sixth and Nineteenth corps to follow behind Wilson's troopers and engage the Confederates on the level ground past the Opequon with the Sixth Corps forming the left of the line. Crook's Eighth Corps was to be held in reserve at first, then move in on the left of the Sixth Corps with Wilson's cavalry to seize control of the Valley Pike south of Winchester. While Early was occupied with the infantry attack, General Torbert in command of Merritt and Averell's divisions was to move down from the north and attack the Confederate left and rear. With the part of Early's army at Winchester attacked from three sides and the troops north of town cut off, the destruction of the Confederate army in the Valley seemed certain.[3]

The Federal advance began right on schedule as Wilson's division attacked the Confederate right and quickly pushed the Confederate pickets back to open the road for the infantry. General Wright led his men along the narrow road from Berryville and the Sixth Corps infantry came through and began to form in line of battle just as they were supposed to, but the Nineteenth Corps troops were nowhere to be seen. Somehow, no one had ordered the baggage and supply trains of the Sixth Corps to wait, so they followed right behind their infantry, effectively blocking the Nineteenth Corps from moving for hours. The road was too narrow for them to turn around or pull over to the side so the fighting men could pass. Many men left the road and tried to move forward across the steep hills and underbrush, but they could only creep forward and exhaust themselves with the effort.[4]

One Union soldier remembered the chaos:

> The road was crowded with artillery, ammunition wagons, and ambulances, all hurrying forward. On each side of it a line of infantry in column of march stumbled over the rocky, guttered ground, and struggled through the underbrush. The multitudes of men who belong to an army, yet who do not fight – the cooks, the musicians, the hospital attendants, the quarter-masters, and commissaries people, the sick, and the skulkers – sat on every rock and under every bush watching us pass.[5]

The hours were passing quickly and Early's men were now alerted and forming their defenses with their artillery already firing on the three divisions of the Sixth Corps. Going back to see why the Nineteenth Corps had not deployed, Sheridan came upon the tangle of wagons and men on the narrow road and exploded. Sheridan and Wright went up and down the stalled column and ordered the drivers to do whatever it took to clear the road immediately, resulting in most of the wagons simply being pushed off the road into the woods. Soon the Nineteenth Corps troops were moving forward, but well behind schedule.[6]

Jubal Early had made a mistake in splitting up his army with the enemy so close, but he moved quickly enough when the Federal troops began to advance, using their delay to his advantage:

> At light on the morning of the 19th, our cavalry pickets at the crossing of the Opequon on the Berryville road were driven in, and information having been sent me of the fact, I immediately ordered all the troops at Stephenson's depot to be in readiness to move, directions being given for Gordon, who had arrived from Bunker Hill, to move at once, but, by some mistake on the part of my staff officer, the latter order was not delivered to General Breckinridge or Gordon. I rode at once to Ramseur's position, and found his troops in line across the Berryville road skirmishing with the enemy. Before reaching this point, I had ascertained that Gordon was not moving, and sent back for him, and now discovering that the enemy's advance was a real one and in heavy force, I sent orders for Breckinridge and Rodes to move up as rapidly as possible. The position occupied by Ramseur was about one mile and a half out from Winchester, on an elevated plateau between Abraham's Creek and Red Bud Run.[7]

General Gordon was not too happy with the way Early dispersed his men and later complained about delays in ordering the army to concentrate:

> The reports of the Federal approach, however, did not seem to impress General Early, and he delayed the order for concentration until Sheridan was upon him, ready to devour him piecemeal, a division at a time. When at last the order came to me, on the Martinsburg pike, to move with utmost speed to Winchester, the far-off reverberant artillery was already giving painful notice that Ramseur was fighting practically alone, while the increasingly violent concussions were passionate appeals to the other divisions for help.[8]

It was indeed fortunate that Early did not have to face the entire Federal army at first. His lines were thin but he was able to put his men in the right spot at the right time:

> Nelson's artillery was posted on Ramseur's line, covering the approaches as far as practicable, and Lomax with Jackson's cavalry and part of Johnson's was on the right, watching the valley of Abraham's Creek and the Front Royal road beyond, while Fitz Lee was on the left, across the Red Bud, with his cavalry and a battery of horse artillery, and a detachment of Johnson's cavalry watched the interval between Ramseur's left and the Red Bud. These troops held the enemy's main force in check until Gordon's and Rodes' divisions arrived from Stephenson's depot.[9]

While the men of Ramseur's division and the Sixth Corps traded sporadic musket fire and artillery shells, both sides were feverishly trying to bring the rest of their forces to the field. Gordon's division arrived about ten o'clock and took position behind some woods between Ramseur and Red Bud Run. Rodes soon arrived with three brigades and formed his men behind another wooded area between Gordon and Ramseur. The hours that were lost bringing the Federal troops forward gave the scattered Confederates time to concentrate and form their lines before the full force of Sheridan's army could be brought against Ramseur's small division. "It was a moment of imminent and thrilling danger, as it was impossible for Ramseur's division, which numbered only about 1,700 muskets, to withstand the immense force advancing against it."[10]

It was nearly noon by the time the Nineteenth Corps arrived in line on the right of the Sixth. During the march to the front, James Fitts noticed:

> It was one of the most beautiful of early Autumn days; the air was cool and mellow, the sun shed a tempered warmth, and the whole face of the country smiled in the harvest time. Carelessly, unconsciously, we marched on to the harvest of death and mutilation, the merry laugh and jest of the soldier passing back from company to company, while little children came out of the houses by the way and looked timidly through the fences as we passed....[11]

Confederate Major General Robert Rodes (Virginia Military Institute Archives)

It was a fine day to die.

Sheridan fully realized how costly the delay in bringing up the Nineteenth Corps had been. "General Early was not slow to avail himself of the advantages thus offered him, and my chances of striking him in detail were growing less every moment...."[12]

But the order had to be given and the Union infantry drove forward just before noon. As they advanced, "the Confederates, covered by some heavy woods on their right, slight underbrush and corn-fields along their centre, and a large body of timber on their left along the Red Bud, opened fire from their whole front."[13]

George Stevens later wrote:

> It was an imposing spectacle to watch that line of battle, stretching three miles across the fields, as it moved toward the rebel lines, the men as composed as though on parade, the line straight and compact, the various division, brigade and regimental flags floating gaily in the sunlight. Away in our front we could see Winchester; its gleaming spires and shining roofs, bright with the warm glow of mid-day, and we proudly felt that before night it would be ours. Onward, through the cornfields and over the grassy knolls, now descending into a ravine and now rising upon the open plain, where the rebel artillery swept with terrible effect, the long line pressed forward, regardless of the destructive fire that constantly thinned our ranks.[14]

General Ricketts reported that as soon as the Sixth Corps moved forward they were hit by heavy artillery fire. Major Vredenburgh, who commanded the

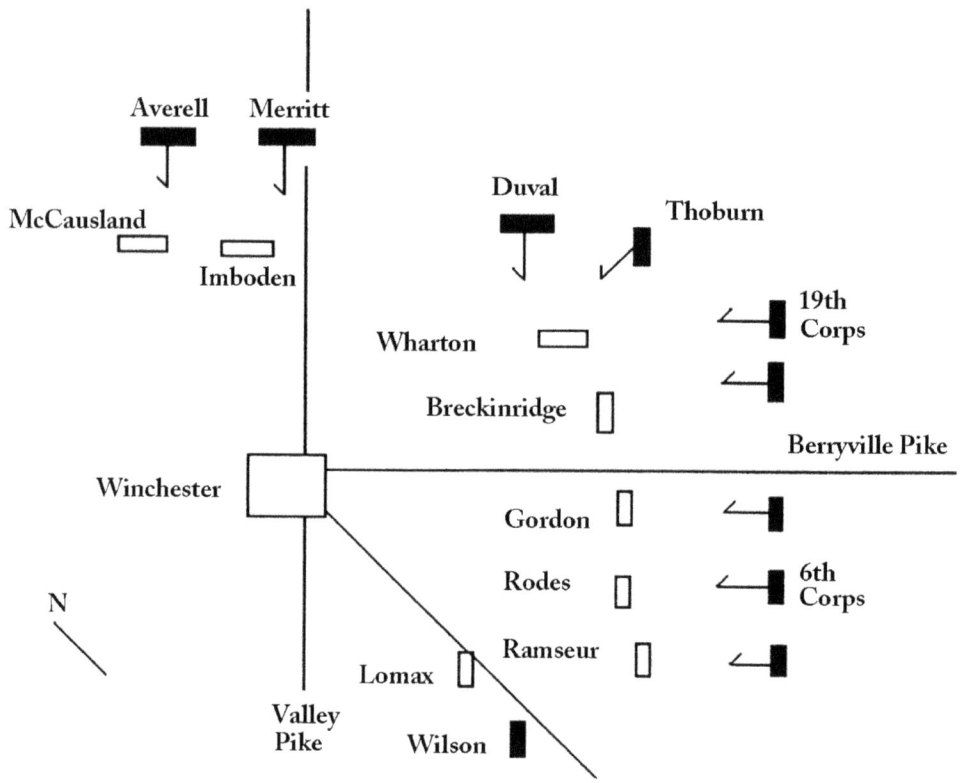

Battle of Winchester

Fourteenth New Jersey Volunteers, was in charge of directing the line as it moved forward. As he led the men forward, he was hit by a shell and killed instantly. His last orders were, "Guide on me, boys; I will do the best I can." At first the advance was moving along quickly and Rickett's troops went forward nearly a mile before encountering serious resistance.[15]

Rickett's division, which was on the right of the Sixth Corps line, had been ordered to follow the Berryville Pike as they advanced, but, "The Nineteenth Corps did not move and keep connection with my right, and the turnpike upon which the division was dressing bore to the left, causing a wide interval between the Sixth and Nineteenth Corps. As the lines advanced the interval became greater."[16]

On the Federal right, Brigadier General Cuvier Grover's division led the attack of the Nineteenth Corps. With their officers in front, the men cheered as they advanced "at double-quick across the clearing, and disappeared into the opposite wood. A roar of musketry, sounding in a thunderous burst of volleys, pealed up from that wood, and smoke and flame streamed out in a long line as though the whole forest had been suddenly ignited."[17] Grover's men had run straight into Gordon's division waiting in the woods.

Brigadier General Henry Birge's brigade reached the woods first and was met with a hail of fire. Colonel Jacob Sharpe's brigade came up for support and a desperate fight began. Gordon launched his own attack and was pushing the Federals back until two more brigades, commanded by colonels Edward Molineux and David Shunk, advanced and stopped the Confederates. Both lines were out in the open firing into each other until Gordon attacked again, "and then the Second division was hurled back into the clearing, stunned, mangled and shattered...."[18]

A soldier in the Nineteenth Corps described what he saw:

> Early restored his formation; and the whole Confederate line swept forward with renewed impetuosity, broke in the whole right of Ricketts and the left of Sharpe, surged around both flanks of Molineux, and swept back Birge. Sharpe's line, thus taken fairly in flank, was quickly rolled up. By this, the left regiment of Molineux, the gallant 22nd Iowa, being in quite open ground, was greatly exposed, so that it, too, was presently swept back. The 159th New York and the 13th Connecticut, after holding on stiffly for a time under the partial cover of a sort of gully, were in like manner swept away.[19]

George Carpenter remembered that

> When Gen. Emory's second division fell back, the first, which had been held in reserve, was ordered to the front, and the Eighth Vermont and Twelfth Connecticut relieved Col. Molineux, who had retreated under a murderous fire.... Over that bloody ground, strewn with the dead and wounded of both armies, these companion regiments advanced at the command of Col. Thomas, amid the most fearful storm of shot and shell they had ever encountered.[20]

Colonel Stephen Thomas led his men forward, "forgetting everything except his determination to take the woods, he rode in front of the colors and shouted, 'Boys, if you ever pray, the time to pray has come. Pray now, remember Ethan Allen and old Vermont, and we'll drive 'em to hell! Come on, old Vermont!' Thomas was so sure of the courage of his men that he never looked back to see if they were following him as he rode toward the enemy.[21]

Still more help was needed to stem Gordon's attack and General Emory ordered Beale's brigade of Dwight's division to move forward to shore up the broken line. A survivor of that terrible fight later wrote:

> To the left and front, far into the open field, through the wreck of Grover's right, into the teeth of the pursuing lines of Gordon, Per Lee led the 114th New York. No sooner had his men emerged from the cover of the wood than they came under the fire of Gordon's infantry and artillery, crossed with the fire of Fitzhugh Lee's guns beyond the Red Bud; yet they were not able to fire a musket in return until their own defeated comrades had passed to the rear. Cruel as the situation was, the 114th marched steadily forward nearly two hundred yards in front of the forest; then, finding himself quite alone and unsupported, confronted by the line of battle of the enemy at the skirt of the timber opposite, Per Lee made his men lie down without other cover than the high grass, and there, loading on their backs and at every moment

losing heavily, without yielding an inch, they held off the enemy until support came.[22]

A soldier from the 114th wrote how he and his comrades were "obliged to stand motionless for ten minutes, fearing to deliver our fire lest we should kill our own men of the Second Division, who were rapidly trying to get to our rear. Standing thus exposed, we lost many men before we had fired a shot."[23]

James Fitts from New York remembered the terror of that day:

> There in that horrible slaughter-pen, for one long hour our regiment held the place that had been given it. For one long hour there was an incessant cross-fire of musketry between those opposing lines, as fast as the men could load and fire. There was no concealment, no shelter; the ground was open, the position of each well understood; our business simply to withstand the Rebel advance, punishing him to our utmost, and receiving his blows as long as they could be endured.
>
> On your right and left, men go down while you are commending their good fighting, and urging them to keep up to the work; they fall in front of you till you find yourself in the ranks, instead of behind them—some lapsing heavily to the ground, stricken with instant death, and others settling slowly down with grievous wounds, and limping or crawling back as best they may. It is a scene of wild confusion, replete with horrors and ringing with unearthly cries and noises.[24]

While the Nineteenth Corps was being battered the Sixth Corps continued to advance, which only widened the gap between them and gave Early exactly the opening he needed to counterattack. Brigadier General Cullen Battle's brigade of Rodes' division launched a ferocious attack and "swept through the woods, driving the enemy before it, while Evans' brigade was rallied and brought back to the charge." It was here that General Rodes was killed by shrapnel.[25]

In his official report, General Ricketts wrote about what happened in the gap between the two Federal corps:

> The enemy discovering this fact, hurled a large body of men toward the interval and threatened to take my right in flank. Col. Keifer at once caused the One hundred and thirty-eighth and Sixty-seventh Pennsylvania Volunteers and One hundred and tenth Ohio Regiment to break their connection with the right of the remainder of his brigade and move toward the advancing columns of the enemy. Those three regiments most gallantly met the overwhelming masses of the enemy and held them in check.[26]

Both Sheridan and Wright saw Rodes' attack and acted quickly to prevent a disaster. Gen. David Russell's division, which had been the reserve, was sent forward. Two brigades commanded by Lieutenant-Colonel Edward Campbell and Colonel Oliver Edwards advanced and hit Battle's Confederates head-on, stalling their attack and pushing them back to the rest of Rodes' division at the edge of the woods. General Russell was mortally wounded leading this counterattack. Brigadier General Emory Upton then brought in his brigade on

Edwards' right and hit the Confederate flank, breaking up their ranks and driving them back into the woods. Upton was wounded in the leg but soon rejoined his troops on a stretcher. Russell's division then pulled back out of range to regroup.[27]

During the desperate fighting Sheridan moved back and forth across his lines encouraging the men. As James Franklin Fitts described:

> Wherever the fight was most furious, there was Sheridan, impetuous, confident, irresistible. He flashed like a meteor at noonday up and down the line of the Sixth Corps, bursting out into quick, energetic appeals as the men recognized him, and half suspended their firing to give "three cheers for Phil Sheridan.
> "Hold this line, men—only hold it an hour longer," he exclaimed to one of the regiments, "and the day is ours! Crook is getting in on the right—you'll hear from him soon—and the cavalry will finish them. Only hold this line and give them the devil a little longer!"[28]

The battle that had looked so promising for Sheridan when Wilson crossed the Opequon had become a bloody stalemate by early afternoon. On the Sixth Corps' line, Upton's charge had pushed Rodes' men back into the woods and the Nineteenth Corps and Gordon's troops had battled each other to a standstill. Sheridan had suffered high losses and had just barely avoided defeat. Now about all his troops could do was to try to hold their current positions and wait for help from Crook or the cavalry. "Along the entire front each side clung to its own positions, too exhausted or too cautious to advance, and too obstinate to recede."[29]

On the other side of the field Jubal Early was feeling very good. His outnumbered army had withstood the Federal attacks and inflicted heavy losses, but he also recognized that he faced a still formidable opponent. He wrote that

> a splendid victory had been gained. The ground in front was strewn with the enemy's dead and wounded, and some prisoners had been taken. But on our side Major General Rodes had been killed, in the very moment of triumph, while conducting the attack of his division with great gallantry and skill, and this was a heavy blow to me.... Had I then had a fresh body of troops to push our victory, the day would have been ours.... Wharton's division and King's artillery had not yet arrived, and Imboden's cavalry under Colonel Smith, and McCausland's under Col. Ferguson, were watching the enemy's cavalry on the left, on the Martinsburg road and the Opequon. The enemy had a fresh corps which had not been engaged, and there remained his heavy force of cavalry. Our lines were now formed across from Abraham's Creek to Red Bud, and were very attenuated. The enemy was still to be seen in front in formidable force, and away to our right, across Abraham's Creek, at the junction of the Front Royal and Millwood roads, he had massed a division of cavalry with some artillery, overlapping us at least a mile, while the country was open between this force and the Valley Pike, and the Cedar Creek Pike back of the latter; which roads furnished my only means of retreat in the event of disaster.[30]

During the morning and early afternoon while the infantry of both armies were forming their ranks and then killing each other, their cavalry was also busy. To the south after clearing the way for the infantry to cross the Opequon, General Wilson's division made several attacks against Ramseur's men and drove them back a short distance before making way for the Sixth Corps. After the fighting began, Wilson remained on the left of the Federal line to guard against a flank attack from Confederate cavalry and look for any opportunity to attack Early's right.[31]

On the other end of the lines, north of Winchester, Merritt and Averell brought their divisions forward against the far left of Early's line. "The battle was fought along the Martinsburg pike, the enemy being flanked or driven from one position to another until all the brigades of Merritt's and Averell's divisions, which had been converging toward a common point, came together about a mile out of Winchester."[32]

Averell brought his men over the Opequon about 5:00 A.M. and engaged the enemy cavalry, which was slowly pushed back to Bunker Hill to make a "determined stand" until being forced to retreat down the Pike toward Stephenson's Depot.[33]

On Averell's left, Merritt, with brigades commanded by Custer, Brig. Gen. Thomas C. Devin and Lowell, moved forward between Averell and the Federal infantry. After pushing McCausland back, Merritt ran into Wharton's infantry, who held the Federal cavalry in check until Early ordered them to withdraw to cover his left flank during the morning infantry battle. Merritt then continued south until he joined with Averell's troopers near Stephenson's Depot.[34]

General Torbert reported that both divisions advanced toward Winchester along the Valley Pike with Averell on the right and Merritt of the left. "We were now about four miles from Winchester; both divisions advanced rapidly, driving the enemy's cavalry pell-mell before them, on and behind their infantry...."[35]

A cavalry trooper from Michigan who took part in the fighting later wrote:

> Moving on over an open country, where the forces of both contending armies were exposed to view in one grand panorama, the divisions of Lomax and Fitzhugh Lee were discovered massed in an open pine wood on the Martinsburg pike, about three miles from Winchester. From the woods they made a formidable charge, driving back our line of skirmishers, but Custer's Michiganders dashed upon them with the sabre, routed them, and captured many prisoners. Dislodging the rebel cavalry from the woods, it struck out in full retreat for the heights west of Winchester, and the chase was on. A stand was made about three-quarters of a mile from the woods, but a sabre charge again put them on the run and they did not stop again until safe behind their infantry lines.[36]

General Breckinridge informed Early that the Federal cavalry was advancing toward Winchester from Stephenson's Depot. Early then ordered one of Breckinridge's brigades "to the left on that road, and directed General Fitz Lee to take charge of all the cavalry on that flank (my left) and check the enemy's cavalry, and moved the other two brigades of Breckinridge's division toward the right...."[37] During the fighting near Stephenson's Depot, Fitzhugh Lee was wounded and unable to continue in command.

15. The Battle of Winchester

While both armies were trying to regroup during the early afternoon:

> Sheridan made up his mind that it would be better to give up his original plan of putting in Crook on the left to cut off Early's retreat by moving against the valley turnpike near Newtown, and instead of this to use Crook and the cavalry on the Red Bud line against Early's left. The time needed for this movement caused a comparative lull in the battle of about two hours. It was not so much that the battle died away, for the fire of artillery and even of musketry was still kept up, as that neither side moved in force against the other.[38]

Crook marched his men behind the Federal lines to the far right where he divided his two divisions. Colonel Thoburn's First Division was on the left, on the right flank of the Nineteenth Corps and opposite the far left of the enemy. Colonel Duval's Second Division was posted even farther to the right so they could swing around the left flank of the enemy. Gordon's troops were on the left of the Confederate line that Crook had now flanked. Breckinridge had formed his men at a right angle to Gordon, making an L-shaped formation.[39]

The Federal forces were now all in place and the battle resumed in earnest.

> As soon as Crook was fairly across the Red Bud, his movement silenced the battery on the left bank that had been enfilading Emory's line, and this served to tell Emory that Crook was in place and at work. Averell and Merritt could be plainly seen surging up the valley road far in Gordon's left and rear, furiously driving before them the main body of Fitzhugh Lee's cavalry. About four o'clock the cheers of Duval's men beyond the Red Bud served as the signal for Thoburn, and now as Crook moved forward, sweeping everything before him, from right to left the whole army responded to the impulse. To meet Thoburn, Breckinridge placed Wharton in position at right angles with Gordon and with the valley road. Duval, having easily driven before him everything on the left bank of the Red Bud, waded through the marsh on his left, crossed the run, and united with Thoburn. Then Crook, with a sudden and irregular but curiously effective half-wheel to the left, fell vigorously upon Gordon, and Torbert coming on with great impetuosity at the same instant, the weight was heavier than the attenuated lines of Breckinridge and Gordon could bear.[40]

It was now late afternoon and as Crook's men advanced on the right, Sheridan launched the rest of his army in an all-out attack. "Crook's success began the moment he started to turn the left flank of the enemy line.... Both Emory and Wright took up the fight as ordered." Soon Early's men were being assailed from front and flank at the same time.[41]

Few commanding generals spent much time on the front lines during a battle, but Sheridan was everywhere, urging the men forward, accompanied only by an orderly who carried his personal battle flag, a small red and white banner with the two stars of a major general.[42] One soldier remembered:

> At length we, of the Sixth corps, heard rapid firing away on the right of the forest. All was attention. Every man stood to his arms ready to advance. Sheridan came to our part of the line. His face all aglow with excitement, the

perspiration rolling down his forehead, his famous black steed spotted with white foam, a single orderly at his back. He rode straight to General Getty, exclaiming, "General, I have put Torbert on the right, and told him to give 'em h—l, and he is doing it. Crook, too, is on the right and giving it to them. Press them, General, they'll run!" and then, using one of those phrases sometimes employed in the army to give additional force to language, he shouted again, *"Press them, General, I know they'll run!"* And then the shout that went up from the men drowned all the other noise of the battle.[43]

One man from Maine felt that "It was all pleasure—this final charge—laying aside the sad scenes around us. We first passed over the field where Grover had retreated; the rebel dead here were very few, and there were fewer still of their wounded. The Union dead and severely wounded from Grover's and Crook's commands were very many...."[44]

Early wrote later that the cavalry attack on the left "was handsomely repulsed. But many of the men on our front line, hearing the fire in the rear, and thinking they were flanked and about to be cut off, commenced falling back, thus producing great confusion."[45]

But it was the Federal cavalry that provided the final blow that finished off the Confederates, Colonel Joseph W. Keifer later wrote:

> Torbert reached the left flank of the Confederate infantry at the moment it was hard pressed by the advancing troops of Wright and Crook. Our cavalry, in deep column, with sabres drawn, charged over the Confederate left, and the battle was won. This charge was the most stirring and picturesque of the war. The sun was setting, but could be seen through the church spires of the city. Its rays glistening upon the drawn sabres of the thousands of mounted warriors made a picture in real war, rarely witnessed.[46]

Sheridan later wrote, "The ground which Breckinridge was holding was open, and offered an opportunity such as seldom had been presented during the war for a mounted attack, and Torbert was not slow to take advantage of it." Merritt's division attacked Breckinridge's infantry and broke the left of the Confederate line, while at about the same time Averell's troopers were coming in from the rear.[47]

Confederate Brigadier General Bryan Grimes tried to keep his troops from running in the face of the advancing Federal troops:

> Upon coming into the open field, I perceived everything to be in the most inextricable confusion—horses dashing over the field, cannon being run to the rear at the top of the horses speed, men leaving their command, and scattering in confusion. My men seeing this state of things began also to show symptoms of alarm, which I in a great measure checked, threatening to blow the brains out of the first man who left ranks, and succeeded in quieting them down and keeping them under control. Then directed my attention to arresting the flight of others, and many a fellow felt the full weight of my best blows from my sword.[48]

General Gordon remembered that "The pursuit was pressed far into the twilight, and only ended when night came and dropped her protecting curtains around us. Drearily and silently, with burdened brains and aching hearts, leaving our dead and many of the wounded behind us, we rode hour after hour...."[49]

Despite the heavy casualties, the Union troops were elated. E. M. Haynes from Vermont said:

Union Major General Alfred T.A. Torbert (Library of Congress.)

> It was not a retreat, but a helpless rout, with our men pursuing and shouting with an impetuosity and vigor that would have been impossible to restrain. Infantry, cavalry and artillery vied in the speed of pursuit, and every man felt that he was a victor. The combined and harmonious movement of all arms of the service, struggling for this achievement through the storm of death that howled around them, without faltering, was a sight for a painter. But when the troops beheld the yielding lines of the rebels, saw their battalions dissolve in their fire, rolling up in fierce enveloping waves, the certainty of victory now impelling them onward, the scene was grand beyond description.[50]

Captain Elisha Hunt Rhodes of the 2nd Rhode Island expressed in a letter home the feelings of many of the veterans:

> After the fight the men were wild with joy. I could have knelt and kissed the folds of the old flag that waved in triumph. We captured several Rebel flags which were displayed along the front of our line. I cried and shouted in my excitement and never felt so good before in my life. I have been in a good many battles but never in such a victory as this. "Hurrah for Sheridan!"[51]

Sheridan had moved out just as he had promised and that night Grant received a triumphant telegram:

> I have the honor to report that I attacked the forces of General Early on the Berryville pike at the crossing of Opequon Creek, and after a most stubborn and sanguinary engagement, which lasted from early in the morning until 5 o'clock in the evening, completely defeated him, and, driving him through Winchester, captured about 2,500 prisoners, 5 pieces of artillery, 9 army flags, and most of their wounded. The rebel General Rodes and General Gordon were killed, and three other general officers wounded. Most of the

> enemy's wounded and all their killed fell into our hands. Our losses are severe, among them General D. A. Russell, commanding division in the Sixth Corps, who was killed by a cannon-ball. Generals Upton, McIntosh, and Chapman are wounded. I cannot yet tell our losses. The conduct of the officers and men was most superb. They charged and carried every position taken up by the rebels from Opequon Creek to Winchester. The enemy were strong in number and very obstinate in their fighting....[52]

It should be noted that Sheridan's message incorrectly reported that General Gordon was killed.

Early's take on the battle and how it was fought was, naturally, quite different from that of his opponent:

> This battle, beginning with the skirmishing in Ramseur's front, had lasted from daylight until dark, and at the close of it we had been forced back two miles, after having repulsed the enemy's first attack with great slaughter to him, and subsequently contested every inch of ground with unsurpassed obstinacy. We deserved the victory, and would have had it, but for the enemy's immense superiority in cavalry, which alone gave it to him.
>
> A skillful and energetic commander of the enemy's forces would have crushed Ramseur before any assistance could have reached him, and thus ensured the destruction of my whole force; and, later in the day, when the battle had turned against us, with the immense superiority in cavalry which Sheridan had, and the advantage of the open country, would have destroyed my whole force and captured everything I had. As it was, considering the immense disparity in numbers and equipment, the enemy had very little to boast of. I had lost a few pieces of artillery and some very valuable officers and men, but the main part of my force, and all my trains had been saved, and the enemy's loss in killed and wounded was far greater than mine. When I look back to this battle, I can attribute my escape from utter annihilation to the incapacity of my opponent.[53]

After the battle, messages of congratulation for Sheridan poured in. From President Lincoln on the 20th: "Have just heard of your great victory. God Bless you all, officers and men. Strongly inclined to come up and see you."[54]

From Secretary of War Stanton:

> Please accept for yourself and your gallant army the thanks of the President and this Department for your great battle and brilliant victory of yesterday.
>
> The President has appointed you a brigadier-general in the Regular Army, and you have been assigned to the permanent command of the Middle Division. One hundred guns were fired here at noon to-day in honor of your victory.[55]

From General Grant:

> I congratulate you and the army serving under you for the great victory just achieved. It has been most opportune in point of time and effect. It will open again to the Government and to the public the very important line of road from Baltimore to the Ohio, and also the Chesapeake canal. Better still, it wipes out much of the stain upon our arms by previous disasters in that locality. May your good work continue is now the prayer of all loyal men.[56]

Sheridan's "good work" came with a high price tag for both armies. In his official report, Sheridan counted casualties of 697 killed, 3,983 wounded, and 338 missing, for a total of 5,018.[57] Early reported infantry and artillery losses of 226 killed, 1,567 wounded, and 1,818 missing, for a total of 3,611. Confederate cavalry losses for the month of September were reported separately, increasing Early's total casualties for the battle to nearly 4,000.[58] Although the Federal casualties were numerically larger, if the sizes of the armies are taken into account, Early actually lost a higher percentage of his men, a loss the Confederates could ill afford.

Despite suffering high casualties, the Federal army had won a major battle in the Shenandoah Valley against some of the best troops the Confederacy could put into the field. After talking to some Confederate prisoners, a Union officer reported, "They were much depressed in spirits, for their defeat was a great surprise to them."[59]

16. The Battle of Fisher's Hill

After the disaster at Winchester, the disorganized Confederates fled south about thirty miles to the fortified positions on Fisher's Hill. Sheridan wrote, "The enemy having kept up his retreat at night, presented no opposition whatever until the cavalry discovered him posted at Fisher's Hill, on the first defensive line where he could hope to make any serious resistance."[1]

After moving to Fisher's Hill on the 20th, Early's troops occupied the old defensive positions,

> Wharton's division being on the right, then Gordon's, Ramseur's and Rodes', in the order in which they are mentioned. Fitz Lee's cavalry, now under Brigadier General Wickham, was sent up the Luray Valley to a narrow pass at Millford, to try and hold that valley against the enemy's cavalry. General Ramseur was transferred to the command of Rodes' division, and Brigadier General Pegram, who had reported for duty about the 1st of August, and been in command of his brigade since that time, was left in command of the division previously commanded by Ramseur. My infantry was not able to occupy the whole line at Fisher's Hill, notwithstanding it was extended out in an attenuated line, with considerable intervals. The greater part of Lomax's cavalry was therefore dismounted, and placed on Ramseur's left, near Little North Mountain, but the line could not then be fully occupied.[2]

The Confederate positions at Fisher's Hill had been originally selected and fortified by "Stonewall" Jackson. A series of hills provided a natural defensive barrier between Massanutten Mountain and the North Mountains where the Valley narrows to less than four miles wide. The eastern side and part of the front is protected by the north fork of the Shenandoah River. The only way to attack the position was from the west over broken terrain, filled with large rocks, steep ravines and thickly wooded areas. Fisher's Hill was the strongest defensive position in the Valley and if the center and left flank were properly manned, it was nearly impregnable. Early recognized that there was the possibility of a cavalry attack through the Luray Valley, but Brigadier General William Wickham's cavalry was to protect this back door to the position.[3]

Although his army had been seriously weakened by the defeat at Winchester, Early was too tough a fighter to abandon the Valley to Sheridan's control without putting up more of a fight. The contest would be renewed:

> This was the only position in the whole Valley where a defensive line could be taken against an enemy moving up the Valley, and it had several weak points. To have retired beyond this point would have rendered it necessary for me to fall back to some of the gaps of the Blue Ridge, at the upper part of the Valley, and I determined therefore to make a show of a stand here, with the hope that the enemy would be deterred from attacking me in this position, as had been the case in August.[4]

Sheridan was already familiar with the strength of the defenses at Fisher's Hill. "A reconnaissance made pending these movements convinced me that the enemy's position at Fisher's Hill was so strong that a direct assault would entail unnecessary destruction of life, and, besides, be of doubtful result."[5]

Not one to waste time in getting at the enemy, Sheridan quickly formulated a plan of attack to use his advantage in manpower against the only real weakness of Early's position:

> In consequence of the enemy's being so well protected from a direct assault, I resolved on the night of the 20th to use again a turning-column against his left, as had been done on the 19th at the Opequon. To this end I resolved to move Crook, unperceived if possible, over to the eastern face of Little North Mountain, whence he could strike the left and rear of the Confederate line, and as he broke it up, I could support him by a left half-wheel of my whole line of battle. The execution of this plan would require perfect secrecy, however, for the enemy from his signal-station on Three Top could plainly see every movement of our troops in daylight. Hence, to escape such observation, I marched Crook during the night of the 20th into some heavy timber north of Cedar Creek, where he lay concealed all day the 21st.[6]

In front of the main Confederate lines on Fisher's Hill was a smaller hill defended by skirmishers behind barricades. This hill obstructed the view of much of the Confederate position from the Federal lines and had to be captured so that Sheridan could see what he was facing before launching the attack. Three regiments from the Sixth Corps moved up the hill that afternoon but were repulsed until reinforced by the First Brigade of the Second Division, commanded by Colonel J. M. Warner. This force drove the defenders back and, although it was a tough little fight, the advantages of controlling this hill were obvious. General Wright reported, "This movement was of the greatest importance to the operations of the next day, as it gave us a view of the enemy's line and afforded excellent positions for artillery...."[7]

During the night of the 21st while Early's men tried to rest or improve their fortifications, the Federal troops of the Sixth and Nineteenth Corps were busy moving closer to Fisher's Hill and digging in on the hill they had captured that day. Crook's men spent the day camped under cover in the woods north of Cedar Creek so that the Confederate lookouts wouldn't discover their location. Once it was dark, they quietly moved farther to the right toward Little North Mountain, where they were to stay hidden until launching the attack. It took all night, but they were able to make the move unnoticed. By dawn they took up position on Early's left, with the Confederates having no idea they were already flanked.[8]

There was little action along the lines at Fisher's Hill during the morning of the 22nd, some skirmishing and artillery fire. The Confederates were expecting Sheridan to launch a frontal assault, which they had every confidence of defeating. Unknown to them, however, Crook was slowly working his corps into position to launch the surprise attack on their left. Colonel Thoburn reported:

> About 2 o'clock in the afternoon we were moved, under the supervision of General Crook, through woods and ravines, so as to be unobserved by the enemy, until we gained a position on the eastern slope of the Little North Mountain, upon the left of the enemy's line of works. The First Division moved by the right flank in two lines and to the left of the Second Division—Colonel Wells' brigade composing the first line and Colonel Harris' the second; our lines being at right angles to that of the enemy, which extended through the open field up the mountain slope to the edge of the woods, under the cover of which our troops were moving.[9]

While Crook was moving around the Confederate left, Sheridan made a move to keep their attention focused on the front lines and hopefully not notice Crook until it was too late:

> Ricketts's division was pushed out until it confronted the left of the enemy's infantry, the rest of the Sixth Corps extending from Ricketts's left to the Manassas Gap railroad, while the Nineteenth Corps filled in the space between the left of the Sixth and the North Fork of the Shenandoah.
> When Ricketts moved out on this new line, in conjunction with Averell's cavalry on his right, the enemy surmising, from information secured from his signal-station, no doubt, that my attack was to be made from Ricketts's front, prepared for it there....[10]

It was now late in the afternoon. The Confederates on Fisher's Hill probably felt that if Sheridan were going to attack, he would have by then and they must have been feeling pretty safe in their strong fortifications. It was then that Crook launched his attack. Colonel Thoburn's men moved forward:

> When the left of my line had nearly passed the left of the enemy's line of works the order was given "by the left flank," and the whole command moved in two lines down the slope to the edge of the woods. A few minutes before this the enemy had discovered our position and had commenced shelling us from their

16. *The Battle of Fisher's Hill* 163

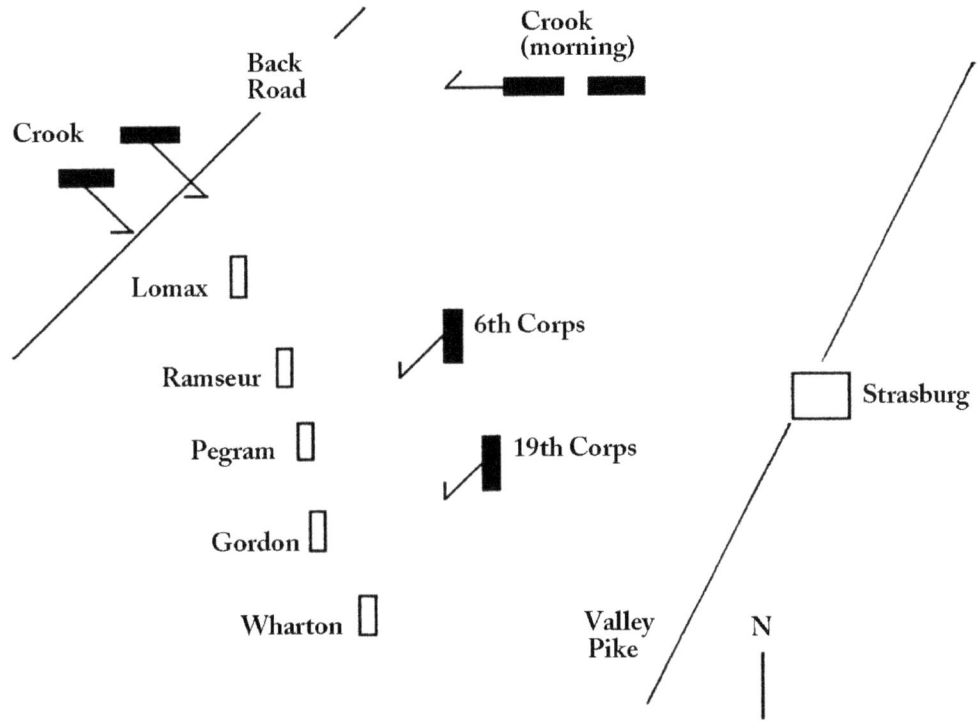

Battle of Fisher's Hill

works on the opposite hill. The command emerged from the woods yelling and firing, and found the enemy running from their works in disorder.[11]

The Eighth Corps had hit the Confederates at the perfect spot. Major General Lunsford Lomax's dismounted cavalry held that portion of the Confederate line and when the Federals descended on their flank and rear, few of them hesitated to quickly leave their positions and run for their lives. Colonel Thomas M. Harris, commanding the Third Brigade, reported:

> The charge was made in gallant style, accompanied by deafening cheers and a rapid discharge of musketry at the onset. So sudden, unexpected, and demonstrative was this charge, and so fairly directed against the enemy's flank, that he was at once stricken with terror, and that portion of his infantry stationed on his left and near to us fled at the first discharge of arms and cheer from our men, and by their confused and rapid flight carried panic and consternation with them as they went.[12]

A colonel in Crook's command and future president of the United States, Rutherford B. Hayes, recalled, "We just yelled as we came down at the top of our voices and the enemy were taken with a panic and fled like sheep. We got every gun they had."[13]

As Crook's men were driving in from the Confederate left flank, Rickett's division attacked from the front, quickly followed by the rest of the Sixth and the Nineteenth corps. A Union officer recalled, "So rapidly did the men dash up the hill that the enemy had no time to reload their pieces, after the first discharge, before our men were upon them, and receiving a heavy fire they broke and fled in utter confusion...."[14]

One artilleryman with a view of the battle wrote:

> We could see the whole line as it went up the slope. The flanking attack of the Eighth Corps on the Rebel left, which was most gallantly made under great difficulties, contributed largely to the demoralization of the enemy, but nothing could dim the splendor of the assault of the Sixth and Nineteenth Corps. The ground in front of the Rebel works was so steep in many places that it amounted to a natural scarp, and from where we were we could plainly see the infantry digging their bayonets into the ground to climb up by.[15]

A Union soldier from Maine remembered the charge. "Again and again the orders were shouted, 'Forward!' 'Go on!' 'Don't stop!' and still on we climbed, many men actually crawling up the steep hill-side on their hands and knees."[16]

James Fitts wrote a colorful account of what he saw that afternoon:

> "There go the infantry!" sang out one of the men. "There they go—there they go!"
>
> I looked and saw, with beating heart, and with a soldier's instant desire to be among his comrades in action, the compact lines of the Nineteenth and Sixth, moving up against the hill, with arms at a right-shoulder-shift gleaming in the setting sun. The left of the line rested on Strasburg; its right was thrown around the hill beyond my range of sight; and steadily, yet swiftly, it went up, like a wall of gleaming steel—up, up, and right on! It never staggered nor slacked, although from points half way down the hill, and from all the long line of its crest, angry spits of flame flashed in its face, and volleys of lead were hurled down upon it. Our artillery still kept up its tremendous diapason, and shot and shell now flew shrieking and humming over the heads of the advancing army, while shell from the Confederates burst along the line, and grape and bullets came thickly down, smiting their victims here and there. But on, still on and right on went that magnificent line, at least fifteen thousand strong as I saw it, rising higher and higher, like a great blue wave, sometimes swallowed in places by the clumps of trees and hollows into which it penetrated, and again emerging into the light of sunset—but on, on—sternly and unfalteringly on![17]

As at Winchester, the Federal columns going up the slope found Sheridan dashing across their front, orderly and battle flag at his heels. Sheridan was everywhere yelling and cursing, urging the men forward. As the Vermont Brigade was making its way up the hill and after the fleeing enemy, they found unexpected company in their midst:

> General Sheridan with long black streamers waving from his hat joined our own division, exclaiming, "Run boys, run! Don't wait to form! Don't let

'em stop!" and when some answered, "we can't run, we're tired out," his reply was perhaps unmilitary but certainly under the circumstances judicious, "If you can't run, then holler!" and thus the wild pursuit was continued....[18]

Up on top of Fisher's Hill the Confederates barely knew what had hit them. Early made every effort to put up a fight, but it was hopeless:

> Ramseur made an attempt to meet this movement by throwing his brigades successively into line to the left, and Wharton's division was sent for from the right, but it did not arrive. Pegram's brigades were also thrown into line in the same manner as Ramseur's, but the movement produced some disorder in both divisions, and as soon as it was observed by the enemy, he advanced along his whole line, and the mischief could not be remedied. After a very brief contest, my whole force retired in considerable confusion....[19]

Soldiers of the Army of Northern Virginia had never been beaten so badly so quickly. Sheridan felt that they collapsed because of "an indescribable panic, precipitated doubtless by fears of being caught and captured in the pocket formed by Tumbling Run and the North Fork of the Shenandoah River."[20]

The Southern army fled up the Valley Pike in complete disorder, closely pursued by the Union infantry. General Wright reported:

> Nothing but night saved his army from utter annihilation. Some of the positions assaulted by the corps were almost unassailable, the approaches being difficult to climb, and the works covered by abatis of no mean strength. Yet our men, flushed with the victory of the Opequon, disregarding all obstacles, and under a heavy fire of artillery and infantry, moved gallantly forward, carried the works, and pursued the enemy till after dark....[21]

The battle turned into a footrace with the Confederates flying down the Valley Pike as fast as they could run and the exhausted but triumphant Union infantry chasing them in the darkness. A small rear guard with two cannon tried to delay the pursuing Federals but was quickly overwhelmed, only adding to the number of captured guns. The infantry was moving so quickly that it took a few hours for Devin's cavalry to catch up to the frontrunners. "The chase was then taken up by Devin's brigade as soon as it could be passed to the front, and continued till after daylight the next morning, but the delays incident to a night pursuit made it impossible for Devin to do more than pick up stragglers."[22]

That night, Sheridan sent a message announcing another victory to Grant:

> I have the honor to report that I achieved a most signal victory over the army of General Early at Fisher's Hill to-day. I found the rebel army posted with its right resting on the North Fork of the Shenandoah, and extending across the Strasburg valley westward to North Mountain, occupying a position which appeared almost impregnable. After a great deal of maneuvering during the day, General Crook's command was transferred to the extreme right of the line on North Mountain and he furiously attacked the left of the enemy's line, carrying everything before him. While Crook was driving the enemy in the greatest confusion and sweeping down behind their breast-works, the Sixth

and Nineteenth Army Corps attacked the rebel works in front, and the whole rebel army appeared to be broken up. They fled in the utmost confusion. Sixteen pieces of artillery were captured; also a great many caissons, artillery horses, &c. I am to-night pushing on down the Valley.... The First and Third Cavalry Divisions went down Luray Valley to-day, and if they push on vigorously to the main valley, the result of this day's engagement will be still more signal.[23]

The next day Early reported the outcome of the battle to Lee:

> Late yesterday the enemy attacked my position at Fisher's Hill and succeeded in driving back the left of my line, which was defended by the cavalry, and throwing a force into the rear of the left of my infantry line, when the whole of the troops gave way in a panic and could not be rallied. This resulted in a loss of twelve pieces of artillery, though my loss in men is not large. I am falling back to New Market, and shall endeavor to check the enemy if he advances. Kershaw's division had better be sent to my aid, through Swift Run gap, at once.[24]

General Wright's official report contained an enthusiastic opinion of the fight at Fisher's Hill. "The annals of the war present, perhaps, no more glorious victory than this. The enemy's lines, chosen in an almost impregnable position, and fortified with much care, had been most gallantly carried by assault ... with an absurdly small loss on our part."[25]

In a message to Grant, Sheridan gave a shorter and more direct assessment: "I do not think that there ever was an army so badly routed."[26]

Unlike most Civil War battles, the casualties for both sides were relatively low. Sheridan's official report listed only 52 men killed, 457 wounded and 19 missing for a total of 528 casualties.[27] Early admitted to 30 killed, 210 wounded and 995 missing for a total of 1,235.[28] The obvious reason for the small number of killed and wounded was that the quick exit of the Confederates kept the bloodletting to a minimum.

Although Sheridan had achieved a great victory at very low cost, he was far from satisfied with the final results:

> Our success was very great, yet I had anticipated results still more pregnant. Indeed, I had high hopes of capturing almost the whole of Early's army before it reached New Market, and with this object in view, during the manoeuvres of the 21st I had sent Torbert up the Luray Valley with Wilson's division and two of Merritt's brigades, in the expectation that he would drive Wickham out of the Luray Pass by Early's right, and by crossing the Massanutten Mountain near New Market, gain his rear.[29]

Sheridan received no news from Torbert on the day of the battle, so there was every reason to believe that Early's fleeing army would be trapped between the advancing infantry and the waiting cavalry. In fact, Torbert made only a halfhearted attempt to get by Wickham at Milford, then turned around and went back to Front Royal. Sheridan was "astonished and chagrined on the morning of the 23rd, at Woodstock, to receive the intelligence that he had fallen back to Front Royal and Buckton ford. My disappointment was extreme...."[30]

16. The Battle of Fisher's Hill

In his memoirs, Sheridan stated:

> I have been unable to account satisfactorily for Torbert's failure. No doubt, Wickham's position near Milford was a strong one, but Torbert ought to have made a fight. Had he been defeated in this, his withdrawal then to await the result at Fisher's Hill would have been justified, but it does not appear that he made any serious effort at all to dislodge the Confederate cavalry....[31]

Colonel James H. Kidd from Michigan thought that

> Torbert made a fiasco of it. He allowed Wickham, who succeeded Fitzhugh Lee after the latter was wounded, with, at most, two small brigades, to hold him at bay and withdrew without making any fight to speak of. I remember very well how the Michigan brigade lay in a safe position in rear of the line listening to the firing and was not ordered in at all.[32]

Sheridan halted the army at Woodstock on the morning of the 23rd. The men had marched all night after the battle and needed rest and food. One New Yorker admitted, "To say that we were tired would not in any measure express our condition. We were exhausted with the hard and constant duties of the preceding four days."[33] Devin and Averell were to continue harassing the fleeing Confederates, but Averell and his men were nowhere to be found. It turned out that Averell had not joined in the pursuit and had actually spent the night in camp while the exhausted foot soldiers were following Early's men. It was almost noon when Sheridan saw Averell, "We had some hot words, but hoping that he would retrieve the mistake of the night before, I directed him to proceed to the front at once, and in conjunction with Devin close with the enemy."[34]

When Sheridan learned that Averell was going to withdraw because of a report that there was a large body of Confederates on his flank, Sheridan sent the following message:

> I do not want you to let the enemy bluff you or your command, and I want you to distinctly understand this note. I do not advise rashness, but I do desire resolution and actual fighting, with necessary casualties, before you retire. There must now be no backing or filling by you without a superior force of the enemy actually engaging you.[35]

One of Devin's troopers who spent most of the day after the battle chasing the disorganized Confederates recalled:

> At daybreak of the 23d the brigade had reached Woodstock, and without waiting for rest or breakfast moved on by Edinburg, picking up a number of stragglers and finding several burning wagons and one piece of artillery on the road. Continued the pursuit until arriving at the creek, about two miles north of Mount Jackson, where we found the bridge burning and a small force of the enemy to dispute over crossing. The Ninth New York, in a spirited dash, soon "ousted" them and we went on to within half a mile of Mount Jackson, where we found them inclined to make a stand. The Ninth and Sixth New York and First New York Dragoons continued skirmishing until 2 P.M.,

Union Brigadier General William W. Averell (Library of Congress).

when Averill [sic] came up with his division. After skirmishing for about two hours General Averill ordered the line to withdraw, and the brigade went into camp near the creek.[36]

Later that afternoon, Sheridan learned that despite his note Averell had withdrawn and gone into camp for the night. This was enough for Sheridan. He relieved Averell of his command, replacing him with Colonel William H Powell. On the 25th, Sheridan wrote to Grant informing him of the failure of the cavalry:

Torbert's cavalry overtook me this evening. Its operations in the Luray Valley, on which I calculated so much, were an entire failure. They were held at Milford by two small brigades of Fitz Lee's cavalry, and then fell back toward Front Royal until after they had learned of our success at Fisher's Hill…. The part that I expected the cavalry to accomplish at Fisher's Hill was a complete failure. I have relieved Averell from his command. Instead of following the enemy when he was broken at Fisher's Hill, so that there was not a cavalry organization left, he went into camp, and let me pursue the enemy for a distance of fifteen miles with infantry during the night.[37]

Averell had done good work on a number of occasions in the past, but with Sheridan came a new aggressive attitude and higher expectations than those of previous commanders in the Valley. He demanded action and accepted no excuses from those who hesitated.

General Torbert kept his command even though his unwillingness to force the issue with Wickham turned out to be far more costly than Averell's lack of aggressiveness. The failure of the Federal cavalry to carry out Sheridan's plan seems like a minor point when compared to the major victories at Winchester and Fisher's Hill. In fact, however, the goal of both battles was to trap and destroy Early's army. Sheridan was not looking to win a war of maneuver to force Early from the Valley, he wanted to hit hard and smash the enemy at every opportunity. The total destruction of Early's army was the goal. Even though the Confederates had been beaten twice, they were tough fighters and Early was as dedicated and tenacious as any soldier in either army. It would not be long before the poor performance of Sheridan's cavalry after Fisher's Hill would come back to haunt the Federal army.

What was left of Early's shattered army moved south along the Valley Pike, staying just ahead of the pursuing Federals. A tired and dejected Confederate from Georgia wrote that

> the retreat continued for about three days, until the army reached a point near Harrisonburg, where it quit the main pike and turned eastward toward Port Republic, where it took up a strong position at the foot of the Blue Ridge Mountains. The enemy continued to follow the pike and left off the pursuit. Here Early rested his army and reorganized his shattered forces. Though always brave and true, he was never a popular leader, even when victorious; but now no one had any confidence in him, and the spirit of his army was at a low ebb. For these misfortunes he blamed the army, while the soldiers blamed him.[38]

On September 25, Early sent Lee an account of the defeats at Winchester and Fisher's Hill:

> In the fight at Winchester I drove back the enemy's infantry, and would have defeated that, but his cavalry broke mine on the left flank, the latter making no stand, and I had to take a division to stop the progress of the former and save my trains, and during the fighting in the rear the enemy again advanced, and my troops fell back, thinking they were flanked. The enemy's immense superiority in cavalry and the inefficiency of the greater part of mine has been the cause of all my disasters. In the affair at Fisher's Hill the cavalry gave way, but it was flanked. This could have been remedied if the troops had remained steady, but a panic seized them at the idea of being flanked, and without being defeated they broke, many of them fleeing shamefully. The artillery was not captured by the enemy, but abandoned by the infantry.
> My troops are very much shattered, the men very much exhausted, and many of them without shoes.
> I deeply regret the present state of things, and I assure [you] everything in my power has been done to avert it. The enemy's force is very much larger than mine, being three or four to one.[39]

Sheridan's second victory in four days thrilled the people of the North. At last, a Federal army was having success in the Shenandoah Valley. After all the disappointment with the bloody offensive against Lee that seemed to produce nothing but casualties, the victories in the Valley and Sherman's capture of Atlanta provided hope that the war was being won after all. In just a few short days, the anguish of three years of defeat and humiliation suffered by the Federal armies in the Shenandoah Valley had been replaced with joy and optimism. It was not very often that Federal troops saw Confederate soldiers running away from them. Now Sheridan's army had routed some of the best men the South had to offer, not once but twice. A new feeling of confidence filled the men. They believed that with Phil Sheridan leading, victory was assured.[40]

17. The Burning and Tom's Brook

While Early's army was still retreating up the Valley, General Lee wrote to William Smith, the governor of Virginia, on the 24th. Knowing that he could not afford to lose the Valley to Federal control and unable to spare troops from his own army, Lee appealed for assistance in rebuilding Early's force using whatever manpower could be found. "General Early has again met with a reverse.... I have written to him to call to his aid all the local troops, and have thought that there may be some who are not within reach of the Confederate authorities. I hope you will do all in your power to increase his strength...."[1]

One of the many problems facing Jubal Early that summer was that Lee did not seem to understand the heavy odds he was facing in the Valley. In his report after Fisher's Hill, Early had informed Lee that Sheridan's army was vastly larger than his own but apparently Lee simply did not believe him. On September 27, General Lee sent Early a letter combining support, suggestions and some mild criticism. Coming from Lee, who was seldom critical of his subordinates, this was indeed an admonition:

> I very much regret the reverses that have occurred to the army in the Valley, but trust they can be remedied. The arrival of Kershaw will add greatly to your strength, and I have such confidence in the men and officers that I am sure all will unite in the defense of the country. It will require that every one should exert all his energies and strength to meet the emergency. One victory will put all things right. You must do all in your power to invigorate your army. Get back all absentees; maneuver so, if you can, as to keep the enemy in check until you can strike him with all your strength. As far as I can judge,

> at this distance, you have operated more with divisions than with your concentrated strength. Circumstances may have rendered it necessary, but such a course is to be avoided if possible. It will require the greatest watchfulness, the greatest promptness, and the most untiring energy on your part to arrest the progress of the enemy in his present tide of success. All the reserves in the Valley have been ordered to you.... I have given you all I can; you must use the resources you have so as to gain success. The enemy must be defeated, and I rely upon you to do it.... Set all your officers to work bravely and hopefully, and all will go well.... The men are all good and only require instructions and discipline. The enemy's force cannot be so greatly superior to yours. His effective infantry, I do not think, exceeds 12,000 men. We are obliged to fight against great odds. A kind Providence will yet overrule everything for our good.[2]

In other words, make do with what you have and hope for the best.

Early fled south to Port Republic and Waynesboro followed by the jubilant Federal army. George Stevens remembered:

> Our march had been a grand triumphal pursuit of a routed enemy. Never had we marched with such light hearts; and, though each day had found us pursuing rapidly from dawn till dark, the men seemed to endure the fatigue with wonderful patience. Our column, as it swept up the valley, was a spectacle of rare beauty. Never had we, in all our campaigns, seen anything to compare with the appearance of this victorious little army.[3]

Sheridan ended his march at Harrisonburg where the infantry rested for about a week, but the cavalry was kept busy harassing Early and destroying supplies. Merritt was sent to Port Republic as a diversion while Torbert took Wilson's division and Lowell's brigade on a raid to Staunton. Merritt ran into infantry at Port Republic and had to fall back while Torbert only partially destroyed a railroad bridge near Waynesboro before being forced out by a superior Confederate force, but did destroy a large quantity of supplies at Staunton.[4]

While the armies were inactive, Sheridan had to decide what action to take next. He was well aware that Grant still wanted what he had always wanted, to cut the railroads leading to Richmond and Petersburg. On the 26th Grant had telegraphed, "Your victories have created the greatest consternation. If you can possibly subsist your army to the front for a few days more, do it, and make a great effort to destroy the roads about Charlottesville and the canal wherever your cavalry can reach it."[5]

Sheridan saw too many difficulties in pursuing Grant's idea at this time. The main reason he didn't want to make a movement to Charlottesville was that it would entail reviving the Orange and Alexandria Railroad. "To protect this road against the raids of the numerous guerrilla bands that infested the region through which it passed, and to keep it in operation, would require a large force of infantry, and would also greatly reduce my cavalry...." In addition, he would have to leave behind another strong force to protect the Baltimore and Ohio from attack, not leaving enough fighting men in the army to pursue a campaign against Richmond.[6]

On October 1, Sheridan reported on his progress and made a proposal:

> I have devastated the Valley from Staunton down to Mount Crawford, and will continue. The destruction of mills, grain, forage, foundries, &c., is very great. The cavalry report to me that they have collected 3,000 head of cattle and sheep between Staunton and Mount Crawford. The difficulty of transporting this army through the mountain passes onto the railroad at Charlottesville is such that I regard it as impracticable, with my present means of transportation. The rebels have given up the Valley excepting Waynesborough, which has been occupied by them since my cavalry was there. I think that the best policy will be to let the burning of the crops of the Valley be the end of this campaign, and let some of this army go somewhere else.[7]

Sheridan's hesitation to cross the Blue Ridge to destroy the railroad was not because of apprehension about what Early might do, but because of food, or rather the lack of it. "I was satisfied, moreover, that my transportation could not supply me further than Harrisonburg, and if in penetrating the Blue Ridge I met with protracted resistance, a lack of supplies might compel me to abandon the attempt at a most inopportune time."[8]

This was a reasonable caution, considering the difficulty in transporting supplies for so many men and animals over the rough terrain, and the virtual guarantee that guerillas would be attacking the wagon trains at every opportunity. But what Sheridan suggested in place of what Grant wanted done was remarkable:

> I therefore advised that the Valley campaign be terminated north of Staunton, and I be permitted to return, carrying out on the way my original instructions for desolating the Shenandoah country so as to make it untenable for permanent occupation by the Confederates. I proposed to detach the bulk of my army when this work of destruction was completed, and send it by way of the Baltimore and Ohio railroad through Washington to the Petersburg line, believing that I could move it more rapidly by that route than by any other.[9]

The idea that the commander of an independent army would offer to dismantle it was truly remarkable and Grant had to seriously consider Sheridan's proposal. Sheridan pressed his case for several days:

> Considerable correspondence regarding the subject took place between us, throughout which I stoutly maintained that we should not risk, by what I held to be a false move, all that my army had gained. I being on the ground, General Grant left to me the final decision of the question, and I solved the first step by determining to withdraw down the valley at least as far as Strasburg, which movement was begun on the 6th of October.[10]

During the time Sheridan and Grant were deciding what the army would do next, an event occurred that only increased Sheridan's resolve to destroy as much of the traitorous Valley as possible. On October 3rd, one of Sheridan's favorite staff officers, Lieutenant Meigs, who had been so helpful when Sheridan first took command, was killed while riding in the countryside doing some surveying work. The facts of his death are murky. Either he ran across a band of Confederate cavalry on a scouting mission and was shot in a fair fight, or he was brutally murdered by bushwhackers without warning. Sheridan chose to believe the latter and issued orders for Custer (who had taken over the Third Cavalry Division when Wilson was sent to command Sherman's cavalry) to destroy all the homes, barns and other buildings in a five-mile radius. Sheridan relented after just a few buildings were burned and instead ordered that all the able-bodied men in the area should be taken as prisoners. It was the frequency of incidents such as this that put a brutal edge on the way the Federal soldiers would treat the Valley residents.[11]

On Thursday morning, October 6th, the Army of the Shenandoah started back to Cedar Creek. The army stretched across the entire Valley with the infantry moving along the Valley Pike and the cavalry as rear guard and on both wings. Custer's Third Division was on the far west moving along the Back Road, while Merritt's First Division occupied the west and center, behind the infantry, and Powell's Second Division was on the east. Every effort was made to see that nothing was left that might be of use to the Confederacy.[12]

Even before the destruction started in earnest, a Confederate soldier wrote to his wife, "The enemy have desolated this country burnt nearly all the ground & barns. It is horrible. I have never seen anything to equal it. I do not know what will become of the people. They must suffer. We can't subsist in this Valley this winter."[13]

The people of the Shenandoah Valley had never before seen destruction on this scale. One man reported:

> The cavalry swept across the whole breadth of the valley of the Shenandoah from the Blue Ridge to the Eastern slope of the Allegheny. The order to transform the valley into a barren waste and leave nothing which would tempt the enemy to return was carried out with unsparing severity. Before the army was a fertile region filled with the stores of an abundant harvest just gathered; behind was a devastated region.[14]

Most of Sheridan's men saw the destruction simply as a means to an end, the end of the war. Union Private Wilbur Fisk wrote:

> A great many of the inhabitants have declared their intention of going North to escape the rigors of war which have become almost intolerable. The Government has offered to furnish transportation, and many families are packing up to avail themselves of the offer. Many others are heartily praying for peace, let it come in what way it will. They have tasted the bitter fruit of secession, and have had enough of it. They find that it does not satisfy, that it was a poor remedy for their imaginary grievances. They see the grim determination of the North and they begin to feel that to hold out longer is to fight against inevitable destiny.[15]

To his wife, Colonel Lowell wrote, "Though if it will help end bushwhacking, I approve it, and I would cheerfully assist in making this whole Valley a desert from Staunton northward,—for that would have, I am sure, an important effect on the campaign of the Spring...."[16]

But some doubted the wisdom or results that would be derived from the wholesale destruction. A chaplain in the 5th New York Cavalry felt that the anguish the men were causing would have a demoralizing effect on them and it remained to be seen how it would affect the Valley residents. "It seems to me that the ultimate result of such a burning on our cause, must be very doubtful. It will exasperate some, inciting them to deeds of greater barbarity, while it will intimidate others, but it is difficult to determine now, where will be the preponderance."[17]

From one side of the Valley to the other, day and night, the burning went on. "Nobody who was one of that army will ever forget the scenes of our retreat. By day the smoke obscured the sun; by night a lurid sky reflected the glare of burning barns and stacks of grain and hay for twice twenty-four hours."[18]

Following Sheridan's men down the Valley, Henry Kyd Douglas saw "great columns of smoke which almost shut out the sun by day…" and "mothers and maidens tearing their hair and shrieking to Heaven in their fright and despair, and little children, voiceless and tearless in their pitiable terror."[19]

While burning a flour mill in Port Republic, Colonel Kidd of the Michigan Brigade witnessed a scene that "is burned into my memory." The flames from the mill had begun to spread to nearby homes and, although he ordered his men to fight the fire, some homes were lost. "Women with children in their arms, stood in the street and gazed frantically upon the threatened ruin of their homes, while the tears rained down their cheeks." This tough and courageous soldier admitted that "It was too much for me and at the first moment that duty would permit, I hurried away from the scene."[20]

Although it probably mattered very little to the people who were losing everything they had worked for their whole lives, keeping the Confederate army from receiving food from the Valley was not the only reason for the Union troopers to swoop down on their homes. There was also an element of revenge in the burning. General Merritt later wrote that the area was a "paradise of bushwhackers and guerrillas. Officers and men had been murdered in cold blood on the roads, while proceeding without a guard through an apparently peaceful country."[21]

One Union captain searching for weapons may have saved the life of a comrade or possibly his own:

> Today I took the 2nd R. I. Vols. And the 5th Wisconsin Vols. and went into the country to search the houses for arms. The people are honest farmers during the day, but at night they arm themselves and mounting their horses are guerilas and fire upon our pickets and destroy our wagon trains if they can overpower the guards. The work was not pleasant, but we had to perform our duty. The people were often wild with rage, but we found that those who professed their innocence the loudest had the most contraband arms. At one house, after putting the family under guard in a room, we found in various places all the equipments of a soldier except the gun. This after much searching we found in the grain room, hid in a barrel which was filled with grain. We loaded a six mule wagon with arms, equipment and saddles and returned to camp.[22]

Whatever their personal feelings about the suffering of civilians, most of Sheridan's men felt that the devastation they brought to the Shenandoah Valley was warranted. As one of them wrote, "This destruction, cruel as it seemed, was fully justified as a matter of military necessity. For so long as a rebel army could subsist in the valley, so long a large force must remain to guard the frontier of Maryland."[23]

On the 7th, Sheridan sent Grant a progress report from Woodstock:

> In moving back to this point the whole country from the Blue Ridge to the North Mountains has been made untenable for a rebel army. I have destroyed over 2,000 barns filled with wheat, hay, and farming implements; over seventy mills filled with flour and wheat; have driven in front of the army over 4(,000) head of stock, and have killed and issued to the troops not less than 3,000 sheep. This destruction embraces the Luray Valley and Little Fort Valley, as well as the main valley. A large number of horses have been obtained, a proper estimate of which I cannot now make.... To-morrow I will continue the destruction of wheat, forage, &c., down to Fisher's Hill. When this is completed the Valley, from Winchester up to Staunton, ninety-two miles, will have but little in it for man or beast.[24]

As Sheridan's troopers went about their business of destruction, Confederate cavalry under General Thomas Rosser followed close behind. Rosser had brought Early cavalry reinforcements, including the Laurel Brigade, which was well known in the Valley for "boasting and swaggering."[25] The smoke from hundreds of fires darkened the sky as Rosser's men rode past farm after farm that had been burned to the ground. Their hunger and exhaustion was replaced by the desire for revenge, and this hatred made the Confederates bolder.[26]

Colonel Kidd remembered:

> The pursuit was rather tame for a couple of days but the sight of the destruction going on must have exasperated the Confederate troopers, many of whom were on their native heath, and put them in a fighting mood, for on the 8th they began to grow aggressive and worried the life out of our rear guard.... Thus it went, alternately halting, forming and facing to the rear, and falling back, until Tom's Brook was reached late in the afternoon.[27]

Confederate Brigadier General Thomas L. Rosser (Library of Congress).

When Sheridan heard about the frequent attacks on the rear guard, his Irish temper got the better of him. He called Torbert in and ordered him to unleash Custer and Merritt, who had been under orders to protect the rear of the army but avoid any major engagements. Sheridan wrote:

> As we proceeded the Confederates gained confidence, probably on account of the reputation with which its new commander had been heralded, and on the third day's march had the temerity to annoy my rear guard considerably. Tired of these annoyances, I concluded to open the enemy's eyes in earnest, so that night I told Tolbert I expected him either to give Rosser a drubbing next morning or get whipped himself, and that the infantry would be halted until the affair was over; I also informed him that I proposed to ride out to Round Top Mountain to see the fight.[28]

On the morning of October 9th, Custer and Merritt turned their divisions around and moved toward the Confederate cavalry. Merritt moved along the Valley Pike with the First Division to attack Lomax, who had about 1,000 to 1,500 men. Custer and his Third Division advanced down the Back Road, parallel with and about three miles north of the pike, to engage Rosser, who commanded over 3,000 troopers.[29]

From his vantage point, Sheridan was able to see the battle develop:

> Custer's division encountered Rosser himself with three brigades, and while the stirring sounds of the resulting artillery duel were reverberating through the valley Merritt moved briskly to the front and fell upon Generals Lomax and Johnson on the Valley pike. Merritt, by extending his right, quickly established connection with Custer, and the two divisions moved forward together under Torbert's direction, with a determination to inflict on the enemy the sharp and summary punishment his rashness had invited.[30]

On Custer's front, he pushed back the enemy's skirmishers to the main lines. Rosser had set up a good defensive position on the hills along Tom's Run (Tom's Brook) with dismounted troopers behind stone walls and rails at the base, another line of barricades near the top, and artillery on the crest. Custer then tried to get around Rosser's left while launching an attack along the road at the same time[31]:

> The entire line was ordered forward, and when sufficiently near the enemy the charge was sounded. The enemy seeing his flank turned and his retreat cut off broke in the utmost confusion and sought safety in headlong flight. The pursuit was kept up at a gallop by the entire command for a distance of nearly two miles, where a brigade of the enemy was formed to check our farther advance.[32]

While Custer was attacking Rosser's position, Merritt had sent Colonel Lowell's brigade to advance along the Pike and was using the Second Brigade to attack the center and his First Brigade on the right to connect with Custer, presenting the Confederates with a sea of blue clad troopers that were coming at them from the front and both sides.[33]

The fighting became general, with both sides charging and countercharging for about two hours. Rosser sent two brigades against Custer and forced him back about half a mile and then set up another defensive position supported by his artillery. Custer then sent his First and Second brigades forward. He said: "The whole line moved forward at the charge. Before this irresistible advance the enemy found it impossible to stand. Once more he was compelled to trust his safety to the fleetness of his steed rather than the metal of his saber."³⁴

Along the Pike, the fighting between Lowell and Lomax went back and forth with neither side able to gain the upper hand. About the same time that Custer made his final attack Merritt got a brigade around Lomax's left and, attacking in front and on the flank, drove him up the Pike toward Woodstock, capturing five pieces of artillery along with wagons and ambulances.³⁵

Custer's fanciful prose tells how the Confederate retreat

> soon became a demoralized rout. Vainly did the most gallant of this affrighted herd endeavor to rally a few supports around their standards and stay the advance of their eager and exulting pursuers, who, in one overwhelming current, were bearing down everything before them. Never since the opening of this war had there been witnessed such a complete and decisive overthrow of the enemy's cavalry. The pursuit was kept up vigorously for nearly twenty miles, and only relinquished then from the complete exhaustion of our horses and the dispersion of our panic-stricken enemies.³⁶

Although the battle took place around Tom's Brook, because of the stampede of the Confederates, it later came to be known as the "Woodstock Races."³⁷

On October 9, Early sent Lee a message notifying him of the defeat at Tom's Brook and complaining about his cavalry:

> Rosser, in command of his own brigade and the two brigades of Fitz Lee's division, and Lomax, with two brigades of his own cavalry, were ordered to pursue the enemy, to harass him and ascertain his purposes, while I remained here, so as to be ready to move east of the Ridge if necessary, and I am sorry to inform you that the enemy, having concentrated his whole cavalry in his rear, attacked them and drove them back this morning from near Fisher's Hill, capturing nine pieces of horse artillery and eight or ten wagons. Their loss in men is, I understand, slight....
>
> This is very distressing to me, and God knows I have done all in my power to avert the disasters which have befallen this command; but the fact is that the enemy's cavalry is so much superior to ours, both in numbers and equipment, and the country is so favorable to the operations of cavalry, that it is impossible for ours to compete with his.... It would be better if they could all be put into the infantry; but if that were tried I am afraid they would all run off.³⁸

Also on the 9th, Sheridan sent a message from Strasburg to Grant informing him of the cavalry battle:

> The attack was handsomely made. Custer, commanding Third Cavalry Division, charged on the Back road, and Merritt, commanding First Cavalry Division, on the Strasburg pike. Merritt captured five pieces of artillery. Custer captured six pieces of artillery, with caissons, battery forge, &c. The two divisions captured thirty-seven wagons, ambulances, &c. Among the wagons captured are the headquarters wagons of Rosser, Lomax, and Wickham, and Colonel Pollard [Munford?]. The number of prisoners captured will be about 330. The enemy after being charged by our gallant cavalry were broken, and

ran; they were followed by our men on the jump twenty-six miles through Mount Jackson and across the North Fork of the Shenandoah.... Some of the artillery captured was new and never had been fired before. The pieces were marked, "Tredegar Works."[39]

The day after the cavalry battle, Sheridan's army continued moving north, crossed Cedar Creek and made camp, planning to stay for awhile.[40]

18. Camping at Cedar Creek

For the Federal troops who had been marching and fighting up and down the Valley since early August, the camp at Cedar Creek was most pleasant. The clean, cool air was invigorating and the men had time to relax and put the war behind them, at least for a few days. George T. Stevens said, "Our army was thus resting in apparent security along the banks of Cedar Creek. The men were amusing themselves in visiting the numerous caverns in the vicinity, strolling among the pleasant groves or wandering by the shady borders of the stream."[1]

The men had time to rest and spent a lot of it just taking it easy and talking with friends. Being no different from any soldiers who had ever served in any army, their talk was mostly of going home, but often the discussion turned to politics and the coming election. Wilbur Fisk wrote home that while talking with a friend about the candidates for president:

> A fellow by his side said he wanted peace too, but it was no McClellan peace that he wanted. He had served one three years already, and had begun on his second three. He was as anxious to go home as any man could be, but he didn't want to go till the rebels were whipped out clean and smooth. He said he had always stood up for McClellan, was a McClellan man clear to the bone, but he couldn't vote for him on the Chicago platform. Rather than have peace by surrendering to the rebels, he would let his bones manure the soil of Virginia.[2]

During this conversation, a sergeant from another regiment walked by and joined the debate:

> No sir, said he, there is no use in talking of armistices and conventions. We have got to fight this thing out. There is no other way. The North and South must find out who is master. Timid people might cry peace, peace, but there would be no peace until we had fought and gained it. The South had rebelled against our common Government, and the Government must compel them to cry Enough, or it would be no Government at all. A Government that couldn't vindicate itself, wasn't worth having, and he didn't believe the people of the North was quite ready yet to vote for any such.[3]

When the men doing the fighting didn't want the war to end until victory was achieved, there was little hope for the success of the South's strategy—prolonging the bloodshed until the Union decided it was not worth the price.

Another man writing home was Colonel Lowell. In one of his letters to his wife, he wrote, "I don't want to be shot until I've had a chance to come home. I have no idea that I shall be hit, but I want so much not to now, that it sometimes frightens me."[4]

While most of the army was camped at Cedar Creek, the Sixth Corps was on its way back to Petersburg:

> Monday, October 10th, the Sixth corps, leaving the Eighth and Nineteenth guarding the line of Cedar Creek, turned toward the left and proceeded to Front Royal.... Here, in the enjoyment of lovely weather, pleasant associations, a bountiful supply of lamb and honey, and untold quantities of grapes of delicious flavor, the corps remained several days, and the men even flattered themselves that in the enjoyment of these luxuries they were to pass the winter. But, as usual with bright anticipations, these were suddenly dispelled by the order to march, on the morning of the 13th, toward Ashby's Gap.
>
> From the direction of our march it was evident that we were on the road to Washington, and rumor had it that we were to be shipped at once for Petersburgh [sic].[5]

While Sheridan was dispersing his army and figuring out what to do next, his opponent was also very busy. After the defeats at Winchester and Fisher's Hill, there was some debate about Early's ability to lead his army and the willingness of his men to follow. Back on October 6th, Governor Smith, had written Lee to complain about Early and offered the comments of an unnamed officer as proof that Early's men had lost confidence in his leadership. "The army once believed him a safe commander, and felt that they could trust to his caution, but unfortunately this has been proven a delusion and they cannot, do not, and will not give him their confidence."[6]

General Lee did not hesitate to defend Early:

> The results of operations is usually the only test the people have of the merit of him who conducts them and their judgment is generally made up accordingly. I think you will agree with me that this is not as safe a guide as a knowledge of all the circumstances surrounding the officer, his resources as compared with those of the enemy, his information as to the movements and designs of the latter, the nature of his command, and the object he has in view....
>
> General Breckinridge, who was present on that occasion, informed me that in his opinion the dispositions made by General Early to resist the enemy were judicious and successful until rendered abortive by a misfortune which

he could not prevent and which might have befallen any other commander. He also spoke in high terms of General Early's capacity and energy as displayed in the campaign while General B. was with him.... So far as my information extends General Early has conducted his operations with judgment, and until his late reverses rendered very valuable service considering the means at his disposal. I lament those disasters as much as yourself, but I am not prepared to say that they proceeded from such want of capacity on the part of General Early as to warrant me in recommending his recall.[7]

Confederate President Davis also was hearing complaints and wrote to Secretary of War Seddon on the 18th. "With the knowledge acquired after the events it is usually easy to point out modes which would have been better than those adopted. General Early ... might have changed his operations to advantage, but this does not prove that another would have foreseen what he did not."[8]

While no one could seriously question Early's courage or devotion to the Confederate cause, two major defeats and the smoldering ruins of large parts of the Valley were apparently sufficient proof for some that he was unable to cope with Sheridan's army. It is unlikely that any other commander could have done much better against Sheridan's overwhelming superiority in all things and the reality of the situation was obvious. A member of the Fourth Georgia Volunteers who had recently returned to duty after being wounded relates:

> I found the morale of the army very bad. It was not disaffection or disloyalty to the cause for which they had so long fought, but they reasoned this way: "We are confronted with an army four times that of our own; Lee is besieged at Richmond and Petersburg; Sherman is marching through Georgia; we are cut off from the Trans-Mississippi Department; our ports are blockaded; our army is daily diminishing, with no material for recruiting; our families are in want and destitution at home, while the Federal government has abundant resources at home and all Europe from which to recruit their armies." With these conditions, they felt and maintained that there was no hope for our success. As sensible men, then why should they sacrifice their limbs or lives for a hopeless cause, however righteous? This was plain to every sensible man....[9]

Despite the growing doubts about their chances for success, there were no serious thoughts of abandoning the "cause." Lee wrote a long letter to Early offering support and suggestions for future operations:

> My regret is equal to your own at the reverses that occurred at Winchester and Fisher's Hill, but I hope our loss can be redeemed. To do this it will be necessary for you to keep your troops well together, to restore their confidence, improve their condition in every way you can, enforce strict discipline in officers and men, keep yourself well advised of the enemy's movement and strength, and endeavor to separate and strike them in detail.... The last defeat of your cavalry (on the 9th) is much to be regretted. It may have proceeded from bad management, and I wish you to investigate it. I would not for the present send them too far from your main body, or allow them to hazard too much. Although the enemy's cavalry may exceed ours in numbers, and I know it does in equipment, still we have always been able to cope

with them to advantage, and can do so again by proper management. You have the greater proportion of the cavalry in Virginia and it must be made effective. The men are good and only require to be properly commanded.... I am not so satisfied that it is Sheridan's intention to leave the Valley. It may be so, but I do not think his burning the bridges behind him and laying waste the country proves it. That might have been to cripple you.... It is impossible at this distance to give definite instructions; you can only proceed on the principle of not retaining with you more troops than you can use to advantage in any position the enemy may take and send the rest to me. I have weakened myself very much to strengthen you. It was done with the expectation of enabling you to gain such success that you could return the troops if not rejoin me yourself. I know you have endeavored to gain that success, and believe you have done all in your power to insure it. You must not be discouraged, but continue to try. I rely upon your judgment and ability, and the hearty co-operation of your officers and men still to secure it. With your united force it can be accomplished. I do not think Sheridan's infantry or cavalry numerically as large as you suppose; but either is sufficiently so not to be despised and great circumspection must be used in your operations.[10]

While Lee's letter is mainly supportive and positive, it is interesting to note that nowhere does he admit the possibility that Sheridan simply has too many men for Early, or anyone else for that matter, to face successfully. Or that the Federal troops, especially the cavalry, are at least as capable as his own.

Despite the disappointments of the last month, one thing Lee need not be concerned about was Early giving up. When Early learned that Sheridan was sending part of his army to Petersburg, he "moved down the Valley again on the 12th. On the morning of the 13th we reached Fisher's Hill, and I moved with part of my command to Hupp's Hill, between Strasburg and Cedar Creek, for the purpose of reconnoitering."[11]

Early's men arrived at Hupp's Hill about 10 A.M. and set up a battery of artillery near the Pike that was well within range of the Federal camp. Colonel Thoburn's First Division was the closest, and suddenly shells began to rain down on the unsuspecting troops. Thoburn quickly sent out Colonel Wells' First Brigade and Colonel Harris' Third Brigade to brush aside what they thought was probably just some harassing fire from a few artillery units.[12]

Colonel Harris reported what happened when the two brigades advanced:

> The Third Brigade had no sooner made its appearance in line at the top of the hill than it was seriously assailed by the enemy's shells, aimed with such accuracy as to do it considerable damage at every discharge, and was hence moved by the right flank at a double-quick for 200 yards to gain the shelter of a wood. In the meantime the First Brigade was moved rapidly forward, through a wood at first and afterward through an open field, and took a position behind a stone wall, within a few hundred yards of the enemy's position, having been exposed from the time it emerged from the wood in front of the enemy's guns to great annoyance from the explosion of his shells, which were aimed with great accuracy. Simultaneously with this advance of the First Brigade the Third was also moved forward and so maneuvered as to place it in connection with the First in a continuous line on the right of the road.[13]

What Harris and Wells didn't know was that they were advancing toward a large part of Early's army. Kershaw's Division was out of sight behind the hill and Gordon and Wharton were in the woods on the left of the Pike. Very quickly, the two Federal brigades were attacked in front by Conner's brigade of Kershaw's division with Gordon and Wharton sending in a skirmish line against the flank. "The whole line had now become fiercely engaged with the enemy's infantry, and it soon became apparent that he was there in such force as to enable him to turn our right, and that he had already initiated movements to this end."[14]

It was time for Harris and Wells to pull their troops back before they were overwhelmed by the Confederates coming at them from two directions. Harris was able to keep his men together long enough to retire, but unfortunately Wells didn't receive word to pull back. The First Brigade "consequently became exposed to an enfilading fire from the right as the enemy's lines advanced, and, being thus finally compelled to withdraw without orders, was so hotly pressed from the front and flank as to throw it in some disorder."[15] While trying to rally his men and retire in good order, Colonel Wells was mortally wounded and found later by Early's men.[16]

Although the fight on Hupp's Hill was not much as battles go, there were two important results. After a month of losing every fight, Early's men finally had a victory to improve their morale. Also, Sheridan discovered to his surprise that Early was much closer than he believed and took steps to bring his army back to full strength. "The day's events pointing to a probability that the enemy intended to resume the offensive, to anticipate such a contingency I ordered the Sixth Corps to return from its march toward Ashby's Gap. It reached me by noon of the 14th...."[17]

Sheridan was still trying to get his own plan for the use and dispersal of his army approved when the fight on Hupp's Hill took place. That same day, a series of messages between Sheridan and Washington muddied the water even further.

From Secretary Stanton: "If you can come here a consultation on several points is extremely desirable. I propose to visit General Grant, and would like to see you first."[18]

From Sheridan to Halleck: "If any advance is to be made on Gordonsville and Charlottesville, it is not best to send troops away from my command, and I have therefore countermanded the order directing the Sixth Corps to march to Alexandria.[19]

And later, Halleck sent another message advising Sheridan that "The Secretary of War wishes you to come to Washington for consultation, if you can safely leave your command." One of the topics to be discussed was Grant's plan to move on the railroad at Gordonsville and the problems of bringing supplies to the expedition through the winter.[20]

Coincidently, on the 14th, Grant sent a message to Sheridan outlining his wishes for the remainder of the Valley campaign:

> What I want is for you to threaten the Virginia Central Railroad and canal in the manner your judgment tells you is best, holding yourself ready to

advance if the enemy draw off their forces. If you make the enemy hold a force equal to your own for the protection of those thoroughfares, it will accomplish nearly as much as their destruction. If you cannot do this, then the next best thing to do is to send here all the force you can. I deem a good cavalry force necessary for your offensive as well as defensive operations. You need not, therefore, send here more than one division of cavalry.[21]

Now there was real confusion. Sheridan was planning on attacking Early when the Sixth Corps returned, but after the fight on the 13th, Early withdrew to Fisher's Hill. Sheridan reported, "concluding that he [Early] could not do us serious hurt from there, I changed my mind as to attacking, deciding to defer such action till I could get to Washington, and come to some definite understanding about my future operations."[22]

On the 15th, Sheridan set out for Front Royal accompanied by Torbert's cavalry, which was continuing on to make a quick raid on the Virginia Central Railroad at Charlottesville. Arriving at Front Royal the next day, Sheridan found that a message was waiting from General Wright, who was in command of the army in Sheridan's absence.[23] Wright forwarded an intercepted Confederate message and informed Sheridan, "I shall hold on here until the enemy's movements are developed, and shall only fear an attack on my right, which I shall make every preparation for guarding against and resisting." The really important part of the communication was a message to Early: "Be ready to move as soon as my forces join you and we will crush Sheridan." It was signed "Longstreet, Lieutenant-General."[24]

Sheridan decided that such a message could not be ignored, whether it was true or not:

> I first thought it a ruse, and hardly worth attention, but on reflection deemed it best to be on the safe side, so I abandoned the cavalry raid toward Charlottesville, in order to give General Wright the entire strength of the army, for it did not seem wise to reduce his numbers while reinforcement for the enemy might be near, and especially when such pregnant messages were reaching Early from one of the ablest of the Confederate generals.[25]

Sheridan telegraphed Halleck asking if he had any information on Longstreet's whereabouts and received in return, "General Grant says that Longstreet brought with him no troops from Richmond, but I have very little confidence in the information collected at his headquarters." Once again Halleck displayed his lack of confidence in Grant and those around him.[26]

Sheridan decided to continue on to Washington with one regiment of cavalry for an escort, the rest having been sent back to Wright. From Front Royal, he telegraphed to Wright:

> The cavalry is all ordered back to you; make your position strong. If Longstreet's dispatch is true, he is under the impression that we have largely detached.... Close in Colonel Powell, who will be at this point. If the enemy should make an advance I know you will defeat him. Look well to your ground and be well prepared. Get up everything that can be spared. I will bring up all I can, and will be up on Tuesday, if not sooner.[27]

Sheridan and his staff continued on to Washington, arriving on the morning of the 17th. At the meeting with Secretary Stanton and Halleck, they ended up agreeing to almost everything he had requested. Sheridan was anxious to return and a special train took him to Martinsburg that evening. Accompanied by a cavalry escort, they arrived at Winchester on the afternoon of the 18th and stopped for the night. After dark a courier from the army arrived, bringing word that everything was all right at Cedar Creek and that "the enemy was quiet at Fisher's Hill, and that a brigade of Grover's division was to make a reconnaissance in the morning, the 19th, so about 10 o'clock I went to bed greatly relieved, and expecting to rejoin my headquarters at my leisure next day."[28]

In the Confederate camp at Fisher's Hill, Early had a decision to make, and quickly. The surrounding area had so little food available that he would have to fall back to the south, or attack and drive the enemy from their position. Knowing that he was not strong enough to make a frontal assault, Early "determined to get around one of the enemy's flanks and attack him by surprise if I could." He sent General Gordon and his topographical engineer, Captain Hotchkiss, to the signal station on Massanutten Mountain to examine the Federal position. At the same time, Brigadier General John Pegram was ordered to study the Federal right and see if there was any chance of a surprise attack on that side.[29]

General Gordon gave an account of his view from the signal station:

> It was an inspiring panorama. With strong field-glasses, every road and habitation and hill and stream could be seen and noted.... Not only the general outlines of Sheridan's breastworks, but every parapet where his heavy guns were mounted, and every piece of artillery, every wagon and tent and supporting line of troops, were in easy range of our vision. I could count, and did count, the number of his guns. I could see distinctly the three colors of trimmings on the jackets respectively of infantry, artillery, and cavalry, and locate each, while the number of flags gave a basis for estimating approximately the forces with which we were to contend in the proposed attack.[30]

What Gordon saw made it clear to him that an attack on the right of Sheridan's army would probably fail. The Federals were just too strong and fully prepared to defend that portion of their lines. However, as Gordon expected, the Federal line on the left was weakly defended. It was believed by everyone that the natural barrier of the mountain made it impossible to get a large body of troops around to that side. Almost all the Federal cavalry was on the right, ready to protect the flank or quickly move out to go on the offensive.[31]

The action that needed to be taken was obvious to Gordon:

> It required, therefore, no transcendent military genius to decide quickly and unequivocally upon the movement which the conditions invited. I was so deeply impressed by the situation revealed to us, so sure that it afforded an opportunity for an overwhelming Confederate victory, that I expressed to those around me the conviction that if General Early would adopt the plan of battle which I would submit, and would press it to its legitimate results, the destruction of Sheridan's army was inevitable.[32]

Excited by the possibilities of an attack on the undefended left, Gordon had Hotchkiss make a sketch of the Federal camps and hurry back to Early with the information they had discovered. Hotchkiss returned to headquarters that night and, in addition to the discoveries made on the mountain, he also reported that "from information he had received, he thought it was practicable to move a column of infantry between the base of the mountain and the river, to a ford below the mouth of the creek."[33]

The next morning, the 18th, Gordon returned and confirmed what Hotchkiss had told Early. Pegram also returned to inform Early that the Federal right was too well protected for them to assault successfully, leaving an attack on the left as the only viable opportunity. Early decided to accept Gordon's plan and ordered that the army prepare to move that night. A meeting of the division commanders was set for two o'clock that afternoon to finalize the plans.[34]

The final plan of attack was as complex as it was daring:

> General Gordon, in command of the Second Corps (Gordon's, Ramseur's, and Pegram's divisions), was to cross the river at Fisher's Hill and go round the end of the mountain and cross again at Bowman's Ford, turn the enemy's left and press on to the pike to his rear. Kershaw was to go through Strasburg, go to Bowman's Mill near the mouth of Cedar Creek, and cross and advance over the front of the enemy's line of breast-works. Wharton, followed by the artillery, was to go along the turnpike to Hupp's Hill and cross after the others and press up the pike. Rosser was to cross Cedar Creek at Mohamy's Mill and engage the Yankee cavalry.[35]

At the two o'clock meeting, Early gave his division commanders, except for Pegram, who was still on the mountain, their final instructions for the coming fight:

> Gordon was directed to cross over into the bend of the river immediately after dark, and move to the foot of the mountain, where he would rest his troops, and move from there in time to cross the river again and get in position at Cooley's house in the enemy's rear, so as to make the attack at the designated hour, and he was instructed, in advancing to the attack, to move for a house on the west side of the Valley Pike called the "Belle Grove House," at which it was known that Sheridan's headquarters were located.[36]

It was essential that all the Confederate units arrive at their jumping-off points undetected so that the attack in the morning could be coordinated. Rosser was to move his cavalry forward early enough so that he could launch his attack by 5:00 A.M. in an attempt to surprise the Federal cavalry. Kershaw and Wharton, accompanied by Early, were to start their men toward Strasburg at one o'clock in the morning. The artillery was to hold back so that the noise caused by the wheels and horses would not alert the Federal sentries. When the attack began, the guns were to move quickly to Hupp's Hill.[37]

Gordon was the first to start his move around the mountain since he had the farthest to go to reach his point of attack:

> The movement was begun with the coming of the darkness. The men were stripped of canteens and of everything calculated to make noise and arouse Sheridan's pickets below us, and our watches were set so that at the same moment the right, the centre, and the left of Sheridan should be assaulted. With every man, from the commanders of divisions to the brave privates under them, impressed with the gravity of our enterprise, speaking only when necessary and then in whispers, and striving to suppress every sound, the long gray line like a great serpent glided noiselessly along the dim pathway above the precipice. Before the hour agreed upon for the simultaneous attack, my entire command had slowly and safely passed the narrow and difficult defile.[38]

The rest of Early's army began to move out at their appointed times. Kershaw and Wharton split up at Strasburg with Kershaw going to the right and Wharton following the Valley Pike to Hupps' Hill, where he was to wait for the artillery when the attack began and then capture the bridge over the creek. Early stayed with Kershaw and about 3:30 A.M. they came within sight of the Federal campfires. While they waited for the time to launch the attack, Early gave Kershaw some last minute instructions on the nature of the ground and directed him to "cross his division over the creek as quietly as possible, and to form it into column of brigades as he did so, and advance in that manner against the enemy's left breastwork, extended to the right or left as might be necessary."[39]

The journey across the mountain for Gordon's men was bad enough, but after they had negotiated the rugged trail came the worst part of the night—waiting:

> For nearly an hour we waited for the appointed time, resting near the bank of the river in the middle of which the Union vedettes sat upon their horses, wholly unconscious of the presence of the gray-jacketed foe, who from the ambush of night, like crouching lions from the jungle, were ready to spring upon them. The whole situation was unspeakably impressive. Everything conspired to make the conditions both thrilling and weird. The men were resting, lying in long lines on the thickly matted grass or reclining in groups, their hearts thumping, their ears eagerly listening for the orders: "Attention, men!" "Fall in!" "Forward!"[40]

Across Cedar Creek the men in blue passed a peaceful day. The 18th of October had been another beautiful fall day in the Shenandoah Valley:

> crisp and bright and still in the morning; mellow and golden and still at noon; crimson and glorious and still at the sun setting; just blue enough in the distance to soften without obscuring the outline of the mountains, just hazy enough to render the atmosphere visible without limiting the range of sight.[41]

The feeling in the Union camp was that Early's army was beaten and no longer a serious threat, but General Wright was not totally ignoring the enemy. That evening, General Crook reported that he had sent a brigade out on a reconnaissance during the day which found no Confederates in the immediate vicinity and he concluded that they had probably retreated due to lack of supplies. Wright later wrote that "we had been expecting for some days that he would either attack us or be compelled to fall back for the supplies.... This view of the matter, which is still believed to have been sound, lent the stamp of probability to the report of the reconnoitering party." But just to be on the safe side, he ordered another reconnaissance early in the morning.[42]

That evening, the Union soldiers gathered around the campfires to talk and read and then re-read letters from home until it was time for sleep. General A. B. Nettleton later wrote:

> The letters were all read and their contents discussed, the flute had ceased its complaining, the eight o'clock roll-call was over, taps had sounded, lights were out in the tents, cook-fires flickered low, the mists of the autumn night gathered gray and chill, the sentinels paced back and forth in front of the various headquarters, the camp was still—that many-headed monster, a great army, was asleep. Midnight came, and with it no sound but the tramp of the relief guard as the sergeant replaced the tired sentinels. One o'clock, and all was tranquil as a peace convention; two, three o'clock, and yet the soldiers slept.[43]

19. Cedar Creek, the Morning

It began about 4:30 A.M. There was a faint bit of light before dawn when the Confederates rolled forward. On Gordon's front General Payne led his cavalry across the ford to clear the Federal pickets. Following close behind the troopers, General Clement Evans led his division, including the old Stonewall Brigade, across the creek. Gordon reported, "The brave fellows did not hesitate for a moment. Reaching the eastern bank drenched and cold, they were ready for the 'double quick,' which warmed them up and brought them speedily to the left flank of Sheridan's sleeping army."[1]

Gordon's men hit the left flank of Crook's Eighth Corps like lightning out of a clear blue sky. The sleeping Federals had no idea what was happening until it was too late. Colonel Hayes was in command of the Second Division, on the far end of the Federal line, which was lined up parallel with the Pike and at right angles with the First Division facing Cedar Creek. They were overwhelmed in a matter of minutes.[2] Evans' division, with Ramseur on the right and Pegram in support, fell on the unsuspecting enemy, many of whom were still asleep. The few men who were awake and able to make some kind of stand "were thrown into the wildest confusion and terror by Kershaw's simultaneous assault in front."[3]

Kershaw's assault on the front of the Federal line along the creek produced the same effect as Gordon's flank attack:

> Nearer and nearer came the roll of battle as each succeeding brigade was put in action. We were moving forward in double-quick to reach the line of the enemy's breastworks by the time the brigade on our right became engaged.

> Now the thunder of their guns is upon us; the brigade on our right plunges through the thicket and throw themselves upon the abattis in front of the works and pick their way over them. All of our brigade was not in line, as a part was cut off by an angle in Cedar Creek, but the Second and Third charged through an open field in front of the enemy's line. As we emerged from a thicket into the open we could see the enemy in great commotion, but soon the works were filled with half-dressed troops and they opened a galling fire upon us.... This did not continue long, for all down the line from our extreme right the line gave way, and was pushed back to the rear and towards our left, our troops mounting their works and following them as they fled in wild disorder.[4]

Colonel Thoburn commanded the First Division when it was hit by Kershaw's men, and was killed early in the battle trying to rally his troops. Kershaw's troops had been concealed by the early morning fog and captured the pickets in their front without raising the alarm. Few of the Union soldiers could see what was going on until it was too late. One man remembered, "There was a bloody struggle over the breast-works, but it did not last five minutes. Through the unmanned gaps in the lines poured the Rebels in a roaring torrent; and then came a brief massacre followed by lasting panic and disorganization."[5]

> The surprise was complete.... Sheridan's brave men had lain down in their tents on the preceding night feeling absolutely protected by his intrenchments and his faithful riflemen who stood guard. They were startled in their dreams and aroused from their slumbers by the rolls of musketry in nearly every direction around them, and terrified by the whizzing of Minie balls through their tents and the yelling of exultant foemen in their very midst. They sprang from their beds to find Confederate bayonets at their breasts. Large numbers were captured. Many hundreds were shot down as they attempted to escape.[6]

The attack happened so quickly that few of Crook's men could do anything but surrender or run. "The second battalion of the Fifth New York Heavy Artillery was taken on the picket line almost entire; and the resistance of the whole command was so momentary that, while it lost seven hundred prisoners, it had hardly a hundred killed and wounded."[7] Major Henry Withers of the Tenth West Virginia Infantry had risen earlier than normal and was just sitting down to breakfast when he heard sporadic firing, but he believed that "the pickets were disturbed by some unimportant event, until I heard a volley fired apparently from the left, where the Second Division were fortified; then almost immediately I heard a volley from our part of the fortifications...."[8]

The experience of Lieutenant Colonel Thomas Wildes of the 116th Ohio Infantry on Thoburn's front was typical that morning. It seemed that the enemy was coming from every direction at the same time:

> The line was scarcely closed up when a heavy volley of musketry was fired on my right.... I found the works of the Third Brigade occupied by the enemy, and that the Thirty-fourth Massachusetts Regiment, being flanked in its position, had left the works in its front. Just at this time I heard brisk firing on my left. Seeing that I was flanked on my right, and apprehending that my left

19. *Cedar Creek, the Morning* 191

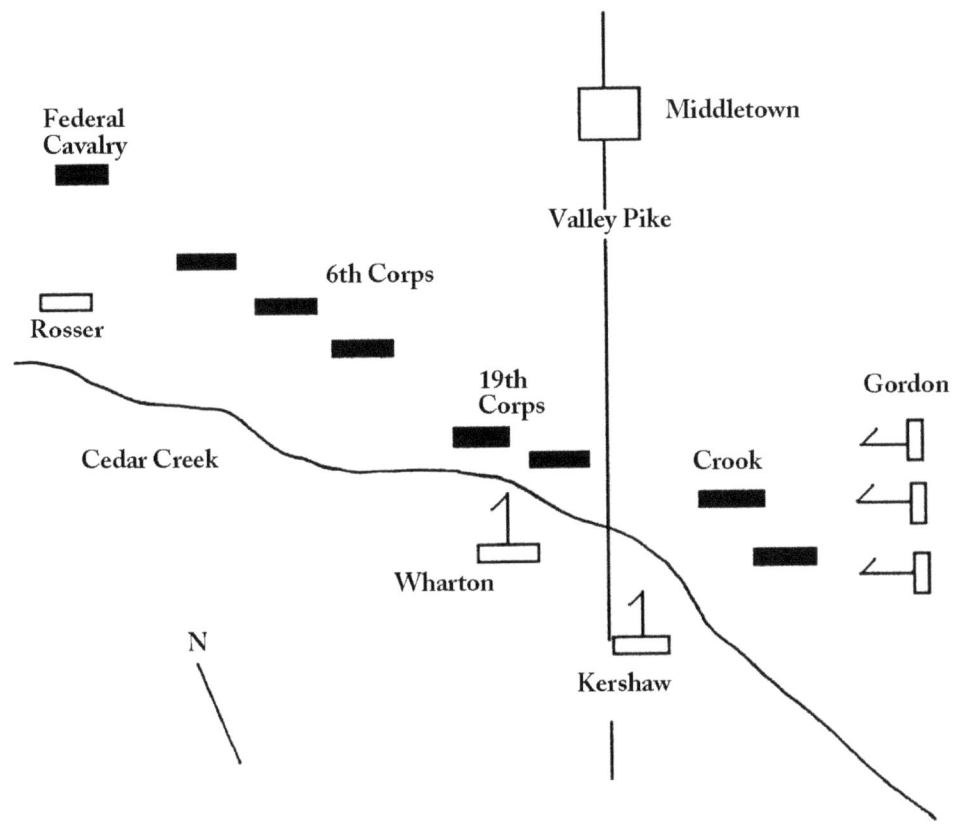

Battle of Cedar Creek—Morning

was also threatened, I ordered the One hundred and sixteenth and One hundred and twenty-third Ohio Regiments to move by the left flank and form line of battle in the field on my left, fronting the position lately occupied by the Third Brigade. I had scarcely formed this line when I heard firing in the woods immediately in my rear.[9]

Colonel T. M. Harris took over command of the First Division after Colonel Thoburn was killed, but he could do nothing that would have stopped or even slowed the Confederate tide. The First and Third brigades were split by the attackers and hit by heavy fire from the front and flanks. Colonel Harris reported that "these two brigades were driven from the works, and so heavy and impetuous was the enemy's advance that their retreat was soon, for the most part, converted into a confused rout, a large proportion of the men flying across the fields to the rear in great disorder."[10]

The Eighth Corps had virtually ceased to exist as a fighting unit. The men who were able to flee headed for the rear past the Nineteenth Corps with the triumphant Confederates right behind them. Several pieces of the Eighth Corps artillery were captured before they could be of any use, except to the Confederates who turned them around to fire on their previous owners. Captain DuPont had so little time to save his guns that he ordered one of his batteries to abandon the caissons and roll the guns down a hill to keep them out of the enemy's hands.[11]

The Eighth Corps collapsed so quickly that almost before they realized what had happened, the men of the Nineteenth Corps were under attack. George Putnam's battalion was on the far left of the Nineteenth Corps when the attack began. They had built up a low earthwork that offered minimum protection and in the darkness and fog they could not tell where the firing was coming from, only that it was getting closer every minute. He later wrote, "It is never easy in a fog to make any trustworthy location of the direction of sound. It is particularly difficult to do this when you have been awakened out of a sleep and are hurried with the feeling that something, you do not know what, has got to be done very promptly."[12]

General Emory also had to act promptly and do something to keep the entire army from being destroyed in detail. He realized that

> even at the cost of annihilation, a force must be sent out to hold the enemy in check till the Sixth and Nineteenth Corps had time to form.
> Col. Thomas and his brigade were close at hand, and, just as the gray dawn revealed the terrible slaughter beyond, Gen. Emory ordered them to advance cross the pike—a single, unsupported brigade—against the best divisions of Early's army.... It was a fearful necessity that required a detachment to be sent to almost instant destruction, in order to gain time....[13]

The desperate fighting on the left had forced Emory to transfer the Second Brigade to bolster the flank, thinning the defense on the Cedar Creek line. Wharton had moved at the appointed time with the rest of Early's army but so far he had made little headway against the fortified front of the Nineteenth Corps along the creek. It was becoming daylight now and with Gordon's men pressing from the left and rear, Early ordered Wharton and the artillery forward.[14]

In an attempt to hold on to their original positions, General Emory repositioned his men on the reverse side of their breastworks. An officer on Emory's staff believed that "This shallow ditch on the outside of a redoubt was the final hold that the Nineteenth Corps had on its position. It was in the case of a man who has been pushed out of a window, and who desperately clings to the sill with the ends of his fingers."[15] A soldier in the 159th New York fought for his life as "the enemy in our front moved forward to the assault, and caught between the two fires our army was forced to move back. Our regiment.... was formed in line in front of the rifle pits to oppose the attack in the rear; but it was impossible to resist the rush of the rebels...."[16]

By now Kershaw had joined with Gordon's men coming from the left and Emory had to pull his men out before they were trapped between them and Wharton's men coming from the front. Emory tried to establish a line facing the Pike but soon had to abandon the attempt and fall back about 1,000 yards.

> My command was now pretty well in line, the First Division on the right and the Second Division on the left, and able to hold the enemy's left in check. I was myself on my own left attempting to establish a connection with the Sixth Corps, when I saw my whole line moving to the rear, orders to that effect having been communicated directly to my two division commanders. About 1,500 yards behind the position thus quitted was a commanding crest which overlooked the whole open country in its front. Here I found General Sheridan's staff collecting stragglers, and here I ordered the Nineteenth Corps to halt and form in two lines of battle.[17]

The fight put up by the Nineteenth Corps, although of short duration, enabled the army headquarters at Belle Grove to evacuate and save most of the wagon trains, but most importantly it gave the Sixth Corps some additional time to get ready to meet the Confederate onslaught.

The fate of the army now rested on the shoulders of General Ricketts, in command of the corps while Wright commanded the army in Sheridan's absence, and the veterans of the Sixth Corps, most of whom had no idea what was happening. They knew that a fight was going on from the firing that could be heard, but they had no idea how serious it was. Soon the fields were filled with stragglers making their way to the rear, privates and officers, most without their weapons, some only half dressed, but all in a hurry to get away. "At length the truth flashed upon us. More than half of our army was already beaten and routed, while the remainder had been in ignorance of the fact that anything serious was transpiring."[18]

General Wright ordered the Sixth Corps to fall back to cover the left. General Ricketts was seriously wounded early in the fighting and the command of the corps fell upon General Getty of the Second Division. The troops were moved quickly and able to take up a new position before any serious fighting took place. They were formed with the left of the Second Division resting near the Pike, the First Division in the center and the Third Division on the right.[19]

Colonel Warren Keifer was in command of the Third Division:

> So great were the number of broken troops of the other corps that for a time the lines had to be opened at intervals in order to allow them to pass to the rear. In consequence of the necessary movements of the morning the divisions of the Sixth Corps were separated and were obliged to fight independent of each other. The Third Division, having faced about, became the extreme right of the army.[20]

It was now a little after 7 A.M. and this was the last chance for the Federal army to save itself. Kershaw's division moved north and struck Keifer's Third Division. At about the same time, Gordon's men were attacking the First Division commanded by General Frank Wheaton, which was to the north of the Third. Both divisions of the Sixth Corps held their ground for a brief time, but the weight of the Confederate attack was too much for these two divisions.

One of the Union officers admitted:

> It was Early's continually extending right which turned us out of this, as it had turned us out of every other line that we had attempted to hold. The

Sixth Corps could no more outfront it or resist it than we. All our fighting that morning was fragmentary, and consequently feeble in effect, however gallant in purpose and bloody in character. We never could get men enough into action at once; the enemy forever overlapped our front and doubled back our left.[21]

The signs of the disaster that had befallen the Federal army were everywhere. A soldier from Vermont wrote:

I am utterly unable to describe the universal confusion and dismay that we encountered. Wagons and ambulances lumbering hither and thither in disorder; pack horses led by frightened bummers, or wandering at their own free will; crowds of officers and men, some shod and some barefoot, many of them coatless and hatless, few without their rifles, but all rushing wildly to the rear; oaths and blows alike powerless to halt them; a cavalry regiment stretched across the field, unable to stem the torrent....[22]

Now there was only one division left to hold the line. The Second Division of the VI Corps had been camped on the northern end of the corps when the battle began. General Getty tried to link his right with the left of the First Division, but when those troops fell back he was forced to withdraw also.[23] Getty was technically the corps commander, but with two of his three divisions falling back, he stayed with the Second Division and pulled his men back about 300 yards to the crest of a hill. He put all his troops into one line to cover as much ground as possible. It was obviously too late to worry about holding back a reserve force. There was no support on the right of the division, but on the left was General Bidwell's brigade, which was connected with skirmishers of Merritt's cavalry.[24]

For over an hour the Second Division held its ground against multiple Confederate attacks; in fact, their stand was so fierce that both Gordon and Early believed they were facing the entire Sixth Corps and not just one division. Gordon saw that victory was almost achieved. "Only the Sixth Corps of Sheridan's entire force held its ground. It stood like a granite breakwater, built to beat back the oncoming flood...."[25]

Soon after Getty had established this latest line, they were attacked. The heaviest fighting was on the right defended by Warner's brigade, and the left-center against Bidwell's and Grant's brigades. "The enemy's lines charged to within thirty yards of the crest, when, unable to withstand our fire, they fell back in disorder. Reforming at the foot of the hill they again charged, to be repulsed."[26]

Colonel Thomas Hyde reported:

The fog had been very dense, and the smoke from the guns of our skirmishers, who were warmly engaged with the foe, rendered the atmosphere still more dense, so that it was almost impossible to see through it a short distance, when suddenly the enemy appeared in two lines, within thirty yards of our line of battle.... Instantly upon seeing the lines, ours was ordered to fire, which they did, and which was returned almost simultaneously by the enemy. Seeing the lines waver a charge was ordered, which was executed in fine style, driving the enemy off the hill ... we had scarcely reformed on the hill when the enemy appeared again on the crest within thirty yards of our lines, and, as before, we poured a heavy volley into them, charging, when they fled in the wildest confusion....[27]

During this action General Bidwell was mortally wounded by a shell while leading his brigade. His men were so shocked and dismayed when he fell that it looked as if "they would now give up the contest, when Lieut.-Col. French of the Seventy-seventh New York, next in command, shouted, 'Don't run till the Vermonters do!' and with a cheer of desperation his troops sprang forward...."[28]

Early had by now reached the front and, after consulting with Ramseur and Pegram, ordered Wharton's division forward:

> In a very short time, and while I was endeavoring to discover the enemy's line through the obscurity, Wharton's division came back in some confusion, and General Wharton informed me that, in advancing to the position pointed out to him by Generals Ramseur and Pegram, his division had been driven back by the 6th corps, which he said was advancing.... The fog soon rose sufficiently for us to see the enemy's position on a ridge to the west of Middletown, and it was discovered to be a strong one.[29]

Gordon was determined to remove this last obstacle to a complete victory. "It was at that hour largely outnumbered, and I had directed every Confederate command then subject to my orders to assail it in front and upon both flanks simultaneously."[30] Gordon was making arrangements with the chief of artillery, Colonel Thomas H. Carter, to begin a bombardment of the Second Division's position when Early arrived.

For the rest of his life Gordon remembered the brief conversation that took place:

> "Well Gordon, this is glory enough for one day. This is the 19th. Precisely one month ago to-day we were going in the opposite direction."
>
> His allusion was to our flight from Winchester on the 19th of September. I replied: "It is very well so far, general; but we have one more blow to strike, and then there will not be left an organized company of infantry in Sheridan's army."
>
> I pointed to the Sixth Corps and explained the movements I had ordered, which I felt sure would compass the capture of that corps – certainly its destruction. When I had finished, he said: "No use in that; they will all go directly."
>
> "That is the Sixth Corps, general. It will not go, unless we drive it from the field."
>
> "Yes, it will go too, directly."
>
> My heart went into my boots.[31]

Gordon had to settle for the artillery bombardment, and as he watched the shells exploding the opportunity for a spectacular victory was slipping away.

The shelling of Getty's troops was not as severe as it looked from a distance. The shape of the ground helped protect the men and losses were lighter than the Confederates supposed. Still, Getty decided it was time to go. The exposed right flank had come under fire and there was no good reason to let his men stand under the shelling any longer than necessary. The division pulled back in good order to a new position about one mile north of Middletown, where they established a new line. The left was resting on the Valley Pike with Merritt's cavalry on the other side. The men quickly built up a low wall of rails, stones and anything else they could find. Skirmishers were sent out and the veteran troops were ready to continue the fight.[32]

The Second Division had abandoned its position, just as Gordon wanted, but the situation was now totally changed. For the first time that day the Confederates had been stopped cold. The remnants of Sheridan's army were in a good defensive position and Getty had sent orders for the First and Third divisions to join him north of Middletown. No one knew it at the time, but the Federal army had taken its last backward steps.[33]

So far it had been mainly an infantry battle, but the cavalry had also played a part. Since the first shots were exchanged, the troopers had been keeping busy. The majority of the Federal cavalry was massed on the far right of the line to protect against being flanked in the open landscape. Rosser had attacked the pickets and moved forward on the right, but quickly met with resistance. Colonel Kidd remembered:

> In a moment, a staff officer from General Merritt dashed up with orders to take the entire brigade to the support of the picket line. Moving out rapidly, we were soon on the ground. The Seventh Michigan had made a gallant stand alone, and when the brigade arrived, the enemy did not see fit to press the attack, but contented himself with throwing a few shells from the opposite bank....[34]

Merritt had sent Lowell's brigade to assist Kidd's First Brigade in defending against Rosser, who surprisingly just stayed where he was. General Devin's Second Brigade was ordered to the left to hold on to the pike and try to stem the flow of refugees.[35] Except for a few units trying to stop, or at least slow down, the flood of infantry heading north, the Federal cavalry spent most of the early morning hours on the right of the Federal line protecting the flank of the Sixth Corps as they gradually fell back.[36]

When the Sixth Corps and the remnants of the Nineteenth Corps set up their lines north of Middletown, General Wright ordered the cavalry to move over to the left of the lines, with Merritt's division north of Middletown across the Pike, Custer's division to the left of them and the First Brigade of the Second Division on Custer's left. The Second Brigade of the Second Division was confronting Lomax's cavalry on the Front Royal and Winchester pike. They spent most of the day there preventing Lomax from attacking the trains and the Federal rear.[37]

Now the cavalry began to take an active part in the battle. General Merritt reported:

> Orders were then sent to each brigade to press the enemy warmly, and Lowell was cautioned to watch his opportunity and charge a battery of the enemy

which seemed exposed in the open country to the left of the pike. Never did troops fight more elegantly than at this time; not a man shirked his duty, not a soldier who did not conduct himself like a hero.... Twice or thrice by movements in the infantry line on our right the enemy got in the flank of the division line and subjected it to a murderous fire; but there was no movement on the part of the men save that demanded by superior judgment for a fresh disposition to meet the contingency; no running, no confusion....[38]

About 11:00 o'clock Custer's division was ordered to move back to the right of the infantry lines. There was a large gap between the left of the Confederate infantry and Rosser's cavalry. Custer was able to move "a portion of my command, the battery included, to a position almost in rear and overlooking the ground upon which the enemy had massed his command."[39] Early was now faced with the one thing he feared most, Federal cavalry divisions on both his flanks.

By now the fighting was pretty much over for the morning. Early was getting cautious and when it came time to attack the Federal position north of Middletown, he found that Ramseur and Kershaw were ready but Gordon's troops were still coming up. By the time all was ready Early had become aware of the Federal cavalry on his left. Realizing what they could do to his troops if the attack failed, he "directed General Gordon, if he had found the enemy's line too strong to attack with success, not to make the assault." The Confederate skirmishers moved out but soon returned to report the Federal line was indeed strong. Gordon decided not to press the attack.[40]

Early now had a decision to make:

> It was now apparent that it would not do to press my troops further. They had been up all night and were much jaded. In passing over rough ground to attack the enemy in the early morning, their own ranks had been much disordered, and the men scattered, and it had required time to reform them. Their ranks, moreover, were much thinned by the absence of the men engaged in plundering the enemy's camps. The delay which had unavoidably occurred, had enabled the enemy to rally a portion of his routed troops, and his immense force of cavalry, which remained intact, was threatening both of our flanks in an open country, which of itself rendered an advance extremely hazardous. I determined, therefore, to try and hold what had been gained, and orders were given for carrying off the captured and abandoned artillery, small arms and wagons.[41]

Gordon was beside himself at the delay. He wanted to continue the attacks regardless of what the Federal cavalry might or might not do. "We waited – waited for weary hours; waited till those stirring, driving, and able Federal leaders, Wright, Crook, and Getty, could gather again their shattered fragments; waited till the routed men in blue found that no foe was pursuing them and until they had time to recover their normal composure and courage...."[42]

One of the reasons Early gave for not continuing the attacks was that many of his men had left their ranks to plunder the Federal camps. While the number of these men is difficult to agree on, it is certain that many did. One of the Confederates who made the early morning attack gives his view of why some of his comrades stopped to loot the Union camps. "Hundreds of the men who were in the charge and captured the enemy's works were barefooted, every one of them was ragged, many had nothing but what they had on, and *none* had eaten a square meal for weeks! …the temptation to stop and eat was too great…."[43]

It would be easy to blame the men who fell out of the Confederate ranks to get something to eat or shoes to cover their bare feet for the decision to end the offensive. The large numbers of Federal cavalry on each flank was an even better reason to be careful. Certainly, as Early pointed out, the men were probably exhausted. Perhaps Early had just taken on too big a task. One of his staff remembered that Early later stated, "The Yankees got whipped; we got scared."[44] He had already won a spectacular victory against enormous odds and perhaps he should have taken the spoils and left the field to the dead and dying. Instead he simply held his ground and waited.

20. Cedar Creek, the Afternoon

While the Army of the Shenandoah was being flung back by the ferocious Confederate attacks at Cedar Creek, its commander was still in bed nearly twenty miles away in Winchester:

> Toward 6 o'clock the morning of the 19th, the officer on picket duty at Winchester came to my room, I being yet in bed, and reported artillery firing from the direction of Cedar Creek. I asked him if the firing was continuous or only desultory, to which he replied that it was not a sustained fire, but rather irregular and fitful. I remarked: "It's all right; Grover has gone out this morning to make a reconnaissance, and he is merely feeling the enemy." I tried to go to sleep again, but grew so restless that I could not, and soon got up and dressed myself. A little later the picket officer came back and reported that the firing, which could be distinctly heard from his line on the heights outside of Winchester, was still going on. I asked him if it sounded like a battle, and as he again said that it did not, I still inferred that the cannonading was caused by Grover's division banging away at the enemy simply to find out what he was up to. However, I went down-stairs and requested that breakfast be hurried up, and at the same time ordered the horses to be saddled and in readiness....[1]

It wasn't until about 9 o'clock when Sheridan and his aides headed south to Mill Creek, where they met their escort from the 17th Pennsylvania Cavalry.[2] One of Sheridan's aides was Major George (Sandy) Forsyth and as they rode south, the faint sound of artillery fire could be heard in the distance. It seemed as if Sheridan could sense something was wrong. Forsyth recalled, "He leaned forward and listened intently, and once he dismounted and placed his ear near the ground, seeming somewhat disconcerted as he rose again and remounted." After riding for about a mile, they came upon a wagon train blocking the Pike. The scene was total chaos; some of the wagons sat facing straight ahead while others were going in all directions trying to turn around.[3]

Major Forsyth learned that the quartermaster in charge of the wagon train had been told by an officer coming back from the front that the army had been defeated and he should turn around and head back to Winchester. Leaving most of the escort behind, Sheridan and two aides, Major Forsyth and Captain Joseph O'Keefe, set out to find the army.[4]

During the ride south, Sheridan had time to decide what to do once he reached the front and discovered what had happened:

> My first thought was to stop the army in the suburbs of Winchester as it came back, form a new line, and fight there; but as the situation was more maturely considered a better conception prevailed. I was sure the troops had confidence in me, for heretofore we had been successful; and as at other times they had seen me present at the slightest sign of trouble or distress, I felt that I ought to try now to restore their broken ranks, or, failing in that, to share their fate because of what they had done hitherto.[5]

The small band of riders made their way south on what was becoming a beautiful fall day. The fog had burned off and the sun was shining, the hills were covered with trees displaying all their fall colors, and as Forsyth noted, "over all was the deep blue of a cloudless Southern sky, making it a day on which one's blood ran riot and he was glad of health and life."[6]

The closer Sheridan got to the battlefield, the more he saw the evidence of a defeat. Supply wagons, headquarters wagons and ambulances filled the pike. Mixed in with the wagons and horses were officers and enlisted men, some wounded and some not, but everything was headed north, to Winchester and safety.[7]

Major Forsyth recalled:

> Soon we began to see small bodies of soldiers in the fields with stacked arms, evidently cooking breakfast. As we debouched into the fields and passed around the wagons and through these groups, the general would wave his hat to the men and point to the front, never lessening his speed as he pressed forward. It was enough; one glance at the eager face and familiar black horse and they knew him, and starting to their feet, they swung their caps around their heads and broke into cheers as he passed beyond them; and then, gathering up their belongings and shouldering their arms, they started after him for the front, shouting to their comrades further out in the fields, "Sheridan! Sheridan!" waving their hats, and pointing after him as he dashed onward; and they too comprehended instantly, for they took up the cheer and turned back for the battle-field.[8]

Mile after mile the small group rode toward the battlefield. Occasionally they would stop while Sheridan asked for news about what had happened. Sheridan's horse, a large black charger named Rienzi, soon to be the most famous horse in the country, was able to keep up a very fast pace and most of the escort fell behind. The legend of that ride was that Rienzi galloped the entire way from Winchester to the battlefield without a stop; this simply was not true, there were several stops. But the truth is very close to the legend: a large black horse, white with foam and charging toward the battle, the small dark man waving his hat and yelling at the men as he went by, urging them to follow him.[9] Forsyth remembered that as soon as they met the first stragglers, Sheridan's "appearance and his cheery shout of 'Turn back, men – turn back! Face the other way!' as he waved his hat towards the front, had but one result; a wild cheer of recognition, an answering wave of the cap. In no case, as I glanced back, did I fail to see the men shoulder their arms and follow us."[10]

The Sheridan magic did not work on everyone, however. Outside of Newtown, Sheridan

> met a chaplain digging his heels into the sides of his jaded horse, and making for the rear with all possible speed. I drew up for an instant, and inquired of him how matters were going at the front. He replied, "Everything is lost; but all will be right when you get there;" yet notwithstanding this expression of confidence in me, the parson at once resumed his breathless pace to the rear.[11]

As they got closer to the front, Forsyth noticed a change in Sheridan. "As he galloped on his features gradually grew set, as though carved in stone, and the same dull red glint I had seen in his piercing black eyes when, on other occasions, the battle was going against us, was there now."[12] They finally passed through some woods and came into view of the battlefield. "In our immediate front the road and adjacent fields were filled with sections of artillery, caissons, ammunition-trains, ambulances, battery wagons, squads of mounted men, led horses, wounded soldiers, broken wagons, stragglers, and stretcher-bearers...."[13]

The first organized troops that Sheridan came to were Getty's division of the Sixth Corps, still holding their position like a rock. These veterans had been waiting to see what was going to happen next and were not too happy about the situation. They knew full well that only a portion of the army had been beaten and by a surprise attack at that. One man remembered:

> While thus waiting for the complete re-formation of the army, sulkily and it is to be feared profanely growling over the defeat in detail which we had experienced ... we heard cheers behind us on the pike. We were astounded. There we stood, driven four miles already, quietly waiting for what might be further and immediate disaster, while far in the rear we heard the stragglers and hospital bummers, and the gunless artillerymen actually cheering as though a victory had been won. We could hardly believe our ears.[14]

A soldier in the 3rd Vermont recorded, "Soon we saw Sheridan coming in sight with his black horse, white with foam.... Of all the cheering I ever heard, that beat it. I should have thought it might have frightened Early's army out of the valley."[15]

One officer witnessed the miraculous change that came over the Union troops:

> A deafening cheer broke from the troops in that part of the field, as they recognized in the coming horseman their longed-for Sheridan. Above the roar of musketry and artillery, that shout arose like a cry of victory. The news flashed from brigade to brigade, along our front, with telegraphic speed, and then, as Sheridan, cap in hand, dashed along the rear of the struggling line, thus confirming to all eyes the fact of his arrival, a continuous cheer burst from the whole army. Hope took the place of fear, courage the place of despondency, cheerfulness the place of gloom. The entire aspect of things seemed changed in a moment. Further retreat was no longer thought of. At all points to the rear stragglers could be seen by hundreds voluntarily rejoining their regiments ... order seemed to have come spontaneously out of chaos, an army out of a rabble.[16]

Private Wilbur Fisk believed he saw in Sheridan "a look of confidence and stern determination in his eye that inspired the men with more hope and courage, I believe, than a whole corps of re-enforcements would have done. Somehow everybody felt a sense of relief when they heard that Gen. Sheridan was on the ground."[17]

Now that Sheridan was on the scene, he had to put his army back together. He met with Wright, who had been slightly wounded on the chin and was sitting on the grass, exhausted, with his beard covered in blood. When Sheridan arrived Wright apologized saying, "Well we've done the best we could." But Sheridan kindly responded, "That's all right; that's all right."[18]

Wright had already taken steps to combine what was left of the army into a continuous line and Sheridan ordered basically the same dispositions that Wright had. He ordered the Nineteenth Corps and the two divisions of the Sixth Corps that were behind Getty's division to come forward and join with those troops and extend the line to the right, "for I had already decided to attack the enemy from that line as soon as I could get matters in shape to take the offensive."[19]

It took about two hours to gather the spread out forces and bring them into line as Sheridan wanted. During this time he rode over to the far left to view the field and check on Confederate dispositions. Sheridan had already sent Custer back to the right flank and he wanted to make sure that the returning divisions went into line where he wanted them. One of Getty's men wrote:

> We had taken our new position in the same order we had formed in the morning, the Second division on the left, the First in the center, and the Third on the right, other troops also took position in the line. The cavalry, which had never for a moment faltered, took position, Custer on the right, Merritt on the left and the Nineteenth corps, which had now succeeded in restoring order to its broken ranks, was massed on the right and rear of the Sixth.[20]

After the troops were formed to Sheridan's satisfaction, Major Forsyth urged Sheridan to ride along the line so that all the men could see for themselves that he had returned and was again in command.[21] Hailed everywhere by cheers of delight, he rode along the front studying the ground and occasionally addressing the men. "'Boys, if I had been here this never should have happened,' he said in his animated, earnest way. 'I tell you it never should have happened. And now we are going back to our camps. We are going to get a twist on them. We are going to lick them out of their boots.'"[22]

An officer from Vermont probably summed up the feelings of most of the Federal soldiers on that hill, "Beneath and yet superior to these noisy demonstrations there was in every heart a revulsion of feeling, and a pressure of emotion, beyond description. No more doubt or chance for doubt existed; we were safe, perfectly and unconditionally safe, and every man knew it."[23]

Another man, standing in line with the Nineteenth Corps, felt that

> Sheridan possessed in a degree unequalled the power of raising in the hearts of his soldiers the sort of enthusiasm that, transmuting itself into action, causes men to attempt, impossibilities, and to disregard and overcome obstacles. The feeling of an army for its general is a thing not to be reasoned with or explained away; once aroused, it belongs to him as exclusively as the expression of his face, the manner of his gait, or the form of his signature, and is not to be transferred to his successor or delegated even to the ablest of his lieutenants, whatever the skill, the merit, or the reputation of either. The mere presence of Sheridan in the ranks of the Army of the Shenandoah that day brought with it the assurance of victory.[24]

After Sheridan returned from encouraging the men, he informed Emory that a Confederate force was heading toward the Nineteenth Corps. This was Gordon's halfhearted attack that was easily thrown back. Sheridan wrote, "This repulse of the Confederates made me feel pretty safe from further offensive operations on their part, and I now decided to suspend the fighting till my thin ranks were further strengthened by the men who were continually coming up from the rear...."[25]

Gradually the strength of the army was built up. From the rear the stragglers were returning and they were welcome.

> The tired troops had thrown themselves on the ground at the edge of the woods, and lay on their arms in line of battle, listlessly and sleepily. Every now and then stragglers—sometimes singly, oftener in small groups—came up from the rear, and moving along back of the line, dusty, heavy-footed, and tired, found and rejoined their respective companies and regiments, dropping down quietly by the side of their companions as they came to them, with a gibe or a word or two of greeting on either side, and then they too, like most of the rest, subsided into an appearance of apathetic indifference.... Little was said by officers or men, for the truth was nearly all were tired, troubled, and somewhat disheartened by the disaster that had so unexpectedly overtaken them....[26]

Their commander was also glad to have these men back. Apparently he understood what had made them run and also appreciated what it took for them to return to the fight. In his report Sheridan wrote that "none behaved more gallantly or exhibited greater courage than those who returned from the rear determined to reoccupy their lost camp."[27]

Waiting for the stragglers to return was not the only reason Sheridan delayed his attack: he was worried about James Longstreet. Sheridan admitted that he believed Longstreet's troops were present. How else could his army be thrown back so quickly unless Early had received heavy reinforcements? It wasn't until mid-afternoon that Sheridan found out from prisoners that only Kershaw's division was present, not Longstreet's entire corps. Also, there was a rumor that Longstreet was going to attack the Union rear from Front Royal. Colonel Powell's cavalry division was stationed in that area and soon confirmed that no such troops were in sight.[28]

During this period, Merritt's cavalry on the left flank was making harassing attacks against Kershaw and Pegram while under constant artillery fire. General Torbert wrote that

> General Merritt, who was constantly annoying and attacking the enemy whenever an opportunity presented itself; although his men were completely within range of the enemy's sharpshooters, his shot and shell, and many a horse and rider was made to bite the dust, they held their ground like men of steel; officers and men seemed to know and feel that the safety of the army in no small degree depended upon their holding their position....[29]

Sheridan was now ready to launch his attack. "Between half-past 3 and 4 o'clock, I was ready to assail, and decided to do so by advancing my infantry line in a swinging movement, so as to gain the Valley pike with my right between Middletown and the Belle Grove House...."[30]

Major Forsyth carried the word to General Emory:

> In a few moments the news ran down the lines that we were to advance. Springing to their feet at the word of command, the tired troops stood to arms and seemed to resolutely shake off the depression that had sat so heavily upon them, and began to pull themselves together for the coming fray. Everywhere along the line of battle men might be seen to stoop and retie their shoes; to rebuckle and tighten their waist-belts; to unbutton the lids of their cartridge-boxes and pull them forward rather more to the front; to rearrange their haversacks and canteens, and to shift their rolls of blankets in order to give freer scope to the expansion of their shoulders and an easier play to their arms; to set their forage-caps tighter on their heads, pulling the visor well down over their eyes; and then, almost as if by order, there rang from one end of the line to the other the rattle of ramrods and snapping of gunlocks as each man tested for himself the condition of his rifle, and made sure that his weapon was in good order and to be depended upon in the emergency that was so soon to arise. Then grounding arms, they stood at ease, half leaning on their rifles, saying little, but quietly awaiting orders and grimly gazing straight toward the front.[31.]

About a mile away the Confederates were waiting, and they knew full well what was coming. During the last few hours the Confederate signal station on Massanutten Mountain had been informing them of Federal movements. Gordon wrote, "The flag signals from the mountain and the messages from Rosser became more intense in their warning and more frequent as the hours passed. Sheridan's marchers were coming closer and massing in heavy column on the left, while his cavalry were gathering on our flank and rear...."[32]

Early's army was in position across the Valley Pike a little north of Middletown. As the Confederates chased the fleeing Federals that morning, the alignment of their divisions was changed and now Gordon was on the left with Evans, Kershaw and Ramseur. Pegram and Wharton's divisions made up the right side of the Confederate line near the Pike, which they had to protect from the Federal cavalry.[33] Gordon was not happy with this alignment:

> When the long hours of dallying with the Sixth (Union) Corps had passed, and our afternoon alignment was made, there was a long gap, with scarcely a vedette, to guard it between my right and the main Confederate line.... With that fearful gap in the line and the appalling conditions which our long delay had invited, every Confederate commander of our left wing foresaw the crash which speedily came.[34]

The Federal line moved forward about 4 o'clock. Getty's division moved with their left along the pike with Ricketts and Wheaton in line to their right. The two divisions of the Nineteenth Corps were further to the right and coming in on a bit of an angle swinging toward the Pike. The Sixth Corps advanced straight ahead and ran into a buzzsaw. Ramseur and Kershaw held their ground tenaciously, pouring fire into the ranks of the Sixth Corps from behind stone walls, hastily erected barricades and a few buildings. The entire line came to a halt and began trading fire with the Confederate line.[35]

Colonel Keifer, with the Third Division, reported that

> The enemy opened a deadly fire with artillery and musketry upon the troops, but for a time they continued the advance, although suffering heavy losses.... The greater portion of the division, after returning the enemy's fire vigorously for a short time, temporarily gave way.... The division lost very heavily in this attack.[36]

The Second Division was also engaged in brutal fighting. Colonel Hyde, whose Third Brigade was along the Pike, reported that "we had advanced about 250 yards, when the enemy opened on us with canister from a battery behind the mill, and an infantry fire from a line posted behind a stone wall in our front and right ... also a battery on the left opened directly upon that flank."[37]

The Second Division was supposed to advance slowly so that the other units could pivot on them. The problem was that being out in the open as they were, this only made them better targets. The attack stalled and with casualties growing by the minute, Colonel French told Getty, "I cannot take my brigade over that field slowly." Seeing his division being pounded by musket and artillery fire, Getty told him to go ahead as quickly as they could.[38]

It took nearly an hour before the Sixth Corps' attack was moving forward again. Getty's division surged forward and drove the Confederates from their stone walls and back to a secondary position near Middletown.[39] The other Sixth Corps divisions also advanced and the sheer weight of the attack forced Ramseur and Kershaw back. General Bryan Grimes reported that "Ramseur then ordered the different brigades of this division to fall back and form (behind) a stone fence about 200 yards in rear.... While holding this position the gallant and chivalrous General Ramseur was mortally wounded and brought from the field."[40]

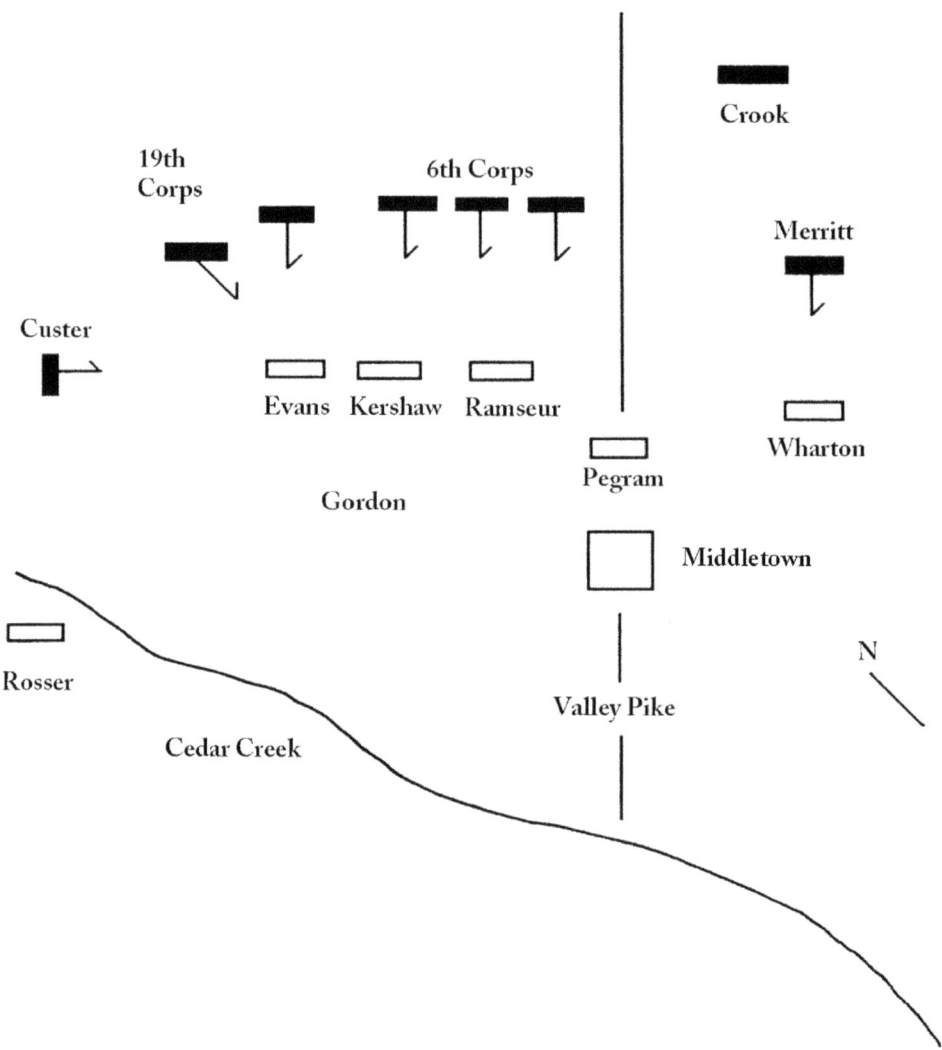

Battle of Cedar Creek—Afternoon

While the Sixth Corps was trading fire with the enemy on the Federal left, over on the right the Nineteenth Corps was also meeting heavy resistance. Emory's First Division was on the right of his corps and their job was to swing around the flank of Gordon's men and drive them into the center of the Confederate line.[41]

Major Forsyth accompanied them as they advanced toward the left of the enemy line:

> Soon the woods become less dense, and through the trees I see just beyond us an open field partly covered with small bushes, and several hundred yards away, crowning a slight crest on its further side, a low line of fence-rails and loose stones, that, as we leave the edge of the woods, and come

into the open, suddenly vomits flame and smoke along its entire length, and a crashing volley tells us that we have found the enemy.[42]

Emory's men held their ground, trading fire with the Confederates until suddenly, they received a volley of musket fire from the right where Gordon's men had moved around to counter-attack. Fortunately for the Federal troops, Brigadier General James W. McMillan's brigade was able to swing around to the right and confront this threat to the flank. They quickly rushed at the defenders and soon the entire line was moving forward, pushing the Confederates back out of their defensive positions.[43]

On the far right of the Federal line, General Custer and his Third Division were protecting the right flank of the Nineteenth Corps and looking for any opportunity to turn the Confederate left flank. When the advance began, he detached three regiments under Colonel Alexander Pennington to confront Rosser, who was on Custer's right. Custer was able to see the infantry battle from a ridge:

Confederate Brigadier General John Pegram (Library of Congress).

> It was apparent that the wavering in the ranks of the enemy betokened a retreat, and that this retreat might be converted into a rout. For a moment I was undecided. Upon the right I was confident of my ability to drive the enemy's cavalry with which I was then engaged across the creek; upon the left my chances of success were not so sure, but the advantages to be gained, if successful, overwhelmingly greater; I chose the latter. With the exception of three regiments this entire division was wheeled into column and moved to the left at a gallop, Peirce's battery following at a brisk trot.[44]

On the Nineteenth Corps line the men could see Custer's troopers moving across the field. "General McMillan ordered the advance, and we pushed forward, driving the enemy ahead of us through the wood, and came out to the left and rear of the Confederate line, enabling our left to pour in a fearful fire on their exposed flank." The Confederates tried to hold on behind stone walls and fences, but soon the left of their line broke for the rear.[45]

General Gordon had been conferring with Early when the attack began and hurried back to the front just in time to see his men being assaulted from two sides. General Evans' division was on the left of the Confederate line and he had been in command while Gordon was gone. Gordon found him

> almost completely surrounded by literally overwhelming numbers; but he was handling the men with great skill, and fighting in almost every direction with characteristic coolness. It required countercharges of the most daring character to prevent the utter destruction of the command and effect its withdrawal. At the same instant additional Union forces, which had penetrated through the vacant space, were assailing our main line on the flank and rolling it up like a scroll. Regiment after regiment, brigade after brigade, in rapid succession was crushed....[46]

As the two divisions of the Nineteenth Corps were breaking down the resistance on Gordon's left and pushing the Confederates back, Custer saw his opening and took it. Since he didn't have to worry about Confederate cavalry, Custer led his men around the Confederate left to try and cut off their retreat. In the open fields the Confederates could clearly see his troopers moving around to their rear and fully understood what it meant. George A. Custer said, "Seeing so large a force of cavalry bearing rapidly down upon an unprotected flank and their line of retreat in danger of being intercepted, the lines of the enemy, already broken, now gave way in the utmost confusion."[47]

One of Custer's troopers remembered that

> Every man felt that the decisive moment had come, and grasped his reins tightly. Like figures of iron bolted to our saddles, we pressed forward with pale cheeks, eyes flashing fire, teeth set firm, and revolvers clasped in our right hands. With the impetus of an avalanche, we charged forward through a storm of shot and shell, which sent many a comrade to his last account. While others whose horses were shot under them pressed forward on foot. The rebels could not stand the terrific assault and fled panic stricken from the field....[48]

Over on the Sixth Corps' front, the battle was also nearing its climax. As the Confederates were retreating on their left, General Grimes was being pressed to the limit. He said, "The enemy were then in front and to the left and rear of the left flank of this division, when they began to fall back in the same disorderly manner as those on the left ... the stampede on the left was caught up, and no threats nor entreaties could arrest their flight."[49]

Only on their far right did the Confederate troops hold their positions. Early wrote:

> Pegram's and Wharton's divisions, and Wofford's brigade had remained steadfast on the right, and resisted all efforts of the enemy's cavalry, but no portion of this force could be moved to the left without leaving the Pike open to the cavalry, which would have destroyed all hope at once. Every effort to rally the men in the rear having failed, I had now nothing left for me but to order these troops to retire also.[50]

On Merritt's front, his troopers had been repeatedly attacking the enemy. During one of these charges Colonel Lowell was killed at the head of his brigade riding into heavy fire.[51] But these attacks had taken their toll on the Confederates and when Early ordered Pegram and Wharton back, the men realized all was lost. Merritt timed his last charge perfectly as he and Custer swept around both flanks of the retreating Confederates. Even Gordon knew it was the end:

> As the tumult of battle died away, there came from the north side of the plain a dull, heavy swelling sound like the roaring of a distant cyclone, the omen of additional disaster. It was unmistakable. Sheridan's horsemen were riding furiously across the open fields of grass to intercept the Confederates before they crossed Cedar Creek. Many were cut off and captured. As the sullen roar from horses' hoofs beating the soft turf of the plain told of the near approach of the cavalry, all effort at orderly retreat was abandoned. The only possibility of saving the rear regiments was in unrestrained flight—every man for himself.[52]

During that final charge, a trooper in the Fifth New York Cavalry remembered that there was "No cheering now; nothing but the thundering tread of the columns, announcing our approach to the enemy, as we swept into the fire.... For three miles the charge continued, the bloody ground, the broken muskets, the dead and wounded, told its ferocity."[53]

A Sixth Corps soldier wrote later, "Our men, with wild enthusiasm, with shouts and cheers, regardless of order or formation, joined in the hot pursuit. There was our mortal enemy, who had but a few hours since driven us unceremoniously from our camps, now beaten, routed, broken, bent on nothing but the most rapid flight."[54]

Captain DuPont was able to place two batteries on high ground near Cedar Creek on the west side of the Pike:

> From this position we overlooked the completely disorganized Confederate army in full retreat, the nearest of the fugitives being about 600 yards from our guns. Our shooting was very accurate and almost every shell exploded directly in the midst of the crowded masses before us. After a very few rounds, evidence of complete demoralization could be plainly discerned – field-pieces and caissons, wagons and ambulances, were abandoned by their drivers and dashed along the road in wild confusion, damaging or destroying each other by collisions, while swarms of the retreating enemy left the road and scattered through the fields.[55]

As the cavalry pursued the fleeing Confederates into the night, Custer noted "That which hitherto, on our part, had been a pursuit after a broken and routed army now resolved itself into an exciting chase after a panic-stricken, uncontrollable mob. It was simply a question of speed between pursuers and pursued...."[56]

The darkness ended the chase and slowly the victorious Federal troops returned to the camps they had abandoned that morning. Sheridan had kept the promise he made while rallying his men that morning. Sheridan would receive the lion's share of the credit for the amazing victory, but while sitting around the fire that night he was honest enough to admit to General Crook, "I am going to get much more credit for this than I deserve, for, had I been here

Union Brigadier General Wesley Merritt (Library of Congress).

in the morning the same thing would have taken place, and had I not returned today, the same thing would have taken place."[57]

Early's beaten and dejected troops continued to retreat until they reached Fisher's Hill. Early wrote:

> The infantry moved back towards New Market at three o'clock next morning, and Rosser was left at Fisher's Hill to cover the retreat of the troops, and hold that position until they were beyond pursuit. He remained at Fisher's Hill until after ten o'clock on the 20th, and the enemy did not advance to that place while he was there.... My other troops were halted at New Market, about seven miles from Mount Jackson, and there was an entirely open country between the two places, they being very nearly in sight of each other.[58]

It had been an expensive victory. Sheridan lost 644 killed, 3,430 wounded and 1,591 missing for total casualties of 5,665.[59] A member of Early's staff reported his casualties at 1,860 killed and wounded and about 1,000 captured.[60] In the final analysis, however, it was worth the terrible price for the Union to finally gain control of the Shenandoah Valley. Sheridan had about twice as many casualties as Early, but he could sustain such a loss, Early could not. The surviving Confederates were devastated, not just from the loss of men and equipment—but their morale was shattered beyond repair. No Confederate force in the Valley would be more than a minor irritation for the rest of the war.

21. To the End

At 10 P.M. on the night of the battle, Sheridan telegraphed Grant the following message:

> I have the honor to report that my army at Cedar Creek was attacked this morning before daylight and my left was turned and driven in confusion; in fact, most of the line was driven in confusion, with the loss of twenty pieces of artillery. I hastened from Winchester, where I was on my return from Washington, and joined the army between Middletown and Newtown, having been driven back about four miles. I here took the affair in hand and quickly united the corps, formed a compact line of battle just in time to repulse an attack of the enemy's, which was handsomely done at about 1 P.M. At 3 P.M., after some changes of the cavalry from the left to the right flank, I attacked with great vigor, driving and routing the enemy, capturing, according to last reports, forty-three pieces of artillery and very many prisoners.... General Ramseur is a prisoner in our hands, severely, and perhaps mortally, wounded. I have to regret the loss of General Bidwell, killed, and Generals Wright, Grover, and Ricketts wounded—Wright slightly wounded. Affairs at times looked badly, but by the gallantry of our brave officers and men disaster has been converted into a splendid victory....[1]

When Grant first appointed Sheridan to command the Middle Military Department, the president and Secretary Stanton both were unsure about his qualifications. Now there could be no doubt in anyone's mind. Possibly as a reminder of his reluctance to appoint Sheridan, Grant telegraphed to Stanton, "I had a salute of 100 guns from each of the armies here fired in honor of Sheridan's last victory. Turning what bid fair to be a disaster into glorious victory stamps Sheridan, what I have always thought him, one of the ablest of generals."[2] From President Lincoln came a message of congratulations, "With great pleasure I tender to you and your brave army the thanks of the nation and my own personal admiration and gratitude for the month's operations in the Shenandoah Valley, and especially for the splendid work of October 19, 1864."[3] Even more important than the flood of praise that came Sheridan's way was an appointment as major general in the Regular Army.[4]

Of course, General Early's report of the battle, and its reception, were quite different. When he reached New Market on the 20th, Early sent a preliminary wire to Lee. In it he delayed as long as possible before getting to the point:

> The Sixth and Nineteenth Corps have not left the Valley. I fought them both yesterday. I attacked Sheridan's camp on Cedar Creek before day yesterday morning, and surprised and routed the Eighth and Nineteenth Corps, and then drove the Sixth Corps beyond Middletown, capturing 18 pieces of artillery and 1,300 prisoners; but the enemy subsequently made a stand on the pike, and, in turn, attacked my line, and my left gave way, and the rest of the troops took a panic and could not be rallied, retreating in confusion. But for their bad conduct I should have defeated Sheridan's whole force....[5]

In answer to the obvious question of why, knowing how badly he was outnumbered, Early still attacked such a large force, he later wrote that "we had been fighting large odds during the whole war, and I knew there was no chance of lessening them." It was important that Sheridan not be able to send large numbers of his troops to reinforce Grant at Petersburg. The surprise attack in the morning produced a great victory; Early just didn't recognize when it was time to leave.[6]

On the 21st, Early sent a message to Lee explaining the series of moves that led up to the battle and a lengthy description of the battle itself, adding:

> The state of things was distressing and mortifying beyond measure. We had within our grasp a glorious victory, and lost it by the uncontrollable propensity of our men for plunder, in the first place, and the subsequent panic among those who had kept their places....
>
> It is mortifying to me, general, to have to make these explanations of my reverses. They are due to no want of effort on my part, though it may be that I have not the capacity or judgment to prevent them. I have labored faithfully to gain success, and I have not failed to expose my person and to set an example to my men. I know that I shall have to endure censure from those who do not understand my position and difficulties, but I am still willing to make renewed efforts. If you think, however, that the interests of the service would be promoted by a change of commanders, I beg you will have no hesitation in making the change.[7]

The next day Early published a long and mostly critical message to his troops:

> Had you remained steadfast to your duty and your colours the victory would have been one of the most brilliant and decisive of the war, you would have gloriously retrieved the reverses at Winchester and Fisher's Hill and entitled yourselves to the admiration and gratitude of your country. But many of you including some commissioned officers yielded to a disgraceful propensity for

plunder, deserted your colours to appropriate to yourselves the abandoned property of the enemy, and subsequently those who had previously remained at their post, seeing their ranks thinned by the absence of the plunderers, when the enemy late in the afternoon, with his shattered columns made but a feeble effort to retrieve the fortunes of the day, yielded to a needless panic and fled the field in confusion, thereby converting a splendid victory into a disaster. Had any respectable number of you listened to the appeals made to you and made a stand even at the last moment, the disaster would have been averted and the substantial fruits of victory secured—but under the insane dread of being flanked and a panic stricken terror of the enemy's cavalry, you would listen to no appeal, threat or order, and allowed a small body of cavalry to penetrate to our train and carry off a number of pieces of Artillery and wagons which your disorder left unprotected. You have thus obscured that glorious fame won in conjunction with the gallant men of the Army of Northern Virginia who still remain proudly defiant in the trenches around Richmond and Petersburg.... Arouse yourselves then to a sense of your manhood and an appreciation of the sacred cause in which you are engaged. Yield to the mandates of discipline—resolve to stand by your colours in future at all hazards and you can yet retrieve your reputation and strike effective blows for your country and its cause. Let every man spurn from him the vile plunder gathered on the field of the 19th, and let no man whatever his rank, whether combatant or non-combatant, dare exhibit his spoils of that day. They will be the badges of his dishonor, the insignia of his disgrace. Soldiers of the Army of the Valley! I do not speak to you in anger. I wish to speak in kindness though in sorrow—my purpose is to show you the cause of our late misfortune and point out the way to avoid similar ones in the future and ensure success to our arms....

Fellow Soldiers: I am ready to lead you again in defence of our common cause and I appeal to you be the remembrance of the glorious career in which you have formerly participated, by the woes of your bleeding country, the ruined homes and devastated fields you see around you, the cries of anguish which come up from the widows and orphans of your dead comrades, the horrors which await you and all that is yours in the future if your country is subjugated, and your hopes of freedom for yourselves and your posterity, to render a cheerful and willing obedience to the rules of discipline, and to shoulder your muskets again with the determination never more to turn your backs on the foe, but to do battle like men and soldiers until the last vestige of the footsteps of our barbarous and cruel enemies is erased from the soil they desecrate and the independence of our country is firmly established.[8]

Blaming the defeat on his troops who were hungry, exhausted and outnumbered by more than two to one was probably not the best way for Early to regain his men's respect and confidence, but by now it didn't matter. There was nothing that anyone could say or do that was going to change the fate of Confederate arms in the Valley. Whatever slim chances Early's army had for success had run away with them at Cedar Creek. Most of the anger and frustration of the Southern people for the reverses in the Valley would fall on Early's head, but to be fair, considering the reality of the situation he faced, it is unlikely that anyone else could have achieved much more than he did that summer. He saved Lynchburg from almost certain destruction, won the victory at Monocacy, and came closer to the nation's capital than any other Confederate force. His army spread panic among the citizens of Pennsylvania and Maryland and forced Grant to send five infantry and two cavalry divisions away from Petersburg, which was exactly the goal of Lee's original plan.

The war was not over and General Grant still wanted Sheridan to get on with destroying the railroads between the Valley and Petersburg. He especially wanted the Virginia Central road destroyed, "even if you have to live on half rations. I say nothing about reaching Lynchburg with a portion of your force, because I doubt the practicability of it. If the army at Richmond could be cut off from Southwest Virginia it would be of great importance to us...."[9]

In response to Grant's message, Sheridan reiterated the reasons why he was opposed to attacking the Central railroad. The destruction had been so thorough that there was not enough food for a military expedition down the Valley. Large numbers of troops would have to be left behind to guard against raids and the route through the Blue Ridge was too long and too easily broken by guerrillas. Sheridan also reported that his cavalry had lost large numbers of men when their terms of enlistment expired. After listing all the reasons why he couldn't do what Grant wanted, Sheridan closed with, "Rest assured, general, I will strike, and strike hard, whenever opportunity offers."[10]

But by this time there were few available targets in the Valley that were worth striking. After a tour of the Valley at the end of October, Assistant Secretary of War Dana wrote to General Rawlins on the 29th with his impressions:

> The active campaign in the Valley seems to be over for this year. The enemy is so decidedly beaten and scattered, and driven so far to the South, that he can scarcely be expected to collect his forces for another attempt during the present season. Besides, the devastation of the Valley, extending as it does for a distance of about one hundred miles, renders it almost impossible that either the Confederates or our own forces should make a new campaign in that territory; and when Sheridan has completed the same process down the Valley to the vicinity of the Potomac, and when the stores of forage which are yet to be found in Loudoun County and in some parts of Fauquier, and the animals that are still there, are all destroyed or removed, the difficulty of any new offensive operations on either side will have been greatly increased....[11]

The burning and destruction in the Valley had produced the desired effect for the remainder of the war. There was not enough food to support a Confederate army in the Valley, let alone any to send to Lee at Petersburg. On November 9th, Early wrote to Secretary Seddon: "The supplies are so limited in the Valley that unless they are kept here my troops cannot be subsisted. I have, therefore, directed that all supplies be stopped unless by your special permission. I hope none will be granted, as it is a case of necessity."[12]

A Confederate staff officer wrote about what he saw at the end of October, "No one can imagine how utterly destroyed is this fine country, unless he could see it. Not one of the hundreds of splendid barns, the pride of the people, & promise of the future was left standing from mountain to mountain.... Broad, fertile fields lay open & barren...."[13]

A private in the VI Corps wrote:

21. To the End

> I don't know how the citizens are going to live this winter. They say we have taken away from them everything they have – their wheat, their corn, their cattle, and everything we could find, and now as winter is coming on, they are entirely destitute. Some of these citizens are going North before we leave. The rest I suppose have deliberately embraced the idea, that they are going to starve to death, and become reconciled to it. They say they have, and they ought to know.[14]

One of the more brutal events of the guerrilla war occurred in November, involving Mosby and his retaliation for an equally brutal event a few months before. On November 11, Mosby sent a letter to Sheridan which explains all:

> Some time in the month of September, during my absence from my command, six of my men who had been captured by your forces were hung and shot in the streets of Front Royal, by the order and in the immediate presence of Brigadier-General Custer. Since then another, captured by a Colonel Powell on a plundering expedition into Rappahannock, was also hung. A label affixed to the coat of one of the murdered men declared that "this would be the fate of Mosby and all his men." Since the murder of my men not less than 700 prisoners, including many officers of high rank, captured from your army by this command, have been forwarded to Richmond, but the execution of my purpose of retaliation was deferred in order, as far as possible, to confine its operation to the men of Custer and Powell. Accordingly on the 6th instant seven of your men were, by my order, executed on the Valley pike, your highway of travel. Hereafter any prisoners falling into my hands will be treated with the kindness due to their condition, unless some new act of barbarity shall compel me reluctantly to adopt a course of policy repulsive to humanity.[15]

Sheridan, who considered all partisans to be nothing better than thieves and murderers, wrote to Halleck a few days later:

> I will soon commence work on Mosby. Heretofore I have made no attempt to break him up, as I would have employed ten men to his one, and for the reason that I have made a scape-goat of him for the destruction of private rights. Now there is going to be an intense hatred of him in that portion of the Valley which is nearly a desert. I will soon commence on Loudoun County, and let them know there is a God in Israel. Mosby has annoyed me considerably, but the people are beginning to see that he does not injure me a great deal, but causes a loss to them of all that they have spent their lives in accumulating. Those people who live in the vicinity of Harper's Ferry are the most villainous in this Valley, and have not yet been hurt much. If the railroad is interfered with I will make some of them poor. Those who live at home, in peace and plenty, want the duello part of this war to go on; but when they have to bear their burden by loss of property and comforts they will cry for peace.[16]

Partisan groups were still constantly harassing the Federal forces, but "their destruction or capture being wellnigh impossible, on account of their intimate knowledge of the mountain region."[17] Sheridan decided to unleash Merrit's cavalry on the area east of the Blue Ridge between the Potomac and the Manassas Gap Railroad, where they received much of their support. There had been continued guerrilla activity in this area with frequent attacks on the railroad, wagon trains and small units of troops. Merritt was ordered to "consume and destroy all forage and subsistence, burn all barns and mills and their contents, and drive off all stock in the region...."[18]

Sheridan recounted that "Merritt carried out his instructions with his usual sagacity and thoroughness, sweeping widely over each side of his general line of march with flankers, who burned the grain and brought in large herds of cattle, hogs and sheep, which were issued to the troops."[19]

As partisan attacks brought reprisals and reprisals brought more partisan attacks, Sheridan developed a simple way of dealing with guerrillas and their supporters. In a terse order to Major General Couch, he said, "If you have arrested spies, hang them; if you are in doubt, hang them anyway. The sooner such characters are killed off the better it will be for the community."[20]

Sheridan had no plans for campaigning during the winter months and the army went into permanent camps near Winchester. The infantry pretty much stayed put, but there were frequent patrols by the cavalry to see what Early was doing and chase guerrillas.[21] On November 11, Early moved his army north to see if he could find a situation that he could take advantage of, but he found the Federal infantry safely settled behind their fortifications and "not being willing to attack him in his entrenchments, after the reverses I had met with, I determined to retire, as we were beyond the reach of supplies."[22]

On November 29th, Rosser surprised the garrison protecting the Baltimore and Ohio railroad at New Creek. He returned with about eight hundred prisoners and several hundred cattle and sheep. It was a fine Confederate victory, but too little too late, as Early reported:

> This expedition closed the material operations of the campaign of 1864 in the Shenandoah Valley, and at that time the enemy held precisely the same portion of that valley, which he held before the opening of the campaign in the spring, and no more, and the headquarters of his troops were at the same place, to wit: Winchester. There was this difference, however, at the beginning of the campaign, he held it with comparatively a small force, and at the close, he was compelled to employ three corps of infantry and one of cavalry, for that purpose, and to guard the approaches to Washington, Maryland, and Pennsylvania.[23]

Of course, Early doesn't mention that most of the Valley was in ruins and that the most important source of supplies for Lee's army had been lost.

Sheridan had always been an excellent bookkeeper, and on November 24 he sent a report to Halleck detailing the property his army captured or destroyed. Among the items listed were: 3,772 horses; 545 mules; 1,200 barns; 71 flour mills; 435,802 bushels of wheat; 20,000 bushels of oats; 77,176 bushels of corn; 20,397 tons of hay; 10,918 cattle; 12,000 sheep; 15,000 swine; 12,000 pounds of bacon or ham; 10,000 pounds of tobacco, all this and much, much more that would not be feeding people of the Valley and, more importantly, Lee's army.[24]

There was no good reason to leave veteran troops sitting in the Valley all winter, so General Lee recalled Kershaw's division back to Petersburg in the middle of November and ordered the Second Corps to return in December, leaving Early to occupy Staunton with just Wharton's infantry and the cavalry, some of which was stationed at New Market. Also in December, the Sixth Corps left the Valley and returned to Petersburg. Crook's Corps was dispersed with one division going back to West Virginia to help guard the railroad and the other to City Point.[25]

The weather was very severe that winter with heavy snow and low temperatures. Two cavalry expeditions were mounted to attack the railroads around Gordonsville and Charlottesville. Torbert led Merritt's and Powell's divisions toward the railroad while Custer advanced toward Staunton as a diversion. Both expeditions met with grief. Custer was surprised by Rosser and Payne near Lacy's Springs and had to retreat back down the Valley. Torbert ran into Lomax and a detachment of infantry from Richmond at Gordonsville and was forced to retreat with little to show for his ride except frostbitten troopers.[26]

Just before Christmas, Sheridan's Irish temper got him in trouble with the secretary of war. For most of the war, the authorities of West Virginia had frequently annoyed the War Department with unfounded alarms and frantic appeals for help because of supposed Confederate activity:

> On December 22, 1864, Governor A. I. Boreman telegraphed from Wheeling to Mr. Stanton that the Confederate General Rosser, with some 3000 cavalry, was supposed to be advancing upon Grafton and the western part of the State. This information was without the shadow of a foundation: in view of the military situation and the season, the suppositious movement of Rosser would have been absurd. But however inconsequential such a despatch appeared to be, Mr. Stanton followed his wise and invariable rule of promptly forwarding it to the commander of the department in the field, without suggestion or comment.[27]

Sheridan had received a number of these false alarms recently and when this one arrived, he finally lost his patience. Committing one of the most indiscreet acts anyone possibly could, Sheridan sent the follow telegram to Secretary Stanton:

> Governor Boreman's telegram received. If I were to make disposition of the troops of my command in accordance with the information received from the commanders in the Department of West Virginia, whom I have found, as a general thing, always alarming in their reports and stupid in their duties and actions, I certainly would have my hands full. I believe many of them to be more interested in coal-oil than in the public service. It was only yesterday that Rosser was at Crab Bottom – according to their reports, on which, at the suggestion of General Crook, I sent a regiment to Beverly; it was only two or three days previous that Rosser was at Romney, &c. They have annoyed me until, with your sanction, I would take great pleasure in bringing some of them to grief.[28]

Leslie J. Perry, in "A Shock to General Sheridan," said: "The next morning, when this flippant epistle was placed in the Secretary's hand, he appears to have been deeply incensed, and immediately sent to General Sheridan the following stinging rejoinder."[29]

> No one, that I am aware of, has asked you to make disposition of your troops in accordance with the information received from the commanders in the Department of Virginia. Governor Boreman's dispatch was received in the night, and sent by the operator in accordance with general instructions to give military commanders every report that comes here in respect to movements of the enemy in their commands. They are expected to form their own judgment of its value. It has been supposed that such information might be useful and desired by you, as it is by other commanders who are your seniors in the service, without provoking improper insinuations against the State authorities or disrespectful reply. With your subordinate commanders you will take such action as you please, but such reports as come to this Department in relation to the movements of the enemy will be forwarded as heretofore, and will be expected to be received with the respect due the Department of which you are a subordinate.[30]

Perry wrote, "I am told by one of the staff-officers that on the morning of December 23, 1864, the cold mountain air about military headquarters at Winchester was made blue by the sulphurous ebullitions of the major-general commanding."[31]

Another interesting event occurred at Christmas time showing that perhaps Sheridan was not the ogre many people in the Valley believed him to be. He apparently tried to bring some relief to the suffering citizens in the areas hardest hit by the fighting and destruction, but was rebuffed in Washington, as this message from Halleck shows:

> Your communication of the 25th asking authority to issue rations to people of the country between Winchester and Staunton has been received and submitted to the Secretary of War. I am directed to reply that it is within the authority of a commanding officer to afford temporary relief to those whom the fortunes of war have placed in his hands or under his immediate protection, but that no authority can be given for the subsistence of rebel families outside of our lines, nor even within, any longer than till they can be removed or sent to their friends and natural protectors. The disloyal people of the Shenandoah, south of Winchester and outside of our lines, have been and are now at full liberty to join friends in the rebel service or in other places in the rebel territory. The disloyal within our lines should be sent South to feed upon the enemy. Loyal refugees should be temporarily assisted and sent North, where they can earn a livelihood. While the men of Virginia are either serving in the rebel ranks, or as bushwhackers are waylaying or murdering our soldiers, our Government must decline to support their wives and children.[32]

As the new year opened, Early's role in the Valley became much different than it had been when he first arrived to save Lynchburg. Early met with General Lee in Richmond on January 2nd concerning what, if anything, could be done in the Valley, "and he told me that he had left me there with the small command which still remained, in order to produce the impression that the force was much larger than it really was, and he instructed me to do the best I could."[33]

21. To the End

On February 27 the final campaign in the Shenandoah Valley began. Sheridan had just appointed Merritt as chief of cavalry while Torbert was on leave and he commanded about 10,000 men in two divisions under Custer and Devin.[34]

Sheridan's orders from Grant were

> to destroy the Virginia Central railroad and the James River canal, capture Lynchburg if practicable, and then join General Sherman in North Carolina wherever he might be found, or return to Winchester, but as to joining Sherman I was to be governed by the state of affairs after the projected capture of Lynchburg. The weather was cold, the valley and surrounding mountains being still covered with snow; but this was fast disappearing, however, under the heavy rain that was coming down as the column moved along up the Valley pike....[35]

Not knowing what Sheridan's target was, Early sent Lomax's cavalry toward Lynchburg to slow down the Federals if they were heading there. Early, with Wharton's infantry, went to Waynesboro to try to block the route to Charlottesville. Both detachments were pitifully small and had no real hope of stopping Sheridan's horsemen in a fight.[36]

Sheridan soon discovered how Early had divided his troops and, not wanting any sizable enemy force in his rear while moving on Lynchburg, he sent Custer's division, closely followed by Devin, to confront Early at Waynesboro. The conditions were poor for cavalry: "The rain had been pouring in torrents for two days, and the roads were bad beyond description; nevertheless, the men pushed boldly on, although horses and men could scarcely be recognized for the mud which covered them."[37]

Early fully realized he could do little but delay the horde of horsemen that were approaching his position. "I did not intend making my final stand on this ground, yet I was satisfied that if my men would fight, which I had no reason to doubt, I could hold the enemy in check until night, and then cross the river and take position in Rockfish Gap; for I had done more difficult things than that during the war."[38]

Custer did not waste much time in studying the Confederate defenses. He quickly saw that their left was exposed near the river behind their line and sent Colonel Pennington with three dismounted regiments around that flank while Custer himself, with two brigades, attacked the front of the breastworks. Pennington soon broke the enemy line on the left and Custer broke through the front with the Eighth New York and First Connecticut charging through the lines to the river, where they set up on the opposite bank to trap the fleeing Confederates.[39]

Attacked from front and flank, the Confederates collapsed so quickly that Early was pretty much helpless during the short fight. "I now saw that everything was lost, and after the enemy had got between the mountain and the position where I was, and retreat was thus cut off, I rode aside into the woods, and in that way escaped capture...."[40]

Sheridan immediately sent a force through Rockfish Gap

> to encamp on the east side of the Blue Ridge. By reason of this move all the enemy's stores and transportation fell into our hands, while we captured on

the field seventeen battle flags, sixteen hundred officers and men, and eleven pieces of artillery. This decisive victory closed hostilities in the Shenandoah Valley.[41]

Jubal Early escaped from the disaster at Waynesboro with just his staff and a handful of others and headed east. They first tried to get to Charlottesville, but Federal forces were already there. They then went through Gordonsville and finally reached Richmond. There, Early met with Lee and then headed back to the Valley to try and organize any troops that he could find.[42]

On March 30, Jubal Early's military career came to an end with a letter from General Lee:

> My telegram will have informed you that I deem a change of commanders in your Department necessary; but it is due to your zealous and patriotic services that I should explain the reasons that prompted my action.... I have reluctantly arrived at the conclusion that you cannot command the united and willing co-operation which is so essential to success. Your reverses in the Valley, of which the public and the army judge chiefly by the results, have, I fear, impaired your influence both with the people and the soldiers, and would add greatly to the difficulties which will, under any circumstances, attend our military operations in S. W. Virginia. While my own confidence in your ability, zeal, and devotion to the cause is unimpaired, I have nevertheless felt that I could not oppose what seems to be the current of opinion, without injustice to your reputation and injury to the service....[43]

After the rout at Waynesboro, Sheridan decided to interpret his orders from Grant in a different light. He finally decided to mount an expedition to destroy the James River Canal and the Virginia Central Railroad. Since there was no organized Confederate force to oppose him, the destruction of these targets was now considered feasible. Although it was now a little late in the game, at least Grant would finally get his wish to have these two arteries disabled. Another part of the orders from Grant were simply ignored. After destroying the railroad, Sheridan was supposed to head to North Carolina and join forces with General Sherman. Instead, Sheridan decided to take his cavalry east and join General Grant at Petersburg. He was at least honest about his motivation: "feeling that the war was nearing its end, I desired my cavalry to be in at the death."[44]

Just a few weeks later, it was the hard driving Philip Sheridan who led the Federal troops that cut off the escape route of the Army of Northern Virginia after they abandoned Petersburg, forcing Lee's surrender. The war was finally over, the price paid to keep the nation together had been horribly high, but in the end it had been worth it.

Notes

1. A Long Road Ahead

1. Larry Shapiro, ed., *Abraham Lincoln: Mystic Chords of Memory* (New York: Book-of-the-Month Club, Inc., 1984), 72.
2. Roy P. Basler, ed., *The Collected Works of Abraham Lincoln, Volume VII* (New Brunswick, N.J.: Rutgers University Press, 1953), 395.
3. James M. McPherson, *Ordeal by Fire: The Civil War and Reconstruction* (New York: Alfred A. Knopf, 1982), 456.
4. Bruce Catton, *Bruce Catton's Civil War* (New York: The Fairfax Press, 1984), 629.
5. Thomas A. Lewis, *The Guns of Cedar Creek* (New York: Harper & Row, 1988), 24.
6. John S. Wise, "The West Point of the Confederacy," *The Century: A Popular Quarterly*, January 1889, 464.
7. A.L. Long, *Memoirs of Robert E. Lee* (Edison, N.J.: The Blue and Grey Press, 1983), 635.
8. Robert E. Lee, *Recollections and Letters of General Robert E. Lee* (New York: Konecky & Konecky, 1992), 118.
9. *The War of the Rebellion: A Compilation of the Official Records of the Union and Confederate Armies* (Washington, D.C.: United States War Department, 1880–1901), Vol. 33, 1114.
10. *Official Records*, Vol. 33, 1117.
11. William Blair, *Virginia's Private War* (New York: Oxford University Press, 1998), 125.
12. George Gary Eggleston, "A Rebel's Recollections," *The Atlantic Monthly*, December 1874, 663.
13. James A. Rawley, *Turning Points of the Civil War* (Lincoln, Neb.: University of Nebraska Press, 1989), 174.
14. Bruce Catton, *Grant Takes Command* (Boston: Little Brown, 1968), 119–20.
15. Catton, *Grant Takes Command*, 122.
16. Catton, *Bruce Catton's Civil War*, 482. Catton, *Grant Takes Command*, 104.
17. Horace Porter, *Campaigning with Grant* (New York: Mallard Press, 1991), 1.
18. Catton, *Bruce Catton's Civil War*, 482. Jeffry D. Wert, *Mosby's Rangers* (New York: Simon & Schuster, 1990), 159.
19. Porter, 47.
20. Ulysses S. Grant, *Personal Memoirs of U. S. Grant* (New York: Charles L. Webster & Company, 1885), 127.
21. Catton, *Grant Takes Command*, 167.
22. *Official Records*, Vol. 31, Part 3, 349–50.
23. Adam Badeau, *Military History of Ulysses S. Grant: From April 1861 to April 1865* (New York: D. Appleton and Company, 1885), 9–10. Wert, 159.
24. Catton, *Bruce Catton's Civil War*, 480.
25. Catton, *Bruce Catton's Civil War*, 480.
26. Catton, *Bruce Catton's Civil War*, 480.
27. *Official Records*, Series 3, Vol. 4, 930.
28. *Official Records*, Vol. 33, 776.
29. *Official Records*, Vol. 33, 794.
30. Grant, 130–32. *Official Records*, Vol. 33, 827–28.
31. *Official Records*, Vol. 33, 828.
32. Catton, *Bruce Catton's Civil War*, 495.

33. Clifford Dowdey, ed., *The Wartime Papers of R. L. Lee* (Boston: Little Brown, 1961), 666–67.
34. *Official Records*, Vol. 33, 1291.
35. Lee, 121–22.
36. Catton, *Grant Takes Command*, 175.
37. Basler, 324–25. Catton, *Grant Takes Command*, 177.
38. Basler, 324–25. Catton, *Grant Takes Command*, 177–78.

2. The Valley

1. Orton S. Clark, *The One Hundred and Sixteenth Regiment of New York State Volunteers* (Buffalo, N.Y.: Printing House of Matthews & Warren, 1868), 206.
2. Jubal A. Early, *Lieutenant General Jubal Anderson Early C. S. A.: Autobiographical Sketch and Narrative of the War Between the States* (New York: Konecky & Konecky, 1994), 366–67. Bevin Alexander, *Lost Victories: The Military Genius of Stonewall Jackson* (Edison, N.J.: The Blue & Grey Press, 1996), 51. John C. Bonnell Jr., *Sabres in the Shenandoah: The 21st New York Cavalry, 1863–1866* (Shippensburg, Pa.: Burd Street Press, 1996), 12–13.
3. Catton, *Bruce Catton's Civil War*, 620.
4. Richard R. Duncan, *Lee's Endangered Left* (Baton Rouge, La.: Louisiana State University Press, 1998), 116–17.
5. John Imboden, "To the Farmers of Augusta, Rockingham and Shenandoah," *The Staunton Spectator*, March 8, 1864, Page 1, Col. 7.
6. Duncan, 135. William C. Davis, *The Battle of New Market* (Garden City: N.J.: Doubleday, 1975), 157–58.
7. Catton, *Bruce Catton's Civil War*, 620.
8. Duncan, 10. Davis, *New Market*, 2.
9. Davis, *New Market*, 3.
10. Early, *Lieutenant General Jubal Anderson Early*, 368–69. Davis, *New Market*, 2. Duncan, 10.
11. Davis, *New Market*, 2. Duncan, 10.
12. Thomas A. Ashby, *The Valley Campaigns: Being the Reminiscences of a Non-Combatant While Between the Lines in the Shenandoah Valley During the War of the States* (New York: The Neale Publishing Co., 1914), 298–99.
13. Edwin B. Lufkin, *History of the Thirteenth Maine Regiment* (Bridgton, Maine: H.A. Shorey & Son, Publishers, 1898), 109. Duncan, 11.
14. Richard B. Irwin, *History of the Nineteenth Army Corps* (Baton Rouge, La.: Elliott's Book Shop Press, 1985), 368–69.
15. Catton, *Bruce Catton's Civil War*, 625.
16. *Official Records*, Vol. 33, 1081.
17. *Official Records*, Vol. 33, 1082.
18. *Official Records*, Vol. 33, 1082.
19. *Official Records*, Vol. 33, 1252.
20. *Official Records*, Vol. 33, 1167.
21. *Official Records*, Vol. 33, 1168.

3. The Campaign Begins

1. Duncan, 11. Grant, 131–32.
2. Duncan, 11. Davis, *New Market*, 7.
3. Davis, *New Market*, 7–8.
4. Davis, *New Market*, 8–10.
5. David Hunter Strother, *A Virginia Yankee in the Civil War* (Chapel Hill, N.C.: University of North Carolina Press, 1961), 213.
6. Davis, *New Market*, 11.
7. *Official Records*, Vol. 33, 762.
8. *Official Records*, Vol. 33, 701.
9. *Official Records*, Vol. 33, 764–65.
10. Stephen D. Engle, *Yankee Dutchman: The Life of Franz Sigel* (Fayetteville, Ark.: The University of Arkansas Press, 1993), 172–73.
11. Davis, *New Market*, 13.
12. Davis, *New Market*, 15.
13. Dowdey, 650–51.
14. *Official Records*, Vol. 33, 1124.
15. *Official Records*, Vol. 51, Part 2, 820.
16. Duncan, 34–35.
17. William C. Davis, *Breckinridge: Statesman, Soldier, Symbol* (Baton Rouge, La.: Louisiana State University Press, 1974), 408–09. Duncan, 36.
18. Davis, *Breckinridge*, 409.
19. *Official Records*, Vol. 33, 1318.
20. Davis, *New Market*, 19. *Official Records*, Vol. 33, 1215.
21. *Official Records*, Vol. 33, 765–66. Duncan, 19–21, 27.
22. *Official Records*, Vol. 33, 1275.
23. *Official Records*, Vol. 37, Part 1, 526. Engle, 175.
24. *Official Records*, Vol. 33, 901. Engle, 175.
25. *Official Records*, Vol. 33, 734.
26. Strother, 222.
27. William S. Lincoln, *Life With the Thirty-fourth Mass. Infantry in the War of the Rebellion* (Worcester, Mass.: Press of Noyes, Snow & Company, 1879), 260–61.
28. *Official Records*, Vol. 32, Part 3, 246.
29. *Official Records*, Vol. 33, 1291.
30. Davis, *New Market*, 27.
31. Davis, *New Market*, 28.
32. Duncan, 114–17.
33. William Hewitt, *History of the Twelfth West Virginia Volunteer Infantry* (Twelfth West Virginia Infantry Association, 1892), 332.
34. Hewitt, 332.

35. Bonnell, 48.
36. *Official Records*, Vol. 37, Part 1, 364.
37. John D. Imboden, "The Battle of New Market, Va., May 15, 1864," *Battles and Leaders of the Civil War*, Eds. Robert Johnson Underwood and Clarence Clough Buel (New York: Thomas Yoseloff, 1956), 480. Davis, *Breckinridge*, 414–15.
38. *Official Records*, Vol. 37, Part 1, 712.
39. *Official Records*, Vol. 37, Part 1, 713.
40. *Official Records*, Vol. 37, Part 1, 2.
41. *Official Records*, Vol. 37, Part 1, 372.
42. Engle, 182–83. Duncan, 119.
43. *Official Records*, Vol. 37, Part 1, 69.
44. Davis, *New Market*, 38.
45. *Official Records*, Vol. 37, Part 1, 421. Davis, *New Market*, 39. Strother, 224.
46. Imboden, "The Battle of New Market," 480.
47. Davis, *New Market*, 47.
48. John C. Breckinridge letter to Francis H. Smith, May 10, 1964, Virginia Military Institute Archives.
49. Davis, *New Market*, 50.
50. Engle, 183–84.
51. *Official Records*, Vol. 37, Part 1, 10–12, 41. Davis, *New Market*, 41.
52. *Official Records*, Vol. 37, Part 1, 446. Engle, 185.
53. *Official Records*, Vol. 37, Part 1, 447.
54. Duncan, 110–11. Davis, *Breckinridge*, 417.
55. Davis, *New Market*, 66–67.
56. *Official Records*, Vol. 37, Part 1, 73. Davis, *New Market*, 67–68. Strother, 224.
57. Engle, 185.
58. Duncan, 125. Engle, 186. Davis, *New Market*, 70.
59. Imboden, "The Battle of New Market," 482. Davis, *Breckinridge*, 418.
60. *Official Records*, Vol. 37, Part 1, 79. Davis, *New Market*, 73.
61. Duncan, 125–26. Davis, *New Market*, 76.
62. *Official Records*, Vol. 37, Part 1, 79–80.
63. Davis, *Breckinridge*, 418. Duncan, 126. Imboden, "The Battle of New Market," 481.
64. Davis, *New Market*, 77.
65. Engle, 186. Davis, *New Market*, 77–78.

4. The Battle of New Market

1. Davis, *New Market*, 81–82.
2. *Official Records*, Vol. 37, Part 1, 89.
3. Bonnell, 55. Franz Sigel, "Sigel in the Shenandoah Valley in 1864," *Battles and Leaders of the Civil War*, Eds. Robert Johnson Underwood and Clarence Clough Buel (New York: Thomas Yoseloff, 1956), 488.
4. Duncan, 127. Davis, *New Market*, 93. *Official Records*, Vol. 37, Part 1, 79–80.
5. Imboden, "The Battle of New Market," 483. Davis, *Breckinridge*, 419.
6. Sigel, 488.
7. Davis, *New Market*, 99. Strother, 224.
8. *Official Records*, Vol. 37, Part 1, 90. Davis, *New Market*, 88–89.
9. Davis, *New Market*, 83–85, 89. Davis, *Breckinridge*, 418.
10. Davis, *New Market*, 92.
11. Imboden, "The Battle of New Market," 484. Davis, *New Market*, 99. *Official Records*, Vol. 37, Part 1, 90.
12. *Official Records*, Vol. 37, Part 1, 83. Sigel, 489. Davis, *New Market*, 108–09.
13. H. A. DuPont, *The Campaign of 1864 in the Valley of Virginia and the Expedition to Lynchburg* (New York: J. J. Little & Ives Company, 1925), 20–21.
14. Imboden, "The Battle of New Market," 483.
15. Bonnell, 56. Imboden, "The Battle of New Market," 483–84.
16. Sigel, 489. Davis, *New Market*, 107–09.
17. *Official Records*, Vol. 37, Part 1, 82. Duncan, 129–30. Davis, *New Market*, 108.
18. *Official Records*, Vol. 37, Part 1, 83.
19. *Official Records*, Vol. 37, Part 1, 83–84.
20. Davis, *New Market*, 117–18. Imboden, "The Battle of New Market," 484.
21. *Official Records*, Vol. 37, Part 1, 84.
22. Imboden, "The Battle of New Market," 484. Davis, *New Market*, 118–19. Davis, *Breckinridge*, 425.
23. Davis, *New Market*, 120–21.
24. Davis, *New Market*, 121–22. Davis, *Breckinridge*, 425–26.
25. *Official Records*, Vol. 37, Part 1, 90.
26. Porter Johnson Memoirs, Letter to Henry Wise, June 8, 1909, Virginia Military Institute Archives.
27. Duncan, 131.
28. Davis, *New Market*, 125–28. Duncan, 131. Bonnell, 57.
29. Bonnell, 57–58. Davis, *New Market*, 127–28.
30. Davis, *New Market*, 129–30.
31. Strother, 226.
32. Davis, *New Market*, 132.
33. *Official Records*, Vol. 37, Part 1, 86. Davis, *New Market*, 132.
34. *Official Records*, Vol. 37, Part 1, 86.
35. *Official Records*, Vol. 37, Part 1, 84. Davis, *New Market*, 133.
36. Davis, *New Market*, 134–36. Duncan, 132.
37. *Official Records*, Vol. 37, Part 1, 87. C. J. Rawling, *History of the First Regiment Virginia Infantry* (Philadelphia: J. B. Lippincott Company, 1887), 166–67. Davis, *New Market*, 147.

38. Davis, *New Market*, 140–41.
39. *Official Records*, Vol. 37, Part 1, 84.
40. Sigel, 489–90. Davis, *New Market*, 141.
41. Imboden, "The Battle of New Market," 484–85.
42. Davis, *New Market*, 152. Strother, 227–28.
43. *Official Records*, Vol. 37, Part 1, 80.
44. Bonnell, 58. Sigel, 490.
45. Davis, *New Market*, 149–50.
46. DuPont, 22.
47. Davis, *New Market*, 156.
48. Sigel, 490. Davis, *New Market*, 156.
49. Strother, 229.
50. Davis, *New Market*, 157–58. John W. Wayland, *A History of Shenandoah County Virginia* (Strasburg, Va.: Shenandoah Publishing House, 1927), 317.
51. *Official Records*, Vol. 37, Part 1, 87.
52. *Official Records*, Vol. 37, Part 1, 76.
53. Davis, *Breckinridge*, 429. Sigel, 491. *Official Records*, Vol. 37, Part 1, 76.
54. Davis, *New Market*, 163.
55. *Official Records*, Vol. 37, Part 1, 737.
56. *Official Records*, Vol. 37, Part 1, 738.
57. *Official Records*, Vol. 36, Part 2, 840.
58. Davis, *New Market*, 166.
59. Strother, 229.
60. Imboden, "The Battle of New Market," 485.
61. Strother, 229–30.

5. New Commander, Same Plan

1. *Official Records*, Vol. 37, Part 1, 492.
2. *Official Records*, Vol. 37, Part 1, 524. Duncan, 142–43.
3. Duncan, 138–39. Thomas J. Reed, *Tibbit's Boys: A History of the 21st New York Cavalry* (Lanham, Md.: University Press of America, Inc., 1997), 123–24.
4. DuPont, 37–38.
5. *Official Records*, Vol. 37, Part 1, 507. Duncan, 143.
6. *Official Records*, Vol. 37, Part 1, 500. Bonnell, 63–64.
7. *Official Records*, Vol. 37, Part 1, 516.
8. *Official Records*, Vol. 37, Part 1, 517.
9. *Official Records*, Vol. 37, Part 1, 525.
10. *Official Records*, Vol. 37, Part 1, 525.
11. Duncan, 144–45.
12. *Official Records*, Vol. 37, Part 1, 528.
13. Strother, 236–37.
14. Duncan, 153–54.
15. *Official Records*, Vol. 37, Part 1, 749.
16. Imboden, "The Battle of New Market," 485. John D. Imboden, "Fire, Sword, and the Halter," *The Annals of the Civil War*, Ed. Alexander Kelly McClure (New York: DeCapo Press, Inc., 1994), 171. 17. Imboden, "Fire, Sword, and Halter," 171–72.
18. Reed, 127. Duncan, 174. Marchall Moore Brice, *Conquest of a Valley* (Charlottesville, VA: University of Virginia Press, 1965), 37.
19. Imboden, "Fire, Sword, and the Halter," 173.
20. *Official Records*, Vol. 37, Part 1, 548.
21. Strother, 239. Bonnell, 69. Duncan, 154.
22. Duncan, 155. Imboden, "Fire, Sword, and the Halter," 172.
23. *Official Records*, Vol. 33, 765.
24. Duncan, 152.
25. Strother, 241.
26. *Official Records*, Vol. 51, Part 2, 981.
27. Strother, 241.
28. Imboden, "Fire, Sword, and the Halter," 172.
29. Imboden, "Fire, Sword, and the Halter," 172.
30. Imboden, "Fire, Sword, and the Halter," 172–73.
31. Duncan, 174–75. Imboden, "Fire, Sword, and the Halter," 173.
32. Imboden, "Fire, Sword, and the Halter," 173.
33. Imboden, "Fire, Sword, and the Halter," 173. Duncan, 175.
34. Strother, 242.
35. Imboden, "Fire, Sword, and the Halter," 173.
36. Reed, 129. Duncan, 175.
37. Strother, 243. Brice, 55. Reed, 129.

6. The Battle of Piedmont

1. Bonnell, 71. Reed, 129–30.
2. Imboden, "Fire, Sword, and the Halter," 174.
3. Imboden, "Fire, Sword, and the Halter," 174.
4. Reed, 129. Duncan, 178.
5. Reed, 131, 134. Duncan, 178.
6. Strother, 243.
7. Duncan, 177–78. Reed, 130–32. *Official Records*, Vol. 37, Part 1, 95.
8. Duncan, 179. Bonnell, 72. Reed, 132–33.
9. Duncan, 179. *Official Records*, Vol. 37, Part 1, 117.
10. Duncan, 179. *Official Records*, Vol. 37, Part 1, 95.
11. Strother, 244. *Official Records*, Vol. 37, Part 1, 95. Reed, 133. Duncan, 180.
12. *Official Records*, Vol. 37, Part 1, 118.

13. *Official Records*, Vol. 37, Part 1, 95.
14. Rawling, 173–74.
15. *Official Records*, Vol. 37, Part 1, 95.
16. *Official Records*, Vol. 37, Part 1, 118–19.
17. Duncan, 183. Reed, 135. Imboden, "Fire, Sword, and the Halter," 175.
18. *Official Records*, Vol. 51, Part 2, 990.
19. Duncan, 184. Imboden, "Fire, Sword, and the Halter," 175. *Official Records*, Vol. 37, Part 1, 95.
20. *Official Records*, Vol. 37, Part 1, 95.
21. Reed, 135–36. Duncan, 181.
22. Duncan, 181–82. Reed, 135.
23. Imboden, "Fire, Sword, and the Halter," 174–75.
24. Strother, 246.
25. Strother, 244–45. Reed, 136.
26. *Official Records*, Vol. 37, Part 1, 103.
27. Duncan, 247. Reed, 137.

7. On to Staunton and Lynchburg

1. Duncan, 188. Strother, 246.
2. Duncan, 191. *Official Records*, Vol. 37, Part 1, 153.
3. Strother, 246–47.
4. Duncan, 193. Strother, 247.
5. Duncan, 194.
6. Strother, 248.
7. Strother, 251.
8. Strother, 250–51.
9. *Official Records*, Vol. 37, Part 1, 606.
10. Dowdey, 767.
11. Strother, 252.
12. Imboden, "Fire, Sword, and the Halter," 175.
13. Achilles J. Tynes Letter, June 13, 1864, Virginia Military Institute Archives.
14. Fannie M. Lyle Wilson Letter, June 17, 1864, Virginia Military Institute Archives.
15. Strother, 252.
16. Strother, 253.
17. Strother, 255.
18. *Official Records*, Vol. 37, Part 1, 97.
19. John Letcher, "The Burning of Gov. Letcher's Residence," *The Staunton Vindicator*, July 22, 1864, Page 1, Col. 6. Duncan, 225.
20. DuPont, 69.
21. *Official Records*, Vol. 37, Part 1, 607.
22. *Official Records*, Vol. 37, Part 1, 607.
23. *Official Records*, Vol. 37, Part 1, 628.
24. Lawrence Royster Letter, July 28, 1864, John E. Roller Papers, Virginia Military Institute Archives.
25. Duncan, 254–55. *Official Records*, Vol. 37, Part 1, 598.
26. *Official Records*, Vol. 36, Part 1, 26, 796.
27. Duncan, 257.
28. Duncan, 256. Jubal A. Early, *A Memoir of the Last Year of the War for Independence in the Confederate States of America* (New Orleans: Blelock & Co., 1867), 35.
29. Duncan, 260–62.
30. Henry Kyd Douglas, *I Rode With Stonewall* (Chapel Hill, N.C.: University of North Carolina Press, 1940), 33.
31. John S. Wise, *The End of an Era* (Boston: Houghton, Mifflin and Co., 1899), 228.
32. Douglas, 33.
33. Wise, 228.
34. Duncan, 260–62.
35. Early, *A Memoir of the Last Year of the War*, 35. Duncan, 256. Long, 356.
36. Strother, 258. Bonnell, 83.
37. Achilles J. Tynes Letter.
38. Bonnell, 85. Rawling, 181.
39. Duncan, 243. Strother, 263.
40. *Official Records*, Vol. 37, Part 1, 98.
41. Duncan, 269.
42. John H. Worsham, *One of Jackson's Foot Cavalry: His Experience and What He Saw During the War 1861–1865* (New York: The Neale Publishing Co., 1912), 229.
43. Early, *A Memoir of the Last Year of the War*, 36. Duncan, 262–64. *Official Records*, Vol. 37, Part 1, 761.
44. *Official Records*, Vol. 37, Part 1, 762–63.
45. *Official Records*, Vol. 37, Part 1, 763.
46. *Official Records*, Vol. 37, Part 1, 763.
47. *Official Records*, Vol. 37, Part 1, 765.
48. Early, *A Memoir of the Last Year of the War*, 36.
49. Duncan, 270. Early, *A Memoir of the Last Year of the War*, 36–37.
50. Early, *Lieutenant General Jubal Anderson Early*, 374.
51. Early, *A Memoir of the Last Year of the War*, 36. Duncan, 243, 272.
52. *Official Records*, Vol. 37, Part 1, 141.
53. Bonnell, 87.
54. Duncan, 271–72. Early, *A Memoir of the Last Year of the War*, 37.
55. Bonnell, 82. Duncan, 273.
56. *Official Records*, Vol. 37, Part 1, 99.
57. Early, *A Memoir of the Last Year of the War*, 37–38.

8. Lynchburg and Retreat

1. Bonnell, 88–89. Duncan, 275–77.
2. *Official Records*, Vol. 37, Part 1, 99–100.
3. Duncan, 277. Early, *A Memoir of the Last Year of the War*, 38.
4. Duncan, 278. *Official Records*, Vol. 37, Part 1, 142.

5. *Official Records*, Vol. 37, Part 1, 650.
6. Strother, 265.
7. Duncan, 281. Strother, 265. *Official Records*, Vol. 37, Part 1, 100.
8. Dupont, 78.
9. *Official Records*, Vol. 37, Part 1, 100, 121. Strother, 265.
10. Duncan, 281. *Official Records*, Vol. 37, Part 1, 100, Strother, 265–66.
11. Duncan, 282. *Official Records*, Vol. 37, Part 1, 100.
12. Duncan, 282–83. *Official Records*, Vol. 37, Part 1, 132.
13. William G. Watson Memoirs, *A Union Soldier in the Shenandoah Valley, 1864*, Virginia Military Institute Archives.
14. Duncan, 281. *Official Records*, Vol. 37, Part 1, 148.
15. *Official Records*, Vol. 37, Part 1, 142.
16. *Official Records*, Vol. 37, Part 1, 142.
17. *Official Records*, Vol. 37, Part 1, 100, 142.
18. *Official Records*, Vol. 37, Part 1, 100.
19. DuPont, 83.
20. Duncan, 287. Strother, 266.
21. William G. Watson Memoirs.
22. Duncan, 286. Early, *A Memoir of the Last Year of the War*, 38.
23. *Official Records*, Vol. 37, Part 1, 142–43.
24. *Official Records*, Vol. 37, Part 1, 143.
25. *Official Records*, Vol. 37, Part 1, 143. Bonnell, 89–90.
26. Early, *A Memoir of the Last Year of the War*, 38.
27. *Official Records*, Vol. 37, Part 1, 160.
28. William G. Watson Memoirs.
29. Early, *A Memoir of the Last Year of the War*, 39. Duncan, 290.
30. Strother, 267. Early, *A Memoir of the Last Year of the War*, 39.
31. J. O. Humphreys Diary, Virginia Military Institute Archives.
32. J. O. Humphreys Diary.
33. Duncan, 300. Early, *Lieutenant General Jubal Anderson Early*, 378.
34. Reed, 162. *Official Records*, Vol. 37, Part 1, 101.
35. Rawling, 186.
36. Reed, 162–64. *Official Records*, Vol. 37, Part 1, 101.
37. Bonnell, 94.
38. Strother, 269.
39. Duncan, 300. Reed, 164. *Official Records*, Vol. 37, Part 1, 101–02.
40. Early, *A Memoir of the Last Year of the War*, 40.
41. William G. Watson Memoirs.
42. *Official Records*, Vol. 37, Part 1, 683–84.
43. *Official Records*, Vol. 37, Part 1, 657.
44. Imboden, "Fire, Sword, and the Halter," 183.
45. Douglas, 290.
46. Dowdey, 652.

9. Early Moves North

1. Early, *A Memoir of the Last Year of the War*, 41.
2. Long, 357.
3. *Official Records*, Vol. 37, Part 1, 766.
4. Early, *A Memoir of the Last Year of the War*, 42. Douglas, 290.
5. Douglas, 293–94.
6. *Official Records*, Vol. 37, Part 1, 346.
7. Early, *A Memoir of the Last Year of the War*, 41.
8. Early, *A Memoir of the Last Year of the War*, 41.
9. Early, *A Memoir of the Last Year of the War*, 42–43.
10. Thomas Winton Fisher, Letter dated June 28, 1864, "The McGinley Genealogy Page," December 5, 1998, http://ted.gardner.org. June 10, 2001.
11. Early, *Lieutenant General Jubal Anderson Early*, 382.
12. *Official Records*, Vol. 37, Part 1, 769–70.
13. Early, *A Memoir of the Last Year of the War*, 42–43.
14. Early, *A Memoir of the Last Year of the War*, 43–44. Bonnell, 101–03.
15. *Official Records*, Vol. 37, Part 2, 16.
16. *Official Records*, Vol. 37, Part 2, 20. Bonnell, 104.
17. Early, *A Memoir of the Last Year of the War*, 44.
18. *Official Records*, Vol. 37, Part 1, 176.
19. Worsham, 233.
20. Early, *A Memoir of the Last Year of the War*, 44.
21. *Official Records*, Vol. 37, Part 1, 176. Early, *Lieutenant General Jubal Anderson Early*, 384.
22. Early, *A Memoir of the Last Year of the War*, 45.
23. *Official Records*, Vol. 37, Part 2, 15.
24. Catton, *Bruce Catton's Civil War*, 610. *Official Records*, Vol. 37, Part 1, 768.
25. *Official Records*, Vol. 37, Part 2, 59.
26. *Official Records*, Vol. 37, Part 2, 60.
27. *Official Records*, Vol. 37, Part 2, 60.
28. Margaret Leech, *Reveille In Washington 1860–1865* (New York: Time Inc., 1962), 409. Catton, *Grant Takes Command*, 310.
29. Catton, *Grant Takes Command*, 311. *Official Records*, Vol. 37, Part 2, 60.
30. Leech, 408–09.
31. *Official Records*, Vol. 37, Part 2, 592. Early, *A Memoir of the Last Year of the War*, 44.

32. *Official Records*, Vol. 37, Part 2, 592.
33. *Official Records*, Vol. 37, Part 2, 592.
34. Early, *Lieutenant General Jubal Anderson Early*, 384–86. Douglas, 292. Leech, 408.
35. *Official Records*, Vol. 37, Part 2, 77. Leech, 410. Charles Carleton Coffin, *Four Years of Fighting: A Volume of Personal Observations With the Army and Navy* (Boston: Ticknor and Fields, 1866), 385–86.
36. Early, *A Memoir of the Last Year of the War*, 45.
37. *Official Records*, Vol. 37, Part 1, 767.
38. *Official Records*, Vol. 37, Part 2, 108–10. Vol. 37, Part 1, 194.
39. *Official Records*, Vol. 37, Part 1, 193–94. Leech, 412.
40. Lew Wallace, *Lew Wallace—An Autobiography, Volume 2* (New York: Harper & Brothers, 1906), 726.
41. *Official Records*, Vol. 37, Part 1, 193.
42. E. M. Haynes, *A History of the Tenth Regiment, Vermont Volunteers* (Tenth Vermont Regimental Association, 1879), 90.
43. *Official Records*, Vol. 37, Part 2, 110–11. Leech, 412.
44. *Official Records*, Vol. 37, Part 1, 195–96.
45. *Official Records*, Vol. 37, Part 2, 119–20.
46. *Official Records*, Vol. 37, Part 2, 133.
47. *Official Records*, Vol. 37, Part 2, 134.
48. *Official Records*, Vol. 37, Part 2, 134.

10. The Battle of Monocacy

1. *Official Records*, Vol. 37, Part 1, 196. Early, *A Memoir of the Last Year of the War*, 46–47.
2. *Official Records*, Vol. 37, Part 1, 193.
3. *Official Records*, Vol. 37, Part 1, 195.
4. *Official Records*, Vol. 37, Part 1, 214, 196.
5. *Official Records*, Vol. 37, Part 1, 193–96.
6. Early, *A Memoir of the Last Year of the War*, 46.
7. Early, *A Memoir of the Last Year of the War*, 46.
8. Early, *Lieutenant General Jubal Anderson Early*, 387.
9. *Official Records*, Vol. 37, Part 1, 205. Early, *A Memoir of the Last Year of the War*, 46.
10. *Official Records*, Vol. 37, Part 1, 350. Early, *Lieutenant General Jubal Anderson Early*, 387.
11. John B. Gordon, *Reminiscences of the Civil War* (New York: Charles Scribner's Sons, 1903), 310.
12. *Official Records*, Vol. 37, Part 1, 196.
13. *Official Records*, Vol. 37, Part 1, 350.
14. *Official Records*, Vol. 37, Part 1, 351.
15. Gordon, 311.
16. *Official Records*, Vol. 37, Part 1, 351.
17. *Official Records*, Vol. 37, Part 1, 352.
18. *Official Records*, Vol. 37, Part 1, 205.
19. *Official Records*, Vol. 37, Part 1, 351.
20. *Official Records*, Vol. 37, Part 1, 214.
21. *Official Records*, Vol. 37, Part 1, 351–52.
22. Worsham, 238–39.
23. Gordon, 311–12.
24. *Official Records*, Vol. 37, Part 1, 209.
25. Early, *A Memoir of the Last Year of the War*, 47. *Official Records*, Vol. 37, Part 1, 197.
26. *Official Records*, Vol. 37, Part 1, 217.
27. *Official Records*, Vol. 37, Part 1, 197. Early, *A Memoir of the Last Year of the War*, 47.
28. *Official Records*, Vol. 37, Part 1, 192.
29. *Official Records*, Vol. 37, Part 1, 202, 352. Early, *A Memoir of the Last Year of the War*, 47.
30. Early, *A Memoir of the Last Year of the War*, 47.
31. *Official Records*, Vol. 37, Part 1, 192.
32. Grant, 306.

11. The War Comes to Washington

1. *Official Records*, Vol. 37, Part 1, 348.
2. Worsham, 241.
3. Early, *A Memoir of the Last Year of the War*, 48.
4. Worsham, 241–42.
5. Catton, *Bruce Catton's Civil War*, 612. Leech, 425.
6. Virginia Jeans Laas, ed., *Wartime Washington: The Civil War Letters of Elizabeth Blair Lee* (Urbana, Il.: University of Illinois Press, 1991), 404–05.
7. Early, *A Memoir of the Last Year of the War*, 48.
8. Robert E. Park, "Diary of Robert E. Park, Macon, Georgia, late Captain Twelfth Alabama Regiment, Confederate States Army" *Southern Historical Society Papers*, Vol. I, January–June 1876, ed. J. William Jones (Millwood, N.Y.: Kraus Reprint Co., 1977), 379.
9. Arlene Reynolds, compiler, *The Civil War Memories of Elizabeth Bacon Custer* (Austin, Tex.: University of Texas Press, 1994), 90.
10. Leech, 416. Catton, *Bruce Catton's Civil War*, 610.
11. Leech, 409. Catton, *Bruce Catton's Civil War*, 610.
12. Leech, 410. *Official Records*, Vol. 37, Part 2, 155, 157.
13. *Official Records*, Vol. 37, Part 2, 83. Catton, *Bruce Catton's Civil War*, 609.
14. *Official Records*, Vol. 37, Part 2, 84. Catton, *Bruce Catton's Civil War*, 609.

15. *Official Records*, Vol. 37, Part 2, 84–85.
16. *Official Records*, Vol. 37, Part 2, 155.
17. *Official Records*, Vol. 37, Part 2, 155–56.
18. *Official Records*, Vol. 37, Part 2, 157.
19. Leech, 415–16.
20. Edward W. Emerson, *Life and Letters of Charles Russell Lowell* (Port Washington, N.Y.: Kennikat Press, 1971), 335.
21. *Official Records*, Vol. 37, Part 1, 231–32.
22. *Official Records*, Vol. 37, Part 1, 230–32. Leech, 412–13.
23. Early, *A Memoir of the Last Year of the War*, 48.
24. *Official Records*, Vol. 37, Part 1, 348.
25. Early, *A Memoir of the Last Year of the War*, 48.
26. *Official Records*, Vol. 37, Part 1, 231.
27. Frank Wilkeson, *Turned Inside Out: Recollections of A Private Soldier in the Army of the Potomac* (Lincoln, Neb.: University of Nebraska Press, 1997), 214.
28. Early, *Lieutenant General Jubal Anderson Early*, 390.
29. Worsham, 242.
30. Early, *A Memoir of the Last Year of the War*, 49.
31. Catton, *Bruce Catton's Civil War*, 613.
32. Leech, 416.
33. Catton, *Bruce Catton's Civil War*, 613. Leech, 417.
34. George T. Stevens, *Three Years in the Sixth Corps* (New York: Time-Life Books, 1984), 372–73.
35. *Official Records*, Vol. 37, Part 1, 265.
36. *Official Records*, Vol. 37, Part 1, 265.
37. *Official Records*, Vol. 37, Part 1, 232.
38. *Official Records*, Vol. 37, Part 1, 232.
39. Leech, 418–19.
40. Simon, 231.
41. *Official Records*, Vol. 37, Part 1, 348.
42. Early, *A Memoir of the Last Year of the War*, 49–50.
43. Early, *A Memoir of the Last Year of the War*, 50.
44. *Official Records*, Vol. 37, Part 1, 348.
45. Early, *A Memoir of the Last Year of the War*, 50.
46. Catton, *Bruce Catton's Civil War*, 614–15. Leech, 423.
47. Stevens, 378.
48. Walker, 29.
49. Stevens, 376.
50. Walker, 30.
51. *Official Records*, Vol. 37, Part 1, 348.
52. Douglas, 296.
53. Long, 359–60.
54. Douglas, 295.
55. *Official Records*, Vol. 37, Part 1, 349.
56. Leech, 426–27.

12. Back to the Valley

1. Catton, *Grant Takes Command*, 313. Grant, 315–16.
2. *Official Records*, Vol. 37, Part 2, 223.
3. *Official Records*, Vol. 37, Part 2, 222–23.
4. *Official Records*, Vol. 37, Part 1, 265.
5. Henry H. Houghton, *Recollections of the War: A Personal Account of the Civil War*, Vermont in the Civil War, http://vermontcivilwar.org/1bdg/3/Houghton.shtml.
6. *Official Records*, Vol. 37, Part 1, 267.
7. Grant, 317.
8. Early, *A Memoir of the Last Year of the War*, 52.
9. *Official Records*, Vol. 37, Part 2, 300–01.
10. Catton, *Grant Takes Command*, 315.
11. *Official Records*, Vol. 38, Part 5, 151.
12. Henry A. Shirey, *The Story of the Maine Fifteenth* (Bridgton, Maine: Press of the Bridgeton News, 1890), 134.
13. Samuel S. Dunton Civil War Letters, Samuel S. Dunton Letter, August 3, 1864, September 10, 2000, http://home.pacbell.net/dunton/SSDletters.html, June 10, 2002.
14. Lufkin, 101.
15. Strother, 279–80.
16. Samuel S. Dunton Letter, July 25, 1864.
17. George Perkins, *A Summer in Maryland and Virginia: Or Campaigning With the 149th Ohio Volunteer Infantry* (Chillicothe, Ohio: The Scholl Printing Company, 1911), 24–25.
18. Peter S. Michie, *The Life and Letters of Emory Upton* (New York: Arno Press, 1979), 121–22.
19. *Official Records*, Vol. 37, Part 2, 366.
20. *Official Records*, Vol. 37, Part 2, 374.
21. *Official Records*, Vol. 37, Part 2, 384–85.
22. Reed, 185–87. Early, *A Memoir of the Last Year of the War*, 53.
23. *Official Records*, Vol. 37, Part 1, 290–91.
24. *Official Records*, Vol. 37, Part 1, 291.
25. Early, *A Memoir of the Last Year of the War*, 53. *Official Records*, Vol. 37, Part 1, 291.
26. *Official Records*, Vol. 37, Part 1, 287.
27. *Official Records*, Vol. 37, Part 1, 292.
28. *Official Records*, Vol. 37, Part 1, 321.
29. Reed, 183. *Official Records*, Vol. 37, Part 1, 321.
30. *Official Records*, Vol. 37, Part 1, 321.
31. *Official Records*, Vol. 37, Part 1, 326–27.
32. Early, *A Memoir of the Last Year of the War*, 54. Douglas, 302.
33. Early, *A Memoir of the Last Year of the War*, 54–55.
34. *Official Records*, Vol. 37, Part 1, 323.
35. Bonnell, 123. *Official Records*, Vol. 37, Part 1, 323.

36. Bonnell, 123. *Official Records*, Vol. 37, Part 1, 323.
37. *Official Records*, Vol. 37, Part 1, 290–91. Reed, 186–88.
38. Pharris DeLoach Johnson, editor, *Under the Southern Cross: Soldier Life with Gordon Bradwell and the Army of Northern Virginia* (Macon, Ga.: Mercer University Press, 1999), 191.
39. Early, *A Memoir of the Last Year of the War*, 55.
40. *Official Records*, Vol. 37, Part 1, 311–12.
41. *Official Records*, Vol. 37, Part 1, 297–98.
42. *Official Records*, Vol. 37, Part 1, 293. Early, *A Memoir of the Last Year of the War*, 55.
43. Bonnell, 124–25. Early, *A Memoir of the Last Year of the War*, 55.
44. Terry L. Jones, *Lee's Tigers: The Louisiana Infantry in the Army of Northern Virginia* (Baton Rouge, La.: Louisiana State University Press, 1987), 214.
45. *Official Records*, Vol. 37, Part 1, 290.
46. Early, *A Memoir of the Last Year of the War*, 55.

13. Chambersburg and the Turning Point

1. Early, *A Memoir of the Last Year of the War*, 56.
2. Early, *A Memoir of the Last Year of the War*, 56–57.
3. Bonnell, 129. *A Memoir of the Last Year of the War*, 59.
4. "The Burning of Chambersburg," *Confederate Veteran Magazine*, October 1903, Vol. XI, No. 10. http://members.home. com/civilwarcsa/1903/article16.html.
5. Early, *A Memoir of the Last Year of the War*, 59.
6. Early, *A Memoir of the Last Year of the War*, 59.
7. Frank E. Vandiver, editor, *The Civil War Diary of General Josiah Gorgas* (Tuscaloosa, Ala.: University of Alabama Press, 1947), 131.
8. Bonnell, 129–30. Early, *A Memoir of the Last Year of the War*, 59.
9. Bonnell, 130. Early, *A Memoir of the Last Year of the War*, 59.
10. *Official Records*, Vol. 43, Part 1, 494.
11. *Official Records*, Vol. 43, Part 1, 494–95.
12. Early, *A Memoir of the Last Year of the War*, 59.
13. Bonnell, 131. Grant, 316–17.
14. *Official Records*, Vol. 37, Part 2, 374.
15. *Official Records*, Vol. 37, Part 2, 433.
16. Emil Rosenblatt and Ruth Rosenblatt, editors, *The Civil War Letters of Private Wilbur Fisk 1861–1865* (Lawrence, Kan.: University of Kansas, 1992), 242.
17. Philip H. Sheridan, *Personal Memoirs of P. H. Sheridan*, Vol. 1 (New York: Charles L. Webster & Company, 1888), 461–62.
18. Grant, 317. Sheridan, Vol. 1, 462.
19. *Official Records*, Vol. 37, Part 2, 558.
20. Grant 318.
21. Catton, *Bruce Catton's Civil War*, 618.
22. *Official Records*, Vol. 43, Part 1, 681.
23. Grant, 319.
24. Grant, 319.
25. Grant, 320.
26. Sheridan, Vol. 1, 464. Grant, 320.
27. *Official Records*, Vol. 43, Part 1, 698.
28. Sheridan, Vol. 1, 463–64.
29. *Official Records*, Vol. 43, Part 1, 719.
30. Reed, 191. Richard O'Connor, *Sheridan the Inevitable* (New York: Konecky & Konecky, 1993), 18–19.
31. Reed, 191–92. O'Connor, 55–62.
32. Adam Badeau, "Lieut-General Sheridan," *The Century*, February 1884, 499–500. Reed, 191–92.
33. O'Connor, 22. Reed, 191.
34. Benjamin P. Thomas, ed., *Three Years with Grant: As Recalled by War Correspondent Sylvanus Cadwallader* (New York: Alfred A. Knopf, 1956), 305–06.
35. W.F.G. Shanks, "Recollections of Sheridan," *Harper's New Monthly Magazine*, August 1865, 299.
36. Grant, 316–17.
37. Jeffery Wert, *From Winchester to Cedar Creek: The Shenandoah Campaign of 1864* (Carlisle, Pa.: South Mountain Press, Inc., 1987), 13. Reed, 190.

14. A War of Maneuver

1. *Official Records*, Vol. 43, Part 1, 710.
2. Sheridan, Vol. 1, 471–72. *Official Records*, Vol. 43, Part 1, 61.
3. O'Connor, 196. Catton, *Bruce Catton's Civil War*, 623.
4. Sheridan, Vol. 1, 499–500.
5. C. M. Keyes, editor, *The Military History of the 123rd Regiment Ohio Volunteer Infantry* (Sandusky, Ohio: Register Steam Press, 1874), 84.
6. Stevens, 388.
7. Sheridan, Vol. 1, 467.
8. Sheridan, Vol. 1, 477–80. Early, *A Memoir of the Last Year of the War*, 60–61.
9. Early, *A Memoir of the Last Year of the War*, 60.
10. Sheridan, Vol. 1, 481.
11. *Official Records*, Vol. 43, Part 1, 791–92.

12. Sheridan, Vol. 1, 483–84.
13. *Official Records*, Vol. 43, Part 1, 816.
14. Sheridan, Vol. 1, 487–88.
15. Keyes, 84.
16. Catton, *Bruce Catton's Civil War*, 627. Bonnell, 133–34.
17. Samuel L. Gracey, *Annals of the Sixth Pennsylvania Cavalry* (Lancaster, Ohio: Vanberg Publishing, 1966), 286–87.
18. Catton, *Bruce Catton's Civil War*, 625. O'Connor, 194.
19. Catton, *Bruce Catton's Civil War*, 626. O'Connor, 194.
20. Charles Wells Russell, ed., *The Memoirs of Colonel John S. Mosby* (Boston: Little Brown and Company, 1917), 283–84.
21. Russell, 312.
22. *Official Records*, Vol. 43, Part 1, 811.
23. *Official Records*, Vol. 43, Part 1, 811.
24. Sheridan, Vol. 1, 492.
25. O'Connor, 197. Sheridan, Vol. 1, 488–89.
26. Wesley Merritt, "Sheridan in the Shenandoah Valley," *Battles and Leaders of the Civil War*, Eds. Robert Underwood Johnson and Clarence Clough Buel (New York: Thomas Yoseloff, 1956), 502–03.
27. Merritt, 503.
28. *Official Records*, Vol. 43, Part 1, 880.
29. *Official Records*, Vol. 43, Part 1, 916–17.
30. *Official Records*, Vol. 43, Part 1, 1006.
31. George N. Carpenter, *History of the Eighth Regiment Vermont Volunteers 1861–1865* (Boston: Press of DeLand & Barta, 1886), 159.
32. Archibald Atkinson Jr., *Memoir of Archibald Atkinson Jr.*(Ms 94–022), Special Collections, Digital Library and Archives, University Libraries, Virginia Polytechnic Institute and State University, 39.
33. Early, *A Memoir of the Last Year of the War*, 66–67.
34. O'Connor, 198. Early, *A Memoir of the Last Year of the War*, 67.
35. Sheridan, Vol. 1, 498–99.
36. Sheridan, Vol. 1, 499. O'Connor, 198.
37. Emerson, 336.
38. Emerson, 339–40.
39. *Official Records*, Vol. 43, Part 2, 50.
40. Early, *A Memoir of the Last Year of the War*, 65.
41. *Official Records*, Vol. 43, Part 2, 873–74.
42. Sheridan, Vol. 2, 8–9.
43. Grant, 327.
44. Sheridan, Vol. 2, 9.
45. Grant, 328.
46. Grant, 328–29.
47. *Official Records*, Vol. 43, Part 1, 554.
48. Sheridan, Vol. 2, 10.
49. Douglas, 308–09.

15. The Battle of Winchester

1. Louis N. Boudrye, *Historic Records of the Fifth New York Cavalry* (Albany, NY: J. Munsell, 1868), 171.
2. Irwin, 380–81.
3. O'Connor, 200–01. Sheridan, Vol. 2, 11–14.
4. O'Connor, 201–02. Catton, *Bruce Catton's Civil War*, 633.
5. John William DeForest, "Sheridan's Battle of Winchester," *Harper's New Monthly Magazine*, January 1865, 195.
6. O'Connor, 202. Irwin, 380.
7. Early, *A Memoir of the Last Year of the War*, 70.
8. Gordon, 320.
9. Early, *A Memoir of the Last Year of the War*, 70–71.
10. Early, *A Memoir of the Last Year of the War*, 71.
11. James Franklin Fitts, "The Last Battle of Winchester," *The Galaxy*, October 15, 1866, 325.
12. Sheridan, Vol. 2, 18–19.
13. Sheridan, Vol. 2, 21–22.
14. Stevens, 399.
15. *Official Records*, Vol. 43, Part 1, 222.
16. *Official Records*, Vol. 43, Part 1, 222.
17. Fitts, "The Last Battle of Winchester," 328.
18. *Official Records*, Vol. 43, Part 1, 318–19. Fitts, "The Last Battle of Winchester," 328.
19. Irwin, 385.
20. Carpenter, 170.
21. Carpenter, 181–82.
22. Irwin, 387.
23. Elias P. Pellet, *History of the 114th Regiment, New York State Volunteers* (Norwich, N.Y.: Telegraph & Chronicle Power Press Print, 1866), 253–54.
24. Fitts, "The Last Battle of Winchester," 329.
25. Early, *A Memoir of the Last Year of the War*, 71–72.
26. *Official Records*, Vol. 43, Part 1, 222.
27. *Official Records*, Vol. 43, Part 1, 162–63. Sheridan, Vol. 2, 23. O'Connor, 202–03.
28. Fitts, "The Last Battle of Winchester," 331.
29. DeForest, "Sheridan's Battle of Winchester," 199.
30. Early, *A Memoir of the Last Year of the War*, 72.
31. *Official Records*, Vol. 43, Part 1, 518.
32. J. H. Kidd, *Personal Recollections of A Cavalryman* (New York: Time-Life Books, 1983), 390.
33. *Official Records*, Vol. 43, Part 1, 498.

34. *Official Records*, Vol. 43, Part 1, 427. Early, *A Memoir of the Last Year of the War*, 72–73.
35. *Official Records*, Vol. 43, Part 1, 427.
36. Asa B. Isham, *An Historical Sketch of the Seventh Regiment Michigan Volunteer Cavalry* (New York: Town Topics Publishing Company, 1893), 70.
37. *Official Records*, Vol. 43, Part 1, 555.
38. Irwin, 389.
39. *Official Records*, Vol. 43, Part 1, 361–62. Early, *A Memoir of the Last Year of the War*, 73.
40. Irwin, 390–91.
41. Sheridan, Vol. 2, 25.
42. Catton, *Bruce Catton's Civil War*, 635.
43. Stevens, 401.
44. John M. Gould, *History of the First–Tenth–Twenty-Ninth Maine Regiment* (Portland, Maine: Stephen Berry, 1871), 498.
45. Early, *A Memoir of the Last Year of the War*, 73.
46. Joseph Warren Keifer, *Slavery and Four Years of War* (New York: G. P. Putnam's Sons, 1900), 114.
47. Sheridan, Vol. 2, 26.
48. Pulaski Cowper, compiler, *Extracts of Letters of Major-Gen'l Bryan Grimes to His Wife* (Raleigh, N.C.: Broughton & Co., 1883), 68–70.
49. Gordon, 323–24.
50. Haynes, 114.
51. Robert Hunt Rhodes, *All For the Union: Civil War Diary and Letters of Elisha Hunt Rhodes* (New York: Orion Books, 1991), 185.
52. *Official Records*, Vol. 43, Part 1, 24–25.
53. Early, *A Memoir of the Last Year of the War*, 74–75.
54. *Official Records*, Vol. 43, Part 1, 61.
55. *Official Records*, Vol. 43, Part 1, 61.
56. *Official Records*, Vol. 43, Part 1, 61–62.
57. *Official Records*, Vol. 43, Part 1, 118.
58. *Official Records*, Vol. 43, Part 1, 555.
59. Rhodes, 186.

16. The Battle of Fisher's Hill

1. Sheridan, Vol. 2, 33.
2. Early, *A Memoir of the Last Year of the War*, 76–77.
3. Irwin, 396–97. O'Connor, 206.
4. Early, *A Memoir of the Last Year of the War*, 77.
5. Sheridan, Vol. 2, 34.
6. Sheridan, Vol. 2, 35.
7. *Official Records*, Vol. 43, Part 1, 152.
8. O'Connor, 207–08. Sheridan, Vol. 2, 35–36.
9. *Official Records*, Vol. 43, Part 1, 370.
10. Sheridan, Vol. 2, 37.
11. O'Connor, 209. *Official Records*, Vol. 43, Part 1, 370.
12. *Official Records*, Vol. 43, Part 1, 390.
13. Ari Hoogenboom, *Rutherford B. Hayes: Warrior & President* (Lawrence, Kan.: University Press of Kansas, 1995), 174.
14. O'Connor, 209. *Official Records*, Vol. 43, Part 1, 170.
15. Augustus Buell, *"The Cannoneer" Recollections of Service in the Army of the Potomac* (Washington, D.C.: The National Tribune, 1890), 279.
16. Gould, 513.
17. James Franklin Fitts, "The Fight at Fisher's Hill," *The Galaxy*, April 1868, 435.
18. Walker, 105.
19. Early, *A Memoir of the Last Year of the War*, 77.
20. Sheridan, Vol. 2, 38.
21. *Official Records*, Vol. 43, Part 1, 153.
22. O'Connor, 210. Sheridan, Vol. 2, 40.
23. *Official Records*, Vol. 43, Part 1, 26–27.
24. *Official Records*, Vol. 43, Part 2, 878.
25. *Official Records*, Vol. 43, Part 1, 153.
26. *Official Records*, Vol. 43, Part 2, 152.
27. *Official Records*, Vol. 43, Part 1, 124.
28. *Official Records*, Vol. 43, Part 1, 556.
29. Sheridan, Vol. 2, 40.
30. O'Connor, 211. Sheridan, Vol. 2, 41.
31. Sheridan, Vol. 2, 42.
32. Kidd, 396.
33. Clark, 230.
34. O'Connor, 212. Sheridan, Vol. 2, 43.
35. Sheridan, Vol. 2, 44.
36. Hillman A. Hall, compiler, *History of the Sixth New York Cavalry* (Worcester, Mass.: The Blanchard Press, 1908), 225–26.
37. *Official Records*, Vol. 43, Part 1, 28–29.
38. Johnson, 199.
39. *Official Records*, Vol. 43, Part 1, 557–58.
40. Catton, *Bruce Catton's Civil War*, 637. O'Connor, 211.

17. The Burning and Tom's Brook

1. Dowdey, 857.
2. *Official Records*, Vol. 43, Part 1, 558–59.
3. Stevens, 409.
4. Sheridan, Vol. 2, 49–50.
5. *Official Records*, Vol. 43, Part 2, 177.
6. Sheridan, Vol. 2, 53–54.
7. *Official Records*, Vol. 43, Part 2, 249.
8. Sheridan, Vol. 2, 54.
9. Sheridan, Vol. 2, 54–55.
10. Sheridan, Vol. 2, 55.

11. O'Connor, 214. Sheridan, Vol. 2, 50–52.
12. John L. Heatwole, *The Burning: Sheridan in the Shenandoah Valley* (Charlottesville, Va.: Rockbridge Publishing, 1998), 131. Kidd, 399.
13. Issac White, *Issac White Letters* (Ms 97–013), Special Collections, Digital Library and Archives, University Libraries, Virginia Polytechnic Institute and State University.
14. John W. Elwood, *Elwood's Stories of the Old Ringgold Cavalry 1847–1865* (Coal City, Pa.: John W. Elwood, 1914), 246.
15. Rosenblatt, 261–62.
16. Emerson, 353.
17. Richard E. Beaudry, ed., *War Journal of Louis N. Beaudry, Fifth New York Cavalry* (Jefferson, N.C.: McFarland & Company, Inc., 1996), 175.
18. Benjamin W. Crowninshield, "Sheridan at Winchester," *The Atlantic Monthly*, December 1878, 686.
19. Douglas, 315.
20. Kidd, 399.
21. Merritt, 512–13.
22. Rhodes, 189–90.
23. Stevens, 411.
24. *Official Records*, Vol. 43, Part 1, 30–31.
25. O'Connor, 215. Sheridan, Vol. 2, 59.
26. O'Connor, 215.
27. Kidd, 400–01.
28. Sheridan, Vol. 2, 56.
29. *Official Records*, Vol. 43, Part 1, 431.
30. Sheridan, Vol. 2, 57.
31. *Official Records*, Vol. 43, Part 1, 520–21.
32. *Official Records*, Vol. 43, Part 1, 521.
33. *Official Records*, Vol. 43, Part 1, 431.
34. Sheridan, Vol. 2, 57. *Official Records*, Vol. 43, Part 1, 521.
35. Hagemann, 283–84. *Official Records*, Vol. 43, Part 1, 431.
36. *Official Records*, Vol. 42, Part 1, 521.
37. Sheridan, Vol. 2, 59.
38. *Official Records*, Vol. 43, Part 1, 559.
39. *Official Records*, Vol. 43, Part 1, 31.
40. O'Connor, 217.

18. Camping at Cedar Creek

1. Stevens, 414.
2. Rosenblatt, 264–65.
3. Rosenblatt, 266.
4. Emerson, 357–58.
5. Stevens, 412.
6. *Official Records*, Vol. 43, Part 2, 894.
7. *Official Records*, Vol. 43, Part 2, 897–98.
8. *Official Records*, Vol. 43, Part 2, 893.
9. "Fisher's Hill and Sheridan's Ride," *Confederate Veteran Magazine*, Vol. IX, No. 4. April 1902. http://members.home.com/civilwarcsa/1902/article5.html.
10. *Official Records*, Vol. 43, Part 2, 891–92.
11. Early, *A Memoir of the Last Year of the War*, 82.
12. *Official Records*, Vol. 43, Part 1, 579, 371.
13. *Official Records*, Vol. 43, Part 1, 371.
14. *Official Records*, Vol. 43, Part 1, 579, 371.
15. *Official Records*, Vol. 43, Part 1, 371–72.
16. Early, *A Memoir of the Last Year of the War*, 82.
17. Sheridan, Vol. 2, 61.
18. *Official Records*, Vol. 43, Part 2, 355.
19. *Official Records*, Vol. 43, Part 2, 355.
20. *Official Records*, Vol. 43, Part 2, 355.
21. *Official Records*, Vol. 32, Part 2, 363.
22. Sheridan, Vol. 2, 62.
23. Sheridan, Vol. 2, 62.
24. *Official Records*, Vol. 43, Part 2, 389.
25. Sheridan, Vol. 2, 63–64.
26. *Official Records*, Vol. 43, Part 2, 386.
27. *Official Records*, Vol. 43, Part 2, 389–90.
28. Sheridan, Vol. 2, 66–68.
29. Early, *A Memoir of the Last Year of the War*, 83.
30. Gordon, 333–34.
31. Gordon, 334–35.
32. Gordon, 335.
33. Early, *A Memoir of the Last Year of the War*, 83.
34. Early, *A Memoir of the Last Year of the War*, 83–84.
35. *Official Records*, Vol. 43, Part 1, 580.
36. Early, *A Memoir of the Last Year of the War*, 85.
37. Early, *A Memoir of the Last Year of the War*, 85.
38. Gordon, 336.
39. Early, *A Memoir of the Last Year of the War*, 86.
40. Gordon, 337.
41. A. B. Nettleton, "The Famous Fight at Cedar Creek," *The Annals of the Civil War*, Ed. Alexander Kelly McClure (New York: De Capo Press, 1994), 658.
42. *Official Records*, Vol. 43, Part 1, 158.
43. Nettleton, 659.

19. Cedar Creek, The Morning

1. Gordon, 338–39.
2. *Official Records*, Vol. 43, Part 1, 365.
3. Gordon, 339.
4. Augustus D. Dickert, *History of Kershaw's Brigade* (Dayton, Ohio: Morningside Bookshop, 1973), 447–48.

5. *Official Records*, Vol. 43, Part 1, 54. J. W. DeForest, "Sheridan's Victory of Middletown," *Harper's New Monthly Magazine*, February 1865, 354.
6. Gordon, 339–40.
7. DeForest, "Sheridan's Victory of Middletown," 354.
8. *Official Records*, Vol. 43, Part 1, 392.
9. *Official Records*, Vol. 43, Part 1, 380.
10. *Official Records*, Vol. 43, Part 1, 372.
11. DuPont, 157.
12. George Haven Putnam, *Some Memories of the Civil War* (New York: G. P. Putnam's Sons, 1924), 194–95.
13. Carpenter, 209–10.
14. *Official Records*, Vol. 43, Part 1, 284. Early, *A Memoir of the Last Year of the War*, 86.
15. DeForest, "Sheridan's Victory of Middletown," 357.
16. William F. Tiemann, compiler, *The 159th Regiment Infantry, New York State Volunteers, in the War of Rebellion* (Brooklyn, N.Y.: William F. Tiemann, 1891), 107–08.
17. *Official Records*, Vol. 43, Part 1, 285.
18. Stevens, 415–16.
19. Stevens, 419.
20. *Official Records*, Vol. 43, Part 1, 226.
21. DeForest, "Sheridan's Victory of Middletown," 357.
22. Walker, 139–40.
23. *Official Records*, Vol. 43, Part 1, 193.
24. *Official Records*, Vol. 43, Part 1, 193–94.
25. Gordon, 340.
26. *Official Records*, Vol. 43, Part 1, 194.
27. *Official Records*, Vol. 43, Part 1, 215.
28. Walker, 143.
29. Early, *A Memoir of the Last Year of the War*, 87–88.
30. Gordon, 341.
31. Gordon, 341.
32. *Official Records*, Vol. 43, Part 1, 194.
33. *Official Records*, Vol. 43, Part 1, 194.
34. Kidd, 411.
35. *Official Records*, Vol. 43, Part 1, 449.
36. *Official Records*, Vol. 43, Part 1, 433.
37. *Official Records*, Vol. 43, Part 1, 433.
38. *Official Records*, Vol. 43, Part 1, 449.
39. *Official Records*, Vol. 43, Part 1, 523.
40. Early, *A Memoir of the Last Year of the War*, 89.
41. Early, *A Memoir of the Last Year of the War*, 89–90.
42. Gordon, 344.
43. Worsham, 276.
44. Douglas, 319.

20. Cedar Creek, The Afternoon

1. Sheridan, Vol. 2, 68–71.
2. Catton, *Bruce Catton's Civil War*, 642.
3. George A. Forsyth, "Sheridan's Ride," *Harper's New Monthly Magazine*, July 1897, 168.
4. Forsyth, 168. Sheridan, Vol. 2, 80.
5. Sheridan, Vol. 2, 78–79.
6. Forsyth, 170.
7. Catton, *Bruce Catton's Civil War*, 642.
8. Forsyth, 170–71.
9. O'Connor, 226. Catton, *Bruce Catton's Civil War*, 643.
10. Forsyth, 171.
11. Sheridan, Vol. 2, 81.
12. Forsyth, 171.
13. Forsyth, 172.
14. Walker, 146–47.
15. Houghton.
16. Nettleton, 661.
17. Rosenblatt, 268.
18. Hagemann, 291.
19. Sheridan, Vol. 2, 83–84.
20. Stevens, 422.
21. Forsyth, 174.
22. DeForest, "Sheridan's Victory of Middletown," 358.
23. Walker, 147–48.
24. Irwin, 431–32.
25. Sheridan, Vol. 2, 86–87.
26. Forsyth, 176.
27. *Official Records*, Vol. 43, Part 1, 54.
28. Sheridan, Vol. 2, 87–88.
29. *Official Records*, Vol. 43, Part 1, 434.
30. Sheridan, Vol. 2, 88.
31. Forsyth, 177–78.
32. Gordon, 346.
33. Early, *A Memoir of the Last Year of the War*, 90.
34. Gordon, 347.
35. Stevens, 424–25. Deforest, "Sheridan's Victory of Middletown," 359. Sheridan, Vol. 2, 88.
36. *Official Records*, Vol. 43, Part 1, 227–28.
37. *Official Records*, Vol. 32, Part 1, 216.
38. Stevens, 424–25.
39. *Official Records*, Vol. 43, Part 1, 195.
40. *Official Records*, Vol. 43, Part 1, 600.
41. *Official Records*, Vol. 43, Part 1, 285.
42. Forsyth, 178.
43. Forsyth, 179.
44. *Official Records*, Vol. 43, Part 1, 524.
45. Forsyth, 179.
46. Gordon, 348.
47. *Official Records*, Vol. 43, Part 1, 524.
48. Karla Jean Husby, compiler, *Under*

Custer's Command: The Civil War Journal of James Henry Avery (Washington, D.C.: Brassey's, 2000), 118.
49. *Official Records*, Vol. 43, Part 1, 600.
50. Early, *A Memoir of the Last Year of the War*, 90.
51. *Official Records*, Vol. 43, Part 1, 450.
52. Gordon, 348–49.
53. Boudrye, 180–81.
54. Stevens, 425.
55. DuPont, 172.
56. *Official Records*, Vol. 43, Part 1, 525.
57. Martin F. Schmitt, ed., *General George Crook: His Autobiography* (Norman, Okla.: University of Oklahoma Press, 1986), 134.
58. Early, *A Memoir of the Last Year of the War*, 90.
59. *Official Records*, Vol. 43, Part 1, 137.
60. Douglas, 319.

21. To the End

1. *Official Records*, Vol. 43, Part 1, 32–33.
2. *Official Records*, Vol. 43, Part 2, 423.
3. *Official Records*, Vol. 43, Part 1, 62.
4. Sheridan, Vol. 2, 92.
5. *Official Records*, Vol. 43, Part 1, 560.
6. Early, *A Memoir of the Last Year of the War*, 93.
7. *Official Records*, Vol. 43, Part 1, 563–64.
8. Jubal Early, "Gen'l Early's Address to His Army," *The Staunton Vindicator*, October 22, 1864, Page 2, Col. 3.
9. *Official Records*, Vol. 43, Part 2, 436.
10. *Official Records*, Vol. 43, Part 2, 464–65.
11. John Y. Simon, editor, *The Papers of Ulysses S. Grant Volume 12* (Carbondale, IL: Southern Illinois University Press, 1982), 365.
12. *Official Records*, Vol. 43, Part 2, 919.
13. William C. Davis and Meredith L. Swentor, eds., *Bluegrass Confederate: The Headquarters Diary of Edward O. Guerrant* (Baton Rouge, LA: Louisiana State University Press, 1999), 564.
14. Rosenblatt, 275.
15. *Official Records*, Vol. 43, Part 2, 920.
16. *Official Records*, Vol. 43, Part 2, 671–72.
17. Sheridan, Vol. 2, 100.
18. *Official Records*, Vol. 43, Part 2, 679.
19. Sheridan, Vol. 2, 100.
20. *Official Records*, Vol. 43, Part 2, 682.
21. O'Connor, 234.
22. Early, *A Memoir of the Last Year of the War*, 94–95.
23. Early, *A Memoir of the Last Year of the War*, 95.
24. *Official Records*, Vol. 43, Part 1, 37.
25. Early, *A Memoir of the Last Year of the War*, 95–97. Sheridan, Vol. 2, 98–100.
26. Sherian, Vol. 2, 102–04. Early, *A Memoir of the Last Year of the War*, 98.
27. Leslie J. Perry, "A Shock to General Sheridan," *The Century*, August 1896, 637.
28. *Official Records*, Vol. 43, Part 2, 823.
29. Perry, 637.
30. *Official Records*, Vol. 43, Part 2, 824.
31. Perry, 637.
32. *Official Records*, Vol. 43, Part 2, 830–31.
33. Early, *A Memoir of the Last Year of the War*, 100.
34. Sheridan, Vol. 2, 112.
35. Sheridan, Vol. 2, 112–13.
36. Early, *A Memoir of the Last Year of the War*, 102.
37. *Official Records*, Vol. 46, Part 1, 476.
38. Early, *A Memoir of the Last Year of the War*, 102.
39. Sheridan, Vol. 2, 115. *Official Records*, Vol. 46, Part 1, 476.
40. Early, *A Memoir of the Last Year of the War*, 103.
41. Sheridan, Vol. 2, 116.
42. Early, *Lieutenant General Jubal Anderson Early*, 464–65.
43. Early, *Lieutenant General Jubal Anderson Early*, 468–69.
44. Sheridan, Vol. 2, 119.

Bibliography

Books

Alexander, Bevin. *Lost Victories: The Military Genius of Stonewall Jackson.* Edison, N.J.: The Blue & Grey Press, 1996.

Alexander, E.P. *Military Memoirs of a Confederate.* Bloomington, Ind.: Indiana Universty Press, 1962.

Ambrose, Stephen E. *Halleck: Lincoln's Chief of Staff.* Baton Rouge, La.: Louisiana State University Press, 1962.

Anderson, Nancy Scott and Dwight Anderson. *The Generals: Ulysses S. Grant and Robert E. Lee.* New York: Wings Books, 1994.

Ashby, Thomas A. *The Valley Campaigns: Being the Reminiscences of a Non-Combatant While Between the Lines in the Shenandoah Valley During the War of the States.* New York: The Neale Publishing Co., 1914.

Badeau, Adam. *Military History of Ulysses S. Grant: From April, 1861, to April, 1865.* New York: D. Appleton and Company, 1885.

Basler, Roy P., ed. *The Collected Works of Abraham Lincoln, Volume VII.* New Brunswick, N.J.: Rutgers University Press, 1953.

Beaudry, Richard E., ed. *War Journal of Louis N. Beaudry, Fifth New York Cavalry.* Jefferson, N.C.: McFarland & Company, Inc., 1996.

Beck, Brandon H., ed. *Third Alabama! The Civil War Memoir of Brigadier General Cullen Andrews Battle, CSA.* Tuscaloosa, Ala.: The University of Alabama Press, 2000.

Blackford, Susan Leigh, comp. *Letters from Lee's Army.* New York: A. S. Barnes & Company, Inc., 1962.

Blair, William. *Virginia's Private War.* New York: Oxford University Press, 1998.

Bonnell, John C. Jr. *Sabres in the Shenandoah: The 21st New York Cavalry, 1863-1866.* Shippensburg, Pa.: Burd Street Press, 1996.

Boudrye, Louis N. *Historic Records of the Fifth New York Cavalry.* Albany, N.Y.: J. Munsell, 1868.

Brice, Marchall Moore. *Conquest of a Valley.* Charlottesville, VA: University of Virginia Press, 1965.

Brinton, John H. *Personal Memoirs of John H. Brinton, Civil War Surgeon 1861-1865.* Carbondale, Il.: Southern Illinois University Press, 1996. Reprint of 1914 edition.

Buckeridge, J.O. *Lincoln's Choice.* Harrisburg, Pa.: The Stackpole Company, 1956.

Buell, Augustus. *"The Cannoneer" Recollections of Service in the Army of the Potomac.* Washington, D.C.: The National Tribune, 1890.

Carpenter, George N. *History of the Eighth Regiment Vermont Volunteers 1861-1865.* Boston: Press of Deland & Barta, 1886.

Carter, Samuel III. *The Last Cavaliers.* New York: St. Martin's Press, 1979.

Catton, Bruce. *Bruce Catton's Civil War.* New York: The Fairfax Press, 1984.

_____. *Grant Takes Command.* Boston: Little Brown, 1968.

Clark, Orton S. *The One Hundred and Sixteenth Regiment of New York State Volunteers.*

Buffalo, N.Y.: Printing House of Matthews & Warren, 1868.

Coffin, Charles Carelton. *Four Years of Fighting: A Volumne of Personal Observation with the Army and Navy.* Boston: Ticknor and Fields, 1866.

Cooling, Benjamin F. *Symbol, Sword & Shield: Defending Washington During the Civil War.* Hamden, Conn.: Archon Books, 1975.

Cowper, Pulaski, comp. *Extracts of Letters of Major-Gen'l Bryan Grimes to His Wife.* Raleigh, N.C.: Broughton & Co., 1883.

Crist, Lynda Lasswell, ed. *The Papers of Jefferson Davis.* Baton Rouge, La.: Louisiana State University Press, 1999.

Croffut, W. A. and John M. Morris. *The Military and Civil History of Connecticut During the War of 1861-1865.* New York: Ledyard Bill, 1868.

Dana, Charles A. *Recollections of the Civil War.* New York: D. Appleton and Company, 1902.

Davis, Julia. *The Shenandoah.* New York: Farrar & Rinehart, Inc., 1945.

Davis, William C. *The Battle of New Market.* Garden City, N.J.: Doubleday, 1975.

_____. *Breckinridge: Statesman, Soldier, Symbol.* Baton Rouge, La.: Louisiana State University Press, 1974.

_____. and Meredith L. Swentor, eds. *Bluegrass Confederate: The Headquarters Diary of Edward O. Guerrant.* Baton Rouge, La.: Louisiana State University Press, 1999.

DeForest, John William. *A Volunteer's Adventures: A Union Captain's Record of the Civil War.* Hamden, Conn.: Archon Books, 1970.

Denison, Frederic. *Sabres and Spurs: The First Regiment Rhode Island Cavalry in the Civil War 1861-1865.* The First Rhode Island Cavalry Veteran Association, 1876.

Derry, Joseph T. *Story of the Confederate States.* New York: Arno Press, 1979. Reprint of 1895 edition.

Dickert, D. Augustus. *History of Kershaw's Brigade.* Dayton, Ohio: Morningside Bookshop, 1973. Reprint of 1899 edition.

Douglas, Henry Kyd. *I Rode With Stonewall.* Chapel Hill, N.C.: University of North Carolina Press, 1940.

Dowdey, Clifford, ed. *The Wartime Papers of R. E. Lee.* Boston: Little Brown, 1961.

Duke, Basil W. *Reminiscences of General Basil W. Duke, CSA.* Freeport, New York: Books For Libraries Press, 1969. Reprint of 1911 edition.

Duncan, Richard R. *Lee's Endangered Left.* Baton Rouge, La.: Louisiana State University Press, 1998.

DuPont, H. A. *The Campaign of 1864 in the Valley of Virginia and the Expedition to Lynchburg.* New York: J. J. Little & Ives Company, 1925.

Dyer, Frederick, H. *A Compendium of the War of the Rebellion.* New York: Thomas Yoseloff, 1959.

Early, Jubal A. "Early's March to Washington in 1864." In *Battles and Leaders of the Civil War.* Ed. by Robert Underwood Johnson and Clarence Clough Buel. New York: Thomas Yoseloff, 1956.

_____. *Lieutenant General Jubal Anderson Early C.S.A.: Autobiographical Sketch and Narrative of the War Between the States.* New York: Konecky & Konecky, 1994. Reprint of 1912 edition.

_____. *A Memoir of the Last Year of the War for Independence in the Confederate States of America.* New Orleans: Blelock & Co., 1867.

_____. "Winchester, Fisher's Hill, and Cedar Creek." In *Battles and Leaders of the Civil War.* Ed. by Robert Underwood Johnson and Clarence Clough Buel. New York: Thomas Yoseloff, 1956.

Elwood, John W. *Elwood's Stories of the Old Ringgold Cavalry 1847-1865.* Coal Center, Pa.: John W. Elwood, 1914.

Emerson, Edward W. *Life and Letters of Charles Russell Lowell.* Port Washington, N.Y.: Kennikat Press, 1971. Reprint of 1907 edition.

Engle, Stephen D. *Yankee Dutchman: The Life of Franz Sigel.* Fayetteville, Ark.: The University of Arkansas Press, 1993.

Evans, Clement A., ed. *Confederate Military History, Vol. III.* Atlanta: Confederate Publishing Company, 1899.

Fletcher, Henry C. *History of the American War, by Lieut.-Colonel Fletcher.* London: Richard Bentley, New Burlington Street, 1866.

Foote, Shelby. *The Civil War A Narrative: Red River To Appomattox.* New York: Random House, 1974.

Fox, William F. *Regimental Losses in the American Civil War 1861-1865.* Albany, NY: Albany Publishing Company, 1889.

Freeman, Douglas Southall. *Lee's Lieutenants: A Study in Command, Vol. 3.* New York: Charles Scribner's Sons, 1972.

_____. *R. E. Lee: A Biography,* Vol III. New York: Charles Scribner's Sons, 1935.

Gallagher, Gary W. *Stephen Dodson Ramseur: Lee's Gallant General.* Chapel Hill, N.C.: University of North Carolina Press, 1985.

_____, ed. *Struggle for the Shenandoah: Essays on the 1864 Valley Campaign.* Kent, Ohio: Kent State University Press, 1991.

Glazier, Willard. *Battles for the Union.* Hartford, Conn.: Dustin, Gilman & Co., 1875.

Goldsborough, W.W. *The Maryland Line in the*

Confederate Army. Gaithersburg, Md.: Butternut Press, 1983. Reprint edition.

Gordon, John B. *Reminiscences of the Civil War*. New York: Charles Scribner's Sons, 1903.

Gorham, George C. *Life and Public Services of Edwin M. Stanton*. Boston: Houghton, Mifflin and Company, 1899.

Goss, Warren Lee. *Recollections of a Private: A Story of the Army of the Potomac*. New York: Time-Life Books, 1984. Reprint of 1890 edition.

Gould, John M. *History of the First—Tenth—Twenty-Ninth Maine Regiments*. Portland, Maine: Stephen Berry, 1871.

Gracey, Samuel L. *Annals of the Sixth Pennsylvania Cavalry*. Lancaster, Ohio: Vanberg Publishing, 1996. Reprint of 1868 edition.

Grant, Ulysses S. *Personal Memoirs of U. S. Grant*. New York: Charles L. Webster & Company, 1886.

Greeley, Horace. *The American Conflict: A History of the Great Rebellion in the United States of America, 1860–'65*. New York: Negro Universities Press, 1969. Reprint of 1866 edition.

Hagemann, E.R., ed. *Fighting Rebels and Redskins: Experiences in Army Life of Colonel George B. Sanford 1861-1892*. Norman, Okla.: University of Oklahoma Press, 1969.

Hale, Laura Virginia. *Four Valiant Years in the Lower Shenandoah Valley, 1861–1865*. Strasburg, Va.: Shenandoah Publishing House, Inc., 1968.

Hall, Hillman A., comp. *History of the Sixth New York Cavalry*. Worcester, Mass.: The Blanchard Press, 1908.

Harwell, Richard B., ed. *The Union Reader*. New York: Longmans, Green and Co., 1958.

Haynes, E. M. *A History of the Tenth Regiment, Vermont Volunteers*. Tenth Vermont Regimental Association, 1870.

Heatwole, John L. *The Burning: Sheridan in the Shenandoah Valley*. Charlottesville, Va.: Rockbridge Publishing, 1998.

Hergesheimer, Joseph. *Sheridan—A Military Narrative*. Boston: Houghton Mifflin Co., 1931.

Hewitt, William. *History of the Twelfth West Virginia Volunteer Infantry*. Published by the Twelfth West Virginia Infantry Association, 1892.

Hoogenboom, Ari. *Rutherford B. Hayes: Warrior & President*. Lawrence, Kan.: University Press of Kansas, 1995.

Husby, Karla Jean, comp. *Under Custer's Command: The Civil War Journal of James Henry Avery*. Washington, D.C.: Brassey's, 2000.

Imboden, John D. "The Battle of New Market, Va.., May 15th, 1864." In *Battles and Leaders of the Civil War*. Ed. By Robert Underwood Johnson and Clarence Clough Buel. New York: Thomas Yoseloff, 1956.

———. "Fire, Sword, and the Halter." *The Annals of the Civil War*. Ed. Alexander Kelly McClure. New York: De Capo Press, Inc., 1994. Reprint edition.

Irwin, Richard B. *History of the Nineteenth Army Corps*. Baton Rouge, La.: Elliott's Book Shop Press, 1985. Reprint of 1892 edition.

Isham, Asa B. *An Historical Sketch of the Seventh Regiment Michigan Volunteer Cavalry*. New York: Town Topics Publishing Company, 1893.

Johnson, Pharris Deloach, ed. *Under the Southern Cross: Soldier Life With Gordon Bradwell and the Army of Northern Virginia*. Macon, Ga.: Mercer University Press, 1999.

Jones, Terry L. *Lee's Tigers: The Louisiana Infantry in the Army of Northern Virginia*. Baton Rouge, La.: Louisiana State University Press, 1987.

———, ed. *The Civil War Memoirs of Captain William J. Seymour*. Baton Rouge, La.: Louisiana State University Press, 1991.

Jones, Virgil C. *Gray Ghosts and Rebel Raiders*. New York: Promontory Press, 1995. Reprint of 1956 edition.

Judge, Joseph. *Season of Fire: The Confederate Strike on Washington*. Berryville, Va.: Rockbridge Publishing Co., 1994.

Katcher, Philip. *The Civil War Source Book*. New York: Facts On File, 1992.

Keifer, Joseph Warren. *Slavery and Four Years of War*. New York: G. P. Putnam's Sons, 1900.

Keyes, C. M., ed. *The Military History of the 123rd Regiment Ohio Volunteer Infantry*. Sandusky, Ohio: Register Steam Press, 1874.

Kidd, J. H. *Personal Recollections of a Cavalryman*. New York: Time-Life Books, 1983. Reprint of 1908 edition.

Kinsley, D. A. *Custer—Favor the Bold: A Soldier's Story*. New York: Promontory Press, 1988.

Laas, Virginia Jeans, ed. *Wartime Washington: The Civil War Letters of Elizabeth Blair Lee*. Urbana, Il.: University of Illinois Press, 1991.

Lee, Robert E. *Recollections and Letters of General Robert E. Lee*. New York: Konecky & Konecky, 1992. Reprint edition.

Leech, Margaret. *Reveille in Washington 1859-1865*. New York: Time Inc., 1962. Reprint of 1941 edition.

Lewis, Thomas A. *The Guns of Cedar Creek*. New York: Harper & Row, 1988.

Lincoln, William S. *Life With the Thirty-fourth Mass. Infantry in the War of the Rebellion*. Worcester, Mass.: Press of Noyes, Snow & Company, 1879.

Long, A. L. *Memoirs of Robert E. Lee.* Edison, N.J.: The Blue and Grey Press, 1983.

Lufkin, Edwin B. *History of the Thirteenth Maine Regiment.* Bridgton, Maine: H. A. Shorey & Son, Publishers, 1898.

Matloff, Maurice, ed. *The Civil War: A Concise Military History of the War Between the States 1861-1865.* New York: Promontory Press, 1982.

McDonald, Archie P., ed. *Make Me a Map of the Valley: The Civil War Journal Of Stonewall Jackson's Topographer.* Dallas: Southern Methodist University Press, 1973.

McKim, Randolph H. *A Soldier's Recollection: Leaves From the Diary of a Young Confederate.* New York: Longman's, Green, and Co., 1910

McPherson, James M. *Battle Cry of Freedom: The Civil War Era.* New York: Oxford University Press, 1988.

_____. *For Cause & Comrades: Why Men Fought in the Civil War.* New York: Oxford University Press, 1997.

_____. *Ordeal By Fire: The Civil War and Reconstruction.* New York: Alfred A. Knopf, 1982.

Merritt, Wesley. "Sheridan in the Shenandoah Valley." In *Battles and Leaders of the Civil War.* Ed. by Robert Underwood Johnson and Clarence Clough Buel. New York: Thomas Yoseloff, 1956.

Michie, Peter S. *The Life and Letters of Emory Upton.* New York: Arno Press, 1979. Reprint of 1885 edition.

Miller, Edward A. Jr. *Lincoln's Abolitionist General—The Biography of David Hunter.* Columbia, S.C.: University of South Carolina Press, 1997.

Murray, Thomas Hamilton. *History of the Ninth Regiment Connecticut Volunteer Infantry.* New Haven, Conn.: The Price, Lee & Adkins Co., 1903.

Nettleton, A.B. "The Famous Fight At Cedar Creek." *The Annals of the Civil War.* Ed. by Alexander Kelly McClure. New York: De Capo Press, 1994. Reprint edition.

Nevins, Allan. *The War for the Union: The Organized War to Victory 1864-1865.* New York: Charles Scribner's Sons, 1971.

_____, ed. *A Diary of Battle: The Personal Journals of Colonel Charles S. Wanwright 1861–1865.* New York: Harcourt, Brace & World, Inc., 1962.

_____, ed. *Diary of the Civil War 1860-1865: George Templeton Strong.* New York: Macmillian Company, 1962.

Newcomer, C. Armour. *Cole's Cavalry: Or Three Years in the Saddle in the Shenandoah Valley.* Freeport, N.Y.: Books for Libraries Press, 1970. Reprint of 1895 edition.

O'Connor, Richard. *Sheridan The Inevitable.* New York: Konecky & Konecky, 1993. Reprint edition.

Pellet, Elias P. *History of the 114th Regiment, New York State Volunteers.* Norvich, N.Y.: Telegraph & Chronicle Power Press Print, 1866.

Perkins, George. *A Summer in Maryland and Virginia: Or Campaigning With the 149th Ohio Volunteer Infantry.* Chillicothe, Ohio: The Scholl Printing Company, 1911.

Pond, George E. *The Shenandoah Valley in 1864.* New York: Charles Scribner's Sons, 1905.

Porter, Horace. *Campaigning With Grant.* New York: Mallard Press, 1991. Reprint edition.

Power, J. Tracy. *Lee's Miserables: Life in the Army of Northern Virginia From the Wilderness to Appomattox.* Chapel Hill, N.C.: University of North Carolina Press, 1998.

Powers, George W. *The Story of the Thirty Eighth Regiment of Massachusetts Volunteers.* Cambridge Press: Dakin and Metcalf, 1866.

Putnam, George Haven. *Some Memories of the Civil War.* New York: G. P. Putnam's Sons, 1924.

Rawley, James A. *Turning Points of the Civil War.* Lincoln, Neb.: University of Nebraska Press, 1966. New Bison Edition, 1989.

Rawling, C. J. *History of the First Regiment Virginia Infantry.* Philadelphia: J. B. Lippincott Company, 1887.

Reader, Frank S. *History of the Fifth West Virginia Cavalry.* New Brighton, Pa.: Daily News, 1890.

Reed, Thomas J. *Tibbit's Boys—A History of the 21st New York Cavalry.* Lanham, Md.: University Press of America, Inc., 1997.

Reynolds, Arlene, comp. *The Civil War Memories of Elizabeth Bacon Custer.* Austin, Tex.: University of Texas Press, 1994.

Rhodes, Robert Hunt, ed. *All For the Union: Civil War Diary and Letters of Elisha Hunt Rhodes.* New York: Orion Books, 1991.

Robertson, James I. Jr. *The Stonewall Brigade.* Baton Rouge, La.: Louisiana State University Press, 1963.

Rodenbough, Theodore F., Henry C. Potter, and William P. Seal, eds. and comps. *History of the Eighteenth Regiment of Cavalry Pennsylvania Volunteers.* New York: Wynkoop Hallenbeck Crawford Co., 1909.

Rosenblatt, Emil and Ruth Rosenblatt, *Hard Marching Every Day: The Civil War Letters of Private Wilber Fisk 1861–1865* University Press of Kansas, 1992.

Russell, Charles Wells, ed. *The Memoirs of Colonel John S. Mosby.* Boston: Little Brown and Company, 1917.

Sandburg, Carl. *Abraham Lincoln: The War*

Years. New York: Harcourt, Brace, World Inc., 1939.

Schmitt, Martin F., ed. *General George Crook: His Autobiography*. Norman, Okla.: University of Oklahoma Press, 1986.

Scott, John. *Partisan Life With Col. John S. Mosby*. New York: Harper & Brothers, Publishers, 1867.

Shapiro, Larry, ed. *Abraham Lincoln: Mystic Chords of Memory*. New York: Book-of-the-Month Club, Inc., 1984.

Sheridan, Philip H. *Personal Memoirs of P. H. Sheridan*. New York: Charles L. Webster & Company, 1888.

Shirey, Henry A. *The Story of the Maine Fifteenth*. Bridgeton, Maine: Press of the Bridgeton News, 1890.

Sigel, Franz. "Sigel in the Shenandoah Valley in 1864." In *Battles and Leaders of the Civil War*. Ed. by Robert Underwood Johnson and Clarence Clough Buel. New York: Thomas Yoseloff, 1956.

Simon, John Y., ed. *The Papers of Ulysses S. Grant*. Carbondale, Il.: Southern Illinois University Press, 1982.

Slease, William Davis. *The Fourteenth Pennsylania Cavalry in the Civil War*. Butler, Pa.: Mechling Associates, Inc., 1999. Reprint edition.

Sprague, Homer B. *History of the 13th Infantry Regiment of Connecticut Volunteers*. Hartford, Conn.: Lockwood & Co., 1867.

Stevens, George T. *Three Years in the Sixth Corps*. New York: Time-Life Books, 1984. Reprint of 1866 edition.

Strother, David Hunter. *A Virginia Yankee in the Civil War*. Chapel Hill, N.C.: University of North Carolina Press, 1961.

Tankersley, Allen P. *John B. Gordon: A Study in Gallantry*. Atlanta: The Whitehall Press, 1955.

Taylor, Richard. *Destruction and Reconstruction: Personal Experiences of the Civil War*. New York: De Capo Press, 1995. Reprint of 1879 edition.

Tenney, Luman Harris. *War Diary of Luman Harris Tenney 1861-1865*. Cleveland, Ohio: Evangelical Publishing House, 1914.

Tenney, W. J. *The Military and Naval History of the Rebellion in the United States*. New York: D. Appleton & Company, 1866.

Thomas, Benjamin P., ed. *Three Years With Grant: As Recalled By War Correspondent Sylvanus Cadwallader*. New York: Alfred A. Knopf, 1956.

Tiemann, William F., comp. *The 159th Regiment, New York State Volunteers, in the War of the Rebellion, 1862-1865*. Brooklyn, N.Y.: William F. Tiemann, 1891.

United States War Department. *The War of the Rebellion: A Compilation of the Official Records of the Union and Confederate Armies*. Washington, D.C.: Government Printing Office, 1880-1901. Series 1 unless noted.

Vandiver, Frank E. *Jubal's Raid: General Early's Famous Attack on Washington in 1864*. New York: McGraw-Hill, 1960.

_____, ed. *The Civil War Diary of General Josiah Gorgas*. Tuscaloosa, Ala.: University of Alabama Press, 1947.

Waite, Otis F. R. *New Hampshire in the Great Rebellion*. Claremont, N.H.: Tracy, Chase & Company, 1870.

_____. *Vermont in the Great Rebellion*. Claremont, N.H.: Chase and Company, 1869.

Walker, Aldace F. *The Vermont Brigade in the Shenandoah Valley 1864*. Burlington, Vt.: The Free Press Association, 1869.

Wallace, Lew. *Lew Wallace—An Autobiography*. New York: Harper & Brothers, 1906.

Warner, Ezra J. *Generals in Blue*. Baton Rouge, La.: Louisiana State University Press, 1964.

_____. *Generals in Gray*. Baton Rouge, La.: Louisiana State University Press, 1959.

Wayland, John W. *A History of Shenandoah County Virginia*. Strasburg, Va.: Shenandoah Publishing House, 1927.

Wellman, Manly Wade. *Rebel Boast: First at Bethel—Last at Appomattox*. New York: Henry Holt and Company, 1956.

Wert, Jeffry D. *Custer: The Controversial Life of George Armstrong Custer*. New York: Simon & Schuster, 1996.

_____. *From Winchester to Cedar Creek: The Shenandoah Campaign of 1864*. Carlisle, Pa.: South Mountain Press, Inc., 1987.

_____. *Mosby's Rangers*. New York: Simon & Schuster, 1990.

Wiley, Bell Irvin. *The Life of Billy Yank: The Common Soldier of The Union*. Baton Rouge, La.: Louisiana State University Press, 1978.

_____. *The Road to Appomattox*. New York: Atheneum, 1977.

Wilkeson, Frank. *Turned Inside Out: Recollections of a Private Soldier in the Army of the Potomac*. Lincoln, Neb.: University of Nebraska Press, 1997. Reprint of 1887 edition.

Williams, T. Harry. *Lincoln and His Generals*. New York: Alfred A. Knopf, 1952.

_____. *McClellan, Sherman and Grant*. New Brunswick, N.J.: Rutgers University Press, 1962.

Williamson, James J. *Mosby's Rangers: A Record of the Operations of the Forty-Third Battalion Virginia Cavalry, From Its Organization to the Surrender*. New York: Time-Life Books, Inc., 1982. Reprint of 1896 edition.

Wise, John S. *The End of an Era*. Boston: Houghton, Mifflin and Co., 1899.

Worsham, John H. *One of Jackson's Foot Cavalry: His Experience and What He Saw During the War 1861-1865*. New York: The Neale Publishing Co., 1912.

Periodicals, Newspapers, Letters, and Other Documents

Atkinson, Archibald, Jr. *Memoir of Archibald Atkinson Jr.* (Ms 94-022). Special Collections, Digital Library and Archives, University Libraries, Virginia Polytechnic Institute and State University.

Badeau, Adam. "Lieut-General Sheridan." *The Century*. February 1884.

Baker, Isaac Norval. *Isaac Norval Baker Memoirs*. Virginia Military Institute Archives.

Black, William J. *William J. Black Diary*. Virginia Military Institute Archives.

Brisbane, Napoleon B. *Napoleon B. Brisbane Letters*. Virginia Military Institute Archives.

Breckinridge, John C. John C. Breckinridge letter to Francis H. Smith, May 10, 1864. Virginia Military Institute Archives.

Brown, James Earl. "Life of Brigadier General John McCausland." *West Virginia History*. Vol. 4.

"The Burning Of Chambersburg." *Confederate Veteran Magazine*. Vol. XI, No. 10. October 1903. http://members.home. com/civilwarcsa/1903/article16.html.

Burr, C. Chauncy (editor). "Lieutenant-General Early." *The Old Guard*. December 1866.

Carpenter, Henry. *Henry Carpenter Letters* (Ms 96-008). Special Collections, Digital Library and Archives, University Libraries, Virginia Polytechnic Institute and State University.

Crowninshield, Benjamin W. "Sheridan at Winchester." *The Atlantic Monthly*. December 1878.

DeForest, J. W. "Sheridan's Battle of Winchester." *Harper's New Monthly Magazine*. January 1865.

———. "Sheridan's Victory of Middletown." *Harper's New Monthly Magazine*. February 1865

Duncan, Richard R. "The Raid on Piedmont and the Crippling of Franz Sigel in the Shenandoah Valley." *West Virginia History*. Vol. 55.

Dunton, Samuel S. Civil War Letters. September 12, 2000. http://home.pacbell.net/dunton/SSDletters.html (June 10, 2002).

Early, Jubal A. "Gen'l Early's Address to His Army." *The Staunton Vindicator*. October 28, 1864, page 2, col. 3.

Eggleston, George Cary. "A Rebel's Recollections." *The Atlantic Monthly*. December 1874.

Fisher, Thomas Winton. Letter dated June 28, 1864. The McGinley Genealogy Page. http://www.dianne.mcginley.com. June 10, 2001.

"Fisher's Hill and Sheridan's Ride." *Confederate Veteran Magazine*. Vol. IX, No. 4. April 1902. http://members.home/ civilwarcsa/1902/article5.html.

Fitts, James Franklin. "The Fight at Fisher's Hill." *The Galaxy*. April 1868.

———. "The Last Battle of Winchester." *The Galaxy*. October 15, 1866.

Forsyth, George A. "Sheridan's Ride." *Harper's New Monthly Magazine*. July 1897.

Fuller, Edward. Paper read at the 59th reunion of the 77th New York State Foot Volunteers. Saratoga Springs, New York. June 26, 1915.

Houghton, Henry H. *Recollections Of The War: A Personal Account Of The Civil War*. Vermont in the Civil War. http://vermontcivilwar.org/1bgd/3/ houghton.shtml.

Humphreys, J. O. *J. O. Humphreys Diary*. Virginia Military Institute Archives.

Imboden, John D. "To The Farmers of Augusta, Rockingham and Shenandoah." *The Staunton Spectator*. March 8, 1864, Page 1, Col. 7.

Johnson Family Papers. Mortimer Johnson Letter. Virginia Miliary Institute Archives.

Johnson, Porter. *Porter Johnson Memoirs*. Virginia Military Institute Archives.

Letcher, John. "The Burning of Gov. Letcher's Residence." *The Staunton Vindicator*. July 22, 1864, Page 1, Col. 6.

Long, A.L. "General Early's Valley Campaign." *Southern Historical Society Papers, Vol. 3, January–June 1877*. Ed. J. William Jones. Millwood, N.Y.: Kraus Reprint Co., 1977.

Marlin, Sidney. Sidney Marlin Letter. Virginia Military Institute Archives.

Park, Robert E. "Diary of Robert E. Park, Macon, Georgia, late Captain Twelfth Alabama Regiment, Confederate States Army." *Southern Historical Society Papers, Vol. I, January–June 1876*. Ed. J. William Jones. Millwood, N.Y.: Kraus Reprint Co., 1977.

Perry, Leslie J. "A Shock to General Sheridan." *The Century*. August 1896.

Roller, John E. Papers. Lawrence Royster Letter. Virginia Military Institute Archives.

———. Papers. Peter S. Roller Letter. Virginia Military Institute Archives.

Shanks, W. F. G. "Recollections of Sheridan." *Harper's New Monthly Magazine*. August 1865.

Tynes, Achilles J. Captain Achilles J. Tynes Letter, June 13, 1864. Virginia Military Institute Archives.

Watson, William G. *William G. Watson Memoirs: A Union Soldier in The Shenandoah Valley, 1864*. Virginia Military Institute Archives.

White, Isaac. *Isaac White Letters* (Ms 97-013). Special Collections, Digital Library and Archives, University Libraries, Virginia Polytechnic Institute and State University.

Whitehorne, Joseph W. A. *The Battle Of New Market*. Center of Military History. United States Army. Washington, D. C., 1988.

Wilson, Fannie M. Lyle. Fannie M. Lyle Wilson Letter, June 17, 1864. Virginia Military Institute Archives.

Wise, John S. "The West Point of the Confederacy." *The Century*. January 1889.

Index

Abraham's Creek, near Winchester 146, 148, 153
Alexander, Union Lt. Col. B.S. 106
Alexandria, Virginia 183
Allegheny Mountains 13
Anderson, Confederate Lt. Gen. Richard 123, 137, 140, 141, 142, 143; Lee recall of 144
Aqueduct Bridge, over Potomac, defenses 106
Arlington Heights 104
Arlington National Cemetery 10
Army of Northern Virginia 6, 8, 9, 10, 17, 65, 66, 71, 135, 165, 220
Army of the Ohio 132
Army of the Potomac: spring campaign 9; 10, 24, 64, 65, 89, 92, 93, 94, 129, 133
Army of the Shenandoah: Hunter commands 47; moves south 48; 135, 136, 173, 199, 203
Army of the Valley 84, 86
Army of West Virginia 67, 77; becomes Eighth Corps 135
Ashby's Gap, Virginia 122, 183
Atkinson, Archibald, Confederate soldier 142

Augur, Union Maj. Gen. Christopher C.: commands Washington 106; 111, 116, 117
Averell, Union Brig. Gen. William W.: troops 21; advances to Saltville 25; 27; Saltville 29; 44–45, 47, 60; in Staunton 61; to Lynchburg 70; 71, 74, 76, 80; fights near Winchester 123; Kernstown 125; 127; Moorefield attack 128; 135, 147, 154, 155, 156, 167; relieved 168

Back Creek, Virginia 87; 145
Back Road, near Valley Pike 173, 176
Backwater Creek, near Lynchburg 74, 76
Baltimore, Maryland: headquarters Middle Department 89; 92, 93, 95, 101
Baltimore & Ohio Railroad: route 17; 20, 21, 26, 46, 86, 87, 89; Monocacy bridge 93; 96, 121, 141, 144–145, 171, 172, 216
Baltimore Pike 96; 101
Barnard, Union Gen. J. G. 106
Beale's Brigade: at Winchester 151

Belle Grove: Sheridan's HQ at Cedar Creek 186; 193, 204
Berryville, Virginia 123, 136, 142, 143, 145; road to Winchester 146–147; 148; troops along road 150; Berryville Pike 157
Bidwell, Union Col. Daniel: Third Brigade, Sixth Corps at Fort Stevens 113; at Cedar Creek 194; killed 195; 211
Big Otter Creek, Virginia 68
Binkley, Union Lt. Col. O. H.: at Monocacy 100
Birge, Union Brig. Gen. Henry: at Winchester 151
Blackwater Creek, near Lynchburg 71, 76
Blair, Francis P. 104
Blair, Montgomery, Postmaster General 104
Blue Ridge Mountains 13, 16, 67, 119, 141, 143, 168, 172, 173, 175, 214, 215
Bolivar Heights, near Harpers Ferry 88
Boreman, A. I., Governor of West Virginia 217
Boteler's Ford 90
Bowman's Ford 186
Boyd, Union Col. William: at New Market 30; 37

243

Breckinridge, Confederate Maj. Gen. John C. 23; command of department and tour 23; 24, 26; where to fight 27; increases manpower 29; message to VMI 29; at Staunton 30; moves to New Market 32; battle plan 33; use of cadets 33; decides to attack at New Market 34; 35, 37; uses cadets 39; 40; final attack at New Market 41; rests troops 42; message to Lee 43; casualties 44; leadership 45; 48, 49, 65, 66; in Lynchburg 68; messages from Early and to Vaughn 69; 70, 87, 90, 97, 122, 124, 148, 154, 155, 156, 180
Brown, Union Col. Allison L.: Monocacy report 100; 101
Browne, Confederate Col. William 54
Buchanan, Virginia 67
Buckton Ford, Virginia 166
Buford's Gap, Virginia 79
Bunker Hill, West Virginia 26; Mosby raid 28; 125, 136, 145, 148, 154
Bushong's Hill, near New Market 34, 35–36, 37
Butler, Union Maj. Gen. Benjamin 10

Cadwallader, Sylvanus: about Sheridan 133
Campbell, Union Lt. Col. Edward: at Winchester 152
Campbell, Union Col. Jacob M.: led 54th Pennsylvania forward 40–41; attack at Piedmont 56–57
Campbell Court House, near Lynchburg 76
Carlin's West Virginia Battery: at New Market 37
Carpenter, George, Union soldier: movements of 142; Winchester fight 151
Carter, Confederate Col. Thomas H. 195
Catawba Mountain, Virginia 80
Cedar Creek, Virginia 25, 48, 136; at Valley; Pike 153; 161, 162, 173, 178, 179, 180, 182, 185, 186; Early's instructions 187; beautiful day 187; 189, 192, 199, 209; casualties 210; 211, 213
Cedarville, Virginia 140
Chain Bridge: defenses 106; 119
Chambersburg, Pennsylvania 126, 127, 128, 129
Charlestown, Virginia 141, 142
Charlestown, West Virginia 24
Charlottesville, Virginia 47, 64, 65, 118, 120, 171, 172, 183, 184, 217, 219, 220
Chesapeake and Ohio Canal: route 17; damage to 91
Chickamauga, Battle of 132
City Point, Virginia: Grant's headquarters 116; 130, 217
Clark, Confederate Lt. Col. J. Lyle: with 30th Virginia Battalion at New Market 34
Clendenin, Union Lt. Col. David: cavalry outside Washington 92; 96
Cloyd's Mountain, Battle of 29
Couch, Union Maj. Gen. 216
Crook, Union Brig. Gen. George: leads advance 24; new plan 25; 27; Cloyd's Mountain 29; 47, 60; in Staunton 61; conduct of troops 64; 71, 75; commands Hunter's army 121; 122, 123, 124, 125, 135, 141, 142, 147, 153; advances on right 155; 156, 161; troops move during night 162; 164, 165, 187, 189, 190, 197, 209, 217
Cross Road, at Piedmont 54
Cullen, Brig. Gen. 106
Culpepper Court House, Virginia 137
Cumberland, Maryland 21; 127
Custer, Union Brig. Gen. George A. 58; wife describes Washington 104–105; 154; Third Cavalry Division 173; 175; Tom's Brook 176–177, 196–197, 202; decides to attack 207; leads cavalry attack 208–209; 215, 217; at Waynesboro 219

Custis, Mary, wife of Robert E. Lee 10

Dana, Union Assistant Secretary of War Charles: conditions at Fort Stevens 112; confusion at Washington 116–117; 118; to Rawlins about Valley 214
Davis, President Jefferson 10, 22, 62, 83, 86, 92; defends Early 181
Derrick, Confederate Lt. Col. Clarence: commands 23rd Virginia at New Market 38; 40
Devin, Union Brig. Gen. Thomas C. 140, 154; Pursuit from Fisher's Hill 165; 167; at Cedar Creek 196; 219
Douglas, Confederate Maj. Henry K.: with Early on raid 114; on Early's moves 145; on damage 174
Dublin, Virginia: Department of Western Virginia headquarters 23; 29
Duffié, Union Brig. Gen. Alfred: near Lynchburg 70–71; advance 74; at Lynchburg, enemy reinforcements 76; waits for orders 78; 79, 80; at Ashby's Gap 122–123; Kernstown 124–125
Dunton, Samuel, Union soldier: following Early 119, 120
DuPont, Union Captain Henry: at New Market 34; left behind 36; covers retreat 42–43; describes Hunter 46–47; at Piedmont 54; 55, 56; artillery 58; VMI destruction 63; 76; leaves Lynchburg 77; abandons guns 192; shells retreating enemy 209
Duval, Union Col. 155
Dwight's Division: at Winchester 151

Early, Confederate Lt. Gen. Jubal Anderson: Shenandoah Valley in 1863 4–5; on Imboden letter 19; commands Second Corps 65; information about 65–66; plan to attack Washington

66–67; messages to Breckinridge 69; troops to Lynchburg and fortifications 69–70; at Lynchburg 71; decides actions 74; 77; Union retreat 78; message to Lee, chases Hunter 79; 80; ends pursuit 81; 82, 83; pursuit 84; staff opinion 84–85; damage, message from Lee 85; describes advance 86; to Martinsburg 87; at Harpers Ferry 88; 89; about discipline 90–91; 92, 93, 95; Union position 96; McCausland attacks 97; 101; time factor 102; toward Washington 103; 104; Washington defenses 108–109; his troops 109; decides to attack 110; delays attack on Fort Stevens 112; official report 113–114; on supplies 115; 116; route south 118; 119, 120, 121, 122; Kernstown 123–124; explains Chambersburg 126–127; damage to cavalry 128; 134, 135; reinforcements 136–137; 140, 141; opinion of Sheridan 142; troop movements 143; 144; scatter troops 145; troops back to Winchester 147–148; sets defense 148; 149, 151, 152; Winchester morning 153; begins retreat 154; 155, 156, 157; message to Lee 158; position on Fisher's Hill 160–161; 162; effort to fight 165; message to Lee 166; 168; troops blame him 168; message to Lee 169; 170, 171; message to Lee about Tom's Brook 177; leadership 180; 181; to Hupp's Hill 182; 183; to Fisher's Hill 184; decides to attack 185; uses Gordon's plan 186; issues orders for move 186; 187, 192; meets Gordon 195; calls off attack 197–198; 204, 207; has to retreat 208–209; to Fisher's Hill 210; details to Lee 212; message to troops 212–213; blame and accomplishment 213–214; to Seddon 214; moves north 216; ends campaign 216; 217; meets Lee 218; to Waynesboro 219; escape from Waynesboro, end of career 220

East Road, at Piedmont 52, 53, 54, 56
Echols: brigade at New Market 33–34; 122
Edgar, Confederate Col. George M.: at New Market 33
Edinburg, Virginia 167
Edwards, Union Col. Oliver: at Winchester 152
18th Connecticut: at New Market 33; 35, 37; Piedmont 54; 55, 76
18th Virginia Cavalry 24; at New Market 29; 30, 53
Eighth Corps: Winchester plan 147; attack at Fisher's Hill 163; 164; at Cedar Creek 189, 191, 192; disperses troops 217
Eighth Illinois Cavalry 92
Eighth New York: at Waynesboro 219
8th Vermont: at Winchester 151
Eleventh Maryland: at Monocacy 96
Emerson, Union Col. William, 151st New York: at Monocacy 97
Emory, Union Brig. Gen. William H. 135; at Winchester 151; 155; at Cedar Creek 192; 203, 204, 205, 206, 207
Evans, Confederate Brig. Gen. Clement A.: at Monocacy 98; at Winchester 152; at Cedar Creek 189; 205, 207

Fifteenth Maine, Union soldier's letter 119
15th New York Cavalry 28
5th New York Cavalry 55; Winchester 146; chaplain on damage 174; at Cedar Creek 209
5th New York Heavy Artillery: Piedmont 54; 55; at Cedar Creek 190
5th U.S. Artillery: at New Market 34

5th West Virginia: at Piedmont 75
5th Wisconsin 174
51st Virginia: at New Market 34–35; 37, 38, 40–41
54th Pennsylvania: at New Market 34; 37, 40–41; Piedmont 54; 56, 76
First Cavalry Division: commanded by Merritt 140
First Connecticut: at Waynesboro 219
First Infantry Brigade, New Market 31
First Maryland Potomac Home Brigade: at Monocacy 96
First New York Dragoons 167
1st New York (Lincoln) Cavalry 22; 48, 53
1st West Virginia: at New Market 31; 33, 35, 37, 40–41; at Piedmont 56
Fisher, Thomas Winton, Confederate soldier, letter home 85–86
Fisher's Hill, Virginia 136; 137; Confederate retreat to, description 160; 161, 162, 165; battle casualties 166; 167, 168; Early's report 169; 170, 175, 177, 180, 181, 182, 184, 185, 186, 210
Fisherville, Virginia 57
Fisk, Union Private Wilber, letter home 129; on destruction 173; at Cedar Creek 179; Sheridan return 202
Fitts, James Franklin: beautiful day 149; fighting at Winchester 152; describes Sheridan 153; Fisher's Hill attack 164
Forest Road, near Lynchburg 70, 73, 74, 78
Forsyth, Union Maj. George (Sandy): Sheridan aide 199; troops follow 200–201; Sheridan seen by army 202; men prepare for attack 204; during attack 206
Fort Jackson, outside Washington 106
Fort Massachusetts, outside Washington 116
Fort McHenry, Maryland 139

Fort Reno, outside Washington 116
Fort Stevens, outside Washington 104, 108, 110, 111, 113, 116
45th Virginia Battalion: at Piedmont 54–55
45th Virginia Infantry Regiment: at Piedmont 54
43rd Battalion Virginia Cavalry, Mosby's men 139
Fourteenth New Jersey Volunteers: Maj. Vredenburgh at Winchester 149–150
14th Pennsylvania Cavalry: at Piedmont 54; Moorefield 128
Fourth Georgia Volunteers, soldier's letter 181
Fourth Pennsylvania Cavalry: at Snicker's Ferry 122
Franklin, Union Maj. Gen. W. B. 128–129
Frederick, Maryland 92; ransom 95; 115, 119
French, Union Lt. Col.: at Cedar Creek 195; during attack 205
Front Royal, Virginia 13, 16, 27, 137, 143, 148; road 153; 166, 168, 180, 184, 204, 215

Garrett, J.W., president Baltimore & Ohio: message to Stanton 87; meets Grant 144–145
Georgetown Pike, to Washington 93, 96, 98
Getty, Union Brig. Gen. 156; command Sixth Corps at Cedar Creek 193; 194, 195–196, 197, 201–202; starts attack 205
Gibson, Union Maj. 128
Gordon, Confederate Maj. Gen. John B. 70, 71, 75, 76, 91; attack at Monocacy 97–98; 99; tribute 100; 101, 122, 145; delay at Winchester 148; 150, 151, 153, 155; pursuit from Winchester 156–157; 160, 183; to Massanutten 185; sees way to victory 185–186; moves to Cedar Creek 187; Cedar Creek attack 189; 192, 193, 194; victory slips away 195; 196; delays attack 197; 203; warning of attack 204; Confederate line 205; 207; troops surrounded 208; retreat 209
Gordonsville, Virginia 69, 118, 183, 217, 220
Gorgas, Josiah, on Chambersburg 127
Grant, Lt. Gen. Ulysses Simpson: previous victories 3–4; description of 7; previous victories, war effort, to Halleck 8; 9; objective for Meade 10; reply to Lincoln 11–12; eliminates Lee's army 18; 24, 25; letter to Sherman 26; to Halleck about Sigel 44; appoints Hunter 46; plan for Hunter 47; 48, 49; orders for Hunter 50; 64, 67; Hunter's route 82; 84, 86, 88; troops from Washington 89; to Meade about Early 89; plan to destroy Early before he returned south 90; 93; messages to Halleck 94; 101; comments on Monocacy 102; 104, 106; to Lincoln, sending troops 107; 114; pursuit of Early 116; Wright in command 117; blames Halleck and Stanton 118; orders for Halleck 118; 119, 120; orders for Hunter 121; combines departments 128–129; Sheridan orders 130–131; with Hunter 131; instructions for Sheridan 131–132; Shenandoah Valley 134; 135, 137; orders to Sheridan 139; information to Sheridan 141; 143; plan for Sheridan 144; to Sheridan 158; 165, 166; to Sheridan about railroads 171; orders to Sheridan 183–184; 211, 212; cuts railroad 214; to Sheridan about railroads 219; 220
Grimes, Confederate Brig. Gen. Bryan: troops retreat 156; defense 205; under attack at Cedar Creek 208
Grover, Union Brig. Gen. Cuvier 150, 151, 156; Cedar Creek 199; 211

Hagerstown, Maryland 115
Halleck, Union Maj. Gen. Henry W.: Grant's proposed attack in deep south 8; tells Grant of defeat 25; 44, 46, 47; reply to Hunter 48; warning to Grant 88; report on Early 89; 90, 91; to Ricketts 93; to Grant 93; examines defenses 106; to Grant, capital defenses 107; 117, 118; to Sherman 119; 120; message to Grant 121; 130, 132, 144; to Sheridan 183; Longstreet information 184; 185, 215, 216; food for civilians 218
Halltown, Virginia 137, 139, 140
Hampton, Confederate Maj. Gen. Wade: Trevilian Station 65
Harpers Ferry 13, 17, 87, 88, 89, 92, 119, 131, 136, 137, 140, 141, 142
Harris, Union Col. Thomas M. 162; Fisher's Hill 163; report on Hupp's Hill 182; at Hupp's Hill 183; at Cedar Creek 191
Harrisonburg, Virginia 13, 50, 168, 171, 172
Hayes, Union Col. Rutherford B.: Kernstown 124–125; at Fisher's Hill 163; 189
Haynes, E.M.: delays Early 93; Winchester victory 157
Higgins, Union Col. Jacob: intercepts McNeill 28; ambushed 29; 37, 124
Hill, Confederate Gen. D. H. 70
Hotchkiss, Confederate Captain Jed: to Massanutten 185; information to Early 186
Humphreys, J. O.: retreat from Lynchburg 80
Hunter, Union Maj. Gen. David 46; follows Sigel plan 47; to Halleck for replacements 47–48; positive message to Sullivan 49; 50, 51, 52; at Piedmont 54; 56, 57, 58, 59; moving south 60; 61; army size 62; report on VMI 63; on supplies 64; 65, 66, 67; about Lynchburg 68; 69; indecision at Lynchburg 71–72; Lynchburg defenses 73;

74; 75; 76; enemy forces 77; 78, 79, 80; chooses route 81; report, hatred by civilians 82; 83, 84, 85, 86, 87, 90; moving slowly 91; 102; orders from Halleck 120; 121, 126, 130; relieved 131; 142
Hupp's Hill, near Cedar Creek 182, 183, 186, 187
Hyde, Union Col. Thomas: at Cedar Creek 194–195; describes attack 205

Imboden, Frank 53
Imboden, Confederate Col. George 53
Imboden, Confederate Brig. Gen. John D.: message in *Staunton Spectator* 15; on Early statements 19; defends Valley 24; 26, 27; ambush at Lost River Gap 29; attacks Boyd 30–31; leaves New Market 32; 35; artillery at New Market 37; comments on New market 45; force 50; facing Hunter, description of Jones 49; troops from Jones, dire circumstances 51; position at Mowry's Hill 52; fight before Piedmont 53; 57; fails to act 58; 60; slows Hunter 68; 70; at Lynchburg 71; 91, 153

Jackson, Thomas "Stonewall": 1862 campaign 16, 17, 65
James River and Kanawha Canal: route 16; destruction 64–65; 219, 220
Jenkins, Confederate Brig. Gen. Albert: fight at Cloyd's Mountain 29
Johnson, Confederate Brig. Gen. Bradley 87, 92, 127, 148; Tom's Brook 176
Jones, Confederate Col. Beuhring: First Brigade at Piedmont 53–54
Jones, Confederate Brig. Gen. Samuel 22
Jones, Confederate Gen. William E. 29; description 49; takes command 51; 52, 53, 54; killed 56; 57, 58

Kanawha River 25

Keifer, Union Col. Warren 152; at Cedar Creek 193; describe attack 205
Kelly, Union Maj. Gen. Benjamin F. 20, 127
Kernstown, Virginia 123; Early's plan 124; casualties 125; 126
Kershaw 137, 140, 143, 144, 166, 170; at Hupp's Hill 183; 186, 187, 189; at Cedar Creek 190–192; 193, 197, 204, 205; to Petersburg 216
Keyes, C. M.: Sheridan as commander 136; new warfare 138
Kidd, Union Col. James H.: on damage 174; rear guard 175; orders from Merritt 196

Lacey Springs: Breckinridge meets Imboden 31; 32; Imboden harasses Hunter 50; 217
Laurel Brigade 175
Lee, Confederate Col. Edwin G. 60
Lee, Elizabeth Blair 104
Lee, Confederate Maj. Gen. Fitzhugh: Trevilian Station 65; 140, 141; at Winchester 148; 151, 154, 155, 160, 167, 168, 177
Lee, "Light Horse Harry 10
Lee, Confederate Gen. Robert Edward: Army of Northern Virginia 3; lack of supplies 5; Gen. Orders No. 7 5; family 10; to Davis about Union plans 10–11; on guerrillas 18; 20; importance of western Virginia 22–23; to Davis about supplies 24–25; unable to send aid to Valley 26; puts Breckinridge in charge 27; message to Breckinridge 44; 48, 49, 57, 59, 61; to Davis about Lynchburg 62; 64, 65; plan for Early 66–67; 79, 81, 82; plan for Early to Davis 83; message to Early 84; explain Early's orders 85; to Davis about Early 86; troops to Grant 89; 90; prisoner release 91–92; 101, 114, 115, 116, 119, 134; message to Early 141; 143; recalls troops 144; 169; to Governor Smith 170; suggestions to Early 170–171; 177; to Governor Smith 180; to Early on future 180–182; 212, 214, 216, 218; ending Early's career 220
Leesburg, Virginia 118, 119
Letcher, John, Governor of Virginia 63
Lexington, Virginia 13, 24; home of VMI 29; 62, 67
Liberty, Virginia 67, 68, 78, 79
Lincoln, Abraham: at Gettysburg 3; second term, Philadelphia speech 4; letter to Grant wishing success 11; to Grant 20; 67; safety of capital 106–107; to Fort Stevens 111; in Fort Stevens 113; 129; Sheridan orders 130; meets Sheridan 132; 141; to Sheridan 158; to Sheridan 211–212
Little Fort Valley 175
Little North Mountain, near Fisher's Hill 160, 161, 162
Lomax, Confederate Maj. Gen. Lunsford 145, 148, 154, 160, 163; Tom's Brook 176–177; 196, 217, 219
Long, A. L.: on raid 114
Long Bridge, over Potomac, defenses 106
Longstreet, Confederate Lt. Gen. James: Grant warning 8; 133, 184, 203–204
Lost River Gap 29
Loudoun County, Virginia 20, 118, 139
Louisa Court House, Virginia 69
Lowell, Union Col. Charles Russell: on confusion 108; about Sheridan 143; 154, 171; on destruction 173; Tom's Brook 176–177; to wife 180; 196; killed 208
Luray Valley 13, 160, 161, 166, 168, 175
Lynchburg, West Virginia 16, 24, 47, 51, 61, 64, 65, 66, 67, 68, 69, 71, 73, 74, 77, 78, 80, 82, 84, 115, 125, 214, 218, 219

Manassas Gap Railroad, route 16; 162, 215
Manor Hill, near New Market 35
Martinsburg, West Virginia 16, 17, 86; Pike 87; 88, 89, 90, 126, 145; pike 148; road 153; pike 154; 185
Maryland Heights: Union position 87; 88, 90, 91
Massanutten Mountain 13, 16, 29, 31, 32, 137, 160, 166, 185, 204
McCausland, Confederate Brig. Gen. John 29; opposes Hunter 61–62; slows Hunter 67–68, 70, 71, 73, 74, 80, 87; leads attack 97; Chambersburg 126–127; after raid 127; 128, 154
McClanahan, Confederate Captain, John H.: artillery at New Market 37; Piedmont 57
McClellan, Union Maj. Gen. George B. 4; advance to Richmond 16; 179
McCook, Union Maj. Gen. Alexander: command of Fort Stevens 108; 110; at Fort Stevens 111; 116
McMillan, Union Brig. Gen. James W.: at Cedar Creek 207
McNeill, Confederate Captain John H.: description of raid 28; 29
Meade, Union Maj. Gen. George G.: Army of the Potomac's re-enlistment 9; 10; prisoner report 89; 129
Mechanicsville, Virginia 69
Meem's Bottom, near New Market 31
Meigs, Union Lt. John R. 136; killed 172–173
Meigs, Union Quartermaster-Gen. M. C.: employees to front 108
Merritt, Union Brig. Gen. Wesley 135; fights at Cedarville, confidence 140; 147, 154, 155, 156, 166, 171; First Cavalry Division 173; on partisans 174; 175; Tom's Brook 176–177; 194; at Cedar Creek 196; 204; attacks 208–209;

attacks civilian area 215–216; 217
Michigan Brigade 174
Middle Military Department 92, 211
Middle River, near Piedmont 53
Middleton, Union Lt. Col. 123
Middletown, Maryland 92
Middletown, Virginia, near Cedar Creek 196, 197, 204, 205, 211, 212
Middleway, Virginia 141
Milford, Virginia 160, 166, 167, 168
Mill Creek, Virginia 199
Millwood, Virginia 137; road 153
Missouri, Department of the 132
Mohamy's Mill 186
Molineux, Union Col. Edward: at Winchester 151
Monocacy, Battle of: casualties 101; 105, 114
Monocacy, Maryland 92; roads converged 93; 94, 121, 131
Monocacy River 20, 93, 95, 96
Moor, Union Col. August: sent to New Market 31; 33–34, 35; first line at New Market 36–37; 40; report on reinforcements 42; arrives at Piedmont 54; 55, 56
Moorefield, West Virginia 127, 128
Morgan Confederate Brig. Gen. John Hunt: assists Breckinridge 26; stops Averell 29
Mosby, Confederate Lt. Col. John 18; harasses Sigel 28; operations 139; executions 215
Mount Crawford: Imboden defends 49; 50, 51, 172
Mount Jackson, near New Market 31, 34, 49, 50, 128, 167
Mowry's Hill, Virginia 52, 53, 58
Mulligan, Col. 87; Kernstown 124; killed 125

National Road: to Baltimore 93; 101

New Creek, West Virginia 127, 216
New Creek Bridge 25
New Hope, Virginia: retreat from Piedmont 57
New London, Virginia 70
New Market, Virginia 13; description of 31–32; 33, 34, 35; battle of, casualties 43–44; 45, 46, 48; Hunter arrives at 49; 50, 59, 62, 64, 82, 142, 166, 212, 217
New Market Gap: road through Massanutten 16; 30, 32
Newtown, Virginia: threatened by Hunter 48; 144, 155, 201, 211
Nineteenth Corps, Union Army: from New Orleans 93; 116, 117, 118, 119, 121, 128, 135; Winchester plan 147; road blocked 147; 149, 150, 151, 152, 153, 155, 162; at Fisher's Hill 164; 166, 180; Cedar Creek 191–192; 193, 196, 202, 203, 205; attack 207–208; 212
Ninth New York 167
North Mountain 87, 160, 165, 175

O'Keefe, Union Captain Joseph, Sheridan aide 200
Old River Road, near New Market 33
Old Town, Maryland 127
151st New York: at Monocacy 97
159th New York: at Winchester 151; at Cedar Creek 192
114th New York: at Winchester 151; 152
144th Ohio National Guard: at Monocacy 96
149th Ohio National Guard: at Monocacy 96
149th Ohio Volunteer Infantry 101; chasing Early 120
116th Ohio Infantry: at New Market 34; 42; Piedmont 54; 55, 75; at Cedar Creek 190–191
110th Ohio Volunteer Infantry: at Monocacy 100; at Winchester 152
One Hundred and thirty-eighth Pennsylvania Volunteers: at Winchester 152

Index

123rd Ohio Infantry: at New Market 31; 33, 35, 37, 57; at Cedar Creek 190–191
Opequon Creek 136; 141; crossing to Winchester 146; 147, 148, 153, 154, 157, 158, 161
Orange and Alexandria Railroad 171
Ord, Union Maj. Gen. E.O.C.: union advance 24; argues with Sigel, asked to be relieved 25; 116

Page Valley 30
Patton, Confederate Col. George S.: commands 22nd Virginia at New Market 38; 40–41
Peaks of Otter, Virginia 67
Pegram, Confederate Brig. Gen. John 160, 165, 185, 186, 189, 195, 204, 205, 208, 209
Pennington, Union Col. Alexander: at Cedar Creek 207; at Waynesboro 219
Perry, Leslie J.: in "A Shock to Gen. Sheridan" 217–218
Perryville, Battle of 132
Petersburg, Virginia: rail center 65; 67; supply problem 83; 84, 89, 90, 101, 104, 114, 116, 119, 134, 135, 141, 142, 143, 171, 172, 180, 182, 212, 214, 216, 217, 220
Petticoat Gap, Virginia 137
Piedmont, Virginia: description of 52; 53; Confederate defenses 54; casualties 57; 58; significance of 59; 60, 64, 67, 70, 82, 86
Point Lookout, Union prison camp 91
Poolesville, Maryland 117, 118
Port Republic, Virginia 51, 52, 53, 54, 168, 171; damage to 174
Potomac Home Brigade: at Monocacy 96
Potomac River 13, 17, 83, 84, 86, 87, 88, 89, 92, 110, 118, 119, 120, 126, 143, 215
Powell, Union Col. William H.: replaces Averell 168; Second Cavalry Division 173; 178, 184, 204, 215, 217

Putnam, George, Union soldier: at Cedar Creek 192

Quinn, Union Maj. Timothy: at New Market 31; burns house 48

Ramseur, Confederate Maj. Gen. Stephen D. 71, 75, 76, 88, 95, 99, 101, 145; at Winchester 148; 154, 158, 160, 165, 186, 189, 195, 197; wounded 205
Rawlins, Union Brig. Gen. John A.: Grant chief of staff 112; 214
Red Bud Run, near Winchester 146, 148, 151, 153, 155
Reserve Division 86
Rhodes, Elisha Hunt, 2nd Rhode Island 157
Richmond, Virginia 16, 64, 65, 84, 105, 171, 184, 214, 217, 218, 220
Ricketts, Union Brig. Gen. James B.: Third Division 6th Corps to Washington 90; to Monocacy Junction 93; 94, 96, 97–98, 99, 100, 102, 122; at Winchester 149–150; describes battle 152; 162, 164; wounded at Cedar Creek 193; 205, 211
Rienzi (Sheridan's horse) 200–201
Rockfish Gap, Virginia 219
Rockingham County, Virginia 50
Rockingham Register: report on locals 43
Rockville, Maryland 103, 118, 119
Rodes, Confederate Maj. Gen. Robert E. 70, 71, 88, 122, 145, 148; dies in attack 152; 153, 157, 160
Rosser, Confederate Brig. Gen. Thomas: on guerrillas to Lee 18; follows federals 175; Tom's Brook 176; 177, 186; at Cedar Creek 196–197; 204, 207, 216, 217
Round Top Hill: Imboden and Vaughn sent to 53; 54, 57, 176
Rude's Hill, near New Market 30, 31, 41–42
Russell, Union Brig. Gen. David A.: killed 152; 153, 157

Salem, Virginia 80
Salem Pike, near Lynchburg 73, 74, 75
Saltville, Virginia: salt mines 23; 24, 25
Second Cavalry Division, Army of the Potomac: at Washington 108
Second Corps Army of Northern Virginia 65–66; route to Lynchburg 69; 71, 78, 79, 80; crosses Potomac at Boteler's Ford 90; 103, 186; to Petersburg 217
Second Division, Sixth Corps: defense at Cedar Creek 194
Second Michigan Cavalry 132
2nd New York Cavalry: at Winchester 146
2nd Pennsylvania Cavalry 28
2nd Rhode Island 157, 174
Second Virginia Cavalry 128
Seddon, Confederate Secretary of War: letter from Lee 5; 23, 57, 181, 214
17th Pennsylvania Cavalry: Sheridan escort 199
Seventh Street, Washington, D.C. 103, 104, 108, 111
Seventy-Seventh New York: at Cedar Creek 195
Sharpe, Union Col. Jacob: at Winchester 151
Shenandoah County, Virginia 50
Shenandoah River 13, 32; North Fork at New Market 36; 42; North Fork 49; 50, 119, 160; North Fork at Fisher's Hill 162; 165
Shenandoah Valley (the Valley): description of 7; 10, 13; value in war 15–17; "Breadbasket of the Confederacy" 17; guerrillas 18; 23, 26, 59, 64, 66, 86, 115, 120, 128, 131, 134, 137, 169; destruction of 173; 187, 210, 214, 216, 217
Shepherdstown 88, 90
Sheridan, Union Maj. Gen. Philip H.: cavalry commander, raid to join Hunter 64; 65; combines

departments 129; 130, 131; meets Lincoln 132; about 132–134; report to Grant 135; 135–136; orders to Torbert 137; total war 137–138; 139; criticism, holds back 140; describes movements 141; 142; orders to troops 143; information from Rebecca Wright 144; meets Grant 144; moves on Winchester 145; Winchester plan 147; 148; costly delay 149; 152; on battlefield 153; 155; cavalry attack 156; victory message to Grant 157–158; 160; strength of Fisher's Hill, plan of attack 161; movement at Fisher's Hill 162; on the battlefield 164; enemy panic 165; victory message 165–166; message to Grant 166; cavalry plan 166; cavalry failure 167–168; message to Averell 167; relieves Averell 168; confidence of 169; 170, 171; destruction and future plans 172; death of Meigs 172–173; progress report 175; rear guard fighting 175–176; Tom's Brook 176–177; to Grant on Tom's Brook 177–178; 180, 181, 182; Sixth Corps return 183; to Halleck 183; Longstreet message 184; to Wright at Cedar Creek 184; Washington meeting 185; 186, 189, 196; in Winchester 199; stops retreat, rallys army 200–201; rides among troops 202–203; starts attack 204; credit for victory 209; to Grant 211; promotion of 212; new targets 214; to Halleck 215; lists damage 216; about West Virginia 217–218; 219; ends Lee's escape 220
Sherman, Union Maj. Gen. William T.: spring campaign 10; 119, 169
Ship, Cadet Col. Scott: VMI cadet commandant 29; 33; report on New Market 39
Shirley's Hill, near New Market 31, 34, 35

Shunk, Union Col. David: at Winchester 151
Sigel, Union Maj. Gen. Franz: spring campaign 10; appointment as department head 21; political general 21; description of 21; complains about troops 22; 24; argues with Ord 25; new plan to advance 25; leaves Martinsburg 26; to Grant about enemy 27; escorts on Valley Pike 28; leaves Winchester 29; Breckinridge dispatches 29–30; cautious 30; leaves Woodstock for New Market 33; decides to fight at New Market 34; 36, 37, 39; launches attack 40; orders retreat 42–43; report on battle 44; leadership 45; 46, 47, 48, 64, 86; at Martinsburg 87
Silver Spring, Maryland 104
Sixth Army Corps, Union 90, 96, 97, 99, 101; arrives in Washington 110; 112, 116, 117, 118, 121, 122, 128, 135, 141; Winchester plan 147; 148, 149, 150, 152; at Winchester 153; 154, 161, 162; at Fisher's Hill 164; 165, 180, 183, 184, 193, 196, 201, 202; begins attack 205; 208; pursuit 209; 212; to Petersburg 217
Sixth New York 167
Sixth Street, in Washington 110
60th Virginia Regiment: at Piedmont 54; 56
62nd Virginia: at New Market 34; 38, 40, 41
Sixty-seventh Pennsylvania Volunteers: at Winchester 152
Smith, Confederate Maj. Gen. Francis H., superintendent of VMI 26
Smith, Confederate Col. George: with 62nd Virginia Mounted Infantry at New Market 34; 38, 41
Smith, William, Governor of Virginia: about Early 170; 180
Smithfield, Virginia 141
Smith's Creek, near New Market 30, 31, 32, 34, 35; Union flank 36
Snicker's Ferry, Virginia 122
Snicker's Gap 119
Snow's Maryland Battery: at New Market 33; 35, 37
South, Union Department of 46
Stahel, Union Maj. Gen. Julius: cavalry commander at New Market 34; 37; cavalry attack 39–40; 48; Medal of Honor 58; 86
Stanton, Edwin M., Union Secretary of War 46; message to Hunter 59; 87, 90, 91, 117, 118, 130; meets Sheridan 132; to Sheridan 158; meets Sheridan 183; 185, 211; to Sheridan about West Virginia 217–218
Staunton, Virginia 16, 24, 26, 27, 29, 30, 44, 47, 51, 52, 53, 56, 57, 59, 60, 61, 62, 67; Early arrives 85; 86, 171, 172, 173, 175, 217, 218
Stephenson's Depot, Virginia 125, 145, 148, 154
Stevens, George T.: Sheridan as commander of 136; at Winchester 149; through Valley 171; at Cedar Creek 179
Stones River, Battle of 132
Stonewall Brigade 71, 189
Strasburg, Virginia 13, 16, 25, 44, 123, 177, 182, 186, 187
Strother, Union Col. David Hunter 21; complains about Sigel 25; Sigel's staff 40; blames Sigel 43; compares Sigel and Averell 44–45; opinion of Sigel 45; occupies Woodstock 48; occupies Harrisonburg 50; advises to flank enemy 51; describes Confederate position at Piedmont 54; in Staunton 60; confusion and destruction 61; at Lexington 62; about Lynchburg 68; to attack 74; retreat from Lynchburg 80–81; confusion 120
Stuart, Confederate Maj. Gen. J.E.B. 18, 58
Sullivan, Union Brig. Gen. Jeremiah: at New Market

34; 36; arrives at Rude's Hill 42; 48, 49; bravery of 58; 71, 75
Sweet Springs 81

Tenallytown, Maryland 119
Tenth Vermont Volunteers: at Monocacy 99
Tenth West Virginia Infantry 190
Terry, Confederate Brig. Gen. William R.: at Monocacy 99; 100
3rd Battalion Valley Reserves: at Piedmont 54
Third Cavalry Division 173
Third Division, Sixth Corps: to Washington 90
3rd Vermont: at Cedar Creek 201
13th Connecticut: at Winchester 151
Thirteenth Maine: following Early 119–120
Thirteenth United States Infantry 132
30th Virginia Battalion: at New Market 34; 38
34th Massachusetts: at New Market 31; 33–34, 37, 38, 41; Piedmont 54; 56; at Cedar Creek 190
Thoburn, Union Col. Joseph: at Piedmont 54; 56, 58, 76; Snicker's Ferry fight 122; Kernstown 124–125; 155; at Fisher's Hill 162; at Hupp's Hill 182; killed at Cedar Creek 190; 191
Thomas, Union Col. Stephen: charge at Winchester 151; sacrifice at Cedar creek 192
Three Top Mountain, near Fisher's Hill 161
Tibbits, Union Col. 123; Kernstown 124
Tom's Run (Brook) 176, 177
Torbert, Union Brig. Gen. Alfred T. A. 135; Winchester plan 147; cavalry advance to Winchester 154; 155; cavalry attack 156; 166, 167, 168, 171, 175; Tom's Brook 176; 184; cavalry attacks 204; 217
Tredegar Works, Confederate foundry 178
Trevilian Station, Virginia: cavalry battle 65

Tumbling Run, near Fisher's Hill 165
Twelfth Connecticut: at Winchester 151
12th West Virginia: at New Market 34; 37; Piedmont 54; 76
Twentieth Pennsylvania Cavalry: Maj. Anderson commander 123
28th Ohio Infantry 22; at New Market 34; 42; at Piedmont 54
21st New York Cavalry 53; at Piedmont 54; Col. Tibbits 123
Twenty-second Corps: around Washington 106
22nd Iowa: at Winchester 151
22nd Virginia Regiment: at New Market 34, 38, 41
26th Virginia Battalion: at New Market 33, 34, 38, 41
23rd Virginia Battalion: at New Market 34, 38, 41
23rd Virginia Cavalry: at New Market 30; 34
Tyler, Union Brig. Gen. Erastus B.: at Monocacy 96
Tynes, Achilles J.: opposing Hunter 62; letter 67

Upton, Union Brig. Gen. Emory: describes Valley 120; at Winchester 152–153

Valley Turnpike: route 16; Union graves along road 27; 31, 32, 42, 50, 51, 83, 85, 136; Winchester plan 147; 153, 165, 168, 173, 176, 186, 187, 204
Vaughn, Confederate Gen. John C. 51, 52, 53, 54; at Piedmont 57; fails to act 58; 60, 69
Vermont Brigade: at Fisher's Hill 164
Veteran Reserve Corps 106
Virginia & Tennessee Railroad: route 16; 24; destruction of 25; 45
Virginia Central Railroad: route 16; 26, 64, 183, 184, 214, 219, 220
Virginia Military Institute (VMI) 26; cadets at New Market 34; 38; attack in line 39; 41, 62; cadet attitude 64

Von Kleiser: artillery at New Market 37; at Piedmont 55
Vredenburgh, Union Maj.: at Winchester 149–150

Wallace, Union Maj. Gen. Lew: commander Middle Department 92; 93, 94; describes position 95; situation 95–96; bridge 100–101; enemy strength 102; 142
Warner, Union Col. J. M.: at Fisher's Hill 161
Washington, D.C. 16; plan to capture 66–67; 84, 86, 89, 90, 92, 94, 99, 101, 103; headquarters of war effort 104; surrounding forts 105; 110, 111, 113, 114, 118, 119, 120, 121, 130, 134, 135, 144, 172, 180, 183, 184, 185
Washington, Department of 106
Washington Pike, at Monocacy 98, 100
Watson, William G.: about Lynchburg 76; retreat from Lynchburg 77, 79; conditions on retreat 81–82
Waynesboro, Virginia 51, 57, 60, 171, 172, 219, 220
Weber, Union Brig. Gen. Max: defends Harpers Ferry 87; 88
Weddle, Union Col.: attack at Piedmont 56
Welch's Spring, Virginia 141
Wells, Union Col. George D., commander 34th Massachusetts: described scene at New Market 37–38; New Market 41; 75, 122; Kernstown 125; 162; at Hupp's Hill 182; killed 183
West Virginia, Union Department of: description of 20; headquarters at Cumberland, Maryland 21; 217
West Virginia Horse Artillery: at New Market 33
Western Virginia, Confederate Department of: description of 22
Wharton, Confederate Brig. Gen. Gabriel C.: arrived

in Valley 26; at New Market 33–34; 35, 39, 74, 124, 153, 154, 155, 160, 165, 183, 186, 187; at Cedar Creek 192; 195, 205, 209, 217, 219
Wheaton, Union Brig. Gen. Frank: at Fort Stevens 111; at Cedar Creek 193; 205
White, Confederate Col. Robert: with 23rd Virginia Cavalry at New Market 34
White's Ford 118, 119
Wickham, Confederate Brig. Gen. William C. 160, 161, 166, 167, 168, 177
Wildes, Union Lt. Col. Thomas: at Cedar Creek 190–191
Williamson's Hill, near New Market 33
Williamsport Pike 125
Wilson, Union Brig. Gen. James: crosses Opequon 146; 147, 153, 154, 166, 171, 173
Winchester, Virginia 17; 26; Second Battle of 27; mock battle 28, 29, 86, 121, 123, 125, 136, 137, 142, 143, 145, 147, 154, 157, 158; casualties 159; 160, 161, 164, 168; Early's report 169; 175, 180, 181; Sheridan arrives at 185; 199, 200, 201, 211, 216, 218, 219
Wise, John S.: feelings of people 4; Early description 66
Withers, Union Maj. Henry: at Cedar Creek 190
Wolfe, Confederate Lt. Col. John P.: with 51st Virginia at New Market 34
Woodstock, Virginia 27, 29, 30, 31, 33; Union troops occupy 48; 49, 50, 166, 167, 175, 177
Woodstock Races, Tom's Brook 177
Worsham, Confederate Sgt. John H.: arrives in Lynchburg 68–69; Fourth of July 88

Wright, Union Maj. Gen. Horatio: commands Sixth Corps 110; 111; Lincoln visits Fort Stevens 113; report to Halleck 117; 118, 119, 121, 122, 135; toward Winchester 147; 152, 155, 156; at Fisher's Hill 161; attack at Fisher's Hill 165; official report 166; in command 184; reconnaissance 187–188; in command at Cedar Creek 193; 196; 197; begins organizing 202; 211
Wright, Rebecca, teacher in Winchester 144
Wynkoop, Union Col. John E: cavalry at New Market 31; at Piedmont 57
Wythe County, Virginia, lead mines 23

York, Confederate Brig. Gen. Zebulon: at Monocacy 98; 100
Young, Union Lt. Col. 122